Bouquets from the Cannon's Mouth

*Soldiering with the Eighth Regiment
of the Pennsylvania Reserves*

By
Robert E. Eberly Jr.

with Foreword by
Edwin C. Bearss

For Roger Smith –
A fellow Civil War buff.

Robert E. Eberly

9 Jan 06

WHITE MANE BOOKS
SHIPPENSBURG, PENNSYLVANIA

Grateful acknowledgment is made for permission to reprint excerpts from the following works:

Images and text from the Thomas W. Springer Diary (#7093-v), Special Collections, University of Virginia Library. Reprinted by permission of the University of Virginia Library.

Aida Craig Truxall, editor, "Respects to All": Letters of Two Pennsylvania Boys in the War of the Rebellion (University of Pittsburgh Press: 1962). Reprinted by permission of the University of Pittsburgh Press.

Dear Folks at Home, The Civil War Letters of Leo W. and John I. Faller (Carlisle, Pa.: Cumberland County Historical Society, 1963). Reprinted by permission of the Cumberland County Historical Society.

Stephen W. Sears, *Landscape Turned Red* (Houghton Mifflin Company: 1983). Reprinted by permission of Houghton Mifflin Company. All rights reserved.

Stephen W. Sears, *George B. McClellan: The Young Napoleon* (Houghton Mifflin Company: 1988). Reprinted by permission of Houghton Mifflin Company. All rights reserved.

John Michael Priest, *Antietam: The Soldiers' Battle* (Shippensburg, Pa.: White Mane Publishing Co., 1989). Reprint, New York: Oxford University Press, 1993.

Noah Andre Trudeau, *Bloody Roads South: The Wilderness to Cold Harbor, May–June 1864* (Boston: Little, Brown & Co., 1989).

Bell Irvin Wiley, *The Life of Johnny Reb: The Common Soldier of the Confederacy* (Louisiana State University Press: 1994). Reprinted by permission of Louisiana State University Press.

This White Mane Books publication
was printed by
Beidel Printing House, Inc.
63 West Burd Street
Shippensburg, PA 17257-0708 USA

The acid-free paper used in this book meets the guidelines for permanence and durability of the Committee on Production Guidelines for Book Longevity of the Council on Library Resources.

For a complete list of available publications
please write
White Mane Books
Division of White Mane Publishing Company, Inc.
P.O. Box 708
Shippensburg, PA 17257-0708 USA

Library of Congress Cataloging-in-Publication Data

Eberly, Robert E., 1944-
    Bouquets from the cannon's mouth : soldiering with the Eighth Regiment of the Pennsylvania Reserves / by Robert E. Eberly Jr. ; with foreword by Edwin C. Bearss.
        p. cm.
    Includes bibliographical references and index.
    ISBN 1-57249-373-9 (acid-free paper)
    1. United States. Army. Pennsylvania Infantry Regiment, 37th (1861-1864) 2. Pennsylvania-History-Civil War, 1861-1865--Regimental histories. 3. United States-History-Civil War, 1861-1865--Regimental histories. 4. Soldiers-Pennsylvania-History--19th century. 5. United States. Army-Military life-History--19th century. 6. United States-History-Civil War, 1861-1865--Sources. I. Title.

E527.537th .E24 2005
973.7'448--dc22

                                                                                    2005042222

PRINTED IN THE UNITED STATES OF AMERICA

Contents

Illustrations & Maps

Illustrations

Maps

MAP KEY

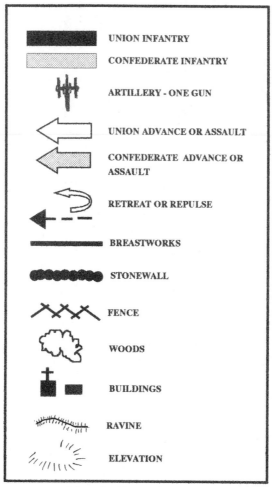

UNION INFANTRY

CONFEDERATE INFANTRY

ARTILLERY - ONE GUN

UNION ADVANCE OR ASSAULT

CONFEDERATE ADVANCE OR ASSAULT

RETREAT OR REPULSE

BREASTWORKS

STONEWALL

FENCE

WOODS

BUILDINGS

RAVINE

ELEVATION

Maps by Karl Feldmeyer

The maps focus primarily upon the movements and/or actions of the various brigades/regiments of the Pennsylvania Reserves. Thus, in many instances, the movements and/or actions of other Federal and/or Confederate units present or engaged are not depicted. For example, Map 7 depicts the action between two brigades of Meade's Pennsylvania Reserves and two brigades of Hood's division in the Cornfield at Antietam. By the time these units clashed (circa seven o'clock in the morning), seven Union brigades from Doubleday's, Ricketts's, and Meade's divisions had already engaged seven brigades from Jackson's division and Ewell's division. The reader wishing a more complete account of the movements and/or actions of all opposing forces in particular battles is invited to review the Bibliography and the Endnotes describing those works that provide definitive accounts of the same.

Foreword

During more than 40 years as a National Park Service historian, including 13 as the Service's Chief Historian, it was my good fortune to visit and become familiar with all of the Civil War battlefields and sites administered by the Department of the Interior. Since my retirement in 1995, I have continued to walk in the footsteps of history as a tour leader for the Smithsonian Institution, the National Geographic Society, History America, the Blue and Gray Education Society, and innumerable Civil War Round Tables. These tours, which focus on our nation's military and political past, have given me an opportunity to interact with many knowledgeable and interesting participants, thus affording all of us a two-way learning experience.

Early in my Park Service career, during visits to the Antietam National Battlefield and the Gettysburg National Military Park, I became aware of a number of Union regiments that belonged to a division known as the Pennsylvania Reserves. At both of these sites a great many unit memorials have been erected. Those commemorating Pennsylvania Reserve regiments are unusual in that they carry two regimental numbers—the first, in bold lettering, indicating the unit's state identity, and the second reflecting its designation in Federal service. For example, the regiment that forms a principal focus of this book is characterized both as the "8th Regt. Pennsylvania Reserve Volunteer Corps" and as the "37th Regiment of the Line" on the monument honoring its service at Antietam.

This peculiar numbering system sparked what has become for me a longstanding interest in the exploits of the Pennsylvania Reserves. Accordingly, I set out to learn about them—none too soon as it turned out—because the dual designations invariably aroused the curiosity of tour participants.

Given this background, I was delighted to learn during a 2002 visit to Hilton Head Island, South Carolina, to speak to the Lowcountry Civil War Round Table, that Robert E. Eberly Jr. had researched and written a manuscript entitled *Bouquets from the Cannon's Mouth.* Having become familiar with Mr. Eberly's background and credentials, I agreed to read his manuscript and, if it warranted publication, to write the foreword. My motive in taking on this task was not entirely altruistic. Reading the manuscript would further enrich my knowledge of the trials and tribulations of the officers and the rank and file of the Pennsylvania Reserves as drawn from a wide range of primary and secondary sources. While reading through the manuscript, I discovered a big bonus—the inclusion by Eberly of the "Prison Diaries of Sergeants Thomas W. Springer and James W. Eberhart."

As is my practice, I read the manuscript word for word and, in recommending its publication, noted that it more than met my personal criteria. Most significantly, it enhanced my knowledge of the Pennsylvania Reserves and their service in the Army of the Potomac—knowledge that I can now share with battlefield tour participants as we walk the ground where the soldiers of the 8th Regiment camped, marched, fought, and died. Through his judicious use of many primary sources, Eberly allows the soldiers to speak for themselves. In doing so, he integrates their words into an informative and graceful narrative.

Organized at the behest of Pennsylvania's great wartime governor, Andrew Curtin, in May 1861, the "Reserve Volunteer Corps of the Commonwealth" was conceived as a bulwark against an enemy who, following Virginia's secession, lay uncomfortably close to Pennsylvania's southern border. Mustered into Federal service after the disaster at First Bull Run (Manassas), the 13 infantry regiments making up the Pennsylvania Reserves gained renown as the only Federal division consisting entirely of troops from one state to fight together throughout their three-year term of service. It counted among its commanders such luminaries as John F. Reynolds and George G. Meade.

The soldiers of the Pennsylvania Reserves were center-staged at nearly all the major battles fought by the Army of the Potomac from the Seven Days through First Fredericksburg. The division missed Chancellorsville, but two of their three brigades were in action at Gettysburg. The Reserves also participated in Grant's 1864 Overland Campaign through the Battles of Spotsylvania Court House and Bethesda Church. Their original terms of enlistment expired on the eve of the fighting at Cold Harbor.

A great many of the soldiers whose enlistments had expired, including a majority of those from the 8th Regiment, reenlisted as veteran volunteers. They, together with those soldiers who had not yet served their full three-year term, were reorganized into the 190th and 191st Pennsylvania Infantry Regiments. This sets the stage for the next part of the book, which begins with a brief overview of the service of Sergeants Springer and Eberhart and their comrades from Company G of the old 8th Regiment, with the newly constituted 191st Pennsylvania Infantry. These veteran soldiers fought their way through from Cold Harbor to Petersburg where, on August 19, 1864, they were captured during the successful Union effort to cut the rail line running into that besieged city from Weldon, North Carolina.

Thereafter, Eberly allows Springer and Eberhart "to speak to us in their own words of the bitter days that were their lot as prisoners of war." The two sergeants and their comrades who were captured during the fight for the Weldon Railroad were confined initially in Richmond's Libby Prison, and later in a makeshift pen on Belle Isle in the James River. In early October they were sent to Salisbury, North Carolina, where they were held inside a stockade built around an old cotton mill. Springer died there in November 1864. Eberhart survived and continued to make diary entries into the following March, when he was set free and began the long journey home.

Day-by-day diaries maintained by Civil War soldiers held in prison pens are uncommon, so the inclusion of the Springer and Eberhart diaries in Part Three of the book, together with the appendices relating to conditions at Salisbury, will be welcomed by those interested in an aspect of the Civil War that graphically underscores the tragic inhumanity of the conflict. I applaud Eberly on his decision to include the diaries, along with his inclusion of explanatory notes pertaining thereto where necessary. In annotating the diaries, he has avoided the heavy hand that too many editors employ.

Since his retirement from a distinguished career as a lawyer in the public and private sectors, Bob Eberly has pursued his long-standing interest in the Civil War by delving into reenacting (with a Pennsylvania regiment, of course), and more recently by serving as the first president of the Lowcountry Civil War Round Table. He is a champion of battlefield preservation and is a member of the Board of Directors of the Friends of the National Parks at Gettysburg. To these many accomplishments he now adds that of published author. His initial work will prove to be a valuable addition to the libraries of those members of the Civil War community who savor "the soldiers' story."

Edwin C. Bearss
Chief Historian Emeritus
National Park Service

Preface

In 1911, on Christmas Eve, an old man rose from his chair at a family gathering and read aloud a letter he had composed for the occasion. He spoke eloquently of his Christian faith and of the remarkable life he had led. In recalling the events of some fifty years earlier, he said: "[T]here is one portion [of my life] that shines bright on memory's tablet, that is, four years engaged in the service of God and my country. I say in the service of God, because I behold that a man who serves his country loyally and faithfully, renders acceptable service to God."[1]

That old man was my great-great-grandfather, Isaac Andrew Moore. He was celebrating his 71st Christmas in a county that, in 1911, boasted more millionaires per capita than any other county in Pennsylvania. Thanks to the vast coal deposits that fed the burgeoning steel mills of nearby Pittsburgh, Fayette County was a very different place from the one in which young Isaac Moore grew to manhood. In 1860, Fayette County was overwhelmingly rural, its total population not exceeding 40,000. The legions of coal miners who would dominate the local labor force at the turn of the century had not yet arrived. Farmers and day laborers—with a smattering of clerks, tradesmen, and professionals—predominated, and those farmers and laborers were staunch Democrats. Indeed, the great majority of Fayette Countians had voted for the Democratic Party's nominee in every presidential election from 1828 through 1856.

Surprisingly, that tradition would be abandoned in the presidential election of 1860. In that momentous year, Abraham Lincoln, the nominee of the new Republican Party, carried the county by a slender margin. He carried the state as well and went on to become the 16th president of the United States. Lincoln's election proved to be the last straw for many of the Southern states whose economies were inextricably bound up with the "peculiar institution" of chattel slavery. By the time the new president gave his first inaugural address in March of 1861, seven Southern states had seceded from the Union. With the firing on Fort Sumter the following month, President Lincoln called for 75,000 volunteers to suppress the rebellion and preserve the Union.

Thousands of young men from towns, villages, and farms throughout the North rushed to the colors, answering Lincoln's call. Among them were three young volunteers from Uniontown, the county seat of Fayette County: Isaac A. Moore, George W. Darby, and Thomas W. Springer. Isaac Moore was a 20 year-old tanner, born in a log cabin at the foot of Laurel Mountain. George Darby, also a tanner, was 19. Thomas Springer, my great-granduncle, was a student just 16 years of age. His father, D. M. Springer, operated a small tailor's shop. The three young men joined the "Fayette Guards," the first volunteer company organized in Uniontown, and marched for Pittsburgh before the month was out. They were joined there by Ashbel F. Hill, an 18-year-old Fayette Countian from Masontown, and by James W. Eberhart, a 17-year-old Fayette City store clerk. Hill had enlisted in the "Brownsville Grays," another of the early Fayette County companies, while Eberhart fell in with the Fayette Guards.

In June 1861, the two companies were combined with eight others to form the 8th Regiment of the Pennsylvania Reserve Volunteer Corps. The Pennsylvania Reserves would go on to establish a sterling record of achievement in the Army of the Potomac under such renowned commanders as George A. McCall, John F. Reynolds, George Gordon Meade, and Samuel Crawford. From the Seven Days Battles in 1862 to the Battles of the Wilderness and Spotsylvania Court House in 1864, the Reserves were invariably in the thick of the fight. Indeed, on the very last day of their three-year term of service the soldiers of the Pennsylvania Reserves were in action at Bethesda Church. By that time, many of them had reenlisted, determined to see the war through to a successful conclusion.

Thomas Springer and James Eberhart were among those veteran soldiers who decided to reenlist. So too were George Darby and Isaac Moore. After surviving the carnage of Cold Harbor, all four crossed the James River and took part in the siege of Petersburg. It was there they had the misfortune to be captured during the fighting along the Weldon Railroad. Springer and Eberhart kept personal diaries of their prison experiences from their initial incarceration in Richmond's notorious Libby Prison through their ultimate detention in the Confederate military prison at Salisbury, North Carolina. Relatively unknown to present-day readers, Salisbury would prove as deadly as the infamous prison at Andersonville, Georgia, during the harsh winter of 1864–65. Springer's diary ends November 29, 1864, the day he died in the Salisbury prison. Eberhart was among the fortunate few to survive. He was paroled in February 1865 and reached the Union line near Wilmington, North Carolina, in early March. Later that month, he made his way home to Pittsburgh. The final entry in his diary reads simply: "18 March 1865 Thanks be Mercifull God that brought me Home again."[2]

In a war notable for the large number of written accounts produced by its protagonists, perhaps it is not surprising that four of these five young men wrote of their experiences—two in the diaries mentioned above and two in the books mentioned below. What is surprising, given the wealth of regimental histories covering scores of units on both sides, is that so little has been written about the 8th Regiment of the Pennsylvania Reserves. Ashbel Hill's memoirs, together with George Darby's, provide the only book length accounts of the regiment's service. In the absence of a formal regimental history, these two books provide a rare glimpse into the lives of the young volunteers who went to war with the 8th Reserves.

Ashbel Hill, severely wounded at Antietam and mustered out of the service shortly thereafter, published an engaging personal account of his soldier life entitled *Our Boys* in 1864. Written while the scourge of war still haunted the land, Hill's memoir presents a nearly contemporaneous account of the events to which he was witness. His anecdotes, recounting not only the terror of battle, but also the mundane occurrences common to life in camp and on the march, bring the story of the 8th Regiment to life. While couched in the vernacular of the era, and often penned with a flair for the dramatic, they clearly have the ring of truth about them.

George Darby fought through the first three years of the war, reenlisted in 1864, and was captured near Petersburg, Virginia, in August of that year. He survived his imprisonment and, in 1896, authored a vivid account of his ordeal entitled *Incidents and Adventures in Rebeldom*. Darby's book, published some thirty years after the war, must be appraised with somewhat greater circumspection than Hill's, the passage of time often serving to embellish recollection. Moreover, it is representative of a genre common at the close of the 19th century in which Confederate military authorities were depicted as devils bent upon intentionally abusing and starving Yankee prisoners in hellish "prison pens." While instances of such conduct undoubtedly did occur, modern research has largely refuted this characterization. These caveats aside, *Incidents and Adventures in Rebeldom* tells the story of the soldiers who marched and fought with the 8th Regiment in an evocative style not often found in formal regimental histories. It also serves as a valuable reminder of the price too often paid by those who go to war.

It should be noted that while I focus on the 8th Regiment of the Pennsylvania Reserves, and on the five young men introduced above, *Bouquets from the Cannon's Mouth* is not a traditional regimental history. For example, I have drawn upon letters, diaries, and books written by soldiers from other Reserve regiments in those instances where a paucity of 8th Regiment primary source material otherwise would have precluded a full account of its service. Also, I have chronicled the fortunes of those veterans who reenlisted and served beyond the end of the regiment's three-year term of service. Indeed, had I not done so, the tragic story of life and death in Confederate military prisons recounted in Chapters Fourteen and Fifteen would have remained untold.

Throughout the book, I have sought to portray events using the words of the participants themselves whenever possible. From senior generals to lowly privates, from newspaper editors and politicians to loved ones writing from home, their words infuse the story with an immediacy and a sense of time and place that no one writing more than 140 years after the fact could hope to achieve.

Many of the words may seem strange to the modern reader. Indeed in certain cases—as, for example, George Darby's accounts of his interactions with Negroes—they may prove disturbing. In many other cases, however, the words spoken by those recalling the defining event in our nation's history are inspiring and timeless. One need look no further than the words uttered by North Carolina Governor William Kitchin and Pennsylvania Lieutenant Governor Robert Murphy at the dedication of Pennsylvania's monument to her fallen sons at Salisbury in 1910. Commenting upon the many monuments erected throughout the country honoring those who served during the Civil War, Governor Kitchin said: "What matters it whether they commemorate Northern or Southern heroism, whether Lee or Grant, whether blue or gray? They all typify noble, sincere, brave American impulse, spirit, endurance, devotion to duty, love of country, and fidelity to faith...."[3] In reply, Lieutenant Governor Murphy paid homage to those Americans who fought for the Confederacy: "[Governor Kitchin's] words of splendid tribute to those who died here [at Salisbury] and to the bravery of the men in blue, who with their blood maintained the integrity of the Union, is only matched by our high esteem for the unflinching devotion of those soldiers who gave to the Army of Northern Virginia the laurel of imperishable renown. To say that there was anything but sincere belief upon the part of those contending on both sides...in the righteousness of their cause is an insult to the honesty of the intelligent and the brave, who risked and lost their all in support of their conviction of right."[4] Such words still speak to us today, if we will open our hearts to hear them.

This, then, is the story of five soldiers and of their comrades in the regiment and the division they served with—the 8th Regiment of the Pennsylvania Reserves. In a larger sense, it is the story of a generation of young men caught up in the maelstrom of war—a war finally triggered by a presidential election that doomed North and South to four years of unimaginable suffering and sacrifice. It is not the only irony of their story that many of those young men were not old enough to vote in that fateful election.

Introduction

On July 4, 1776, as a new nation was being created in Philadelphia some three hundred miles to the east, a young Quaker from Virginia placed a notice on his gristmill in the Monongahela country west of the Allegheny Mountains. Henry Beeson's notice advised would-be settlers that 54 building lots would be offered for sale in three weeks' time. The lots sold quickly, and the little village of Beeson's Mill was born. Known over time as Beesontown, the Town of Union, and, ultimately, Uniontown, the community prospered and, in 1783, became the county seat of Fayette County, Pennsylvania. Named in honor of the Revolutionary War hero, the Marquis de Lafayette, the newly created county lay entirely within lands finally ceded to Pennsylvania by Virginia in 1780. In that year, a long-simmering boundary dispute between the two states was finally resolved when both of them accepted a border surveyed by Charles Mason and Jeremiah Dixon. The Mason-Dixon Line soon came to be regarded as an informal boundary between North and South and served as a de facto dividing line between free states and slave states.

The question of slavery was never far from the minds of the citizens of the Monongahela country. Many of the earliest immigrants had come over the Laurel Hill from Maryland and Virginia, bringing their slaves with them. They settled on lands that had been claimed by Virginia since 1754 when Governor Robert Dinwiddie ordered a young militia officer named George Washington to occupy the Forks of the Ohio—then under French control. Pennsylvania countered Virginia's claim by asserting that it owned the contested lands by virtue of the British Crown's 1681 grant to William Penn.[1]

Despite their disagreement over the border, the legislatures of the two states were in complete accord on one fundamental matter—the institution of chattel slavery, legally recognized and protected in both jurisdictions prior to 1780. That year, however, marked a dramatic change in the status quo when the General Assembly of Pennsylvania passed an "Act for the Gradual Abolition of Slavery."[2] The final resolution of the border dispute and Pennsylvania's action on the slavery issue, all within the space of less than 12 months, persuaded many of Fayette County's earliest immigrants that it was time to move on. As one commentator noted: "The passage of this law...about the same time that [Fayette County] was [found to be] Pennsylvania territory combined to induce many of our early settlers to sell out and migrate to Kentucky, which about this date had opened her charms to adventure, settlement and slavery.... These early removals to Kentucky brought to our county overpowering numbers of settlers from Eastern Pennsylvania and New Jersey.... Of this class of new settlers were the Friends, or Quakers...and the Scotch-Irish Presbyterians...."[3]

Many of these new settlers were opposed to slavery, and the debate became increasingly acrimonious in the years leading up to the election of 1860.[4] As early as the 1820s, Fayette Countians were bitterly divided on the issue, with some organizing societies for the abolition of slavery, while others went even further, arguing that slaves should be freed and repatriated to Africa. On the other hand, defenders of the "peculiar institution" were loath to interfere with the rights of slave owners in the Southern states, believing the institution of slavery to be protected by the Constitution. As the radical abolitionist movement spread outward from the New England states, tensions increased: "In 1836, [United States Senator] Daniel Sturgeon of Uniontown presided at an organization meeting for a colonization society in his home town. [Reverend] Samuel Gould, a radical abolitionist, was refused permission to speak and [tried to] set up his own meeting at the courthouse. The crowd shouted him down, and when someone mentioned 'tar and feathers' Gould had to beat a retreat. The next year, local newspapers reported that another meeting at the courthouse had adopted resolutions calling for non-intervention with slavery in the South."[5]

By the early 1850s, Uniontown had come to serve as an important stop on the Underground Railroad. Two routes, one out of Maryland via the National Road and another out of western Virginia through Morgantown, intersected in the Fayette County seat, located just 15 miles north of the Mason-Dixon line.

Meanwhile, the rise of national political parties in the first half of the 19th century also colored Fayette Countians' attitudes toward slavery. While Fayette County had been staunchly in the Democratic fold for years,[6] the new Republican Party, organized nationally at an informal convention in Pittsburgh early in 1856, quickly gained numerous adherents from the ranks of the county's antislavery proponents. Thus, while Fayette County—and Pennsylvania—voted overwhelmingly for their native son, Democrat James Buchanan,[7] in the election of 1856, the growing strength of the Republican Party made the outlook for the 1860 election much less predictable.[8] The fracture in the national Democratic Party at the 1860 nominating convention over the slavery issue only served to complicate matters further.

The question of slavery, and in particular its extension into the western territories, continued to vex the nation throughout President Buchanan's term. Indeed, the issue dominated the 1860 presidential campaign. Having split irreconcilably over this issue, the Democrats went their separate ways. Southern Democrats, calling for Federal protection of slavery in the territories, nominated John C. Breckinridge of Kentucky. The Northern Democrats, opposed to the extension of slavery into the territories, nominated Stephen A. Douglas of Illinois. A new political party, the Constitutional Union party, comprised of Whigs unwilling to join the Republicans and the remnants of the defunct Know-Nothing party, nominated John Bell of Tennessee. Bell, a pro-slavery Southerner who nonetheless opposed its extension into the territories, campaigned against secession and supported the Union. The Republicans, of course, nominated Abraham Lincoln of Illinois. Lincoln ran on a platform that called for the prohibition of slavery in the territories, while upholding the practice as it existed in the Southern states.

And so, amid threats of secession and civil war, the election came. In November 1860, Fayette Countians went to the polls. In the closest presidential vote in the county's history, Abraham Lincoln defeated John Breckinridge with 49.8 percent of the vote to Breckinridge's 47.7 percent.[9] Lincoln won a majority of the electoral votes in Pennsylvania and 17 other states to become the 16th president of the United States.[10] The Rubicon had been crossed.

Part One

The Young Volunteers

Our flag is unfurl'd, and our arms flash bright, As the sun wades up the sky;
But ere I join the doubtful fight, Lovely maid I would say "Good-bye,"
I'm a young volunteer, and my heart is true To our flag that woos the wind;
Then three cheers for that flag and our country too, And the girls we leave behind.

When over the desert, thro' burning rays, With a heavy heart I tread;
Or when I breast the cannon's blaze, And bemoan my comrades dead,
Then, then will I think of my home and you, And our flag shall kiss the wind;
With huzza for our cause and country too, And the girls we leave behind.

Then adieu, then adieu, 'tis the last bugle's strain That is falling on the ear;
Should it so be decreed that we ne'er meet again, Oh, remember the Young Volunteer.

"The Young Volunteer" (1863)
Words and Music: John H. Hewitt

"Headed for the Seat of War"

Uniontown to Pittsburgh

The ominous events surrounding the election of 1860 cast a pall over Fayette County as bleak as the snowstorms that blanketed its farms and towns. But while winter gave way to spring in 1861, neither section of a bitterly divided country appeared willing to give way to the other. Fayette Countians, too, increasingly gave voice to opinions so strongly held as to seem irreconcilable.

In the months following Lincoln's election, the nightmare that so many had predicted came to pass. Led by the "fire-eaters,"[1] South Carolina seceded from the Union on December 20, 1860. Mississippi, Florida, Alabama, Georgia, and Louisiana followed her out in January 1861, and Texas joined them in early February. On February 8, 1861, deputies from the seven Southern states met in Montgomery, Alabama, and adopted a "Constitution for the Provisional Government of the Confederate States of America."

Fayette County Republicans who had voted for Abraham Lincoln were heartened by his inaugural address. In it, the new president acknowledged the "[a]pprehension [that] seems to exist among the people of the Southern States that by the accession of a Republican administration their property and their peace and personal security are to be endangered." He sought to allay their fears by reiterating his previously stated position on the momentous question of slavery: "I have no purpose, directly or indirectly, to interfere with the institution of slavery in the States where it exists. I believe I have no lawful right to do so, and I have no inclination to do so." At the same time, he left no one in doubt regarding his position on the issue of secession: "I hold that in contemplation of universal law and of the Constitution the Union of these States is perpetual.... We cannot remove our respective sections from each other nor build an impassable wall between them."[2]

Those who believed that the Union could be preserved without war must have been given pause, however, by the clear warning Lincoln issued to those secessionists who would hear it: "In *your* hands, my dissatisfied fellow-countrymen, and not in *mine*, is the momentous issue of civil war. The Government will not assail *you*.

3

You can have no conflict without being yourselves the aggressors. *You* have no oath registered in heaven to destroy the Government, while *I* shall have the most solemn one to 'preserve, protect, and defend it....'"[3]

Fayette County Democrats, on the other hand, were much less sanguine in their assessment of the political situation. Their views were reflected in a letter to the editor of the *Genius of Liberty*, Fayette County's largest newspaper:

> MR. EDITOR: —The republican party is no less surely ruining the country than it is ruining itself. Its fanaticism caused the original disruption of the Union, and its folly will make the disruption permanent. Before the election they falsified the facts to the people, and told them that disunion was a mere threat, never to be executed. The South, they said, would live contented under a government which made a savage war upon the very basis of their society and their wealth.... Though many leaders disavowed the intention to interfere by legislation with slavery in the States; still, the fiercest abolitionists were led to believe that the moral effects of the triumph would ultimately make them the masters of slavery even there....
>
> The republicans are indulging their folly at a bitter cost to the country.... They have been implored from the beginning to this moment to present some feasible basis of settlement. They have insultingly rejected every compromise, every plan which promised to become a foundation on which to build anew the superstructure of union, strength and peace. Whenever the hopes of the country were settled upon any measure of conciliation, they have uniformly used their congressional majority to vote it down....
>
> The abolitionists have the power, and they will enforce their doctrine...whether the people like it or not. Abundantly able to save, they are distracting and rending the country. Mr. Lincoln—if he thinks at all—seems to be halting between the present fear of his party on the one hand, and the fear of prospective infamy on the other. Radical and imbecile at once, he seems utterly unable to comprehend or alleviate the evils which afflict us for the sin of electing him.... History will record, that in eighteen hundred and sixty-one the Black Republicans had the power to save the country, and *would not*.
>
> LUZERNE[4]

In that same issue, the editor, while railing against the "evils of republicanism," nonetheless made clear the paper's position regarding the question of secession:

> Our opinions on the question of Union or Disunion are as distinct and clear as they are deeply felt. We are for the Union, *unconditionally*. The masses of the Cotton states, we believe and feel, have fallen into the darkest of errors on this most vital question. A revolutionary right to break up governments, and institute new ones, resides in every people and cannot be taken away. The Virginia and Kentucky resolutions of Jefferson and Madison affirm nothing more than this

right, giving no sanction whatever to the *constitutional* right of secession. These resolutions have always been the soul of the Democratic faith, and to them we still hold. We have thought from the first that the South was taking the wrong mode to save themselves from the evils with which republicanism threatened them. But they were not wholly without excuse. The republicans are their bitter and open enemies. They were elected on the principle that robbing and stealing property legally and rightfully belonging to the South is a moral duty; on the principle of refusing them their just rights in the Territories. The Republican party has broken the compact of Union in every State where they had the power. They have foisted on the country an administration which threatens to live in daily violation of the Constitution as expounded by the Supreme Court—an administration whose bosum is filled with malice and hatred towards the South. During the whole campaign, the lips of Republican speakers were foul with abuse against a whole section.... These acts palliate, but do not justify, the course of the cotton states. There can be no justification for that man who would sunder the American Union. Great as are the wrongs of the South, we believe they could have been redressed within the Union....

While Democrats have unceasingly labored to arrive at some just compromise with the Southern people, the Republicans seem bent on permanent dissolution. They agree with the *Tribune*, that the nation had better go to destruction, than that the South should enjoy any rights which are distasteful to them, however clear and just these rights may be. Democrats have always struggled for the 'equality' of the Southern States, and the protection of their property. Republicans are against both. They have defeated the friends of law and justice, and the result speaks so loudly in the distress of the country, that we need not speak of it.[5]

All eyes soon turned to a beleaguered Federal garrison in Charleston harbor. The editor of the *Genius of Liberty* commented on the worsening situation in the weekly edition dated April 11, 1861:

The dangers of civil war seem greater every hour, whilst both Lincoln and Davis declare their policy to be peace, and each avers he will not be the aggressor. It will be nearly a miracle if hostilities between the two sections shall not have taken place before this is read by many of our readers.

The present month promises to be an eventful one, and we shall await its developments with great solicitude. If it shall proclaim our escape from a war with our own kinsmen and friends, none will rejoice more sincerely than we. If on the other hand, its close shall find us embroiled in a bloody contest, whose end and result cannot be foreseen, we shall endeavor, calmly and dispassionately, to consider the momentous questions which it must involve, and contribute, as far as in us lies, to mitigate its evils.[6]

Less than 24 hours later, just past three o'clock in the morning, all efforts at negotiating a peaceful evacuation of Fort Sumter having failed, representatives of Confederate Brigadier General P. G. T. Beauregard delivered a fateful message to Major Robert Anderson, the fort's commander: "SIR: By authority of Brigadier-General Beauregard, commanding the Provisional Forces of the Confederate States, we have the honor to notify you that he will open the fire of his batteries on Fort Sumpter [*sic*] in one hour from this time. We have the honor to be very respectfully, Your obedient servants, JAMES CHESNUT, Jr., *Aide de Camp.* STEPHEN D. LEE, *Captain, C. S. Army, Aide de Camp.*"[7]

At 4:30 a.m. April 12, 1861, a shell from a Confederate 10-inch mortar burst over Fort Sumter. The Civil War had begun. Details of the momentous events in South Carolina reached Uniontown with the publication in the next issue of the *Genius of Liberty* of the following dispatch from Charleston:

> CHARLESTON, April 12. —The bombardment has commenced, and War is inaugurated. The batteries on Sullivan's Island, Morris Island, and other points opened on Sumpter [*sic*] at 4 o'clock this morning. Major Anderson has returned the fire, and a brisk cannonading has been kept up during the day.
>
> We have no information from seaward yet with regard to the movement of the United States vessels outside [the harbor]. The militia are under arms, and the whole of our population are on the streets. Every available space facing the harbor is filled with anxious spectators.[8]

President Lincoln's proclamation of April 15 calling for volunteers to put down the rebellion was reprinted on page one of the *Genius of Liberty*, right next to the Charleston dispatch:

> WASHINGTON CITY, April 14 [*sic*]. —Whereas, the laws of the United States have been, for some time past and are now, opposed, and the execution thereof obstructed in the States of South Carolina, Georgia, Alabama, Florida, and Mississippi, Louisiana and Texas, by combinations too powerful to be suppressed by the ordinary course of judicial proceedings, or by the powers vested in the Marshals by law.
>
> Now therefore I, ABRAHAM LINCOLN, President of the United States, in virtue of the power vested in me by the Constitution and the Laws, have thought fit, to call forthwith, and hereby do call forth the MILITIA of the several States of the Union, to the aggregate number of SEVENTY FIVE THOUSAND, in order to suppress the said combination, and cause the laws to be duly executed....
>
> I appeal to all loyal citizens to favor, facilitate and aid this effort to maintain the honor, the integrity and existence of our National Union, and the perpetuity of the popular Government, and to redress the wrongs already long enough endured. I deem it proper to say that the first service assigned to the forces hereby called forth will probably be *to repossess the forts*, places and property which

have been seized from the Union;... And I hereby command the persons composing the combinations aforesaid to disperse and retire peaceably to their respective abodes, within twenty days from this date.[9]

The news from South Carolina electrified Fayette Countians and galvanized hundreds of young men to rally to the flag. S. Duncan Oliphant, a prominent local lawyer with militia experience, immediately undertook to raise a company of volunteer infantry in Uniontown. By April 22, Oliphant's company, known as the Fayette Guards, marched northward toward Pittsburgh, 98 strong.

One of the volunteers, George Darby, recalled his response and his feelings upon hearing the news: "With patriotic motives burning high within me, I with many thousands of my country's sons, donned the blue of a soldier boy with a faint conception of the hardship, danger and exposure we were to endure, but with a rugged and unfaltering determination to sustain our beloved country in its struggle with the cohorts of rebellion to the bitter end. I was nineteen years old, strong and vigorous, and my comrades were all young and hearty men.... On April 22d, 1861, [I] enlisted in Captain S. D. Oliphant's company, which was organized at Uniontown...for the three months service. On our arrival at Pittsburgh...we found the quota for the three months' men already filled, so we at once re-enlisted for three years, or during the war."[10]

S. Duncan Oliphant was 34 years old when the war broke out. Born in Fayette County in 1826, he was graduated from Jefferson College in Washington County, Pennsylvania, in 1844 and entered Harvard Law School in October of that year. Following his graduation from Harvard, he was admitted to the bar in Fayette County and began his practice in the law offices of his uncle, E. P. Oliphant. In 1849, Oliphant was commissioned as a lieutenant colonel commanding a battalion of uniformed militia in Fayette County. The *Genius of Liberty* noted the departure of Oliphant's Fayette Guards for Pittsburgh and reflected upon the character of the man:

> Col. S. D. Oliphant left here on Tuesday last with a full company, about 100 men, enlisted under the call of Gov. Curtin, for the defense of the National Capitol. This is a noble company, composed of substantial citizens, and many of our most promising young men.
>
> We feel no hesitation in saying that the company has been exceedingly fortunate in the selection of a Captain.... S. D. Oliphant is a gentleman of character and intelligence, a fine military man, and possessed of a kind and generous heart; his command will find him not only an urbane and genial companion, but [also] a skillful and efficient commander.
>
> Whilst we regret most deeply that the necessity exists which has called them out, we rejoice to record the fact that our citizens have so promptly and nobly responded to the call. We shall watch their movements with the most anxious

George W. Darby enlisted in the Fayette Guards (Co. G of the 8th Reserves) April 22, 1861. He served through the war and was honorably discharged June 28, 1865.

Author's Collection

S. Duncan Oliphant organized the Fayette Guards in April 1861 and served as the company's first captain. He was later elected lieutenant colonel of the 8th Reserves.

National Archives

solicitude, and inform our readers from time to time of all matters of interest that come to hand. We have no doubt that if an opportunity offers, that both officers and men will nobly acquit themselves.

The *Genius* is represented in the person of W. H. Leithead, a good Printer, a good Democrat, and a clever and agreeable fellow in all the relations of life. He will no doubt make a good soldier.[11]

As the young printer went about the business of learning to become a good soldier, he did not forget his prior training as a good newspaperman. On April 29, he penned the following letter to the *Genius of Liberty* from his unusual barracks in the city of Pittsburgh:

Dear Sir—The Company from Uniontown is still here, and all are enjoying themselves, and appear to be in excellent spirits. We are now [housed] on a boat at the wharf, but expect to leave...tomorrow for the Fair Grounds, where arrangements have been made for the several companies now here.... All the members composing the 'Fayette Guards' are much pleased with Col. Oliphant as Captain of the Company....[12] The Pittsburghers say that it is composed of the best looking lot of men that have entered the city since the campaign opened, and that they have the best martial music that is in the city. It is not known how long we will remain here, but wherever we go, I will try and give you all the information I can.

But as I am on the boat, and there is so much noise and confusion, I will have to close. Excuse a soldier's haste.

Yours, Respectfully,
W. H. L.[13]

George Darby also commented on the company's riverfront accommodation: "We were temporarily quartered on board the river steamer *Marengo*, which lay at the foot of Market Street [on the Monongahela River], and were drilled in a public hall at the corner of Market and Water streets. We were [next] boarded at the Girard House, on Smithfield Street.... We were afterwards removed to Camp Wilkins, (the old fair grounds), which we occupied for some length of time, in common with Colonel McLain's Erie Regiment."[14]

Camp Wilkins was organized in late April 1861,[15] when Pennsylvania Governor Andrew G. Curtin,[16] in response to a plea from the mayor of Pittsburgh, decided to form a military camp in the western part of the state. Volunteer companies from the outlying counties in western Pennsylvania, together with the numerous companies formed in Pittsburgh itself, were marched to the old Fair Grounds, located on the south side of Penn Avenue between present-day 29th and 32nd Streets. Colonel Phaeon Jarrett, appointed by the governor to organize the camp, arrived April 29 and proceeded forthwith to put it on a firm military footing. One of his first actions was to post a set of rules for the camp, which quickly became known as "Jarrett's Twelve Commandments." These set out a daily schedule for the troops and provided for roll call, company drill, instruction in the military arts, and policing the camp.

By May 3, 16 companies, comprising some 1,200 volunteers, were in camp. For many of them, the journey to Camp Wilkins marked the first time they had ever traveled any distance from their homes. There was little time for homesickness, however, as the fledgling soldiers passed their days with drill and dreams of martial glory. For the loved ones they left behind, however, those days would pass slowly and would be filled with worry and prayer. One young volunteer, Joseph McQuaide of Greensburg, received a letter from his father and mother that gave voice to the fears common to parents across the breadth of a divided nation:

Pennsylvania's great wartime governor, Andrew G. Curtin, was the prime architect of the Pennsylvania Reserve Volunteer Corps and championed it throughout the war.
Library of Congress

May the 23rd 1861

My Dear Joseph as this is the first letter that I ever comensed to Rite to you my youngest son: The one that I thought would watch over my dying pillow.... You may be assured that I rite with no ordinary feelings. You do not quite know how hard it is for a parent to part with a favorite Child. But I would be the last person on Earth to Discourage you, you are there moved to follow the Dictates of your own conscience.... One thing I wish you to be Careful of your health in Damp, Wet days.... Keep warm, Keep your neck well secured from Cold.... Do not above all other things neglect to hold Communion with that kind heavenly father who created you....

Do not be afraid to lean on the strong arm of our Blessed Jesus for he is everywhere present.... It was good advice the old preacher gave when he said trust in God [and] Keep your powder dry. Much may depend on the Justness of our cause [and] the strength and discipline of our army but much more depends on that God who rules in the armies of heaven.... I hope that this war will terminate in less time than one year. We are all well.... If there is anything you want rite or let us know. We will endeavour to send it to you.

May the Blessings of Allmighty God be with you wherever you may be called to go is the Daily prayer of your father & mother.

John and Mary McQuaide[17]

A typical Union infantry company at "Parade Rest." Note the company's musicians at the right of the formation.

National Archives

If there was one topic that commanded the attention of these fledgling soldiers more than the arrival of mail from home, it was the matter of food. In this regard, it is interesting to peruse the following list, describing the daily rations for one company of 77 men: "95 ½ lbs Fresh and Salt Beef, or 67 ½ lbs Pork; 86 ¾ lbs Soft Bread or Flour, or 57 ¾ lbs Hard Bread; 11 ½ lbs Beans or 7 ¾ lbs Rice; 8 ¾ lbs Sugar; 4 ¾ lbs Coffee, ground; 3 ¾ quarts Vinegar; 3 pecks Potatoes; 13-16 lbs Candles; 3 ¾ lbs Soap; 1 quart Salt; 3 pints Soft Soap."[18]

Many local civic societies and religious organizations were quick to "adopt" the various companies encamped at Camp Wilkins. In addition to supplying the soldiers with uniforms and blankets, these groups supplemented the basic fare described above with culinary delights much more likely to remind the boys of home. For instance, "the Ladies of the Liberty Methodist Episcopal Church on Saturday evening presented the Erie Regiment...with 500 pies which were distributed at a rate of fifty to each company."[19]

While all undoubtedly appreciated the baked goods, some of the Erie soldiers had more pressing needs. George Darby recounted an amusing incident involving one such unfortunate: "The Erie Regiment had been uniformed in suits of gray consisting of jacket and pants, and they soon became worn and ragged, and all appeals for clothing had been refused. One genius among them, whose pants had been entirely worn away at the seat, determined to appeal to the public, which he did in the following original manner. It was the custom for crowds of visitors to come to camp on Sunday and the Erie man having painted the words 'The last resort' in big black letters on a large shingle, attached a cord to it and hanging it over the seat of his pants, went parading around camp among the visitors. This novel walking advertisement of their necessities soon brought the desired clothing...."[20]

In that innocent springtime of 1861, before the reality of war commanded the undivided attention of the Fayette Guards, thoughts of home often led to sojourns home, particularly by the company's officers:

> Lieutenants Gardner and Ramsey of the Fayette Guards, now at Camp Wilkins, near Pittsburgh, paid our town a flying visit a few days since. They were warmly greeted by their fellow townsmen and carried back with them various and goodly packages that will doubtless be welcome to the boys. They represent the company as being comfortably situated—all in good health and spirits, and rapidly progressing in their military lessons.... Whilst in town, Lieut. Ramsey was engaged in collecting the Wide-Awake and Little Giant Capes that had seen service during the Presidential Campaign to take to the soldiers at Camp Wilkins. The idea is a good one, and we hope all who have any of either kind on hand, will send them in, as they will prove very acceptable to our brave boys when standing guard on inclement nights. It is gratifying that any remnants of the

campaign can be made to minister to the comfort of the volunteers. Send on the water-proof capes.[21]

The soldiers' visits home were reciprocated with great frequency, as related by the editors of the *Genius of Liberty*:

Among the most pleasant incidents of our life, was our visit last week to Camp Wilkins, and the communication we had with our brave 'soger boys....' There are now at Camp Wilkins twenty-six companies, and three more ordered in this week, viz: Capt. Bierer's of Uniontown, Capt. Cuthbert's of New Brighton and Capt. Adams', of Beaver. The Erie Regiment is already organized, and when one more company is accepted they will organize two more. The troops are making rapid improvement in drilling. The precision with which they execute movements is very creditable considering that many of them knew nothing about them a few days ago.

Capt. Oliphant, as we predicted, is very popular with his company, and also throughout the camp. First Sergeant John Bierer, ex-editor of the *Genius*, seems to be in excellent spirits. He devotes himself assiduously to the discharge of his duties and the comfort of his men. The men all seem to enjoy camp life exceedingly, and with one or two exceptions they enjoy excellent health. Should an opportunity occur during the period of their enlistment, there need be no fears but that the high character of the Fayette County soldiery will be fully sustained.

Since our visit two informal regiments of eight companies each, have been formed, and Capt. S. D. Oliphant has been elected Lieut. Colonel of one of them.

Camp Wilkins is a great resort for Pittsburghers and the people from the surrounding counties. Thousands go out every pleasant afternoon, when the gates are thrown open to the public to witness the regimental parade.

Without any disparagement to any of the rest, we thought that the Fayette Guards were decidedly the best looking company in camp.[22]

The reality of war intruded soon enough; but, curiously, it impacted Fayette Countians on the home front more than it did those preparing for it at Camp Wilkins. On May 30, 1861, the *Genius of Liberty* reported that:

[f]or several days past, the people of Uniontown, and of Fayette County, have been under a high state of excitement, produced by reports received from Western Virginia. On Monday afternoon [May 27] messengers arrived here from Morgantown, Va. [just 25 miles southwest of Uniontown], confirming the news that Virginia secessionists had military possession of Grafton, and that Morgantown and the Pennsylvania border were threatened with violence and raids, and that armed men to the number of 1,200 or 1,500 were marching in that direction.... [It was reported that] two villages in the southwestern part of Preston

County [Virginia] had been seized and occupied by the troops from Grafton, that depredations had been committed on individuals and property, and that Kingwood and other towns, as well as various prominent individuals had been severely threatened. Families were said to be leaving. Merchants leaving or boxing up their goods, and that the greatest alarm existed among the Union men....

Upon hearing these reports...the greatest excitement, enthusiasm and alarm seemed to take hold of our citizens. Meetings of the local authorities, citizens and military organizations were called...and means were taken to secure arms. Companies expressed a willingness to go as soon as armed to the defense of the border [a mere fifteen miles south of Uniontown].... Capt. F. H. Oliphant [S. Duncan Oliphant's father, then 61 years of age] on Tuesday morning [May 28], at the head of three companies of cavalry, armed with rifles...took up the line of march for the border.... [A]n immediate attack upon Uniontown was expected, and our fellow citizens throughout the county, with a patriotism and promptness that entitles them to the everlasting esteem and gratitude of our citizens, dropped all their business...and commenced collecting their men, and preparing to come to the defense of the town, or if needs be, go on to the border. On Tuesday afternoon the sound of martial music was heard approaching the west end of town, and it was soon discovered to be accompanied by the New Salem Guards...in wagons and on horseback, armed with rifles, pistols, &c. They were a bold, brave, fine looking set of men to the number of 60 or 70, and although they were not expected, it gave our citizens a joyful and agreeable surprise. They marched to the Clinton House [where they were] tendered the thanks and hospitalities of the town. During the afternoon they again formed into line and paraded through the streets, and seeing the town was in no danger, determined to return home. Our Home Guards, under command of Capt. A. Giler, turned out, well-armed, and received Capt. Herbert's Guards in front of the Court House and escorted them out of town....

[In the evening] the sound of a bugle and the tramp of horses was heard and the 'Dunlap's Creek Cavalry'...fully armed and equipped, made their appearance in our streets.... Our citizens then quietly retired, feeling deeply grateful, and amply secure against attack. About 11 o'clock, Tuesday night, the 'Dunbar Cavalry'...with a strong force, fully uniformed and well armed, came into town, and finding everything quiet, put up at the Clinton House. On Wednesday morning, the two Cavalry Companies paraded through our streets and were everywhere greeted with demonstrations of gratitude and respect. Halting in front of the McClelland House, they were eloquently addressed by our Burgess...after which the companies returned to their homes, carrying with them the most affectionate regards, and best wishes of our entire people.

Although these demonstrations in one sense, may seem to have been unnecessary, yet they have been highly important in showing the loyalty and patriotism of our citizen soldiery, and the promptness with which they responded to
the call of duty, and also in more closely cementing the bonds of union and
fraternal feeling among our own citizens of Pennsylvania and Western Virginia.[23]

While the elder Oliphant was leading his band of troopers southward toward
the enemy border, his son was preparing to lead the Fayette Guards northward to a
new camp. As the number of volunteers at Camp Wilkins grew ever larger, so, too,
did concern among the citizens of Pittsburgh regarding its perceived shortcomings:
"[T]here were a number of valid reasons advanced by the press for removal of
Camp Wilkins to a more suitable site. The papers pointed out that the Fair Grounds
were too small to drill the 2,000 troops; that the proximity of the camp to the city
had a demoralizing effect; that it was impossible to enforce proper discipline while
the facilities for reaching the city were easy and available; that drunken brawls and
fierce assaults were not infrequent among the volunteers, and that the area was
unsanitary."[24]

With volunteer companies continuing to pour into Wilkins and other camps
across the Commonwealth, Governor Curtin addressed a message to an emergency
session of the legislature in Harrisburg on April 30. In it, he stated: "It is impossible
to predict the length to which the madness that rules the hour in the rebellious states
shall lead us, or when the calamities which threaten our hitherto happy country
shall terminate.... We have a long line of border on States seriously disaffected,
which should be protected. To...protect our borders we should have a well-regu-
lated military force. I, therefore, recommend the immediate organization, disciplin-
ing, and arming of at least fifteen regiments of cavalry and infantry, exclusive of
those called into the service of the United States; as we have already ample warning of the necessity of being prepared for any sudden exigency that may arise. I
cannot too much impress this upon you."[25]

Heeding the governor's warning, on May 15 the legislature passed "An Act
to...Provide for Arming the State." Andrew Curtin signed it into law the same day.
The act called for the creation of a military corps, to be known as the Reserve
Volunteer Corps of the Commonwealth, consisting of 13 regiments of infantry, one
of cavalry and one of light artillery. These regiments were filled quickly with men
from the numerous volunteer companies that had arrived in camps throughout the
state too late to be included in the regiments previously tendered to the national
government in response to President Lincoln's call for volunteers.

Also on May 15, Governor Curtin appointed George Archibald McCall of
Philadelphia to command the troops of the newly created Pennsylvania Reserve
Volunteer Corps (as the corps had come to be called).[26] Born in 1802, McCall was
a West Point graduate who had distinguished himself in the Seminole and Mexican

Wars. He received two brevets in the latter for "gallant and distinguished conduct" at the battles of Palo Alto and Resaca de la Palma. In 1850, he was appointed inspector general of the army with the rank of colonel of cavalry. McCall resigned his commission in 1853 due to ill health and settled on a farm in Chester County, Pennsylvania. He remained active in military affairs, however, serving as a major general in the state militia. When Fort Sumter was attacked, Governor Curtin summoned McCall to Harrisburg to advise him on military affairs within the Commonwealth and, shortly thereafter, offered him command of the Reserves. McCall readily accepted Curtin's offer and was commissioned as a major general of volunteers.

In one of his first actions after taking command, General McCall recommended that a new camp be established north of Pittsburgh on the line of the Allegheny Valley Railroad. This site, he believed, would go far toward alleviating the unsanitary conditions that prevailed at Camp Wilkins. There, according to McCall, the troops would "have every facility for bathing in the pure waters of the Allegheny [River]."[27] The new site was named Camp Wright in honor of John A. Wright, Governor Curtin's military aide, and the Fayette Guards were among the early companies to be transferred there from Camp Wilkins. Before long, the boys from Uniontown were making their way back home: "Our town has been visited during the past few days by quite a number of our brave soldier boys from Camp Wright. Lieut. H. W. Patterson, W. H. Leithead, Isaac Moore, Thos. W. Springer, William Searight, John R. Rutter, and others, of Capt. Oliphant's company. Lieut. T. Hudson Hopwood, A. Gorley, S. D. Sturgis and others

George Archibald McCall of Philadelphia served as the first commander of the Pennsylvania Reserves with the rank of major general of Pennsylvania Volunteers. He was later commissioned a brigadier general of United States Volunteers.

National Archives

of Capt. Bierer's company, all of whom have been accepted and sworn into service. They all appear to enjoy good health and spirits, and appear determined to give a good account of themselves.... We are rejoiced to hear them speak so well of their Captains, (Bierer and Oliphant), which is alike creditable to these gallant and generous officers and brave men."[28]

Also among the early arrivals at Camp Wright was a company of volunteers from Brownsville, Pennsylvania. Known in its earliest years as Redstone Old Fort, Brownsville lay on the northwestern border of Fayette County, just 12 miles from Uniontown. Astride the National Road along the right bank of the Monongahela

River, it had once rivaled Pittsburgh as an early gateway to the West, with access via the Monongahela to the Ohio River and thence to the Mississippi.

Many young men from the surrounding farms and villages flocked to Brownsville in response to President Lincoln's call for troops. Among them was 18-year-old Ashbel Fairchild Hill, a student from nearby Masontown. Hill enlisted May 1, 1861, in the infantry company recruited by Captain Cyrus L. Conner, a Brownsville native who had served with the Fayette County Volunteers during the Mexican War. The new recruits were forced to bide their time in Brownsville, drilling without arms or uniforms, awaiting the call to go into camp. As he recounted in his book, *Our Boys*, Hill and his young comrades were elated when their orders finally came:

> Marching orders! Hurrah! Hurrah! The sun was just sinking beneath the wild old hills west of Brownsville, when a glad cheer rang out on the mild evening air; it came from a company of Volunteers— they stood in line in one of the principal streets of the town. Our company had been organized as soon as the first call for troops to crush the rebellion was made; and for weeks we had been anxiously awaiting orders to go into camp. It was now June [1861], and the welcome order had just come. Early next morning we embarked for Pittsburg, at which place we arrived after a journey of sixty miles, down the beautiful Monongahela. We were ordered to Camp Wright, which was about twelve miles from the city, on the left bank of the Allegheny [River]. On our arrival thither, we found barracks constructed of pine boards, and we unhesitatingly took possession of one of the buildings, and moved in. Not long after, a board might have been seen swinging above, on which was inscribed in huge letters—THE BROWNSVILLE GRAYS.[29]

Ashbel Fairchild Hill enlisted in the Brownsville Grays (Co. D of the 8th Reserves) May 1, 1861. He was wounded severely at the Battle of Antietam and was honorably discharged on surgeon's certificate December 20, 1862.

Author's Collection

The Grays learned their first lesson on their very first night in camp: "When nine o'clock came, the 'tattoo' was beaten. At ten came the 'taps.' We were just wondering what it meant, when a man who was called the 'officer of the day,' came round and looking into our quarters, said, in an authoritative tone—'Lights out!' Then we understood it—no lights were to be burning in camp after taps. Our candles were at once extinguished, and we retired to our bunks."[30]

While Hill undoubtedly slept soundly that night, dreams of martial glory crowded into his mind: "I was just dreaming of advancing stealthily upon a rebel masked battery, when a loud report burst upon the air, shook the barracks, and caused me to spring up and strike my head against the bunk above, with such force that the flash of a hundred cannon seemed to be exhibited to my startled senses. I opened my eyes, and found all things bathed in the broad light of day. The report which had so suddenly interrupted my dreams of battle, came from a six-pounder [cannon] which was kept in camp, to be fired every morning at five o'clock."[31]

Reveille and roll call were the first order of business, followed by a breakfast of coffee, bread, beefsteak, and potatoes. Then a surgeon who determined their fitness for military service inspected the new recruits. Hill described what happened next:

> After all had been inspected...we were drawn up in line to be vaccinated. The surgeon passed slowly along the line, performing the operation upon the arm of each with some dispatch. He was scratching away at the arm of a slim, thin-faced young man, called 'Watty,' when I observed that same thin face grow, first, very red, then white as a sheet, and for a few minutes he was quite sick and faint. One of our boys rallied him in the following manner: "Watty, if you are so tender as that, you will never stand it to have your head lifted off by a shell; it would be the death of you." A groan from Watty was the only reply. He certainly couldn't see the joke.
>
> The next thing administered to us was the oath. All the boys took it without the least hesitation; they had offered their services to their country, and they were in earnest. There was no 'backing the patch.' We were sworn into the service of the State of Pennsylvania, with the understanding that we should be subject to a call from the government at any time.[32]

Invariably, in any military camp there are those few characters who endear themselves to their fellow soldiers (if not to their officers) by acting the fool. Levity often serving as the only antidote to the harsh realities of war, it is given to such men to relieve the loneliness and fear which are the soldier's constant companions. The Brownsville Grays' resident character was James Gaskill, from Cookstown on the Monongahela. Gaskill had spent most of his adult life working as a boatman, but he had also traveled with a circus as a clown. Hill related his initial encounter with the man who would bring so much joy to the soldiers and unceasing consternation to their officers:

> [He was] quite a comical chap, of eight-and-twenty, with small, bright, black eyes, black hair, and a growth of stunted, black whiskers and moustache. His

appearance was quite clownish: he was amusing the admiring spectators by playing as many antics as a monkey, and making numerous quaint remarks. But,
what was my surprise when...he abruptly stopped in the midst of a great flow of
loquacity, stood still and erect, deliberately doffed his beaver [hat], and exhibited therein a gentle creature, known as a—*black snake*! The serpent, which was
about thirty inches in length and proportionally thick, reared its head aloft, and
took a mild survey of the audience.... Gaskill at this moment placed his hat upon
his head, minus the snake, which he retained in his hand, and proceeded to
disperse the crowd which was collected around him, by thrusting the monster
right at their faces. Then, such tumbling and scrambling as there was to escape
being touched by the shiny reptile, I never before witnessed.... Having thus dispersed the crowd, Gaskill entered the barracks, deposited his 'pet' in a small
box in his trunk, then came tripping out singing the oddest little song in the
world....[33]

Clowns, professional and otherwise, did not provide all the entertainment in
camp. The fledgling soldiers' efforts to master the military arts also provided comic
relief from time to time. Hill recalled one such instance:

One evening it was announced to us that we were detailed for camp-guard
for the following day.... I was delighted at the prospect of having an opportunity
of trying my hand at 'guard duty' for the first time.... Having been placed on
post on the north side of the camp, by the corporal of the guard, and a musket
placed in my hands, I felt as proud as a king, and I remarked to myself that I
certainly *was* a soldier, *now.*

Just without the camp, near my post, was our drill-ground, and I was kept in
continual merriment by observing the awkward motions of some of the companies on drill.... While I was watching the movements of a platoon which was
being drilled by a youthful lieutenant, an incident occurred which struck me as
being particularly ridiculous.

The platoon had been standing at rest a few moments, when the lieutenant
said: 'Now, boys, I should like to try you on a bayonet charge. Do you think you
can do it up [proud]?' They all said they could. The officer then commanded;
'Shoulder—*arms!*'

They shouldered arms; and he continued: 'Charge—*bayonet!*' They made an
attempt to bring their muskets to the position of charge-bayonet, the points of
their bayonets ranging from the height of the knee to the height of the head. The
officer seemed to think it would do, and he said: 'Now for a charge. Forward!
Double-quick! *March!*'

The platoon made a rush right forward, placing the lieutenant, who was standing in front of them, in imminent danger of being run through. In giving the

command, it seemed he had forgotten that he was standing directly in front of his men. Now they were rushing at him with charged bayonets. He had not the presence of mind to command them to halt; so, under the impulse of the moment, he sprang backward, and fell prostrate over a stump, while the men—they had no orders to halt—rushed on, one or two...falling over the prostrate form of the lieutenant. [He] sprang up, and cried out, after his platoon: 'Oh—a—a—*quit*—stop! That is, a—a—halt!'

But he was too late. In the excitement of the mock charge, the men either heard not, or heeded not. They kept straight on, and not being very well skilled in the noble art of 'keeping step,' they broke up into a disorderly crowd, and, concluding that *that* ought to be the end of the matter, rushed right across the beat I was walking, and bolted into their quarters. The lieutenant followed presently, looking just the sheepishest mortal that I ever saw wearing shoulder-straps.[34]

By mid-June, some forty-three volunteer companies were present in Camp Wright. Just one regiment had been organized, and the deportment of the remaining companies ranged from those with uniforms and arms supplied by their home counties to those that had nothing but their patriotism to display on the parade ground. The Brownsville Grays were among the have-nots in this regard, as Hill noted on the occasion of General McCall's first visit to the camp: "All was stir and excitement in camp. The six-pounder was loaded and fired, with great rapidity—thirteen times. What was up? Why, General McCall was entering Camp Wright, and was going to review us that afternoon. But one regiment was organized, armed and equipped; it was known as the 'Erie Regiment'...commanded by Colonel John McLane. The remainder of the troops in camp...[including the Brownsville Grays and the Fayette Guards] marched into a large field with the Erie Regiment, and were reviewed. We had no arms, no uniforms, no accoutrements of any kind; and when the general appeared on the field, and the command, 'Present—arms' was given, we respectfully raised our hands to our hats, thereby presenting our own arms. We thought it very nice—that review—very military."[35]

On the heels of General McCall's inspection, a number of the unaffiliated companies were organized into an unofficial regiment in order to enhance their prospects for acceptance into the regular army.[36] Shortly thereafter, McCall returned to Camp Wright to attend to the formal organization of two new regiments of the Pennsylvania Reserve Volunteer Corps: "On Friday afternoon [June 28] Gen. McCall went up on the A. V. R. R. to Camp Wright, and proceeded to organize two Regiments—the 8th and 9th. The 8th—Col. G. S. Hays, Lieut. Col. S. D. Oliphant, and Major John W. Duncan—is composed of the following companies: Anderson Cadets, Capt. Gallope; Duncan Guards, Capt. Shoenberger; Fayette Guards, Capt. Gardner; Brownsville Greys, Capt. Conner; Armstrong Rifles, Capt. Cantwell;

Clarion Union Guards, Capt. Lemmon; Jefferson Riflemen, Capt. Johnson; Hopkins Infantry, Capt. Wishart; Hopewell Rifles, Capt. Eichenberger; Greene County Rangers, Capt. Bailey."[37] The Brownsville Grays and the Fayette Guards were incorporated into the 8th Regiment as Company D and Company G, respectively.

Three days later the two new regiments marched from Camp Wright to Camp Wilkins.[38] For the men of the Fayette Guards, the movement heralded a return to familiar environs. For the Brownsville Grays, however, Camp Wilkins provided a new experience—and a new temptation. Hill spoke of both in *Our Boys*:

> Our quarters consisted of a row of rough old cattle-sheds, at the south side of the [fair] ground. The sheds were divided into rooms capable of accommodating, with bunks, five or six each. Here, then, was my first mess formed. They were all young men, none above twenty-four; their names were—Will. Mitchell, Mr. Craft, James Troth, John Woodward, and Will. Haddock....
>
> Our quarters being at the south side of the camp, The Pennsylvania Central Railroad lay directly by us, and the trains went thundering along every fifteen minutes, night and day....
>
> [So] away I went, making for Pittsburg as the first point, to have a look at the fashions.... I could get out of camp at my convenience.... I would here state, that the reason the men were kept in such 'durance vile' was that, were they allowed to pass out *ad libitum*, three-fourths of them would be constantly 'on a high;' in fact, they would spend half their time in the 'smoky city,' Pittsburg.[39]

Such high jinks, of course, were frowned upon. Minor delinquencies often were handled summarily, but more serious infractions were dealt with by courts-martial. Hill's first exposure to a court-martial proceeding left an indelible impression:

> It was evening. The Eighth Regiment stood in line, on dress parade. Our first court-martial had convened, and now the result was being made known. The sentences of several offenders were being read to us by the adjutant. Several had been tried for 'sleeping on post,' and a number for drunkenness and rowdy conduct. There was one very serious case. One Jack Bear, of company 'K,' had grievously offended, in that he went out of camp clandestinely, got drunk, came back making an unreasonable amount of noise, kicked up several rows [of tents] and on being ordered by his captain to desist, cursed him, was put in the guard-house, broke out, and finally concluded this interesting course of procedure by promising most solemnly to shoot his captain as soon as the opportunity should occur.
>
> The adjutant read—
>
> "Private Bear, of company K, charged with mutiny; specifications, that on, or about the fourth day of July, the said Private Bear...did, in open violation of rules and regulations, become intoxicated, during which his conduct was most

disorderly and outrageous, and on being mildly reprimanded by his captain, used toward him the most shameful and insulting language, finally threatening to kill him.

"The court-martial carefully examined the evidence adduced, and, after due consideration, sentenced him, the said Private Bear...to be brought before the regiment while on dress parade, to be then and there publicly dismissed from the service, and drummed out of camp."

The sentence was to be immediately carried out. The regiment was brought to an "open order," and the front rank faced about. Then, entering this avenue at the right of the regiment, came the poor fellow, a guard on either side of him, and following a fifer and drummer playing the "Rogue's March." 'Twas a sad scene. I'll never forget how the poor fellow looked; it was painful to witness such unutterable dejection and shamefacedness.... How then must he have felt while marching along that avenue of men—that gauntlet of a thousand pairs of eyes. I think I should much rather run a gauntlet of knives and tomahawks in the hands of the most relentless savages.[40]

Duly chastened by what they had witnessed, the men of the 8th Regiment returned to their daily routine of regimental maneuvers. Lieutenant Colonel Oliphant was leading them through a bayonet drill one hot July afternoon when a messenger rode up and placed a document in his hand. Oliphant read it and then, waving his sword aloft, shouted: "Marching orders for Washington! Three cheers!" Hill described his comrades' reaction: "[H]ad you been in the vicinity of Camp Wilkins, you would have heard three of the most stirring cheers that ever rang out from the lips of a regiment of volunteers; so welcome those marching orders."[41] The movement was scheduled for Sunday, July 21, 1861:

Sunday morning came. The regiment was in line at nine o'clock.... [At last] we marched from Camp Wilkins toward Pittsburg, where we were to take the cars. In another hour we stood in one of the streets of Pittsburg, slowly embarking on the train that was to convey us to Baltimore. Thousands of spectators, men, women, and children, thronged the sidewalks, talking kindly with us, and bidding us 'good-by.' Many kind wishes followed us as the locomotive screamed, and the streets of the Smoky City began slowly to glide from beneath us.... One beautiful creature told me I must not think of returning without the head of Jeff Davis. I laughed, and informed her that I should certainly bring *that* desirable acquisition, and that if I didn't find him too unhandy to carry, would bring [his] entire body.[42]

Hill summed up the feelings of many of the young soldiers on that memorable day, as they were leaving Pittsburgh for an uncertain future: "We were buoyant with the brightest hopes now. Pittsburg was soon left behind, and we were whirling along the Pennsylvania Central in the liveliest manner. Alas! How many of the brave fellows whom that train carried were destined to return no more forever! How many had looked upon their wives, their children, their fathers, their mothers, their brothers, sisters, and friends for the last time! How many had bidden a last, long farewell, had received the last fond caress, the last kiss from those they loved better than life itself!"[43]

And George Darby recalled the departure of the Fayette Guards for the front: "This was on the 21st day of July, the day of the first battle of Bull Run. The tidings from the bloody field were flashing northward over the magnetic wires, and the news was not of a reassuring character; excitement ran high, and any man or woman, who that day wore a smile, was looked upon with grave suspicion, and in order to put a check upon the exuberance of expression of any sympathizer with the cause of the Confederacy, there were hempen nooses decorating all the lamp-posts along Liberty and Penn avenues.... [A]fter passing that most trying ordeal of leavetaking of the loved ones left behind, we took the cars on Liberty Street and headed for the seat of war."[44]

"We May Have Some Trouble in Baltimore"

Pittsburgh to Washington

Journeys by train in the 1860s, particularly those aboard a military train, were fraught with dangers scarcely imaginable by contemporary rail travelers. The train carrying the 8th Regiment from Pittsburgh to Harrisburg caught fire in the middle of the night as it was descending the eastern slope of the Allegheny Mountains: "Fire! Fire!... The ammunition car—it is on fire!" Hill "thrust [his] head out [of the rail car window] and, looking forward, saw one of the cars near the locomotive blazing up right merrily. It was a car that was loaded with ammunition. It had, it seems, been fired by sparks from the locomotive."[1] One of the Brownsville Grays, Wesley "Fletch" Chess, grabbed an armful of blankets and managed to smother the flames before they reached the ammunition.

After the excitement died down, Hill went back to sleep: "When I awoke it was morning; the train was not in motion. I looked out, and perceived that we were in some town; on inquiry I learned that it was Duncannon, twenty miles west of Harrisburg. The kindness and hospitality of the citizens of this place deserve a word of praise. They no sooner knew that a train of soldiers was standing near the town, than they thronged around us with pies, cakes, bread-and-butter, milk and other like refreshments.... [A]nd we did ample justice to them, for we had not been supplied with provisions, except a few crackers. At length we moved on, and after an hour found ourselves at Harrisburg. Here we remained till near evening, while various equipments were being dealt out. We received knapsacks, haversacks, canteens and cartridge boxes."[2]

While Hill and most of his comrades stayed with the train during the provisioning process, several others, including his messmate, D. L. Craft, decided to take a "cruise about." According to Hill, Craft "went out to a neighboring house and formed the acquaintance of a 'dear angel,' with whom he fell desperately in 'love at first sight,' and with whom he afterward corresponded."[3] Fortunately, Craft made it back to the station in time to catch the train:

It was four o'clock in the afternoon before the train moved on; then we went flying, and soon arrived in little York.

Here a piece of sad news reached us; it was of the battle of Bull Run, and the rout of the Federal army, which had taken place on the previous day.... Printed telegrams were afloat, stating that our troops had been defeated and routed, that they were flying toward Washington in wild disorder, pursued by the victorious rebels, who would probably follow them right into the Capital, that all was confusion there, and Congress had adjourned to meet in Philadelphia. It was said that it would be dangerous for us to pass through Baltimore now, that the secessionists there were growing very bold since our defeat. We moved on. Night found us still in the cars.

As we neared Baltimore, Captain Conner passed through our car and said—

"Men, load your pieces; we may have some trouble in Baltimore...."[4]

We reached Baltimore during the night, and the train stopped; we remained in the cars till morning. It was now discovered that we were to stay in Baltimore for a day or two, and we disembarked and formed line to march through the city to a place of encampment beyond. Before we started, Colonel Hayes addressed us thus—

"Boys, let us pass through the city in a quiet and respectful manner. Offer no insults—disturb no one. You all have your pieces loaded, and if we are assaulted, defend yourselves.[5] I have no fear that you will not do your duty."

We marched through the city unmolested, though many a black scowl was cast upon us. Some of the citizens, however, looked pleasantly on, and welcomed us. It was evident that Baltimore was quite a mixture of Union and Secession. One man came to the window, an upper one, and called out to a friend at the opposite side of the street—

"I say, Wilson, they'll never get back, the damned Yankee cusses!"

At a point a few steps further, a beautiful young lady stood at her door, waving a small copy of the Stars and Stripes. Having marched through the city, we repaired to a hill beyond and encamped.[6]

A few days later, while still encamped near Baltimore, Hill and one of his messmates chanced upon a conversation between Colonel George S. Hays, the 8th Regiment's commanding officer, and the Brownsville Grays' company officers:

"And you think we'll go, Colonel?" I heard [Captain Conner] say.

"Yes; oh, yes. I have orders now, to move tomorrow morning;...."

"Is it supposed that Washington is in danger?" asked Lieutenant Jacobs.

"Yes; it is reported that Beauregard...is moving on the capital."

"At what point is he expected to make the onset?" asked Lieutenant Clarke.

"It is supposed to be his intention to cross the Potomac at the Chain Bridge, and enter Washington by way of Georgetown. But a new general has been called to Washington to take command, and Beauregard must be sharp to outwit him."

"Who is that?"

"It is a general who has very ably conducted the campaign in West[ern] Virginia; his name is McClellan."

The Colonel walked away, and the Captain said—"Boys, hold yourselves in readiness to take the cars for Washington tomorrow morning."[7]

Thankfully for the men of the 8th Regiment, their journey from Baltimore to the nation's capital proved less hazardous than the one from Pittsburgh to Pennsylvania's capital. Along the way, however, many of them witnessed for the first time a sight that they had only imagined when reading their hometown newspapers: "We passed many darkeys who were working in the fields, and who cheered us lustily."[8] Maryland, of course, lay south of the Mason-Dixon Line, and the "peculiar institution" was much in evidence in the tobacco fields of the great plantations.

In all probability, there were as many motives for enlisting as there were young men on that train. Undoubtedly some joined for the sake of adventure, seeking the glory they believed could be theirs if only they could get to the front before the war ended. Others, such as Hill and Darby, were driven by patriotism, determined to do their part to crush the rebellion that threatened the Union. But for those young men who donned the blue to end the evils of slavery once and for all, the sights they saw while speeding through the Maryland countryside surely must have stirred their deepest emotions.

At last, the dome of the Capitol Building, then under construction, came into view, and shortly thereafter the train pulled into the depot on New Jersey Avenue. The soldiers disembarked and gathered their gear. They marched through the city and out Seventh Street to Meridian Hill where they pitched their tents at sunset: "Many regiments engaged at Bull Run had been marched to the northeast side of the Potomac, and were encamped in our vicinity. Many came from these regiments to talk with us, and many were the stories they related of the very unbrotherly disposition of the rebels. They told [of] many incidents connected with the battle, all going to prove that the rebels were no cowards and that to fight them was no sport."[9]

Of course, even in the bleak days following that unexpected and disastrous defeat, some of the newly blooded "veterans" could not resist the opportunity to tweak the noses of the "rookies." One of A. F. Hill's comrades related a story allegedly told to him by a Union cavalryman:

"[T]here was a cavalryman telling me something of a story, just now...."

"[He] said that during a hand-to-hand conflict in which he took part, he and a rebel Zouave had it for a spell, but he was too much for Mr. Reb, and at last clipped his head clean square off with his sabre. Now, one would think *that* ought to settle any man, but—"

"What!" [Hill] interrupted, "You don't mean to say that it *didn't* settle him?"

"Yes, so the cavalryman told me; he said that no sooner had he cut the fellow's head off, than the invincible reb threw down his gun, picked up his own head with both hands, and ran right at him. Well, such a thing as that will try any man's nerves, and our hero turned his horse about and retreated. A kind of superstitious horror seized him, and the acephalous rebel, seeing that he could not overtake him, actually flung his head after him, then laid quietly down and kicked the bucket."[10]

Harsh reality commanded the attention of the men of the 8th Reserves soon enough:

The first fatal shooting accident in the regiment occurred while in camp at Meridian Hill. Our muskets had been loaded with buck and ball in anticipation of an attack from the rebel element while passing through Baltimore,[11] and it became necessary to extract these charges. To do this, a ball screw is attached to the end of the ramrod and inserted in the muzzle of the gun, screwed into the bullet and the charge withdrawn by pulling out the ramrod. A man in Company B neglected to remove the cap from the nipple of his gun and in pulling out his ramrod the cock of his piece caught on a small pine tree at the butt of the musket, discharging it. The charge, ramrod and all, struck him in the pit of the stomach and passing obliquely through his body came out at the back of his neck. I was standing nearby and ran to his assistance but he was dead when I reached him.[12]

After several days encamped on Meridian Hill, the soldiers received their first pay. Hill and one of his messmates, William Mitchell,[13] decided to visit Washington to see the sights: "We were not long in reaching the city, which we entered by Seventh Street, and began at once to look about us for *sights*. Independently of the public buildings in Washington, it is far from being an attractive city. But once remove from it the Capitol, the White House, the Treasury Building, the War and Navy Departments, the Post Office, and the Smithsonian Institution, and Washington would be a very common place.... Having wandered about the city, viewing the wonders and eating ice cream every ten minutes till near evening, we made up our minds to return to camp."[14]

A few days later, the 8th Regiment was ordered to Tennallytown, a small village near the northern border of the District of Columbia. Hill recalled the day of their march as "an exceedingly hot one—it was the second of August—and the thermometer stood, I think, at ninety-seven degrees in the shade."[15] The men marched out Pennsylvania Avenue through Georgetown and then proceeded northward, a distance of about eight miles: "We suffered much from the heat. Indeed, many sank down by the way, sunstruck."[16] One soldier from the 9th Reserves provided a graphic description of the march in a letter home: "The sun was high, the day clear, and the road very dry and dusty. It was not long after the word 'Forward' was given, until the sweat commenced to roll in drops from head to foot, chasing one another down my back and breast with such rapidity that I really felt as though subjected to a shower-bath of hot beans.... I have been warm with walking before and have felt the sun, as I thought, in all its glory, but never before experienced the heat thereof to such an extent as on Monday last. It seemed to me as though I was encased, from head to foot, in red hot iron."[17]

After what must have seemed the longest eight miles the men had ever marched, they reached their objective: "We arrived at Tennallytown...at two o'clock in the afternoon. We pitched our tents on the summit of a high hill which was covered with luxuriant clover; it was the most elevated point for miles around. Our camp was called Camp Tennally. It was not many days ere the whole division known as the 'Pennsylvania Reserves' arrived, regiment by regiment, and encamped in the vicinity. Thus, for the first time, our division was together. It consisted of twelve regiments of infantry, a rifle regiment (the Pennsylvania 'Bucktails'),[18] one regiment of cavalry, and one of artillery. We numbered about fifteen thousand men, and were commanded by General George A. McCall."[19]

The large number of troops gathered near Tennallytown particularly impressed one young Pennsylvania soldier. Albert Rake, a private in the Reserves' 5th Regiment, wrote to his wife on August 11, 1861:

> Dear wife and children I again send you a few lines to let you know how and where I am. We are now 5 ½ miles from Washington We left Harrisburgh on last fryday morning and came to Baltimore that night and went through the town in the night and the union sentiment was much stronger there than I expected. We left Baltimore in the morning and came to Washington and staid there til in the evening and then came to our camp here. And what they will do now I can not tel you for we do not find out enny thing.... I got your letter at Harrisburgh and I was glad to hear from you again.... I can not come to see you now but you must be in good hopes for if god spares me I can come some time.... Give my love to all nabours and tel them that if they were here they could not see the country for solgers. I don't know how menny there is but over one hundred thousand enny how. Please rite as soon as you can and tel me what you intend to call the baby as I would like to know.... Tel Grace to give it a kiss for pap and you give all the children a kiss for me. So I will close by sending you a kiss from
>
> > Your Affecinate husband
> > Albert Rake[20]

Like Albert Rake, many of the men who had gathered at Camp Tennally were married and, for the first time in their lives, found themselves far away from their loved ones. Letters from home were eagerly anticipated and, when received, were treasured. Andrew Lewis, a lieutenant in the 11th Regiment of the Pennsylvania Reserves, upon receiving the following letter from his daughter Mary, wrote to his wife that "I was glad to think that Marey at last could make out to send me afiew lines of heirs but as fiew as they were I am proud that I hav a daughter to rite me a letter now:"[21]

Ebensburg [Pennsylvania]

Aug 13 1861

Dear Father

As this is the first time I hav ever wrote a letter and as I think for my first beginning I cant find one more worthey than my one dear Papa I will attempt to scribble a few lins to let you know that we are all well at least as far as helth is conserned but our minds are never easy on your account nor never will be until your safe return Dear papa it is so loansom here with out you O when will this dredfull war be over and when will we have you home with us never to leave us again.

I have just herd that Lousa Myers is ded Mr J Myers youngest daughter She died of something like scarlet fever We were so fread Jackey [Lewis's son] will get it Poor little Jackey wants to see you so bad.

All of our friends here sends love to you We are so sorry we have nothing nice to send you now Papa I want you someday to write me a letter Mamma Jackey and myself sends love to you And now dear Papa for to take good care of yourself is the prayer of your loving daugther Mary.

Mary F. Lewis

To her dear father

Andrew Lewis[22]

As ever, humor served to ameliorate the loneliness felt by soldiers far from home, and it was not long before that notorious boatman and part-time circus clown, James Gaskill, made his presence known:

At Tennally Town our camp was located on a hill side, and one day a man drove in with a covered wagon, in which he had a barrel of ice cream, which he was vending at ten cents per saucer, and Gaskell was very anxious for some of that cream, but he was short the ten cents, but here again his wits stood him in good stead. He secured his game by deftly removing a linch-pin from the hinder axle, and giving the horse a cut with a brush, over went the wagon, out tumbled the barrel, and starting to roll down the hill was arrested in its mad career by the ever present Gaskell, who dived into the contents of that barrel clear up to his middle, and came up smiling with his arms folded low across his breast, and a pyramid of ice cream resting upon them, which towered high above his head, and thus he made for his quarters, eating as he ran, and shedding ice cream at every jump.[23]

Despite the occasional frivolity, the daily life of the men at Camp Tennally largely was taken up with the serious business of improving their knowledge of the manual of arms, participating in battalion drill and becoming proficient in the use of their weapons—all skills that they would need to master if they hoped to prevail in the battles to come.[24] Matters were not destined to proceed smoothly, however. Only four days after their arrival at Camp Tennally, the soldiers of the 8th Regiment precipitated a crisis when they refused to muster for target practice, claiming that their muskets were too dangerous to be fired. General McCall was forced to intervene personally, as he noted in the following letter to Governor Curtin:

Camp Tenally August 6th 1861

Gov'r A. G. Curtin
Harrisburg

Sir: It is with extreme regret and, I must add, mortification that I have to relate an occurrence of this date which reflects most severely upon the executive of the state from which I come: it is this,

Having last evening ordered Col. Hays of the 8th Regt. (Reserve Corps) to form his Regiment for target practice this morning at an early hour, as I desired to witness their proficiency, I was called upon early by the Colonel, accompanied by the ten Captains of his Regiment who reported to me that during the night about three fourths of the men of the Regiment had stacked their arms in front of the Colonel's tent; and that this morning they had refused to take them saying they would never go to the field with arms that endangered the lives of those who fired them: arms that had been pronounced to them unfit for service by Inspector General Coppie: arms that on the firing of one single round in one company had eleven (a fact) made totally useless by the blowing out of cones, or plugs in touch holes or being split either in stocks or barrel.[25]

The Captains, whom I questioned much, said their men had sworn they would not go to battle with these arms. They said they had used every argument in vain and asked what was to be done? I proceeded at once to the ground, having directed the officers to precede me & say that if the arms were not taken immediately and the Regiment brought into line, I would turn out a Regiment and compel them. When I arrived on the ground the men were taking their arms & were very soon formed on the color line. I kept them on drill for some time & their discontent was overcome for the moment. But now, Sir, the time has arrived when the promise of the Executive must be redeemed or the State will be disgraced. These men say, and what they say is corroborated by Colonel Hays

Soldiers of the 8th Pennsylvania Reserves

Ronn Palm's Museum of Civil War Images, Gettysburg, Pa., Private Collection

and others, that your Excellency promised them, when they passed through Harrisburg on their way to Baltimore, to procure for them the best arms to be had, by which they understood you to mean you would purchase arms if they could not be got from the Federal Government.

I have only to say that upon my arrival at Washington I reported to the Secretary of War & to Lieut. General Scott that the arms in possession of these Regiments were unfit for service, & that I have only been able to procure with the entire assent of these high officers of the Government to the urgency of the demand, arms for two Regiments.

It has been reported to me that several other Regiments have said they would not go into the field with their muskets; and officers have told me in bitter terms that they would be disgraced. I candidly say I apprehend something of this kind; and I must say that if they refuse to go with arms, which I do myself from close examination condemn, I shall have no argument to offer against them. I will go with two Regiments if no more be armed, and I will leave to [the Government] for what the Country must be made acquainted with.

I [have], Sir, every respectful Consideration for yourself,

Your Most Obt Servt
Geo. A. McCall[26]

Not all of Colonel Hays's men railed against their firearms. One of them, Private John Strathern of Company C, allowed as how they were "very nice guns" in a letter to his parents:

Headquarters 8th Regt PRVC, Co. C
Georgetown Heights
August 15, 1861

Dear Father and Mother,

Your ever welcome letter reached me last night and I seize the first opportunity of answering it. As far as my health is concerned, I think you have but little to fear. Our Regiment was out on picket guard three miles from this place toward the Potomac for twenty-four hours. We went out on Saturday evening and returned on Lord's Day evening. On our homeward march the rain poured down in torrents and the roads were completely submerged. Our tents were all wet inside, the water having completely overflowed the floor of them—the earth being the only floor we can get—and that was pretty damp.... I never slept more soundly than I did on Lord's Day night, and although my clothes were damp in the morning, I am happy to say that I did not even feel stiff in the morning.... I bought another rubber blanket the other day, so you see that I mean to use all lawful means to preserve my health....

The Reserve is nearly all here. Our men are busy preparing a masked battery. They are making a bad havoc of an old secessionist timber. They have laid down about twenty acres of it since yesterday morning. The other regiments are similarly employed all around the vicinity.... We have got our new guns—they are the improved Harper's Ferry Musket and very nice guns they are....

All the young men from Braddock's Field are well and determined to fight if need be. We are all in good spirits and will try to do our duty if [it] comes to [a] fight.

Give my best respects to all inquiring friends. Write soon and send me more newspapers....

> Your son
> John Strathern[27]

Strathern's favorable view of his musket notwithstanding, General McCall was soon afforded an opportunity to bring his concerns regarding the issue of defective firearms to the attention of his superiors at the highest level. On August 21, 1861, he presided over a formal review of the Pennsylvania Reserves by the president of the United States and the commander of the Army of the Potomac. Jacob Heffelfinger, a corporal in the 7th Regiment, described the ceremony in a letter to his sister:

> Camp Tennally Aug. 22nd 1861.

Dear Sister Jennie,

Yesterday was a gay time for the nine Pennsylvania Regiments stationed here. At 8 O'clock A. M. we marched out of camp having been ordered to be prepared to be reviewed by Maj. Gen. [George B.] McClellan, in whom we all have great confidence. At 10 A. M. we were all in line....

We had not stood very long before Gen. McClellan dashed into the field in fine style, followed by his staff...and a company of U. S. Dragoons who acted as escort. He immediately commenced the review, passing up and down before each line, nothing escaping the notice of his clear keen eye. His face betokes great energy and enthusiasm. He is very young in appearance, much more so than any of the members of his staff. I think that we have the 'right man in the right place,' and that the rebels will find themselves badly whipped one of these days.

To be reviewed by Gen. McClellan was event enough for one day, and we expected no more; but before he had passed the last line several carriages were driven into the field.... I remarked to the men near me that one of the men resembled Pres. Lincoln. Soon Gen. McCall was seen to leave Gen. McClellan & party, and hasten to the party in the vehicles, who proved to be none other than the veritable 'Old Abe,' accompanied by Secys. [Simon] Cameron, [Salmon P.] Chase, & [William H.] Seward. They immediately proceeded to the head of the line and commenced passing in review before the troops who received them with arms presented and bands playing. As the party reached the head of our

regiment, they were joined by General McClellan and proceeded with the review, the Pres. taking the lead followed by Genls. McClellan and McCall. When
the President's carriage was immediately in front of...our company, he halted
for several moments...because the horses became unmanageable and would not
move the carriage. Thus we were honored with a longer sight of his honest face
than any other ones on the ground. As the reviewing party passed to the front,
nine of the most deafening cheers I have ever heard were given by the whole
command for the Pres. who rose in his carriage waving his hat at arms length....
This ended, all troops marched to their camps well satisfied with the events of
the day, and better prepared to fight, not only for the Union, but for the man who
so nobly directs the ship of state in these perilous times....

Yours affectionately,

Jacob Heffelfinger[28]

One can imagine the sense of awe that the young soldiers of the 8th Reserves—
the great majority of whom had never traveled beyond the borders of their own
counties—must have felt, being reviewed in their nation's capital by the president
of the United States. Private Adam Bright, an Allegheny Countian serving in the
9th Regiment, surely echoed the sentiments of thousands of his fellow Pennsylvanians when he recounted his adventures in a letter to his brother in Penn Township:
"I visited the capitol in Harrisburg, The Washington monument at Baltimore, and
the Capitol at Washington, and I have seen more since I started than I ever expected
to see in my life."[29]

After the review, General McCall issued the following order:

> Soldiers of the Pennsylvania Reserves! This day must be recognized as a
> propitious inauguration of your future military history. You have this day passed
> under the scrutinizing inspection of the Commanding General of the Army of
> the Potomac, in whose ability to successfully prosecute this war, the confidence
> of the country is reposed. You have passed in review before the President of the
> United States and his cabinet; both the General and the President have expressed
> to me their most unqualified approbation of your soldier-like appearance in
> review, and of the discipline thus manifestly shown to exist in the corps.
>
> It now rests with you, officers of the Pennsylvania Reserves, to carry out to
> perfection the work so well begun. Upon you devolves the care of your men; let
> that be unremitting. Let every attention to their wants temper the rigid discipline
> necessary to the formation of a soldier, and with one heart we will uphold the
> flag of our State, and place her name among the foremost in the cause of our
> common country.[30]

The men of the 8th Regiment soon returned to their daily ritual of drill and
picket duty, as John Strathern related to his parents in a letter written from Camp
Tennally in early September: "[O]n Tuesday evening, orders were received from

General McCall to march to the Chain Bridge immediately (this was about 9 o'clock in the evening, and in less than five minutes we were in line [with] canteen and forty rounds of cartridges in our cartridge box).... On Wednesday we were ordered out double-quick time to go to the Great Falls on the Potomac 12 miles from this place.... I have just got home and have had only six hours sleep for the last 72 hours, the balance of the time we have been marching all over creation. We must have traveled over seventy miles. It rained most of the time and we slept on the ground.... We exchanged a few random shots with the enemy's pickets without any damage to us."[31]

On September 10, the routine of camp life was broken again by another impressive ceremony. Pennsylvania's governor had traveled to Washington to present stands of colors to the Pennsylvania Reserves. As President Lincoln and General McClellan once again looked on, Governor Curtin "proceeded to formally present the colors to the colonels of the several regiments, at the head of their color companies. Attended by his staff and General McCall, he commenced at the right of the line and placed in the hands of each colonel, the beautiful flag provided by the State of Pennsylvania.... After having received the colors, the companies wheeled by platoons and marched...to the rear, and took their places in the line with their new colors unfurled to the breeze."[32] When the presentations were completed, the governor addressed the assembled soldiers:

General McCall and men of Pennsylvania: I give these flags to you to-day, and I know you will carry them wherever you appear, in honor, and that the credit of the State will never suffer in your hands.... Our people are for peace. But if men lay violent hands upon the sacred fabric of the Government, unjustly spill the blood of their brethren, and tear the sacred constitution to pieces, Pennsylvania is for war—war to the death! [Thousands of Pennsylvanians] follow you with their prayers. They look to you to vindicate a great Government, to sustain legitimate power, and to crush out rebellion.... [Y]our friends in Pennsylvania know of the presentation of these flags to-day; and I am sure that I am authorized to say that their blessing is upon you. May the God of Battles in His wisdom protect your lives, and may Right, Truth and Justice prevail.[33]

General McCall responded:

Governor Curtin: Permit me, in the name of the Pennsylvania Reserve Corps, to return, through your Excellency, to the State of our birth, the thanks with which we receive the splendid banners that...you have this day presented. The bestowal of these noble banners devolves upon the regiments of this division a responsibility they cheerfully accept; and they trust, with the aid of the God of Battles, to bear these Stars and Stripes proudly in the conflict, and to place the banner of our State amongst the foremost in the cause of the Constitution and the Union of our common country.[34]

A typical Union infantry company at rest, their arms stacked. Note the various activities in which the soldiers are engaged.

National Archives

At the conclusion of the ceremony, the several regiments of the Pennsylvania Reserves passed in review before General McClellan, and then marched from the parade ground back to their camp. Before dismissing them, Lieutenant Colonel Oliphant, second in command of the 8th Regiment, drew his men up in line and addressed them:

> "Eighth Regiment, you have this day been presented, by the Governor of your State with a beautiful stand of colors; *will you ever surrender them?*"
>
> "Never! Never! No! Never, never, never!" burst forth from a thousand throats.
>
> We kept our word. That same flag, though pierced by hundreds of bullets, and torn here and there by fragments of shell, continued to wave over the centre of our regiment while it was a regiment.[35]

Shortly after the various regiments received their state colors, they were organized into three brigades, and the brigades, into a division known as McCall's division. The first brigade, commanded by Brigadier General John F. Reynolds, was comprised of the cavalry regiment and the 1st, 2nd, 5th, and 8th Regiments. The second brigade, commanded by Brigadier General George G. Meade, was comprised of the 3rd, 4th, 7th, 11th, and 13th (Bucktail) Regiments. The third brigade, commanded by Brigadier General E. O. C. Ord, was comprised of the 6th, 9th, 10th, and 12th Regiments.

The day following the review by Governor Curtin, the sound of artillery from across the Potomac interrupted the daily routine of the Pennsylvania Reserves. Many of the men gathered on the Camp Tennally parade ground to watch what was evidently a fight of some sort taking place on the Virginia side of the river near Lewinsville. The flash and smoke from cannon fire and exploding shells could be seen, as could clouds of dust presumably thrown up by the movement of cavalry. For over an hour, the Fayette County boys watched the engagement, hoping they might finally be going into action. Just as one of them wondered aloud whether they might be called upon, "the long roll sounded on all sides, in all the surrounding camps. It was the call to arms!"[36] Hill described the soldiers' reaction:

> "Hurrah! Hurrah!" And with a wild shout we rushed to our quarters, buckled on our cartridge-boxes, and seized our muskets.
>
> "Fall in! Fall in!" cried the captain, who made his appearance in our company street, his sword at his side.
>
> In fifteen minutes we were all in line, and the whole division, artillery and all, was en route for the Chain Bridge. We were nearly wild with delight. Could it be that we should yet have an opportunity to try our hand? The prospect certainly was favorable. The cannonading continued. General McCall rode along, was cheered lustily, and was soon at the head of the column. But oh, confusion! The firing suddenly ceased, and we were ordered to halt when near the Chain Bridge. We were told that the rebels had been defeated and had fled precipitously. How provoking! We really wished that they had proved too much for our fellows, that

we might have had a chance at them. But there was no chance now; the fight was over, and we were ordered to return to Camp Tennally, which we did, but certainly not so quickly as we had marched from it to the Chain Bridge.[37]

Just days later, however, Hill's wish to meet the enemy appeared to have been fulfilled, according to a brief article that appeared in the *Genius of Liberty* on September 26, 1861: "The Eighth Pennsylvania Reserve, Col. Hays, have met the enemy, and given them a taste of their quality. After a severe march from Camp Tennally to Point of Rocks...Capt. Johnston's company and the Greene County Rangers were detached as platoons and...put to flight a number of rebels on the road. They moved towards a log house which seemed to be the rebel headquarters, and attacked it after loading with double cartridge. A few shots at the chimney and an open window brought out a woman with the Stars and Stripes, and a few more, a flag of truce. Five rebels were killed, three in the woods and two in the house and several wounded. None of the Eighth were hurt. The Eighth is commanded by Col. Hays, and made up nearly altogether of Pittsburghers."[38]

Any sense of pride this article may have engendered on the home front was short-lived, however, as the true facts concerning the "engagement" were conveyed to Colonel Roddy, the editor of the *Genius of Liberty*, in a letter that he published two weeks later:

Camp Tennally, Oct. 1, 1861

Col. Roddy—Dear Sir:

There is an article going the rounds in the papers giving an account of a skirmish between Company's B and I of the 8th Regiment Penn'a. R. V. C., with a portion of the secession force on the Potomac above Great Falls. Now, Sir, I happen to belong to the 8th Regiment and was out on picket duty when said skirmish should have taken place, and nothing of the kind occurred as related in the article alluded.

A portion of Company B fired a volley at an old house across the river a range of near half a mile, when a woman appeared at the door with what looked like a white rag on a broom-stick, and the firing ceased; and the first we heard of any of the rebels being killed or wounded, we read it in the *Pittsburgh Chronicle*. I believe there was considerable firing done by our men across the river, at what they fired it is hard to tell for I stood my turn on picket for a whole week and was on nearly every post occupied by the Regiment and I saw nothing to shoot at save peaceable citizens following their daily employment and they were at so great a distance off it took a glass to tell what they were. Some of Company G or C swam across the river and went up to the rebel pickets, and one of them returned with our boys and was well treated. A rebel Captain swam across at or near Great Falls, and held a conversation with Lieut. Col. Oliphant, Capt. Gardner and other officers of our Regiment. His name was Capt. Weaver, and [he] commanded a company of Cavalry in the 33rd Virginia Cavalry. He was much of a gentleman and after conversing for some time they drank each other's health, exchanged presents, and he swam back to the Virginia shore well-satisfied that the Union army had been very grossly misrepresented as to its character and object in this war.

If you think this worth notice you can insert it in your paper.

A Soldier of the Eighth Regiment[39]

It would be some time yet before the soldiers of the 8th Regiment would "see the elephant."[40] During the time they spent at Camp Tennally, the Reserves helped to construct Fort Pennsylvania, a substantial fortification that lay on the highest point of elevation along Washington's northern defenses.[41] The fort commanded three major roads that converged at Tennallytown to join the Rockville Road that led into Washington by way of Georgetown. Together with its accompanying battery, the fort, which mounted 27 guns and mortars, protected the northern approaches to Washington, as well as Camp Tennally itself and a major signaling station also located in the area.

John Strathern noted the completion of Fort Pennsylvania in a September 15 letter to his parents in which he displayed a pride in his regiment as yet untarnished by the reality of war:

> Headquarters
> 8th Regiment P.R.V.C.
> Camp Tennally
>
> Dear Mother and Father,
>
> Your letter of the 11th came duly to hand and was perused with pleasure. You must excuse me for not writing oftener and sooner....
>
> I expect that you know about as much about the movements of the Army as we do, if not more, for we know nothing about where we are going when we start on a march til we get to the spot.... You will no doubt see the necessity of this for news travel[s] fast [in] these times as your letters show. A falsehood travels 20 miles before truth gets his boots on.... The rumors you refer to in your letter are afloat here, but we cannot believe the half we hear....
>
> We have to keep two days rations cooked so as to be able to march at any moment. General McCall say[s] that he has but to send the order and before he can turn himself, the 8th Regiment is on its way—double quick time. He say[s] that [in] the other regiments, one-half take to the woods when they get an order to march to any place where there is any chance for fight. Our boys run [out] from the Fort where they were at work when we get marching orders.... The 8th Regiment is allowed by all to be the best regiment of the Reserve....
>
> Fort Pennsylvania is finished and we are going to build another about three miles from here....
>
> Your son,
> John Strathern
> Co. C—8th Regiment Pa. R.V.C.[42]

As Strathern noted, in addition to working on fortifications, the men of the 8th Regiment were often ordered out into the Maryland countryside to perform picket duty. On one such occasion, a young girl and her younger brother walked over to the picket line from a house nearby with some pies to sell. Hill recalled the humorous conversation that ensued:

> "How do ye sell yer pies?" asked one of our boys, whose name was Dennis.
>
> "Nine cents; if we can't get nine, we'll take eight, that's what mother told us," replied the boy, with genuine childlike simplicity.
>
> The little girl, who was a more discreet merchant, whispered "Hush—sh—sh," and addressing us said "Nine cents is the price."
>
> "But I'll not give more nor eight," said Dennis.
>
> "But I want nine," persisted the girl, who was, perhaps, ten years old—two years older than the boy, her brother.
>
> "I can't afford to give it," said Dennis decidedly.
>
> "Then you may take one for eight," said the girl, after some apparent hesitation. And so the bargain was consummated.[43]

On another occasion when a detachment from the 8th Reserves was sent out on picket duty, the men were posted along the northern bank of the Potomac. As the river was only two hundred feet wide at that point, it was possible for the Pennsylvanians to carry on a shouted conversation with their counterparts on the Virginia side. In the course of one such exchange, a captain in the Virginia Cavalry proposed an armistice for the day, to which the Union boys readily agreed:

> By and by one of the rebel soldiers asked: "If I swim over to you, will you allow me to return?"
>
> "Yes, certainly!" was the reply.
>
> "Then I'll come," said he; and walking to a point a little further down the stream, he climbed over the precipice—it was not so steep there—to the water's edge, doffed his clothing, and plunged in.
>
> He was a good swimmer, and soon reached the Maryland shore. We also walked down to the point at which he was crossing, and met him at the water's edge. A great-coat was given him to cast about his shoulders. Then the conversation was opened. He told us that they believed their cause was just—that had we been born south of the Potomac, we, too, had been enlisted in the rebel cause. He expressed his regrets that, in the course of events, Virginia must fight against Pennsylvania, her sister State. He would almost as lief fight the South Carolinians, but he thought he was doing his duty by enlisting in the cause of his State.
>
> Among other things, a green-back was shown him, upon which was the President's likeness.

"Do you know who that man is?" he was asked.

"Yes," replied the Virginian, smiling, "and I wish he and old Jeff Davis were obliged to come here and do picket duty along the Potomac; I don't think the war would last long if that were the case."[44]

It was a wish common to every young soldier who ever fought in a war started by men too old to don the uniform themselves.

"A Brush with the Rebels"

Camp Pierpont and the Battle of Dranesville

As September waned, rumors of an imminent troop movement abounded, and the soldiers of the 8th Regiment were eager to cross the Potomac and put the "secesh" to flight. Young John Strathern wrote to his parents in early October, giving voice to his hopes and fears as the Army of the Potomac commenced its advance:

> Headquarters
> 8th Regt P.R.V.C.
> Fort Pennsylvania
> October 3, 1861
>
> Dear Father and Mother,
>
> Your ever welcome letter of the 28th is before me, and I hasten to answer it. I was happy to hear that you had received the money alright. I think it better, Father, to send my money home to you than to keep it here and lose it, as many have done, or have it stolen.... I may be killed—and if I fall, I would rather have my friends have what I have earned than my foes. Besides, if any person has a right to the use of the money, certainly you have. Should I be spared to return to you, we will talk of recompense. Never want while you have any money belonging to me, for I sent it for your use. I am glad that there is a prospect of a change for the better, and better times expected soon.... The coming month will write the history of the American Rebellion. The Grand Army of the Potomac has made a move forward, and as they advance, the rebel phalanx yield before the Union army. General McClellan is not to be trapped. There appears to be no disposition of Rebel Generals to risk a battle on this side of Manassas, and perhaps not there.... All the Boys here are well.... No more at present....
>
> Your son,
> John Strathern[1]

The Army of the Potomac had indeed begun to stir. Less than a week after writing to his parents, Strathern and his comrades in the 8th Regiment crossed the

Potomac River and entered enemy country. A. F. Hill recalled the excitement of that first advance into Virginia:

> The first week of October had passed away, and we were standing in groups in our company street one evening discussing the prospects of receiving marching orders, when Captain Conner made his appearance and said—"Boys, pack up, and strike your tents...."
>
> Soon the bugle sounded the welcome call of the "assembly," and the cry of "Fall in!" was reiterated on all sides. We marched over the Chain Bridge, and at last were in VIRGINIA.[2]
>
> We halted and bivouacked for the night about four miles out on the Georgetown and Leesburg turnpike. Early the following morning we moved on a mile further, then filed off the road into a clover-field on the right, and encamped. Having pitched our tents, we proceeded to scour the surrounding country to see what we could find in the way of beans, potatoes, fruit, etc. The houses were all deserted; the inhabitants having fled upon our approach, leaving furniture and all, fearing, no doubt, that were they to remain, we would eat them alive, as a matter of course—Yankees that we were.[3]

With their tents erected and pickets posted, Corporal Hill and his comrades in the Brownsville Grays turned their attention to a more mundane endeavor,[4] albeit one that was never far from their minds:

> As soon as the first relief was posted, we proceeded to do our butchering, that is, to collect what stray sheep, hogs or cattle might chance to lurk in that vicinity, and appropriate them to our own use. This was, perhaps, rather arbitrary, but it could not be helped, for as the owners had fled to secessiondom, it was impossible for us to ask their permission to deal thus summarily with their unfortunate animals.... George Wagner, my ex-messmate, was a butcher by trade, and he superintended the proceeding.... We had just strung up the sixth hapless animal...when a body of mounted men was seen on the right moving toward us. Evidently some general, accompanied by his staff, was approaching us. Horror! It would never do for him...to see what kind of work was going on. So we hurriedly took down the bodies of the animals, piled them up in a fence-corner, and covered them with straw taken from a neighboring barn. We had but carried out this nice little arrangement, when the head of the approaching cavalcade passed by. Who should it be riding in advance but General McClellan, accompanied by General McCall.[5]

Fresh water, of course, was even more important than fresh beef, and the area selected for the 8th Regiment's camp seemed to have been blessed with it in abundance. There was, however, one small problem:

Our new camp was called Camp Pierpont, and was situated near the village of Langley. A stream of water wound its way down a gentle valley near its location, and as there were no springs at hand, we used the pure water from the "bubbling brook." Several days had elapsed, when we observed that the water of the stream, though at first clear and transparent, became rather whitish—began to put on a milky appearance. We paid no attention to it, however, supposing it to be a peculiarity belonging to the streams of benighted Virginia. We continued to use the water for a week before we discovered the true cause. Then it came with a startling vengeance. It was simply that the boys of a regiment encamped further up the stream had been all this time industriously *washing their garments* in it, using a superior quality of rosin soap; hence that milky appearance. I need not say that springs came into immediate use, notwithstanding their non-proximity.[6]

Drill continued on a daily basis, with greater emphasis being placed on maneuvers and massed musketry. As ever, certain soldiers simply could not pass up an opportunity for mischief:

The colonel had the regiment out drilling on a gently sloping hillside and gave the command to fire by file from right to left. Now the colonel was mounted on a horse that would not stand fire and at the first crack of a gun he turned tail and fled, notwithstanding the strenuous exertions of the colonel to hold him, but each additional shot lent wings to his flight and he carried the colonel over the hill and out of sight. Meanwhile the firing proceeded and finally the head and shoulders of the colonel could be seen above the brow of the hill excitedly swinging his sword and yelling, "Cease firing! Cease firing," accompanied by numerous cuss words to add emphasis to his orders. But the men were enjoying the situation and could not hear his orders, and whenever they fired a new volley the head and shoulders of the colonel would suddenly disappear again. They finally ceased their fire and allowed the raging colonel to approach, who instantly ordered the regiment to camp, threatening to buck and gag the first man that fired off his gun on the way back.[7]

And that irrepressible master of merriment, Private Gaskill of the Brownsville Grays, found the southern black snakes to be every bit as much to his liking as those of his native Pennsylvania:

While our command lay at...[Camp] Pierpont, Bud in some manner secured two snakes of fair dimensions which he carried constantly about his person; sometimes they were secreted in the sleeves of his blouse, sometimes in his hat, and as revolting as it may seem, I have seen him with his pets in his mouth. Colonel Hayes, of the Eighth, was a special victim of Bud's pranks, and although he frequently expiated his fun by a sojourn in the guardhouse, he was irrepressible. The Colonel being a man of nervous temperament, naturally hated the sight of a snake, yet Bud would approach him, extending his paw for a shake with a genial "how do 'do, Colonel," when down would come one of Bud's snakes into the Colonel's hand, then of course it would become necessary for the redoubtable Bud to adjourn for the time being. I once saw this fellow approach the Colonel with a snake coiled within his mouth, its head protruding from between his lips, its tongue darting out, and in order to secure the officer's attention, he says "Granny! Let me kiss you." On this occasion, the Colonel was the first to beat a retreat.[8]

Ever since marching over the Chain Bridge into Northern Virginia, the Pennsylvania Reserves had been anticipating a "brush with the rebels."[9] Indeed, with the main Confederate army entrenched at Manassas Junction and Centreville, the troops at Camp Pierpont were subject to a standing order to be prepared to muster in fighting trim the moment the long roll should sound. Finally, in early November as Hill was preparing for picket duty, the drummer boys did sound the call to arms in the camp of the 8th Regiment:

> Near this hour I was emerging from my tent, musket in hand, and was about to proceed to the gate [to report for picket duty], when the startling sound of the *long roll* broke upon the sharp morning air.
>
> "Confound it if I go to the gate," I exclaimed; and seeing the boys begin to pack their knapsacks and haversacks, and fall into line, I followed their example....
>
> At length, we filed out of camp and took our position in the brigade, the brigade in the division; and the whole, infantry, cavalry, and artillery, was soon in motion. We took the Leesburg pike, and marched slowly forward; skirmishers were sent out on all sides as we advanced, and scouts were sent in advance. Thus we marched, without interruption, till we reached Drainesville; a village consisting (or did then) of a small grocery store, a dwelling house—two families occupy it—and a blacksmith shop. A corpulent woman was standing on the piazza, while a short, stout, green-looking man in his shirt-sleeves was leaning against the closed door of the grocery establishment.
>
> "I say, old fellow, how far is it to the rebs?" asked one of our boys; for we halted here for a few minutes.
>
> "You'll find them soon enough," retorted the Drainesvillian.
>
> "Aren't you afraid of us Yankees?" was asked.
>
> "No, not a d[amne]d bit," he replied; and he stood there and grinned as though he *wasn't* afraid.[10]

Alas, no "rebs" were to be found, and the soldiers of the 8th Regiment, bitterly disappointed by their failure to have engaged the enemy, returned to Camp

A drummer boy of the 8th Pennsylvania Reserves

Ronn Palm's Museum of Civil War
Images, Gettysburg, Pa., Private Collection

Pierpont. They did not return empty-handed, however: "General McCall's Division of the army have all returned to their quarters at Langley. They found no rebels in their reconnaissance towards Dranesville [but]... brought home large quantities of forage. Gen. McCall's division improved the fine weather yesterday in building huts for winter quarters. They go in bodies into the forests, fell large trees, and split them into planks, with which they are building very comfortable cabins. The forests yesterday were deprived of many a fine oak tree, valued highly, no doubt, by the owners of the soil."[11] Ashbel Hill commented on those "comfortable cabins" while describing the 8th Regiment's winter quarters: "The huts we built were eight by ten feet;... we built them of small logs to the height of four or five feet, and pitched our tents upon the top of the walls, for coverings. A fire-place and chimney adorned a corner of each building, imparting a cheerful, domestic appearance. Such were our castles."[12]

As the men settled into their newly constructed winter quarters, Cordello Collins, a private in the 13th Regiment (the famed "Bucktails"), wrote home about his life in winter quarters and the marching and skirmishing that had frequently occupied the Pennsylvania Reserves since they crossed the Potomac:

Dear Perrants

I received your letter day before yesterday.... I was glad to hear from you and that you was so well there. You wrote to me that you herd that the Pa. solgers was all killed in that hard fite [at Ball's Bluff] but none of the Pa. solgers was there....

We have had 4 or 5 hard frosts heare. Last night was very cold.... Last Monday and teusday we had a genral inspection. The Bucktails had the prais of bein the best drilled regment out of the Pa. reserve....

While I am heare we have had one Skirmish heare. The 20 of Oct. some of this rement had fire one shot a piece at them and killed 4 or 5 of the Secess horse men....

I want you to send me a Bucktail. Put a paper round it and sent it by mail....
I would like to have one from home for the naim of it.

Write how much snow there has binn there and if you has killed eny dear
since I came from home. The 19th, the Pa. solgers marched about 18 miles out
to wards manasas gap. Then we laid down for to stay over night but about 9
oclock we was ordered back 2 miles to the Cross roads to where the most of the
regments was.... Then marched back to our camps Monday. We have had a
peaceiful time since then heare but we expect to move from heare soon.

We have a nuf to eat heare sutch as it is. But I have to buy some sweet
potatoes and py and sweet cakes, butter chease and apples to suit my taste.... I
can lay the sweet potatoes and butter down to a pretty good advantage. But
Fletcher Hamlin can beat me eating....

Write to me as soon as you can. I reming your affectionare Friend

Cordello Collins[13]

While the soldiers of the Pennsylvania Reserves enjoyed the enforced idle-
ness of winter quarters, numerous changes were occurring in their command structure. On November 1, 1861, President Lincoln accepted the resignation of Winfield
Scott, the elderly general in chief of the United States Army, and appointed Major
General George B. McClellan as his successor. In a move of much more immediate
concern to the Fayette Guards, Captain Jesse B. Gardner of Company G was elected
to the position of major of the 8th Reserves. To replace him, the Fayette Guards
elected William Searight of Uniontown. It was a popular choice and was well-
received at home:

Seldom indeed have we been privileged to record an incident that has afforded us as much gratification as it does to inform our readers, that our young
and valued friend, William Searight, has been by a most flattering vote elected
Captain of the Oliphant-Gardner company in the 8th Pennsylvania Regiment.

Captain Searight is an excellent tactician, having spent a considerable time at
West Point. Talented and well educated, he will doubtless make an efficient and
popular officer. This is another promotion entirely upon merit. Captain Searight
from the promptings of that unselfish patriotism of which his nature abounds
was among the first to enlist from this place as a private, and his noble companions in arms appreciating his abilities, have placed him at the head of one of the
finest companies in the service. Success to Captain Searight and the noble old
Company G.[14]

Searight's renowned tactical experience was soon put to good use. On December 20, 1862, Union cavalry scouts reported that a strong Confederate foraging
party was expected to be operating in the area of Dranesville. As the Reserves had
been foraging extensively in this area themselves, General McCall mounted an
expedition to turn back the rebel force, reassert control over the disputed ground

between the two armies, and "procure forage at Gunnell's farm or some other rank secessionist's farm."[15] With these objectives in mind, General Ord's third brigade marched at daybreak, followed by General Reynolds's first brigade. General Meade's second brigade was held in reserve. Hill, marching in Reynolds's brigade, described the day's events:

> Morning came, and all were busy arranging their accoutrements for the projected expedition. I was very lame, but I determined I would not be left in camp, and I limped off with the regiment as it filed out of camp and joined the brigade. This done, we moved into the pike and marched toward Drainesville....[16]

> On reaching Difficult Creek, we...filed off to the left, and taking our position on a high hill, a quarter of a mile from it, we stacked arms and broke ranks. We had lain for several hours, and were just beginning to wonder whether the Third Brigade *would* be so fortunate as to meet with a party of rebels, when the heavy, booming sound of the cannon reached our ears, coming from the direction of Drainesville....[17]

> [W]e hurriedly formed and started toward Drainesville by the pike, at a double quick, with five miles between us and glory.

> Meanwhile the sound of the cannon continued to reach our ears; the firing had become more rapid. We hurried on. Four miles were marched in forty minutes. We then began to meet the forage wagons, which blocked up the road, and somewhat impeded our progress. The drivers informed us that the Third Brigade was "at it out there...." The musketry could be heard. We began to meet ambulances laden with wounded, and now and then brave fellows limping along still carrying their guns. We also met a squad of rebel prisoners under charge of a corporal and two men.

> We were within a few hundred yards of the village where our forces were posted, when the firing suddenly ceased, and a wild shout arose.

> "They're driving the rebels!" was exclaimed; and we rushed madly on.

> We arrived upon the scene just in time to see the rebels disappear down the Centreville road, with the gallant Bucktail Regiment [temporarily attached to the Third Brigade as skirmishers], and the Sixth and Ninth Regiments...at their heels. We sent up a deafening cheer—such as never before rang out among the green pines in the vicinity of Drainesville....[18]

> It was night ere we retraced our steps. As may be imagined, my physical condition was not improved by a march of ten miles, half of which had been done at a double-quick. My foot pained me very much...as it came in contact with the sharp, hard stones of the pike.... I was in a bad humor, too. Here, I had limped ten miles, hoping to have the pleasure of a row with the rebels—had just arrived in time to be too late—and had got a good ducking in Difficult Creek in the bargain. On reaching camp, however, I soon forgot my troubles in a deep

slumber, from which I awoke the next morning, feeling very old. I couldn't get over my disappointment, and in writing a letter to a friend, that day, after detailing the events of the battle, I wound up with:

> I tell you, Tom, we cursed the fate
> That brought us to the field too late—
> That brought us there, just as the foe
> Concluded to get up and go.
>
> The Third Brigade had all the fun,
> It did the fighting that was done;
> And it got all the praise, to boot,
> For making rebels skallyhoot.[19]

His comrades in the first brigade shared Hill's disappointment. Albert **Rake** wrote to his wife shortly after the battle:

Dec 27 61

Dear Wife

I received your letter last night and was very sorry to hear that you was not well. But you must not go out in the cold too much.... I am afraid you expose yourself to save your monny, but you must not do it for if I live and keep well I can send you enough to live on without your doing so much. I got the box you sent to me but I am now where I get good living. We have beef stake, potatoes, milk, tea, coffee, sugar, rice, bread and butter, and molasses as much as we want in the hospittle so you need not send me enny thing at present.... We have 9 sick persons in the hospittle now and there is four nurses of us and 2 cooks.... I like the job better than I did at first. I am not well nor don't expect to get so as long as I am in the army but I will stay as long as I can. I will try and get a furlow in March to come home.... I can get on a raft and come down.... There is none of our boys in the hospittle now nor I don't want enny of them in for it is a bad place. There has four died since Simon died. I suppose you have heard of the fight close to our camp lately. Our boys was not in it for the suns of bitches [the Confederates] had run before they got to the place. But I hope we will have a chance yet at them before long. I have no news of importance to send to you so I will close by sending you all a kiss

From your loving husband, A. Rake[20]

Following the disasters of First Bull Run and Balls Bluff,[21] Dranesville was welcomed as a resounding success for Union arms and provided a much-needed morale boost for the Army of the Potomac. Upon learning of McCall's victory, Governor Curtin visited Camp Pierpont to congratulate the Reserves. John Willoughby, a soldier in the 5th Regiment, described the governor's visit in a letter to his friend, James Randolf Simpson:[22]

Camp Pierpont
Sunday, Dec. 29th '61

Friend Dol

Yours was received last night. Glad to hear from you and would that you had witnessed the sight that I wish thousands of others did this beautiful December afternoon. I was watching the Pennsylvania Reserve Corps while Gov. Curtin and Gen. McCall accompanied by Gen. S. Cameron...and other distinguished persons reviewed them. I was not in the ranks [and] therefore had a very good view of things.... The review passed off very well. After all had...passed [in] review the 1st and 2nd Brigade marched to their respective quarters. The 3rd Brigade, Easton's Battery [and] four companies of [the] 1st Pennsylvania Cavalry, [all] commanded by Brig. Gen. Ord, remained. To them Gov. Curtin made a speech, praising them for their gallantry at the Battle of Dranesville and also ordering that the word Dranesville should be imprinted on their flags.[23] Cheers were given for Curtin, McCall and Pennsylvania.... Oh! That the time may soon come when the Bloody Fifth may leave her mark; and make the...Fifth Pennsylvania a terror in Secession Ranks.

I was on guard part of Christmas;... All the boys were let loose to enjoy themselves as they might.... Great excitement prevails about the destination of Slidell and Mason;[24] today [the] papers say they are to be released.... Miss Swerringer [is] a nice gal; OK no doubt. I wonder if a–well, a young man named James Randolf—is not slightly struck. Bully for her. Give her a soldier's best wishes....

Dol, we have some gay times in [tent] No. 11. We have a stove; a good crowd gets in then for the tales. One of the most welcome guests is Major Hawn (Whitey). He is a brick—liked by all and as good a soldier as can be found in the Army of the Potomac.... I must close. Good night....

Truly yours
John A. Willoughby
Company G, 5th Regt.[25]

While the soldiers of the first and second brigades lamented their late arrival on the field at Dranesville, whatever disappointment Hill and his messmates may have felt at missing out on the engagement was at least partially assuaged a few days later by the arrival of a parcel from home:

On arriving in camp, I was informed, by my messmates, that a "box" had been sent to one of them from home, containing, among other things, two half-gallon tin cans, tightly sealed, one marked in big letters—"PRESERVED PEACHES," the other, "CURRANT JELLY." Now, the one marked "preserved peaches" contained whiskey; that marked "currant jelly" contained whiskey, too. Thus one gallon of the "poison" had walked slyly into camp, beneath the very noses of the provost-marshals, officers of the day, etc.

Haman, Dick, Ort and Enos had been imbibing, and were already right merry when I entered our domicile. They urged *me* to take "something." Well, I do not think it any harm to take a little now and then while in camp, especially in damp and muddy weather, so I did take a "little" three or four times. By and by, all became boozy; Haman and Dick called in everybody that passed by, made everybody drink several times till nearly every man in the company felt right happy.[26]

The soldiers' happiness was short-lived, however, as the harsh reality of life in an army camp intervened the very next morning:

Next morning I was somewhat startled by the information that a friend of mine—Corporal Rinehart, of Company "I"—had been taken ill and conveyed to the regimental hospital...and that he was now supposed to be dying.... I hastened to the hospital, accompanied by Lieutenant Wood...and soon succeeded in gaining admittance. I looked around on the miserable sufferers occupying the various beds, but I could not see my friend. Some...were suffering terribly with one disease or another; one I particularly remember, had some disease of the throat, and he lay constantly struggling and gasping for breath; others lay pale and wan—wasted away to almost nothing—their eyes sunken, their lips thin and white, and their hollow cheeks wearing a deathly pallor. But the patient that most attracted my attention was one who lay in a delirium, struggling for every breath he drew; his face was almost black, as from mortification; his lips dry and parched; and his eyes rolling and staring wildly. I turned away, sickened at the sight.

"But where—" I asked of Lieutenant Wood—"where is Corporal Rinehart...?"

"There!" said he, pointing to the suffering figure I have just described; "Poor fellow, he is nearly gone!"

I was amazed. I could not trace in those features now turned black by disease—those wildly staring eyes—that prostrate form, any resemblance to my dear friend, Corporal Rinehart! Yet it was he. Disease had almost done its work—death stood impatiently waiting for him.[27]

Indeed, Corporal Rinehart did die shortly after Hill found him in the regimental hospital. He described the sad scene that ensued:

Heavy, dismal clouds were flying in wild disorder across the heavens. The cold, chill winds of December were sighing from hill to hill, and through the dark-green pine woods. A solitary snow-flake, here and there, descended lazily—it was too cold to snow much. Slowly, sadly an ambulance, escorted by ten soldiers with arms reversed, and followed by a company of soldiers, as mourners, took its way from camp. The low, solemn, and plaintive notes of a fife, and the dull roll of the muffled drum, told but too plainly what that ambulance contained—the pale corpse of a soldier. 'Twas the cold lifeless form of my friend.

The body was escorted to the pike with military honors, sent thence to Washington, there embalmed and sent to the bereaved ones at home.

As my friend was borne from my view forever, I could not refrain from tears. Yet why? His transition from this world to another could have been no loss to him—it must have been infinite gain; for he was one who could have no reason to fear the Pale Conqueror—to shrink back from the icy waters of the River of Death. He was one of the very few, yes, the *very* few, who besides professing religious principles, carry them out. It has never been my privilege to form the acquaintance of a more honest, honorable, amiable, or upright young man. Such was my friend, Corporal Rinehart.[28]

With the suspension of campaigning for the winter, life soon returned to a semblance of normalcy for Hill and his comrades. Many of the soldiers took advantage of the relative inactivity occasioned by the suspension of campaigning during the winter to catch up on their correspondence. John Strathern, assuming an air of experience that belied his 23 years, offered his younger brother James some sage advice on that most serious of matters—marriage:

> Headquarters 8th Regt. P.R.V.C.
> Camp Pierpont, Virginia
> January 12th 1862

Dear Brother

Your kind and interesting [letter] reached me in due time, and it affords me great pleasure to see that disappointment has not annihilated every vestige of cheerfulness. Why, sir, you bear your troubles like a philosopher. But you ask me what this is all about.

Well, not to keep you longer in suspense; a friend writing to me from Braddock's Field some time ago, informs me that you had laid siege to a Fort near Braddock's Field.... He expressed to me that you were likely to be outgeneraled. Then brother, my advice to you is to escape the siege and beat a retreat as speedily as possible, [for fear] of being cut off from reinforcements.

But laying all jokes aside, and to talk the matter over soberly, my friend informs me that if he may judge from appearances, he thinks that you have some notion of taking a partner for life, and starting for yourself in the world. Now brother, talk the matter over coolly, calmly and deliberately. In the first place, do you think that you could discharge the duties of the married state? If you can, then you have got one step ahead of me. Are you prepared to assume the necessary responsibility of head of the house? I fear that you are premature in this matter. With wedlock, comes care. Now take a brother's advice and let the fair sex alone for a few years yet, at least till you are as old as I am, and then [take] my word for it, you will think differently. If not, you will then be better prepared for the duties of a father and governor of a house. Take my advice and do not do anything rashly. This is a matter not of a day, week or month, but of a lifetime, and on it depends your happiness here.

By all means get Father's and Mother's consent before you act. I think that what I have said will be enough when you accept that my knowledge of the fair sex, and the world generally, is much more extensive than yours. This is by no means [a] trifling matter, therefore, look twice before you take the fearful leap....

No more at present. I remain

Your affectionate brother
John Strathern[29]

When Private Strathern was not busy dispensing marital advice, he and his comrades occupied themselves with those pursuits common to daily life in the army's winter quarters:

The winter wore gradually away. The regular routine of exercise was kept up; save that out-door sports were somewhat eschewed in consequence of the increasing mud. Otherwise, things went on as usual; Gaskill got tight regularly, whenever he could procure anything to get tight on; Winder continued to tell his usual number of solemn untruths daily; Hare stuttered away as usual, getting into a fight alternately with Dave Adams and Bob Young; chuck-o-luck was carried on daily;[30] the mud continued in good swimming order; military funerals were intermixed with other things, the muffled drum becoming a familiar sound; picket duty was done regularly; the captain was tried and acquitted [on a charge of countenancing unauthorized foraging by his men]—released from arrest and restored to his command; rumors, as usual, were afloat; talking was done, and opinions expressed as to the plans for the coming spring's campaign; and, altogether, we looked earnestly forward to the coming spring, when we should surely go forth to meet the defiant rebels. Anxiously, impatiently, we waited, watched and wished for clear windy days to come and dry up the mud, that we might move forward. All was anticipation.[31]

During these weeks of enforced inactivity, one of the Fayette Guards, whose nom de plume was Diomed, took time to write to the editor of the *Genius of Liberty*, apprising him of the news relating to Company G. He also offered an interesting insight on the disappointment his comrades felt at arriving on the field too late to take part in the Battle of Dranesville:

Camp Pierpont
Feb. 8th, 1862

Col. Roddy—At the request of my comrades, and remembering former promises and "Old Lang Syne," I seat myself for the purpose of dropping you a line which I hope may be found to be entertaining to your readers and acceptable to yourself.... So, without further preface, I will "just wade in," and if after reading, you don't like it, then burn the manuscript.

Of Company G and the Eighth Regiment there is not much to write, which would either amuse or interest your readers, except personal incidents; and these are too numerous to think of relating in anything less than a volume. Hence you will perceive at a glance that I am prohibited from gleaning in this field, by the magnitude of the undertaking. Yet I will just observe in passing that the men are all cheerful and well as their friends could wish, and more comfortably housed in their log shanties, than you yourself could believe were I to describe them. Their budget of fun, sport and devilment being absolutely inexhaustible...must be seen and felt before you would venture to believe or tell it....

Col. Hayes is at home on a furlough, and Lieut. Col. Oliphant is in command of the regiment, though for that matter there is not much doing in that line just now, because of bad weather and mud, plenty of which we have had for some time past; and but for a court martial which he is daily attending or conducting at General Reynolds' the Col. would, I think, keep as far away from the roads as we are from the Rebels, and thank his stars that he was so fortunate as not to be compelled to try the experiment of occasionally dropping himself and horse through them. Maj. Gardner is confined to his quarters yet with his sprained ankle, and has for his companions Capt. Searight and Lieuts. Ramsey and Dawson.... Since the accident, he has been presented with a beautiful sword; the ceremonies of which, I understand, will be shortly sent you for publication. Capt. Searight is winning golden opinions from all who know him since his promotion by the suffrages of his comrades....

Of the war and its progress it is unnecessary to say much.... Yet one can't help recurring occasionally to the "change which came o'er the spirit of our dreams," since the era of Camp Wilkins, and the "big muster" at the Pittsburgh fair grounds. Often since has the question been argued in our tents and shanties whether we were the most fools or crazy then; in fact, it has been a prolific theme of discussion ever since. But Carpet Knights, Feathers, Spurs, Spread Eagle Speeches and Glory, disappeared all at once, when the Reserve was ordered to march forthwith to the Federal Capitol to take part in the stirring scenes which were then enacting on the Potomac. And when on the road we heard of McDowell's defeat, and the probable advance of Beauregard upon Washington, our illusions fled forever—and earnest preparations for "battle's magnificently stern array" began, and fixed and riveted our attention. 'Tis true we were doomed to disappointment...but then it was and is a disappointment about which there are few grumblers, because when weighed against life and limb...we are found to be the gainers to an extraordinary extent. For by it, we have lost not a single life, and have improved in drill, discipline, and all that pertains to efficiency as soldiers....

Yours &c.,

Diomed[32]

On February 20, the same day that "Diomed's" letter appeared in the *Genius of Liberty*, General McCall issued an order that called upon his soldiers to commemorate the birthday of the country's first commander in chief and to exert their greatest efforts to ensure the survival of the Union:

> Head Qrs. McCall's Division
>
> Camp Pierpont Feb 20th 1862
>
> A national salute will be fired in front of Stewart's Battery by the Artillery of this Division...at 12 o'clock M. on Saturday the 22nd inst.
>
> The "Declaration of Independence" and the "Farewell Address of Washington" will be read to each Regiment if copies can be procured.
>
> The Congress of the United States have resolved to observe this day and have expressed their wish that the Army of [the] Potomac should also celebrate it.
>
> Let us then commemorate this day, the anniversary of the birth of our great civil Father. He loved his Country and he loved his Countrymen; let us imitate him in his perfection of Patriotism. He bequeathed this Union to their descendants. It is a holy and beautiful heritage. We will defend it. It is worth living for, and it is worth dying for. The Soldiers of the Union have achieved great and important Victories. The Old Flag now waves in almost every Rebel State. Belmont and Dranesville are followed by Port Royal, Roanoke, Fort Henry and Fort Donelson.
>
> Soldiers of the Reserve, your General congratulates you on these victories.
>
> Let us then celebrate this day with Guns, with Music, with Banners and with high resolves
>
> By Order of Brig. Gen. McCall[33]

The news of the Union victory at Fort Henry on February 6 and the Confederate surrender at Fort Donelson 10 days later galvanized the men of the Pennsylvania Reserves:[34]

> Just as the sun was sinking in the west...a mounted messenger dashed into camp, shouting—
>
> "Fort Donelson is ours! It has been surrendered with twenty-five thousand prisoners!"
>
> Every man who heard, shouted—
>
> "Hurrah! Hurrah! Fort Donelson is taken! Three cheers!"
>
> A soul-stirring cheer went up; every man in the regiment shouted with gladness on hearing the welcome news. Other regiments took up the cheer, and ere long fifteen thousand men were yelling at the top of their voices....
>
> Our brass band now came forth, took its position on the most elevated spot in our regimental street, and played all the national airs they could think of; beginning with "Hail Columbia" and winding up with "Yankee Doodle." The whole regiment gathered around, cheering at intervals in a deafening manner.

"Hurrah! The war is about over," shouted one.

"Who wants to buy a good gun?" asked another.

"Or a good knapsack? I'm about done with mine," said another....

"Ah, boys, *the war is not over yet!*" said a youthful soldier, gravely; he was a member of Company "B."

Poor fellow, he was right. Better had it been for *him* if the war *had* been over then. Then he could have returned to his smiling home on the green banks of the Allegheny. But alas! Where is he now? His bones lie buried at Glendale,[35] no stone marks the spot, and his widowed mother...sits, lonely and sad, at her cottage window, gazing sorrowfully upon the glassy surface of the clear river, thinking of her boy—her only boy—her lost Willie![36]

The Union victory at Fort Donelson did not end the war of course, and Private Hill noted that "[i]t was obvious that the time was not far distant when we should do something; the mud began to grow 'beautifully less.' By and by, we received orders to keep three days' rations in our haversacks, and be ready to march at any time."[37]

Not surprisingly, just where the Reserves would march was the subject of much speculation. Private Strathern assured his brother that the 8th Regiment would be in the vanguard of a Federal advance upon Leesburg and Centreville:

> Eighth Regt. P.R.V.C.
> Camp Pierpont
> March 1st 1862

Dear Brother,

There was an illumination in Washington City on the 22nd [in honor of George Washington's birthday], but the public buildings were no[t] illuminated on account of the death of President Lincoln's youngest son, William....

There is no truth in the report that we are to go to Washington city, and as we are the First Brigade of General McCall's Division, we will compose the advance on Leesburg and Centerville. There are enough raw recruits to take care of that place, as there will never be any attack upon the Capitol....

The Braddock's Field Boys are all well....

> Your brother,
> John Strathern[38]

"Away Down South in Dixie"

Manassas to the Rappahannock

Nine days after John Strathern wrote to his brother, the Pennsylvania Reserves did, indeed, move out, but their objective was neither Leesburg nor Centreville. Corporal Hill recalled that:

> [t]he Colonel rode hurriedly into camp, and shouted—"Battalion, shoulder—*arms!*" It was done with alacrity
>
> "Right—*face!*" This command was obeyed with equal agility. Then came the magic—
>
> "*Forward*—March!" The band struck up a favorite air, we moved as one man, and uttering one wild farewell cheer, we marched from Camp Pierpont—forever.[1]

George Darby recalled the march, undertaken in miserable weather, and had few kind words for those who had ordered it:

> On learning that the enemy had evacuated Manassas, the Reserves broke camp at Pierpont...and marched for that point.[2] This march, owing to the inclemency of the weather, was the hardest, most exhausting and fatiguing that the Reserves ever experienced during their term of service and was caused by the stupid blundering of some one high in authority.
>
> This senseless and worse than useless march was made from our camp at Pierpont during one of the most terrific storms of sleet and rain which it was ever my misfortune to encounter, and to add to the aggravation of the situation, when we had almost reached Manassas, our objective point, here came the order to countermarch on Alexandria, and on reaching that point during a heavy snow fall we were loaded upon platform cars, and sent back to Bull Run. This experience was simply awful; it was a regular Burnside stick-in-the-mud with additional horrors.[3] The roads throughout this section of the country had been transformed into rivers of mud, axle deep, and rain and sleet continued in

ceaseless down-pour night and day. Men, completely exhausted, fell out of rank, and dropping down in the fence corners, died of fatigue and exhaustion. I remember one night while on our return march we halted in a piece of woodland, completely fagged out, the down-pour continuing; the ground was reeking with water, so that lying down was impractical, so setting to work we felled a hickory tree and building a fire against it, I sat down before it with my cap drawn over my eyes, and immediately fell asleep. On awakening I found the leathern frontis entirely burned from my cap. On resuming the march, it being impossible to follow the roads on account of the depth of the mud, we were obliged to take to the fields and woods, as the paths formed by the advance became impassable, those in the rear would be obliged to start a new one and thus we struggled on.... Upon reaching Alexandria we were started back to the place whence we came. Now if there was ever an intelligible reason assigned for these blundering, quixotic movements, which cost the Republic vast sums of money, and the sacrifice of many precious lives, I have never heard of it. On reaching Bull Run and finding that the railroad bridge had been destroyed, a foot-way was constructed across the stream and we continued our march to Manassas. At that point several of my comrades and myself were fortunate enough to secure a hut which the rebels had occupied and failed to destroy when they left. We gathered a lot of wood and soon had a fire started within, which dried out the shanty and enabled us to spend a night in comfort, secure against the raging of the elements.[4]

Hill, who had spent his first night in Manassas in a railroad freight car with his messmates, inspected the abandoned Confederate dwellings the next morning: "I took a stroll among some of the old cabins which had constituted the winter quarters of the rebels; I found many relics of the past winter in the shape of broken bottles, Richmond newspapers, etc. In one of the buildings I found an envelope which had once contained a letter. It was addressed—'Captain Edgar Covington, Thirty-Eighth Virginia Regiment, Manassas.' It was a fancy envelope; on it were a five cent rebel stamp, a picture of the rebel flag, and the following patriotic verse—

> On, on to the rescue! The vandals are coming!
> Go, meet them with bayonet, sabre and spear!
> Drive them back to the desolate land they are leaving—
> Go, trusting in God—you have nothing to fear!"[5]

Albert Rake encountered relics of a more tragic nature during a visit he made to the nearby battlefield at Bull Run. He described his experience in a letter to his wife:

Manassas April 20 62

Dear Lucy

    I suppose you think [it] strange that I don't rite oftener but I have been waiting all last week to get a letter from you but I have not got one yet for we don't get our mail regular. Our Regt is all along the Rail Road. I sent you 27 dollars by Express. It is not as much as I could of sent you but some times we don't get our grub regular so I kept some and find it comes in quite good.... I cant say how long we will stay at this place, but I hope it wont be long for it will be awful this summer in this place. I was to see the place where the Battle was [First Bull Run, July 21, 1861] and I don't care about seeing another one, for the bones of the men lay all round and them that was buried was not more than a foot under-ground.... Rite soon again. So good by. No more but

A Kiss to my family one and all

Albert Rake[6]

While awaiting further orders at Manassas, some of Ashbel Hill's comrades had the misfortune to "liberate" a supply of what they supposed to be whiskey from a railroad car bound for General Banks's corps. The train had broken down just past Manassas Junction, and the contents of the car in question proved irresistible to the thirsty Union soldiers. In due course, many of the imbibers, including Hill who had been prevailed upon to "take a horn," became violently ill:[7] "My head ached; my appetite was gone; and as the day wore away, I 'got no better much faster....' In a day or two I had become so weak as to be scarcely able to walk. As I was unable for duty, I found myself obliged to enter the 'sick list'—to place myself under the doctor's care. I was loth to do it, too; for it has ever been my opinion that a man is no better than a dead man when placed under the hands of almost any of our army surgeons. This is startling, but *it is true*. An ordinary army surgeon can, by a course of treatment, bring the stoutest man to the grave; and they seldom fail to do it."[8]

The Pennsylvania Reserves remained at Manassas for several days, during which time Hill's condition improved somewhat. He was still too weak to walk, however, and thus, when the 8th Regiment marched to Catlett Station on April 17, he was forced to ride in an ambulance:

We had been at Manassas a week, when we received orders to move to Catlett Station, on the Orange and Alexandria railroad, twelve miles from Manassas. I was too weak to walk, and was accordingly placed in a vehicle known as a "one-horse ambulance." This was my first ride in an ambulance; and, oh, how de-voutly I prayed that it might be the last!... I verily believe that a vehicle worse adapted to the transportation of sick and wounded soldiers could not be in-vented. Whenever the wheels came in contact with the slightest obstacle, the ambulance would rock, and jump, and spring, and surge, and shake, and quake in a frightful manner. Once, I remember, the wheel went suddenly into a gutter, and the body of the ambulance gave such a fearful leap, that it threw the driver from his seat, and he came down in the mud with a startling grunt. As for me, there I lay within that miserable contrivance, jostled from side to side, my head knocking violently against the frame-work at every revolution of the wheels, while I wondered how it would go to ride in such a jumping, jolting affair with a broken arm or leg.[9]

The march to Catlett Station was the initial movement in a general advance upon Fredericksburg by McDowell's I Corps, to which McCall's division had been attached when General McClellan commenced his Peninsula campaign in mid-March.[10] With the rest of the Army of the Potomac heading for Fort Monroe on the Virginia Peninsula, President Lincoln held the I Corps back to bolster the defenses of Washington. Believing that the best defense is a good offense, McDowell had requested, and been given, permission to take Fredericksburg as part of his "defensive operations" below the Federal capital—hence the advance southward from Manassas.

John Strathern wrote home from Catlett Station on April 22, commenting on the battlefield at Bull Run and alerting his father to be on the lookout for some "secesh tobacco":

Dear Father,

I hope you will excuse the brevity of my last letter, as at the time it was written all was bustle and excitement....

During our stay at Manassas, I had the pleasure of visiting the scene of the Battle of July 21st 1861. The masked batteries, our men talked of, were all a myth so far as I could see. There had never been any fortifications except a rifle pit, here and there....

We are now about ten miles beyond the [Manassas] Junction on our way to Fredericksburg....

We have lain inactive for the last three days, owing to the rainy weather, but this morning it is clear, and the prospect is that [we] will have fine weather again....

On Saturday morning, I boxed my overcoat and took it up to the station and expressed it to you. Enclosed you will find a note, a pipe and [a] secesh tobacco bag....

I believe I must close for present. Hoping to hear from you soon. Let me know how you all are getting along.

Your son,
John Strathern[11]

From Catlett Station, McCall's men continued their march southward toward Fredericksburg, halting at White Ridge, north of Falmouth, along the way. There, Hill and his friend, Dave Malone, took to the countryside in search of a better dinner than they could look forward to in camp:

[A]fter a walk of half a mile [we] found ourselves at the door of a picturesque mansion surrounded by tall green trees. Thinking to call in and try to procure dinner, we knocked at the door. We did so several times before there was any response. At last the door was opened by a pleasant woman of fifty.

"Can you accommodate us with dinner?" I asked, after the compliments of the day had passed.

"Walk in—I will try," was the reply.

We did so, and were ushered into a commonly-furnished room.

"Is your husband at home?" I asked.

"No," she unhesitatingly replied; "he is in the army."

"Ah? The—the"

"The Confederate Army—*you* call it the *rebel army*."

"I perceive that you do not hide the truth. A great many ladies of these parts, on being asked where their husbands are, say they have none—that they are widows."

"Some may say so; but I do not wish to disguise the truth. I am what you call a secessionist; my husband and only son are in the army of the Southern Confederacy. It is nothing to be ashamed of; we believe our cause is just...."

The lady now busied herself about preparing dinner, and when it was ready we sat down. We were treated to a very satisfactory repast, during which the merits of the war were discussed with some warmth. Our entertainer was very intelligent, and she defended the cause of the South with great enthusiasm.... When we offered remuneration for the hospitality we had received, the old lady said—

"No; I ask nothing; I fed our own soldiers when they were here; I have plenty, I will give even to our enemies as long as I can."

"You are very kind, madam," said I "but I would much rather—"

"No," she interrupted, "I wish no pay; one never loses anything by being hospitable."

"I hope I may never meet your husband or son in battle."

"I hope not."

We bade the hostess good-day, and departed. I felt somewhat stung that I had partaken of the hospitalities of one whose soil I was invading."[12]

The Pennsylvania Reserves pressed on toward Fredericksburg. As they neared the village of Falmouth, which lay across the Rappahannock River just upstream of Fredericksburg, Hill conveyed the scene in language that presaged his postwar career as an author:

As we descended the hill which lies north of Falmouth, we looked across the beautiful Rappahannock, and beheld a piece of scenery which I shall never forget. The sun was already mounting up into the blue heavens, and his full, open light shone upon Fredericksburg. That city appeared to our view as a mixture of gable-ends, chimney-tops, and tree-tops. It appeared to be a city built in the midst of a wood.... The leaves upon the trees were now full-grown, and they wore all the verdant freshness that an early spring morning is wont to inspire. Thousands of dewdrops still hung thereon, and sparkled like diamonds in the melting light of the morning sun; while in the midst the blue smoke ascended in curling wreaths from many chimneys. The Rappahannock flowing from between two green hills, half a mile above, and disappearing, in its windings, among the rolling woodlands far below, lay placid and smooth, its glassy surface reflecting the outline of a few white cottages and green trees which stood upon the opposite shore in the full light of the morning sun.[13]

The beauty of the country in which the Reserves found themselves also touched Joseph McQuaide. He reflected on it in a letter to his parents in mid-May:

> 9th Pennsylvania Reserve Corps
> Company C
> Camp near Fredericksburg May 12, 1862

> Dear parents
> I now seat myself to answer your letter...and I now can say in reply that I am well at present and I hope that you are...getting along well. We are now as you can see by the heading handy to Fredericksburg. It looks to be a very nice town but the river is between us and it so we cannot tell mutch about it. There is about fifteen hundred soldiers...[working on] the bridges that are under construction. The Rebels having burned the bridges when they left.[14] The people that are here are secesh of course and tell it pretty plainly.
> We are camped in the nicest place now that ever we were. Plenty of the very best of water and sutch a lovely place I think was never occupied by an army.... Well this is May, beautiful flowery may, the pride of the year. There has been about a week of very beautiful weather. Not a cloud to be seen, clear and warm, and this you may know is good for us to have been exposed to the wet and cold since the 15th of March without tents. You may well say that we hail the warm weather with joy.... We have two company drills a day and dress parade in the evening....

> J. L. McQuaide[15]

While at Falmouth, the men of the 8th Regiment enjoyed a plentiful and varied diet. In addition to the ubiquitous foraging, they also availed themselves of a well-stocked market in the village. And, on occasion, they could persuade certain of the local inhabitants to "invite" them to dinner. The soldiers' lack of social graces, however, sometimes caused them no little embarrassment—witness the tale of John Stewart, a sergeant with Company G:

> The market at Falmouth was well supplied with fish of the herring variety, also with peanuts galore. This latter commodity could be purchased at five cents

per peck, but as they were raw, we were obliged to do the roasting act ourselves. Occasionally some of the boys who had a little remaining money would go to Falmouth and applying at a private house would secure an extra meal of herring and bacon. It had become customary among the boys in speaking of pork and crackers, to call it hard tack and sow-belly, and it had been so long thus designated that these useful articles of army diet were scarcely known by any other name. One day Sergeant Stewart, of Company G, went to Falmouth and induced a lady of the place to get him up a dinner of herring and bacon, so sitting down to the table he proceeded to dispatch his meal...when out of compliment to his hostess' skill as a cook he thoughtlessly remarked, "Madam, this is the best sow-belly I ever tackled." The lady, greatly surprised, said "What did you say, Sir?" Stewart, greatly embarrassed and blushing, said, "Oh! Ah! Excuse me, I mean to say really I think this is the best bacon I have ever tasted...." [H]e did not regain his wonted composure until he was well out of that house.[16]

In the course of their advance upon Fredericksburg, Union troops came into increasing contact with large numbers of fugitive slaves. Runaway slaves who reached Union lines often were referred to as "contrabands."[17] The term generally referred to those slaves who sought the protection of the Union army and were employed by it as cooks, teamsters, or menservants. Hill and Darby both recounted numerous instances of interaction between soldiers of the 8th Reserves and contrabands (widely referred to by the soldiers as "darkies," a term which the contrabands habitually applied to themselves). Hill encountered one runaway slave himself on his way to visit Fredericksburg, and later witnessed an amusing exchange between a Union officer and another slave, a young runaway eager to "see those animals called 'Yankees'" for himself:[18]

I had not yet visited the city of Fredericksburg; there was a stern barrier between us and that city—the Rappahannock River.... One day...learning that the bridge was in a passable condition, I resolved to...visit Fredericksburg at once....[19] When within a quarter of a mile of the river (for the camp lay at some little distance from it) I observed a sable Sambo approaching with his bundle. For about this time the negroes of that vicinity might be seen at all hours, day and night, striking out in various directions, leaving their masters. The gentleman in question was one of this class. Thinking to gain some information from him regarding the geography of that part of the world, I accosted him with—

"Hilloa, Sam! Striking out, eh?"

"Yes, sah—yah-hah! Hah-hah!" replied Sam, seeming to be very much amused at the idea of *striking out*; and he exhibited two rows of immense eaters.

"Where does your master live?" I asked.

"Ober 'cross de riber dar—down below dar," replied Sam, with a voluptuous grin.

"And you've dissolved partnership with him?"

"Oh, yes; lots ob it."

"Well, Sam, can't you tell me something of the country hereabouts?"

"Yes, sah—considable."

"I believe this is Stafford County, is it not?"

"I spec so."

"You came from beyond the river, you say."

"Oh, yes—come from dar dis mornin'."

"And what county is that over there?"

"Oh, it's Vawginny—dat's what dey call it. Wichmond's de capilet ob it—de place dey's fightin', you know."

"Yes—but the *county*, I mean, Sam," said I, with a suppressed smile; Virginia is the *State*, you know."

"Yes—Vawginny am de—de—yes, sah."

Perceiving that it was useless to attempt to gain any information from that ignorant darkey, I bade him good-day, and passed on. I was nearing the bridge when I saw a lieutenant of our division engaged in conversation with a little darkey of twelve years of age. It appeared that little Sambo had been to camp to see those animals called "Yankees," and had not found them exactly what he had expected. Happening to meet with the lieutenant above spoken of, he had now opened a conversation on the subject. As I came within hearing distance, the darkey said:

"Massa, *is* dem de weal Yankees?"

"Yes, certainly—the simon pure—the unsophisticated," replied the officer, somewhat amused at Sam's earnestness....

"But", argued the sable juvenile, "where is der horns I'm heared so much about?"

"Oh, the horns, eh?" replied the lieutenant, readily comprehending the ideas which had prompted this question; "why, you see, they take them off and put them into their knapsacks while about camp; the Yankees are different from other animals in that respect."

"Den do dey put dem on to fite wid?"

"Yes," replied the officer, with difficulty choking down his risibility.

"Oh, golly" exclaimed Sam, turning away horrified.[20]

Hill continued over the river and into Fredericksburg. While there, he made his way to the burial site of Mary Washington, the first president's mother:

From the hill on which we were encamped, I had often observed a marble column, about fourteen feet in height, standing in a green field beyond Fredericksburg. I was told that it was a monument marking the spot where the mother of [George] Washington was buried. I determined, while on that side of the river, to visit it; and thither I bent my steps. After wading through a field of luxuriant clover, I arrived at the monument. What was my indignation and horror, when, on arriving there, I perceived that the white marble was spattered over with hundreds of bullets and shot—that the rebels, during their possession, had been amusing themselves by discharging their muskets against it! What desecration! I cannot think that it was ever tolerated by their officers. Perhaps it was done by the more vulgar ones of the rebel army; yet it was done by rebels. As I stood contemplating the sacrilegious act, I imagined that nothing could afford me greater relief at that moment, than to have a few hundred of them there. I felt that I could whip a whole regiment of such despicable barbarians.[21]

Hill's opportunity to engage the "barbarians" would come soon enough. On May 31, Confederate troops under Joseph E. Johnston engaged McClellan's forces at Fair Oaks (or Seven Pines) less than 10 miles east of Richmond.[22] The two-day battle finally ended in a rebel repulse, and might be largely forgotten today but for the fact that Johnston was seriously wounded on the first day of the encounter. Upon learning of Johnston's wounding, Confederate President Jefferson Davis assigned the overall command of Confederate forces in Virginia to General Robert E. Lee. It was a choice that would have profound consequences for the prosecution of the war in the East. In the aftermath of Fair Oaks, with General McClellan pressing President Lincoln for reinforcements, the Pennsylvania Reserves were ordered to the Virginia peninsula:

Head-Quarters, Pennsylvania Reserve Corps
Camp near Falmouth: June 8, 1862.

General M'Call is happy to inform the soldiers of his command, that he has received orders to embark with his division, at Belle Plain, below Fredericksburg, where transports will be in waiting, sail around to White House landing, and join M'Clellan in front of Richmond.

All will hold themselves in readiness to march this evening for the place of embarkation.

(Signed) Brigadier-General George A. M'Call
H. J. Biddle, Assistant Adjutant General

Such was the order issued on Sunday morning, the eighth of June. To embark in transports for Richmond! Oh, we were in *transports* already! To join M'Clellan in front of Richmond! "Long-looked for, come at last!" Oh, it was glorious![23]

George Darby recalled the 8th Regiment's departure from Fredericksburg:

We were accompanied by a fine brass band, in which the regiment took great pride. Upon boarding the ship, the band struck up a lively air. Soon the banks of the river swarmed with darkies who could not resist the inspiriting strains, and a lively dance among them was the natural result. The young negroes up to the age of sixteen or seventeen, of both sexes, were gowned in a single garment of tow cloth, constructed in the form of an ordinary night shirt and I say to you that there were more shirt skirts fluttering in the wind that day than on the clothes line of a thrifty housewife, after a two weeks' washing. It was a most ludicrous scene and the boys cheered them on to redoubled exertion until the boat sailed away.[24]

And Hill noted: "By and by, the boat let go of her moorings, the machinery began to operate, the wheels revolved with quick splashes, and we glided down the stream—our band striking up the air—

'Away down South in Dixie.'"[25]

Part Two

On to Richmond

Our knapsacks sling, and blithely sing, We're marching on to Richmond;
With weapons bright, and hearts so light, We're marching on to Richmond.
Each weary mile with song beguile, We're marching on to Richmond;
The roads are rough but smooth enough, To take us safe to Richmond.

But yesterday, in murd'rous fray, While marching on to Richmond,
We parted here from comrades dear, While marching on to Richmond;
With manly sighs and tearful eyes, While marching on to Richmond,
We laid the braves in peaceful graves, And started on for Richmond.

Our thoughts shall roam to scenes of home, While marching on to Richmond,
The vacant chair that's waiting there, While we march on to Richmond;
'Twill not be long till shout and song, We'll raise aloud in Richmond,
And war's rude blast, will soon be past, And we'll go home from Richmond.

Then tramp away while the bugles play, We're marching on to Richmond;
Our flag shall gleam in the morning beam, From many a spire in Richmond. Richmond.

"We Are Marching on to Richmond"
Words and Music: E. W. Locke (1862)

"Now, Boys, Let Them Have It!"

The Seven Days

As the steamer *R. Donaldson* made her way down the Rappahannock toward Chesapeake Bay, Sergeant Hill[1] and his comrades in the 8th Reserves were in high spirits: "We were at last off for the scene of action.... Lovely scenes, from time to time, unfolded themselves to our view as we glided down the river. On the green shores stood many a picturesque cottage of snowy whiteness in the midst of a cluster of trees."[2] John Urban, a private in the 1st Regiment was enthralled by the Negroes' reaction to the passing of the vessels:

> On the way down the river we passed a number of very fine plantations, and large numbers of blacks, with a few whites, gathered along the shore to witness the sight. The blacks were wild with joy and excitement, and it was highly amusing to the boys to see their demonstrations of delight. Some of them waded into the water and shouted for "Massa Lincoln" to take them on board; others gathered in groups, and jumped, shouted, and clapped their hands, until they sank down on the ground exhausted. The few whites looked on in sullen silence. We were probably the first Union troops these people had ever seen, and to them, no doubt, we seemed a mighty legion, and to the blacks an army of deliverers who had come to set them free. These poor, ignorant people instinctively knew that the marching of Union troops, or "Massa Lincoln's men"—as they called us—South, would in some way, lead to their good; and no doubt in the privacy of many a humble cabin was discussed that night the joyful news, and many earnest, sincere prayers ascended to Almighty God in thankful praise that the day of deliverance was nigh, and that the promised "Moses" had at last appeared to lead them to freedom.[3]

During the voyage, Hill indulged his penchant for poetry, inscribing the following verse on the white panel wall of his cabin:

> On the Rappahannock River
> Twenty-five miles from the bay;
> June the tenth in two-and-sixty—
> Cloudy, rainy, stormy day.

Who we are, and where we're going,
Reader, would you like to know?
We are of McCall's Division;
And to White House do we go.

There to join the brave McClellan,
And to whip the rebels out;
Then secession and rebellion
Will be 'clean gone up the spout.'"[4]

General George B. McClellan had chosen White House Landing, which lay on the Pamunkey River upstream of its confluence with the York, as a forward base of operations for his grand offensive campaign against the Confederacy. President Lincoln had given command of all Union forces to "the brave McClellan" November 1, 1861. McClellan had been reorganizing, equipping, and restoring the morale of the Army of the Potomac since the Union disaster at Bull Run and, through the autumn and winter of 1861, had honed it into a superb fighting machine. By the spring of 1862, he had come under increasing pressure to employ it.[5]

When he could delay no longer, McClellan finally placed his army in motion. In mid-March, he moved some 120,000 troops by water from the port of Alexandria on the Potomac River to Union-occupied Fort Monroe and the town of Newport News at the tip of the peninsula formed by the York and James Rivers.[6] McClellan's strategic design was to flank the main Confederate army, then entrenched along the line of the Rappahannock River, and march his own army some seventy-five miles up the peninsula to Richmond. McClellan believed that he could take the Southern capital before the Confederates could move to intercept him.[7] If successful, McClellan might well end the war and cement his burgeoning reputation as "The Young Napoleon."[8] The Peninsula campaign began with a cautious, albeit successful, siege of Yorktown, the token Confederate forces abandoning their defenses there on May 3. On May 5, McClellan's troops defeated a rebel rear guard under Major General James Longstreet in heavy fighting at Williamsburg.

When the Army of the Potomac began its seemingly inexorable march toward Richmond, President Lincoln held McCall's division back and attached it to McDowell's I Corps to bolster the defenses of Washington. During April, they were tasked with guarding the line of the Orange & Alexandria Railroad. In early May, McDowell was authorized to attempt the capture of Fredericksburg as an extension of his defensive operations south of Washington, and the Pennsylvanians, together with the rest of the I Corps, advanced to Falmouth, across the Rappahannock River from Fredericksburg. On May 26, General Reynolds's first brigade crossed the river and occupied Fredericksburg. They remained there until June 9 when, as Hill noted, they took to the transports and made for White House Landing. Morale was high among the Pennsylvania Reserves as they set out to rejoin "the brave McClellan"

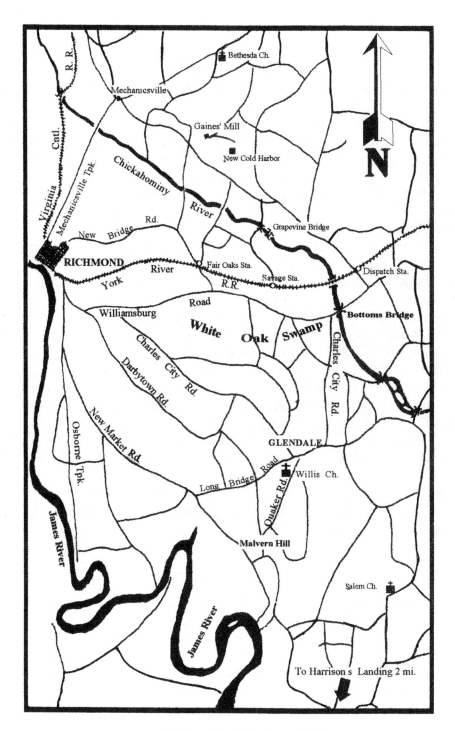

Richmond and Environs, 1862

and his Army of the Potomac. The feelings that Private Urban expressed were typical: "We had been greatly disappointed in being severed from the Army of the Potomac, and prevented from going with it from Alexandria to the peninsula, and the men were wild with delight at the prospect of joining it again.... [T]o judge by the joy and mirth of the men, it might have been supposed that they were going on a grand pleasure excursion instead of to a great battle, and it must not be supposed that these men expected anything else than hard work and severe fighting when they arrived in front of Richmond. They all believed that a grand effort would be made to storm the rebel Capital, and the result would be terrible battles, with great loss of life—but the men were eager for the fray, and rejoiced at the prospect of meeting the enemy."[9]

That prospect appeared much closer than Urban and his comrades might have imagined on June 12. That day, Confederate Brigadier General James Ewell Brown "Jeb" Stuart rode out of Richmond at the head of 1,200 cavalrymen, beginning his legendary ride around McClellan's army. By the next evening, Stuart's troopers were at Tunstall's Station on the York River Railroad, tearing up track and torching a supply train a mere four miles from White House Landing. The men of General Reynolds's first brigade, who had moved on to Dispatch Station on June 12, hurried back to Tunstall's at the double-quick but, by the time they got there, Stuart had disappeared. At White House Landing, Seymour's third brigade had just disembarked, and his men were quickly deployed to defend the landing. Stuart sensed the presence of the Union troops, however, and turned south toward the Chickahominy River. The Federals never did catch up to him, and he returned to a hero's welcome in Richmond on June 15, having ridden entirely around McClellan's bemused army. Along the way, he had gathered valuable intelligence that Robert E. Lee, commanding the newly designated Army of Northern Virginia, would soon put to good use. The Pennsylvania Reserves, in the meantime, pushed ever closer to the Confederate capital:

> Meadow Bridge Virginia
> June the 24th 1862
>
> Dear Parents
>
> I this morning lift my pen to inform you of our whereabouts. Well, since last I wrote you we have been on the move constantly. We arrived at this place [just west of Mechanicsville, a mere six miles northeast of Richmond] on the 19th and next day went on picket at the bridge. Our company was stationed at the end of the bridge and the Rebels at the other. We were not more than three hundred yards apart. We talked with them and exchanged papers on the morning of the 20th.[10] There was three deserters came over to us. They belonged to the Third Louisiana Battalion.... [Y]esterday [June 22] after dinner we were ordered to fall in. The Regiment was formed in a trice and we took up the line of march for

Mechanicville where our cannon were planted to shell the rebels out of their forts on the hill on the opposite side of the [Chickahominy] river. The object was to drive in their pickets, a very dangerous undertaking. When everything was ready, company "C" was chosen to do the work. We threw our haversacks in a pile and started down by [a] circuitous route until we came to the bridge. Then we started pell mell over the bridge, the Rebel pickets rallying and firing from every tree. But their shot all went too high, whistling close over our heads.... We drove them right under us and occupied their line. After the second fire they began to run and did not stop till they were behind their forts and rifle pits. Our cannon were placed so well that they could not come near their cannon to fire on us. When we marched out of the Reg't almost everyone bid goodbye to company "C," but the almighty ruler of the skies covered us with his wings and protected us from the enemies fire. We returned with one man wounded in the arm slightly. There was three Rebels killed and one wounded....

The Rebels put up two pontoon bridges across the river last night so we are looking for an attack every moment as the cannon are constantly booming.... I have not had a full night's sleep since we landed at the Whitehouse. Constantly under arms and marching and counter marching. My friend [Cyrus] Loll is dead. Kelley was certainly killed at Fair Oaks.... I heard from George Kelley about a week ago. He was...very lonely and disconsolate after the loss of his father. His father was shot dead right by him.... The rest of the boys are all well.... Jimmy sends his love to you. Give my respects to all who inquire after me. Nothing more at this time. But remains as ever.

J. L. McQuaide[11]

When they came ashore on the peninsula, the Pennsylvania Reserves were attached to General Fitz John Porter's V Corps. Porter was posted north of the Chickahominy River to guard McClellan's supply line from White House Landing as the rest of the army advanced south of the river.

Having learned from Jeb Stuart's reconnaissance that Porter's troops were isolated north of the Chickahominy, Robert E. Lee determined to take the offensive. In command of the Army of Northern Virginia for less than a month, Lee developed a bold plan to destroy the V Corps before it could be bolstered by reinforcements from south of the river. If successful, the Confederates would not only wreck an entire Union corps, they could also roll up the right flank of McClellan's army and separate him from his base of operations at White House Landing, thereby forcing him to abandon any siege of Richmond before it had even begun.

Behind the Union lines rumors were rife—among them that Beauregard's army had arrived from Mississippi; that the rebels had amassed 200,000 troops to attack McClellan south of the Chickahominy; and, most ominously for the untested men of the Pennsylvania Reserves, that Confederate Major General Thomas J.

George B. McClellan, *center*, and his general officers on the Peninsula. Brigadier General George A. McCall stands immediately to McClellan's left.

"Stonewall" Jackson had left the Shenandoah Valley and was bearing down upon them. Andrew Lewis sensed what was coming and wrote a letter to his wife in Lancaster. In it he gave poignant voice to the hopes and fears common to all soldiers about to go into battle:

> Daspatch [*sic*] Station
> 8 miles from Richmond
> June 15th 1862

> Dear Maria
> I take this opertunity to again send you a fiew lines to let you know that we are all landed safe here and safe and sound.... The whole of the reserve core are heare and on the road hear and I am informed that they are expected to play a very activ part in the coming battle before Richmond for we are to be placed in the center of the line of battle. So I hop that our friends in the North may not be disapointed in what they may expect of the reserv core when the time arrives for them to do their dutey. But maria if I am not mutch mistaken their will be one of the awfulest battles fought here that the world has ever wittnessed for I think that their will not be less than five hundred thousand men will be engaged in it. So that their must be a great maney fall of cours but who they may bee is hard to tell. But if I should be so unfortinet as to be one of the number my onley wish is for you to show yourself capable of baring up against the loss. For Maria recolect that maney wife has the same or will hav the same thing to trouble them and how maney a mother will hav their sones to mourn for the lose of them. And now Maria as I hav evrything squared up or nearly so I shall leav you in [tolerable circumstances] to get along in the world for the balance of your dayes. For even should I escap death from the bullits of the enimey at the most there is but a fiew short years for us to liv together in this world before one or the other of us must be called home. Baring this in mind I hop you may try and do you dutey as a mother and I will try and do mine as a soldier so that you shall not be asshamed of me. So now I must conclud. And now Maria don't forget my advise if enything may happen to me. And I still remain you affectonat husband.
> Andrew Lewis[12]

Lewis was right about the looming conflict, but wrong about the Pennsylvania Reserves' place in it. Rather than posting McCall's division in the center of the Union line, General Porter positioned them along Beaver Dam Creek near Mechanicsville, a small village just six miles northeast of Richmond.[13] There the Reserves constituted the extreme right wing of the Army of the Potomac. Porter ordered cavalry north of Mechanicsville to warn of any approach by the dreaded Stonewall Jackson. He also posted infantry pickets at Meadow Bridge to intercept any Confederate advance from the west.[14] Andrew Lewis took his turn on the picket line, returning to camp the worse for the experience:

Camp before Richmond Virginia
June 25th 1862

Dear Maria

I received your letter yestarday evening and was glad to hear that you were all well and hop that this may find you all enjoying the same blesing. As for myself I have not had as good health as I might of had for I caught cold out on picket on my last turn....

[I]t is all swampy about here and at night there is a kind of due or baither swet that I do not like. For after being out in it a while at night you would think that your face was all over smeared with grease so stickey and muckey is it yet it is warm. But I never got a worse cold in my life than I got the first night I was out. But I am much better now again and shall try and take better care of myselfe on the next time. For one must be very carefull here of a disease they call the swamp feaver wich I find is making sad havock amongst the troops....

I must not forget to let Marey and Jackey [Lewis's daughter and son] know that I got a letter from both of them with yourse and was glad to see how Marey has improved in hier riting and hop that she will not neglect to keep at it now.... So to help you along Marey I shall give you a little job...and that is no less than for you to rit to Mary Litzeinger who lives at Bridensville Westmoreland County Pa. And tell heir for me that heir sone in my company is well and hartey....

And now while I am riting this letter to you I am constantley looking out for the rebbles cannon balls which are flying pritey thick about here for they have built a new fort in the woods nearer to us and are firing at us all the time but as yet hav not hurt eny of us as yet. But I hop that McClenn [McClellan] has things most completed for us to advance and then you will all heare some stiring newse.... For I do tell you that the goverment at this time has a monstrous armey in the field and that armey...are not agoin to be triffled with....

So now I must close quick for some of the companey's expect a fight. So good by. This may turn out to be a fight before [I] get back. Tell Jackey [and] Melly...I hav not forgot them but hav no time to rit to them. So still I remain your affectonated husband

A Lewis[15]

The fight that Lewis's comrades were anticipating erupted the very next day. On June 26, Confederate troops belonging to Major General Ambrose Powell Hill's light division crossed the Chickahominy and poured into Mechanicsville. Porter's pickets retreated into his main defensive line along the bluffs above the east bank of Beaver Dam Creek. The soldiers of the 8th Regiment sprinted to their posts, spurred on by their commander:

"Fall in! Fall in, men! Quickly!"

At the same moment, a startling volley of musketry was heard toward the right of the division. Another followed, and another, and a wild, fierce, continuous rattle ensued. With a wild shout we flew to our arms, and awaited the order, "take arms;" it was given at once by [Lieutenant Colonel] Oliphant. He then rode along in front of the regiment, addressing each company separately; as he rode by our company [the Brownsville Grays], remembering that he was a native of the same county with us, he said: "'Now, boys, you will have an opportunity to show the gray-backs what old FAYETTE COUNTY will do for the UNION. You'll do your county no dishonor—you'll stand by your flag, won't you?—the flag presented you by—' His voice was drowned by a deafening cheer."[16]

Riding on, Colonel Oliphant came to his own company and exclaimed: "Fayette Guard, remember Pine Knob is looking down upon you, and Lafayette is watching you from the dome of the court-house! You will not go back on me today?"[17]

The Brownsville Grays were deployed as skirmishers near the base of the bluff when Confederate artillery began to pound the Union position. "Hundreds of shells, solid shot, and charges of grape [*sic*: case shot] and canister came crashing among the trees about us.... We were truly in the midst of the fight; yet we could take no active part, for the rebels beyond the swamp were hid from our view. They were so near, however, that at times their bugles could be heard among the trees.... 'I suppose our fellows are giving it to them now,' I remarked, just as a solid shot went crashing through the tree above my head, tearing off a large limb which fell near me. The next moment a shell came whizzing over, exploding among the branches of the same tree; and an ugly three-cornered piece came near dropping on my head."[18]

Atop the bluff, the Fayette Guards were being subjected to an equally intense fire from the Confederate batteries. Private Darby recalled the shelling, and its alarming effect upon Richard Crutchfield, a young runaway slave adopted by Darby and his messmates. "Coon," as Crutchfield was known, served as a cook and general utility man for Darby's mess and looked after their haversacks when they went into battle:

> Back of the lines on Beaver Dam Creek, was a considerable strip of timber, and at the first volley the negro contingent took to the woods. The rebel artillery opened upon us, but their aim was high, their shots passing harmlessly over our heads; their shells exploding in the woods, scattered the negroes in every direction. Coon had been made custodian of Lieutenant Macquilkin's fiddle, and two haversacks filled with rations. Next morning Coon put in his appearance minus fiddle or haversacks and in consequence the mess had nothing for breakfast. I took it upon myself to take him to task for the loss of the aforesaid articles when the following conversation ensued:
>
> "Coon where are the haversacks?"
>
> "I dun frode em away."

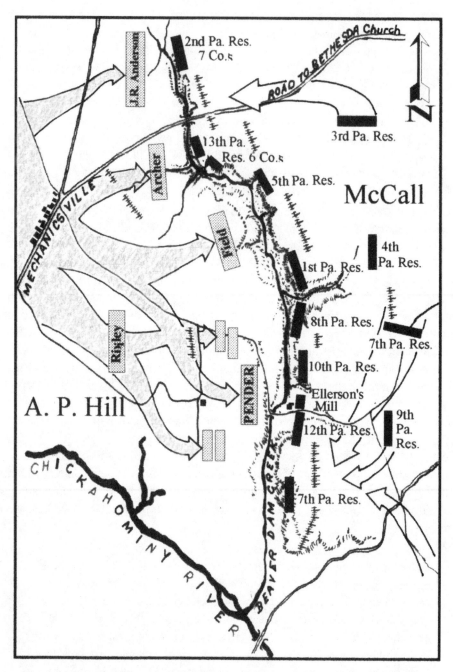

The Battle of Mechanicsville, June 26, 1862. The Pennsylvania Reserves defend the Union left flank on Beaver Dam Creek.

"Why did you throw them away?"

"Gor Amighty, Mr. Darby, nigger couldn't run fas' 'nuf an' tote dem ar habbersacks."

"Well, why didn't you hide?"

"I did get nudder nigger to hide me under a house, but hadn't been dar morn' minnit fo' 'long come one of dem shells an' it says 'Wha is yo'? Wha is yo'?' ker bang, boom zip. Good G[od] Mr. Darby, den I had to get outen dat mighty quick, an' I was runnin' as fas' as I could an' 'long cum nudder of dem ar shells an' he say 'ketch-im, ketch-im' swiss-boom-whiz-z-z. Lord, Massa Darby, nigger had no bizzness roun' dar.... No sar, niggar can't stan' no sich fiten' like dat, no sir. I codn't spar de time, or I'd frode away mi shoes."[19]

Soon after the Southern artillery barrage began, the Brownsville Grays were ordered back to the bluff to protect a Union battery then being threatened by a Confederate advance. Hill described the scene: "Simultaneously with our movement a brigade of rebels...charged madly down the opposite hillside, uttering the most savage yells that ever greeted my ears. Rushing unhesitatingly across the narrow valley that intervened between the two hills, they were about to ascend our hill, when one of our regiments...which lay in a concealed position near the base, arose and poured such a murderous volley into the rebel ranks that they broke and fled.... As they were rushing [back] up the hill they had just descended, [our] battery...sent showers of grape and canister after them; and hundreds fell to the earth torn and bleeding."[20]

Private Urban recounted the action from his vantage point: "In front of the first brigade a part of the ground was low and swampy, making it almost impossible for troops to cross. Into this a part of the rebel column charged, and a scene of the most indescribable confusion, horror and tumult ensued. Hundreds of the men and horses sank into the mire, and were shot down by the deadly rifles of the first brigade. Again and again the enemy advanced to the assault, only to be driven back with the most terrible slaughter."[21]

The Union position above Beaver Dam Creek proved to be impregnable. Secure behind their defensive works, McCall's Pennsylvania Reserves, fighting virtually on their own, held off repeated attacks by A. P. Hill's light division, as well as several assaults by a brigade from another rebel division, inflicting appalling casualties on the valiant but doomed Southerners. The total Confederate loss in killed, wounded, and missing at Mechanicsville was 1,475 men as against only 361 for the Pennsylvanians.[22]

For the great majority of McCall's men Mechanicsville represented their first taste of battle. They had started the day as rookies and ended it as veterans. George B. McClellan was justifiably proud of them. During the evening of June 26, he sent a telegram to Edwin M. Stanton, the secretary of war, in Washington: "Engagement still continues with great vigor. The enemy have not gained a foot & McCall is doing splendidly. He is showing that his Division is equal to the veterans of the Army of the Potomac. Rebel forces very large but our position good & our men as brave as can be."[23]

The newly blooded veterans had little time for accolades, however, for they knew that the rebels would come at them again the next morning. They dug in, replenished their cartridge boxes, and tried to get a little rest. Curiously, many of the men slept quite well:

> There we lay, within rifle-range of the enemy, fully expecting that the morrow would unfold scenes of the most terrible carnage; yet we slept soundly. I know that my sleep was as deep as any I ever enjoyed.
>
> It is, indeed, remarkable that men can lie down and sleep so tranquilly, when they know the danger that awaits them on the morrow—when they hear the cries of the already mangled—when they know that the dead lie strewn around, and that, with the early dawn of the coming day, the work of death will be resumed.
>
> Such is the case—and it is well; for men never so much need repose as on occasions like the one in question.[24]

The rebels did, indeed, press their assault on the Union position the following day, but the Pennsylvania Reserves were no longer there. Despite his terrible losses, Robert E. Lee had prevailed in one critical respect at Mechanicsville—he had wrested the initiative from the cautious McClellan. The guns had barely fallen silent when "the Young Napoleon" concluded that the Army of the Potomac had no choice but to change its base of operations (McClellan's terminology) from White House Landing to the James River. Abandoning his offensive on the very doorstep of Richmond, McClellan began to organize a general withdrawal to the James River where his army could be supplied and protected by the Union navy.[25] Accordingly, Porter was ordered to pull back from Mechanicsville to protect the lower bridges over the Chickahominy until the heavy guns, supplies, and baggage accumulated at White House Landing could be extricated. At 3 o'clock in the morning, McCall's Pennsylvania Reserves silently slipped out of their works above Beaver Dam Creek and withdrew to a new position behind Boatswain's Creek just below Gaines's Mill.[26] Porter posted them there behind the main battle line as a ready reserve.

The Confederates were not long in coming. In the early afternoon of June 27 they attacked in force all along the V Corps' new defensive line. As the battle raged back and forth, gaps began to open in the Union line, and the 8th Regiment was ordered in to stem the rebel tide.

The Brownsville Grays were in the thick of the fight. While forming up with the Second United States Regulars in a sunken road, they were subjected to a fierce shelling. Sergeant Hill vividly recalled the destruction wrought by the rebel artillery: "Suddenly I heard an explosion a little to my right that pierced to my very brain. I naturally turned in the direction and saw a sight that is before my eyes yet. Twenty or thirty feet from me, where the banks were not high enough to afford much protection, I saw a cloud of dust and smoke in the very midst of Company 'A.' I saw a man throw his hands wildly above his head, and fall backward, covered with blood. A moment he lay quivering convulsively, then he lay still—perfectly still. He was dead. Another stooped, and picked up his own arm which had been torn off by the shell...and rushed wildly toward a small hospital some distance to the rear flourishing the dismembered limb above his head, and shouting, in the broad tongue: 'Och, docther, me airm's off!'"[27]

As the enemy shelling continued unabated, Colonel Hays, commanding the 8th Regiment, ordered his men to fall in:

> Our turn had come....
>
> We entered the field. The conflict was gradually nearing us; the Second Regulars [who had advanced first] had been so pressed by overwhelming numbers that they were forced to retire.... Rebel bullets were already beginning to reach us. We had just entered the field and were marching along the valley in order to gain the right of the Second Regulars, when Nick Swearer—brave fellow—who had left us a few minutes before we were called into line for the purpose of filling his canteen, came rushing after us at the top of his speed, exclaiming—
>
> "By jolly, boys, I must be in that scrape!..."
>
> He had but uttered the words when he fell headlong—a bullet in his hip....
>
> We marched to the right of the Second Regulars, and lay down under the hill. We saw many horrid sights while lying there. Men staggering from the field with mangled hand or arm, or limping off—a leg covered with blood; some crawling away, only a few inches at a time; some—an officer now and then—were being carried off, covered with blood, and groaning in agony....
>
> "Now, Company 'D,'" said the captain, remember that you are just as good as any rebel company we may meet. Don't be afraid, boys! Never let them call us *cowards*!"
>
> "Up, boys, up!" shouted Colonel Hayes [*sic*] at that moment. We sprang to our feet as one man.
>
> "Forward!" shouted the colonel.[28]

Private Darby described what happened next:

> The [5th New York] Zouaves were hotly engaged when we arrived and many of them had been killed and wounded. Under a heavy fire of artillery, which killed some of our men, the regiment formed [a] line of battle in rear of the Zouaves and charging forward beyond their lines drove the rebels into a thick pine woods. We encountered here a murderous fire which caused our line to halt. My musket had become foul and I dropped to the ground on one knee and was ramming away at the cartridge with both hands to get the load down when I

felt something spattering over my face and left side, and on turning around I discovered that my comrade, George Proud's head had been dashed to pieces and his brain and fragments of his skull had been scattered over me. William Kendall, another comrade next to me, was also killed while I was ramming at the cartridge, which I did not succeed in getting down.[29]

The fighting at this point was desperate: "We stood within twenty or thirty paces of them, loading and firing at will," Sergeant Hill recalled. "The smoke was so dense that they were but dimly visible. But the flash of their pieces could be distinctly seen, and I each time chose a flash as the object of my aim. I remembered, in this critical hour, the great injunction, 'Fire Low!' and I was ever careful not to elevate my musket too much. Bullets, with their fierce hissing sound, were passing my ears by scores. I wondered that I could escape."[30]

Darby had an even closer call: "I heard my name shouted and upon looking around I saw [Joseph] Sturgiss scooting for the rear, with bullets cutting the ground about him like a storm of hail. The facts were, that in the confusion of the battle, our command had been ordered to fall back, but we had not heard the order, and were banging away at the enemy. Joe had discovered the situation, and sounded the note of warning to me just in time to save me. I hesitated, upon seeing the bullets fall so thick about Joe, as to whether I should try it, but it was death to remain where I was, so I took the chance and for a marvel escaped without a scratch."[31]

The 8th Regiment and the 1st, which had also been thrown into the breach, stood their ground for nearly an hour, forcing the Confederates back into the woods. Desperately short of ammunition, the two regiments were relieved by a New York unit that took their place in line. Private Urban described what happened next: "Our regiment and the 8th Pennsylvania Reserves, which had been engaged on our right, and was also out of ammunition, were now ordered to march to the rear for the purpose of getting a new supply and a short rest. The two regiments marched to the rear, stacked arms, and threw themselves on the ground. We had hardly more than done so, when a wild commotion in our front caused us to jump to our feet, when we discovered that a serious break had taken place in the line we had just vacated. The New York regiment which had relieved us broke and fled as soon as the rebels charged on them...."[32]

General Porter, the V Corps commander, saw the New Yorkers streaming to the rear and rode up to Colonel R. Biddle Roberts, the commander of the 1st Regiment, exclaiming:

"Colonel Roberts, can't you take these two regiments [the 1st and the 8th] and stop those men?" To which Roberts replied, "I will try; but get me some ammunition to stop the enemy."

Colonel Roberts formed the two regiments, and, although the shells from the enemy's batteries fell thick around them, and the shouts of the now victorious enemy, who were in hot pursuit of the broken Union troops, could be heard coming nearer and nearer, they stood as firm as if on dress parade, and presented a solid front of steel to the demoralized fugitives, who tried to pass them and get to the rear. The two regiments succeeded in stopping the most of them, but they were now in a most serious situation, as the rebels would soon be upon them, and they without ammunition to defend themselves.[33]

As J. R. Sypher noted in his *History of the Pennsylvania Reserve Corps*, "[t]he men [of the 1st and 8th Regiments] stood firmly, but were appalled at the situation, being in the face of the advancing enemy without a single round of ammunition."[34] Fortunately, reinforcements arrived on the field just in time to stop the Confederate advance.[35] As the afternoon wore on, however, the Confederates fed more and more troops into the fight, and the Union line finally was broken irreparably: "About sunset the rebels were reinforced, and they made the most energetic onset along the whole lines. Our troops, already exhausted and praying, like Wellington, for night to come, began to give way. The enemy pressed vigorously on; and our whole line fell back.... The rebels followed closely; already their bullets began to sing about our ears."[36]

The day ended with the Confederates in possession of the field and Porter's V Corps retreating across the Chickahominy. Gaines's Mill would prove to be the largest and costliest battle of the entire Peninsula campaign. Between them, the two armies sustained some 15,000 casualties in less than nine hours of combat. McCall's Pennsylvania Reserves lost more than 1,600 men killed, wounded, captured, and missing in their second consecutive day of hard fighting. Among those captured was Union Brigadier General John F. Reynolds, the commander of McCall's first brigade.

June 28 brought a comparative lull in the fighting as the Union army continued its retreat, while the Confederates spent the day consolidating their gains and attempting to ascertain McClellan's intentions. By the following morning, Lee became convinced that McClellan was falling back toward the James River. He pressed the retreating Federals, but a successful rear guard action in the morning at Allen's farm, and a sharp engagement at Savage's Station on the York River Railroad late in the afternoon, delayed the rebel pursuit sufficiently to permit the majority of the Union army to cross White Oak Swamp and continue their march to the James.

The Pennsylvania Reserves were not engaged in either of these actions. They had crossed the Chickahominy the night of June 27, halting at Trent's Hill just south of the river the following morning. Late that evening, General McClellan ordered them to escort the army's reserve artillery to firm ground south of White Oak Swamp: "The magnificent corps of reserve artillery of the Army of the Potomac, commanded by Gen. [Henry] Hunt, and numbering over one thousand guns [*sic*], was still parked on Trent's farm...and it was of the utmost importance that this most valuable auxiliary of the army should be prevented from falling into the hands of

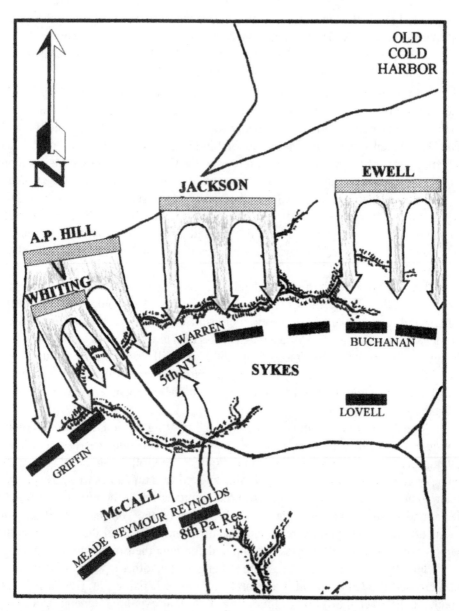

The Battle of Gaines's Mill, June 27, 1862. The Pennsylvania Reserves relieve the 5th New York.

the enemy. This splendid park of artillery consisted of thirteen batteries, its guns being of the most improved pattern, and was intended to be used in the bombardment of Richmond."[37] The Pennsylvanians marched through the night, their regiments posted throughout the artillery train, in a line some seven miles long. They reached firm ground south of White Oak Swamp around noon on June 29. McClellan directed McCall to park the artillery there and set up a defensive position to repel any attack from the direction of Richmond.

Late in the afternoon, McCall's weary soldiers resumed their march, with the 3rd Pennsylvania Cavalry, Benson's battery of the Second U.S. Artillery, and the 8th Regiment in the vanguard. McCall had been ordered to proceed to the intersection of the Willis Church Road with the Charles City and Long Bridge Roads to cover the army's passage through that vital crossroads. Reaching what they supposed to be their destination near midnight, the Pennsylvanians stacked arms and lay down. After four days of nonstop fighting and marching, the soldiers of the 8th Regiment undoubtedly longed for a good night's sleep, but that was not to be—as Private Urban explained:

> [A]s we had now reached [the crossroads], we hoped to get some rest; and weary and almost worn out by the long marching and fighting we had passed through, we threw ourselves on the ground for that purpose.... [W]e had hardly more than nestled down when our brigade [the first, commanded by Colonel Seneca Simmons since General Reynolds's capture at Gaines's Mill] was ordered to fall into line, and marched [westward] down the New Market [Long Bridge] road to picket and watch the movements of the enemy in our front....[38] The night was so intensely dark that it would have been impossible to distinguish an enemy a few steps from us, and...we [were] compelled to move with the greatest caution.... [I]t was certainly a considerable relief when we halted....
>
> A picket line was established a few yards in front of the line, and we were then informed that we might lie down and sleep, but with loaded rifle in hand, and ready in a moment's notice to jump into line and receive the enemy. I soon found out that...sleep was out of the question, for it was a night of constant alarm. At one time a volley of musketry almost in our rear made us spring to our feet in alarm, as we supposed that the enemy was making an effort to cut us off from the army; but it subsequently was learned that two Union regiments had fired into each other by mistake. At another time, a number of artillery horses, which had broken loose, dashed along the line snorting with terror, giving us the impression that a cavalry charge was being made upon us. The almost constant barking of dogs at several farm-houses in our front gave us the impression that the enemy was advancing, keeping us in a state of constant alarm, and preventing us from getting the sleep we so much needed to prepare us for the desperate work on the morrow.[39]

In actuality, as McCall's division trudged onward in the pitch black of that rainy June night, they missed the junction where they should have halted and continued westward on the Long Bridge Road in the direction of Richmond. Their vanguard came into contact with Confederate pickets around midnight, and McCall halted his troops, throwing forward the pickets that Private Urban described.

Sergeant Hill and his comrades in the 8th Reserves who had been out on the Long Bridge Road picket line all night, finally got a few precious hours of rest early the next morning when they "returned to the large field where the whole division lay, and stacked our arms with the rest. The forenoon wore quietly away."[40] It was the lull before the storm. The large field to which a very tired 8th Regiment had returned on the morning of June 30 would, by the end of the day, be littered with the detritus of one of the most fiercely fought battles of the Civil War.

With McClellan's Army of the Potomac strung out between White Oak Swamp and Malvern Hill in a ragged column many miles long, Robert E. Lee sensed that a critical moment had arrived. He knew that the entire Union army had to funnel through Glendale, a country crossroads surrounded by several small farms and houses. The Charles City Road running southeast out of Richmond, the Long Bridge Road running generally in an east-west direction, and the Willis Church Road running north from Malvern Hill all converged there. Lee intended to hurl three Confederate divisions at Glendale in an effort to cut McClellan's retreating army in two.[41] If he succeeded, he stood a very good chance of inflicting a devastating defeat on the Army of the Potomac and forcing McClellan to abandon the Peninsula entirely.

The critical road for General McClellan was the one that led south out of Glendale to Malvern Hill. This was the Willis Church Road, sometimes called the Quaker Road. On June 30, it was clogged with countless wagons, cannon, caissons, and tens of thousands of disheartened Union soldiers. McClellan, of course, appreciated the necessity of defending Glendale and the Willis Church Road until his army reached Malvern Hill and the safety afforded by the Federal gunboats stationed on the James River. Accordingly, he deployed four divisions north and west of Glendale to keep Lee at bay—Henry Slocum's, Philip Kearny's, George McCall's, and Joseph Hooker's.

By all rights, having marched and fought for four days without respite (and having suffered grievous casualties in the process), McCall's men had every right to expect that they would be posted in relative safety along with their comrades in the other two V Corps divisions at Malvern Hill. But, as George Darby explained: "On reaching [the crossroads at Glendale the night of June 29], the column [mis]took an old abandoned road, not shown on the maps, for the Quaker Road which was three miles further on. After marching several miles on this old road it became impassable in the darkness and we went into camp.[42] In the meantime Sykes's and Morrell's divisions of Porter's [V] Corps countermarched and finding a private road passed over our division in the darkness and by this means reached the Quaker Road and proceeded toward the James. [General] Porter neglected to notify our command of this movement and we were thus abandoned...."[43]

While it may be that General Porter never gave any formal orders to McCall regarding the disposition of his troops,[44] nonetheless it was clear to McCall that General McClellan had "instructed the several commanders to maintain their positions, and protect the army trains then moving on toward James River."[45] What McCall could not have anticipated on that last morning of June was that the position his weary troops occupied would, by the end of the day, prove critical to the very survival of the Army of the Potomac.

Evan M. Woodward, sergeant major of the Reserves' 2nd Regiment, set the scene:

> General McCall was ordered to take up a position on the left of the...Long Bridge Road...in front of the Quaker Road leading to Malvern Hill and Turkey Bridge, and to maintain it until the whole of the immense supply trains of the army, then slowly advancing from White Oak Creek, had passed towards [the] James River, and to repel any attack on it. General Meade's brigade [the second] was posted on the right, General Seymour's [the third] on the left, and Reynolds's [the first, which included Woodward's regiment and the 8th Regiment], now [under] Colonel Simmons, held in reserve. The artillery was placed in front of the line....[46] On the right of the Reserves [but not connected with them] was posted Kearny's division, and on the left...was Sumner [actually Sedgwick's Division, also unconnected with the Reserves], and further to the left...was Hooker.[47]

Astonishingly, General McClellan was nowhere to be seen. Perhaps demoralized by Lee's aggressiveness, McClellan had left the front lines for the relative safety of Haxall's Landing on the James River: "With the sounds of battle plainly heard and the clouds of battle smoke plainly seen, McClellan removed himself even further from the scene by boarding the gunboat *Galena* and steaming upriver to investigate a Rebel column reported on the River Road."[48]

Although posted in reserve with Simmons's first brigade, Sergeant Hill clearly anticipated the 8th Regiment being ordered into combat. He prepared accordingly: "Having formed line-of-battle, facing to the west, we stood awaiting the attack. I ever made it a point to go into battle with my canteen full of water, if possible, for the excitement of battle, and the strenuous exertions, together with the fumes of gunpowder, create a burning thirst. I discovered that my canteen was empty. I knew that there was a spring of cold, clear water a few hundred yards to our front, but I did not like to go that distance from the regiment. I looked about me, and presently discovered in the wood a pool of stagnant water; with this water I filled my canteen."[49]

Hill wasn't wrong about his regiment being thrown into the fight. Late in the afternoon, Kemper's brigade of Longstreet's division attacked McCall's left flank, scattering the 12th Regiment, capturing several artillery pieces, and threatening to break through the Union line. McCall immediately ordered Colonel Seneca Simmons to advance two regiments to support the hard-pressed left wing. Simmons, who had assumed command of Reynolds's brigade following that general's capture on June 28, picked the 5th and 8th Regiments for the task. Hill recalled the scene vividly:

> As we lay near the [abandoned] battery, we were much exposed to the projectiles from the rebel guns; and, for awhile, shell were exploding about us, and solid shot were flying over our heads, tearing the trees shockingly; while charge after charge of grape and canister rattled among the trees and spattered the ground in our midst.... [A] regiment of infantry soon emerged from a wood a few hundred paces in our front, and advancing half the intervening distance, prepared to charge. They came so close, in fact, that we heard their colonel give the following command—
>
> "Sixth Georgia [sic], fix bayonets! Give the Yankees a little cold steel!"[50]
>
> We heard the clinking rattle of their bayonets as they placed them on their guns, and we felt that warm work was at hand.
>
> We saw that a charge was about to be made upon us, and we nerved ourselves to resist it; but ere the rebels had well succeeded in fixing their bayonets, one of General M'Call's aides rode hastily up and shouted—
>
> "Eighth Regiment, General McCall orders you to charge!" 'Twas enough. Our bayonets were already fixed; and, with a savage yell, we sprang up and rushed madly upon the Georgians [sic]. They couldn't stand it; away they went, flying hither and thither in the most disorderly style.[51]

The men of the 5th and 8th Regiments pursued the retreating Confederates but were, in turn, assailed by Branch's brigade, which had just reached the field. Sent reeling by the North Carolinians' fire, they fell back toward the Union line and took cover behind a slight swell. It was there that Hill had a poignant encounter with a wounded Southern soldier:

> [G]lancing to my right I saw...a wounded rebel lying under a peach tree—the blood gushing from a wound in the breast. Although the rebels were already beginning to rally on us, I could not refrain from stopping a moment with the sufferer—he was trying to support himself on his elbow. I bent over him and asked—
>
> "Are you much hurt?"
>
> He did not reply, but looked imploringly into my face, and seemed struggling for breath....

He tried to speak, but could not. I observed that his lips were dry and parched, and I did not doubt that he wanted water. So I asked—

"Do you want water?" And at the same moment a bullet whistled by my ear and struck the peach tree.

"Oh, yes! Oh, yes!" he replied with all the energy he could muster.

I placed my canteen to his lips, and he eagerly drank. Then wishing to make a good impression upon him, regarding us *Yankees*, of whose cruelty I had no doubt he had heard the most terrible tales, I said—

"You see, my friend, that we know how to treat even an enemy with kindness."

"Ah," said he..."*you're no enemy of mine....*"[52]

Simmons's men reformed near the 12th Regiment's original position as the Confederates came on with increasing ferocity:

The rebels were now firing as they advanced, and we were ordered to lie down to avoid the bullets. Colonel Simmons stood by his horse within a few feet of where I lay.

"Boys," said the brave old veteran, "Lie still; don't arise or fire till I give you the word. I'll give you the word in time."

The bullets of the rebels were now flying over us in perfect swarms. Every moment I expected to see the gallant Simmons fall. At length the rebels arrived to within thirty paces of us.

"Now, boys, let them have it!" shouted Colonel Simmons, and at the same moment he was struck in the breast, and fell dead....[53]

As the Pennsylvanians rose to fire, the onrushing Southerners delivered a volley of their own that "scattered them and decimated their officers. 'Every officer to whom the troops looked for orders fell almost at the same time,' one man recalled. The Confederates pushed the 5th, 8th and 10th Reserves back and eventually broke them after 'terrific' fighting."[54]

Seneca Simmons was not the only casualty among the senior officers. General Meade had been wounded on another portion of the battlefield, and Colonel Hays, the commander of the 8th Regiment, was seriously injured as well: "Colonel Hayes' [sic] horse was struck and torn to pieces by a cannon shot and the heavier portions of the animal falling upon the colonel, injured him so severely he had to retire from the service."[55]

Of the intensity of the fighting along a portion of his line of battle, General McCall noted in his official report of the day's action: "It was here...my fortune to witness between those of my men who stood their ground and the rebels who advanced, one of the fiercest bayonet-fights that perhaps ever occurred on this continent. Bayonets were crossed and locked in the struggle; bayonet wounds were freely given and received. I saw skulls crushed by the heavy blow of the butt

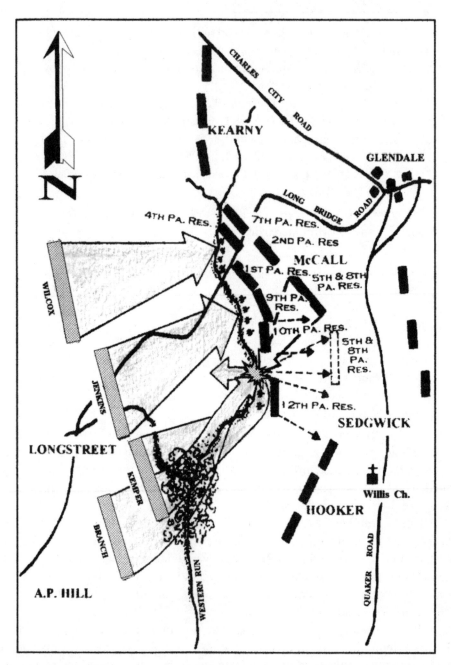

The Battle of Glendale, June 30, 1862. The Pennsylvania Reserves defend McClellan's line of retreat to the James River.

Colonel Seneca G. Simmons commanded the first brigade of the Pennsylvania Reserves at the Battle of
Glendale June 30, 1862, where he was
mortally wounded.

The Historical Society of Dauphin County

of the musket, and, in short, the desperate
thrusts and parries of a life-and-death encounter, proving, indeed, that Greek had met
Greek when the Alabama boys fell upon the
sons of Pennsylvania."[56]

The fight for Randol's battery that
McCall witnessed was unprecedented in its
ferocity. H. R. Hogan of the 11th Alabama
recalled that "[o]n reaching the guns...a desperate hand to hand conflict took place....
Charley McNeil mounted one of the guns
with our regimental colors, but was shot, falling underneath the canon, but still held and
waved the flag in the face of the enemy. His
nephew, Billy McNeil, seeing his uncle's
condition, attempted to relieve him of the
flag, but was shot dead before he could do
so.... When we were forced back, Charley
McNeil was left with his flag, and when we
returned he had been slain by a bayonet thrust
through the heart, and our colors were
gone."[57]

Indeed, the battle raged furiously all
along McCall's line. As noted, his left flank,
where the earlier charge of the 5th and 8th
Regiments had scattered Kemper's brigade,
finally gave way before the Southerners' re-
newed onslaught. The timely intervention of elements of Hooker's and Sedgwick's
divisions saved it from collapse. And on the right flank, troops from Kearny's division helped to stem the rebel tide.[58] Nightfall finally brought the battle to a close,
but not before General McCall himself was captured while trying to rally his troops
in the twilight. The Pennsylvania Reserves had been severely mauled, losing 1,118
men killed, wounded, or missing out of some 6,000 engaged,[59] but McClellan's line
of retreat to the James River was preserved. It had been, as Wellington said of
Waterloo, a very close run thing.

Although the conflict would drag on for nearly three more bloody years, June
30, 1862, would stand out as one of the true turning points of the war. Robert E.
Lee's biographer, Douglas Southall Freeman, commenting on the battle, wrote:
"Frayser's Farm [Glendale] was one of the great lost opportunities in Confederate
military history.[60] It was the bitterest disappointment Lee had ever sustained, and

one that he could not conceal. Victories in the field were to be registered, but two years of open campaign were not to produce another situation where envelopment seemed possible. He had only that one day for a Cannae, and the army was not ready for it."[61]

Confederate Brigadier General Edward Porter Alexander wrote in his memoir that "[n]ever, before or after, did the fates put such a prize within our reach. In spite of all the odds against us, it is my individual belief that on two occasions...we were within reach of military successes so great that we might have hoped to end the war with our independence.... This chance of June 30th '62 impresses me as the best of all. The Confederacy at this moment was about in its prime & had more men available than ever before or after. [T]hink of the moral shock to the North of the destruction & capture of McClellan's entire army...."[62]

While the "destruction & capture" of the entire Army of the Potomac might be characterized as wishful thinking on Alexander's part, it is clear nonetheless that George B. McClellan's army found itself in a position of great peril on June 30 at Glendale. The Union forces engaged west of the Quaker Road that fateful June day did nothing less than deny Robert E. Lee a victory that would have reverberated from the gates of Richmond to the halls of the White House. It was left to Confederate Major General James Longstreet to pay McCall's battered brigades the ultimate compliment. In interviewing a captured Union surgeon the day after the battle, Longstreet asked him what he knew of the fighting and the Union troops that were engaged. The surgeon replied that he knew only of McCall's division, with which he had served, and that it had fought where they were then standing. Longstreet replied: "Well, McCall is safe in Richmond [having been captured late in the evening while reconnoitering along the battle line];[63] but if his division had not offered the stubborn resistance it did on this road, we would have captured your whole army."[64]

The musings of generals were the furthest things from the minds of the privates, corporals, and sergeants who had borne the brunt of the day's fighting and who, as night fell, counted themselves lucky to still be alive. "About dark I began to look about me to see how many of the boys were yet safe," Sergeant Hill recalled.[65] He made his way through the woods, looking for the remnants of his regiment:

> I came out [of the woods] upon a road which I followed a short distance, and found myself near a hospital. Walking to the rear of the hospital, I found a number of men lying beneath a large oak tree against which a flag was leaning.
> "Are any of the Pennsylvania Reserves here?" I asked.
> "Yes. Is that you, sergeant?" was the reply.
> "Yes. Is this the Eighth?"
> "Yes. What's left of it."
> "Is that you, Charley?"
> "Yes. Come and lie down."

It was Charley Brawley, a brave young fellow of our company. I lay down beside him, and, notwithstanding that cries of agony proceeded constantly from the hospital at hand, I was soon wrapped in slumber.[66]

The Fayette Guards and the Brownsville Grays had marched and fought virtually nonstop throughout the first six days of the battles that would come to be known as the "Seven Days." On the seventh day they would rest.

6

"The Sacredness of the Family Circle Is Broken"

A Respite at Harrison's Landing

During the night of June 30, the Pennsylvania Reserves withdrew from Glendale and trudged off down the Quaker Road to rejoin the Army of the Potomac. They left more than three thousand of their comrades behind—dead, wounded, or missing on the fields of Mechanicsville, Gaines's Mill, and Glendale. It was a battered, worn-out division that reached Malvern Hill shortly after daybreak on July 1. While McCall's men were fighting for their lives at Glendale, General McClellan concentrated the remainder of his army on the heights at Malvern Hill. At the same time, Henry Hunt, his artillery chief, posted 171 guns about the crest in a great semi-circle facing northward.[1] As the Pennsylvanians filtered in through the Union lines, they anxiously sought out their comrades, desperate for even the smallest scraps of information pertaining to the previous day's fighting. Sergeant Hill and Charley Brawley, who had become separated from their regiment, learned that McCall's division was posted in reserve on the summit of the hill and headed off to join them:

> Charley and I, on arriving at the crest of the hill, distinguished our regiment by its battalion flag, and found the boys sitting by their stacked arms.
>
> "Why, sergeant, is that you? I feared that you were dead; I felt sure that one of those balls must have hit you and left you lying dead...in that wood." The speaker was Haman.
>
> "Yes, Haman," I replied; "and I feared that one of them might have hit *you* after we were separated. I am glad you are safe.... Why did the regiment go off and leave Charley and me asleep?"
>
> "Oh, we were aroused and hurried off very suddenly; it was not daylight yet."
>
> "Have you learned of the result of the battle?"
>
> "We've heard something. General McCall is missing."
>
> "Then General Meade has command of the division."
>
> "No, he is wounded. General Seymour is in command...."
>
> "How about our company? How many are killed or wounded?"

"Lieutenant Moth is missing."

"Ah, I believe I did not see him after that charge. Who else are missing?"

"Mitchel is missing, and so is Jake Archibald; also Jim Roland, Hen Underwood, John Young, Ike Mayhorn and Will Haddock. Sergeant Zee and McWilliams were killed. John Gue was badly wounded. John Woodward was slightly wounded, too; also Finley Whitmire."[2]

While McCall's weary soldiers enjoyed a well-deserved rest, their comrades in the other Federal divisions prepared to meet the inevitable Confederate attack. It came about three o'clock that afternoon. Despite their gallantry, the rebels were doomed from the outset. Federal artillery arrayed along the crest of the hill swept the half-mile wide slope that the gray-clad infantry had to cross in order to reach the Union breastworks. As if the shot and shell from the Federal gun line were not enough, the Southerners were also subjected to a barrage from several Union gunboats stationed on the James River, well within range of the Confederate lines. The sound of the gunboat fire proved only slightly less terrifying to the Union defenders posted atop Malvern Hill than it did to the Confederate soldiers charging up its slopes: "Suddenly, there arose behind us a stunning report that made the old hill shake; and a monstrous shell went screaming over our heads, dropping in the vicinity of the rebel batteries and exploding with a terrific crash. It was from a [Union] gunboat that lay quietly at anchor on the bosom of the James. In a few minutes another followed—another and another, at intervals. Surely, the shrieking sound of those terrible projectiles, as they hurled through the air, was enough to appal the rebels. The very sound was terrifying; it was like the howl of some wild beast; the scream of a panther is scarcely worthy to be compared to it."[3]

Brigade after brigade of Confederate infantry was pushed forward against the Union position, all to no avail: "No troops ever acted with more desperate courage than the [Confederates] did upon that occasion, but like the storm-lashed ocean, madly dashing its billows against a rock-bound shore, they were hurled back, broken and confused, but to unite and return again to the assault. From batteries upon batteries were vomited forth sheets of flame and smoke, whose storms of grape and canister mowed down the columns of advancing valor, leaving vast gaps, that were filled up by the mad and infuriated masses."[4] Confederate Major General Daniel Harvey Hill recalled the final assault late in the day and bitterly lamented the appalling losses suffered by the Southerners: "I never saw anything more grandly heroic than the advance after sunset of the nine brigades under [General] Magruder's orders. Unfortunately, they did not move together, and were beaten in detail. As each brigade emerged from the woods, from fifty to one hundred guns opened upon it, tearing great gaps in its ranks; but the heroes reeled on and were shot down by the reserves at the guns, which a few squads reached. Most of them had an open field half a mile wide to cross, under the fire of field-artillery in front, and the fire of the heavy ordnance of the gun-boats in their rear. It was not war—it was murder."[5]

Robert E. Lee's last, desperate attempt to destroy McClellan's army had failed. Nonetheless, he emerged the strategic victor of the Seven Days Battles. He had beaten back the invader from the doorstep of the Confederate capital and had wrested the initiative from his cautious adversary. Despite his overwhelming victory at Malvern Hill, George B. McClellan hastened his army away from Richmond toward Harrison's Landing on the James River. He would rest there, a beaten man, under the sheltering guns of the Union flotilla.

It was near midnight when the 8th Regiment began its march to the James. "About eleven o'clock...the sleepy boys were woke up and put in motion, and passing by Haxall's house we slowly wound our way down the hill to the river road, along which we marched, passing over Turkey Bridge. The night was extremely dark, but the road, which for a long distance was exceedingly bad, was lit up by thousands of candles placed in the trees, and bright fires burning upon the wayside.... At daybreak we entered a fine field of standing wheat, where we laid down and rested for an hour and then moved on."[6] Then the rain came: "As the gloom of night melted into the gray of morning dawn, rain began to fall, and it gradually increased in violence till it finally came down in torrents. Slowly, steadily we marched on—the rain beating mercilessly upon us. About the middle of the forenoon we neared Harrison's Landing. As we did so, a forest of masts and steamboat chimneys loomed up to view. It was evident that we were near our journey's end...."[7]

The heavy rains that lashed the Pennsylvania Reserves as they made their way to Harrison's Landing had also inundated the battlefield at Glendale. John Urban, who had been wounded in the fighting there and taken prisoner the following morning when the Confederates overran a nearby Union field hospital, recalled a tragic sequence of events occasioned by the deluge:

> On the morning after the close of the fighting [at Malvern Hill], the most terrible reports commenced to come in about the condition of a large number of Union wounded who were yet lying on the field, who had fallen in the battle on Monday, at Charles City cross roads [Glendale]. It had rained very heavily since the battle, and it was said that the low grounds being overflown with water, some of the men had drowned, and others were in the most wretched condition, and would have to perish if speedy relief was not sent to them. The Union surgeons secured the consent of the rebel authorities at the hospital to fit out an expedition and try to save them, and a number of wagons were furnished for that purpose. A number of prisoners, some of them wounded, but in such a manner as not to interfere with their duties, were selected to go with the train and load the wounded. I was selected to take charge of the squad.... We were accompanied by

a few guards, and to farther protect us from the rebel soldiers who might be rambling over the field, we had white strips of muslin tied around our caps. Thus fitted out, we proceeded on our mission of mercy, and it was not long before we reached the battle field.

The dead had not been buried, and the sight that met our eyes was terrible to behold. They lay thick on the ground, and in some places were heaped on top of each other, and presented a sight so sickening that we could hardly proceed. All had the appearance of being plundered by rebel stragglers, their pockets being turned inside out. Lying among the dead were a number of wounded, and the hope of helping them gave us nerve and strength to do what, under other circumstances, would have been an impossibility. I had been instructed to remove only such as would probably have a chance of recovery, and not disturb those who were past hope; but I soon found it hard to discriminate between them. They begged with tears in their eyes to be taken, and I soon loaded as many as we could take. We lifted quite a number out of the water and mud, and made them as comfortable as we could, and then started with our load for the hospital. On the way, several died, and I was told by one of the doctors that I should not have loaded men who were so hopelessly wounded. We had expected to be sent out again; but, in the meantime, it had been decided to bring no more wounded to our hospital, and we did not get to go.[8]

While Private Urban was endeavoring to save his wounded comrades at Glendale, a remarkable story was unfolding near Harrison's Landing involving another wounded soldier. Jacob Dutton Moore, a sergeant in Company E of the 85th Pennsylvania, recalled his miraculous rescue in a pension application filed after the war: "I trudged along with my Regiment, disabled as I was, until we arrived near Harrison's Landing Virginia when I became so reduced and weak on account of my wounded thumb and ill health that I could not possibly go any further and laid down in the mud expecting there to die. While in this condition my brother belonging to another Regiment and a comrade of his came to me, assisted me to a barn some distance away and got me something to eat and drink when they left me and returned to their respective commands."[9]

The brother who saved Jacob Moore was none other than Isaac Moore of the Fayette Guards. In a postwar affidavit filed in support of his brother's pension application, he recounted the story: "A few days after the Seven Days fight on the Peninsula in Virginia in 1862, I found [my brother] in an open field lying in the mud sick and unable to get up or get food or water. I carried him with the assistance of one of my Company comrades to an old barn or outbuilding near the Hospital at Harrison's Landing and got him some water. I then left him and promised to return next day and bring him something that he could probably eat but on returning next day I could not find him nor learn anything definite about him and didn't learn where he was until several weeks afterward...."[10]

The rains finally abated on July 3, and the bedraggled soldiers at Harrison's Landing spruced themselves up as best they could for a formal review by their "Young Napoleon," safe at last under the lee of the Federal gunboats patrolling the James River:

The following day was the "Fourth of July." The sky was clear, the sun shone forth, and the mud began to dry up. In the afternoon, we were drawn up in line for review, and Little Mac [General McClellan] rode along, wearing his usual smile; and we cheered him enthusiastically, as was our wont. His address as issued to the Army of the Potomac was read to us; it was, as nearly as I can remember, as follows:

Soldiers of the Army of the Potomac:

You have been attacked at your position in front of Richmond by far superior numbers; and, there being no hope of reinforcements, you have succeeded in changing your base of operations by a flank movement—always considered the most hazardous of military operations. You have borne the privations and perils attending you with a fortitude never surpassed; you have repulsed the enemy in every encounter, always holding the field at night; of guns and munitions of war, you have captured more than sufficient to repay you for all that you have lost. Our lines are now reestablished, our position is strong; and if the enemy have the hardihood to attack us, he will be severely punished, and effectually re-pulsed. There can be no longer any doubt that each one of you may say, with pride, 'I belong to the Army of the Potomac!' And on this, our nation's birthday, we declare to our foes who are rebels against the best interests of mankind, that this army *shall yet* enter the capital of their so-called confederacy, at whatever cost of time, treasure, or blood.

Geo. B. McClellan,
Major-General Commanding[11]

For those soldiers, and there were many, who believed McClellan's "change of base" was nothing more than an ignominious retreat by another name, his words surely must have rung hollow. As the army settled in at Harrison's Landing, many of the soldiers took the opportunity afforded by their relative inactivity to catch up on their correspondence. On July 4, John Bierer, a corporal in the Fayette Guards, wrote to the editor of the *Genius of Liberty*, relating the part played by the 8th Regiment in the Seven Days Battles:

Col. Roddy: you have, no doubt, already received news of the battles in front of Richmond. That is, the general results—supposed intentions and objects of the parties—numbers of killed, wounded, prisoners, and missing; and, in fact, all the general outlines and material effects of the struggle. But the particulars of the battles, especially those in which your readers, and the public of Fayette County and Western Pennsylvania, are immediately interested, may not reach you so easily, because this sort of information is usually communicated last. I propose, in this short letter, to give you, as far as is possible, a correct account of the doings of the Eighth Regiment, the companies, and men from your section engaged in it.

The ball opened on Thursday afternoon, June 26th, by the enemy, 30,000 strong, attacking the First and two regiments of the Third Brigade of McCall's Division. The contest was furious but we held our ground, and at half past nine, P.M. when the firing ceased, we laid down and slept on the same ground we had occupied at the commencement and during the progress of the battle. The Eighth supported Easton's Battery, Company G immediately back of it. Here we lost three men, McNamee and Sager killed and Grimes wounded.... Before daylight the firing commenced the next morning, but our battery had only fired a few shots when we were ordered to fall back to a position near Gaines' Mill, about two and a half miles to the rear. Retiring leisurely and in good order, we arrived there about 10 o'clock, A.M., and took position in line of battle in the center. About half past one the contest began in furious earnest and was continued without intermission on the left center until nightfall. The Eighth lay in a road under cover of, and in advance of Easton's guns, until about three o'clock, when it was ordered to relieve the New York Fifth, (Fire Zouaves) and three or four companies of Berdan's Sharpshooters. Under and into a terrible fire of shot and shell they resolutely marched forward until they passed the New York Fifth, when the order to charge was given, and with a wild yell they dashed forward into the wood, and through the fire of a division of the enemy. Here they were met by a direct and enfilading fire, and a fire from the enemy's sharpshooters in the tree tops, as well as grape and canister from their cannon. They unflinchingly endured this murderous fire and would have continued there till the last man, but they were ordered to fall back, which they did in good order leaving the ground strewn with their killed and wounded. Here Co. G lost seven killed and eleven wounded in less than twenty minutes.... This was the first, and was conceded to be the most daring charge of the day. Regiment after regiment cheered us as we passed out to our first position. The next morning we crossed the Chickahominy and continued our retreat (for that's its name) on Sunday toward the new base on the James River. On Monday another terrible battle was fought at White Oak Swamps [Glendale]. McCall's Division as before sustaining the fiercest shock of the battle though it had already melted away to a handful. When the battle opened the 1st brigade was formed in line of battle in a wood to support and protect two batteries about two hundred yards in front of us. The [Confederates] advanced rapidly upon them, and had got within thirty yards of them. The gunners skedaddling when the order to charge was given by Gen. Seymour, and with a shout of exultation at the order we dashed forward, the

Fifth and Eighth in advance, but the enemy, though twice our number, did not wait to receive us, but broke and fled into the woods on the right and left, where we followed and took a number of prisoners. But we were soon recalled from the pursuit and ordered to form in line to repel an attack of the enemy then moving out of the woods, five columns deep, and in numbers so great that I confess (though we stood to it as long as there was a chance of escape from being taken) the chances were all against us. We were compelled to give way after losing Generals McCall and Meade and half the regimental and staff officers. The Eighth being protected by an elevation in front did not lose so many in this as in the previous engagements. Co. G had three men wounded. In the next day's battle [Malvern Hill] we were held in reserve, and were not called upon to participate in the fight. In fact this day's fighting was principally with cannon. But if you desire, Mr. Editor, to know how a man feels after marching and fighting for a week, with but little food and less rest, you can have my place for a day or two. Yours &c.,

John Bierer[12]

Corporal Bierer's letter was published in the Uniontown newspaper July 17, 1862, one week after the editor had noted that "[t]he most distressing anxiety and excitement has existed in this place for several days past in regard to the killed and wounded in the late battles before Richmond."[13] The anxiety that the editor of the *Genius of Liberty* referred to certainly was not misplaced. In the Seven Days Battles before Richmond, Porter's V Corps, to which the Pennsylvania Reserves belonged, suffered more than one-half the total number of soldiers killed in the entire Army of the Potomac and nearly one-half the number of wounded and missing. McCall's Pennsylvania Reserves lost a total of 3,067 killed, wounded, and missing, nearly one-third of its effective strength going in (and nearly 20 percent of the total casualties in the entire army).[14] The 8th Regiment alone suffered 32 men killed, 113 wounded, and 85 missing.[15]

Among the dead was Andrew Lewis of the 11th Regiment—the thoughts expressed in his June 15 letter to his wife having proved tragically prescient. On July 24, Lieutenant Colonel Daniel Porter wrote to Maria Lewis regarding the fate of her husband:

> Mrs. Lewis,
>
> In accordance with my promise to drop you a line, Surgeon DeBenneville returned yesterday. He reports your husband as having died from the wound received in Friday's fight. His leg was amputated, but not withstanding he died. I most sincerely sympathize with you in this your sad bereavement. The stroke is heavy, but we must bow in submission to the will of God. These are times that try men's souls. The sacredness of the family circle is broken, fond hearts are separated and every dear remembrance ignored. I can scarcely realize that he is dead, but alas I fear it is too true.

Allow me to write the inscription of him who now lies in the grave, in a southern clime, surrounded by traitors and demons to the best of governments. In memory of Capt. Andrew Lewis, who died from the effects of a wound received June 27th 1862 at the battle of Gaines Mill, fighting for the maintenance of law and order. No braver man ever lived—no braver man ever fell. No child of his need blush at the name of that patriotic brave man. His character here was without a stain. In all intercourse he was most honest. He stood high in the regiment. Accept my heartfelt sympathy, and may God who pities the widow & orphan enable you to bear your load of grief & sorrow like the true Christian who looks forward to a better & happier world.

> Yours very truly
> Dan G. Porter[16]

Two days later, Joseph McQuaide wrote to his parents, lamenting the death of his close friend and comrade, James K. Thompson, who had been killed in the fighting at Gaines's Mill:

> Camp at Harrison's Landing Va
> July 26th 1862

Dear Father and Mother

I received your letter this morning and now seat myself to frame some kind of answer to it. In the first place I am well and do hope that these few lines may find you all enjoying good health and getting along fast and peaceable with your harvest.... I know that the harvest will look big in the field but remember it is a longtime to Christmas and at that time when the crop is all in the barn it will not look one bit too big. So don't crow of the harvest but just compare it with our harvest that is to enter Richmond and end the war which will be the harvest of death to tens of thousands of us. But withal everyone is eager for the move. No loud clamorous boasting but the solemn resolution of revenge or death for our comrades, our country and our God....

I was quite rejoiced to hear by your letter that you had visited the family of my dear Jimmy...and had tried to console them in their sore affliction. They have lost a son that was an honor to them. He was noble minded and kind hearted and obliging to all—a true Christian and one whose smiling countenance and genial influence spread sunshine all around him.... Tell Mary that she cannot do one a greater favor under Heaven than to raise up a namesake for my comrade. She has already got a James so that she cannot give it the full name but let her call him Thompson McQuaide and she will have my very heart and soul hence forth and for ever. She can do me no greater favor.... Now I will have to think of closing hoping you will answer them other letters and this one as soon as you receive it. I cannot be resigned to the death of my comrade this side of the grave until we meet never to part. Write soon.

Death oft I've feared thy fatal blow
Now fond I bare my breast
I do thou kindly lay me low
With him I loved at rest

J. L. McQuaide[17]

While many soldiers caught up on their correspondence, others replenished the contents of their haversacks, woefully diminished by weeks of hard marching and fighting: "On our coming to the Peninsula, sutlers had been excluded; but now they were allowed to visit us once more, with their usual prices; for instance, butter one dollar per pound; cheese seventy-five cents; eggs sixty cents per dozen; tobacco one dollar and a half per pound; preserved peaches one dollar and a half per pint-bottle; raisins seventy-five cents per pound; ham thirty cents; cards...sixty cents per pack; whiskey (on the sly) two dollars per pint; and...everything else in proportion."[18]

Still other soldiers took advantage of their proximity to the James River and its tributaries to wash their clothes (as well as themselves) and to frolic in the inviting streams: "I walked around [a swamp] and was soon standing on the shore of Heron [*sic*: Herring] Creek.... I suppose there were two hundred soldiers in the water; and they were splashing, and floating, and swimming, and diving among one another, in a manner that reminded me of the tiny creatures seen in a drop of water, through a microscope."[19]

The peaceful existence enjoyed by the soldiers inside the Federal lines was shattered during the night of July 31, when the Confederates sited a number of artillery batteries on the southern bank of the James River opposite Harrison's Landing and fired hundreds of rounds into the Union encampment. Sergeant Hill vividly recalled the ensuing artillery duel:

A terrific discharge of artillery aroused me from my slumber. It was followed by the whizzing of a solid shot and the bursting of a shell over our camp. Another solid shot struck the ground so near that I could feel the shock; and I sprang up. The rain had ceased to fall, but it was pitch dark. Several shells went screaming over, bursting—the fragments flying and singing in all directions.... I sprang from our low tent and stood erect. As I did so, I encountered Mose, a contraband cook. He was much terrified, and he exclaimed—'My Lod! Whar ar dey flingin' dem from?... A battle of some magnitude now took place. One of the rebel batteries turned upon the gunboat, while the others plugged away at us. The picture was a grand one—a terribly grand one. The night being very dark lent great effect to the scene. Flash after flash burst forth from the gunboat, lighting up the surface of the James with a vivid glare; and at each flash a stunning report with a dozen echoes shook the earth, and a shell, with its tail of fire,

A typical sutler's store near a Union camp. The officer appears to be casting a wary eye at the contents of the keg from which his men are imbibing.

National Archives

could be seen making a circle against the gloomy heavens, screaming like a very demon, and bursting near the rebel batteries with a crash. They followed each other so rapidly, that the operations of the rebel batteries were thrown entirely in the shade. The rebels couldn't stand it; their batteries were soon silenced, and they beat a hasty retreat.[20]

In order to prevent any recurrence of this unwelcome surprise, General McClellan ordered that the south bank of the James opposite Harrison's Landing be occupied:[21] "Accordingly...a regiment was sent over to take possession, and to burn several beautiful mansions that stood upon the green shore opposite our camp; for it was supposed that from observatories on these houses the rebels had been, for some time past, keeping watch over our camps.[22] No opposition was offered to their landing, and they burned the houses to the ground."[23] The 8th Regiment, newly armed with Springfield rifled muskets,[24] took its turn at picket duty over the river. As had the other regiments detailed to the south shore, the men of the 8th Reserves "returned at night with an abundance of fruit, vegetables and berries."[25]

A few days after the midnight artillery duel a prisoner exchange was agreed to, and many of the Union soldiers captured during the fighting on the peninsula were paroled and made their way to Harrison's Landing. Their comrades' joy at their safe return was tempered by concern for those as yet unaccounted for. Hill recalled the scene on the Brownsville Grays' company street as he returned from guard duty:

> [T]here stood Jim Roland, John Young, Hen Underwood, and Mr. Ike Mayhorn...surrounded by the boys, who were eagerly asking questions in rapid succession.
>
> "Did you see the captain or Lieutenant Moth in Richmond?" was asked.
>
> "Yes, both of them; and General McCall and General Reynolds...."
>
> "Do you know anything of Mitchel or Jake Archibald?"
>
> "No; but we saw Will Haddock. He is wounded."
>
> It was amusing to hear the returned prisoners relate what they had seen and experienced during their captivity, especially on Belle Island.[26] Mayhorn's activities were particularly interesting. Jim Roland related an amusing anecdote of him of which I will give a brief sketch.
>
> During the first day of their sojourn on the island, Mayhorn observed a rebel lieutenant...wearing a pair of magnificent boots. It at once occurred to him that he would like to possess those boots.... [H]e watched the officer, followed him from place to place, and haunted him like a shadow till night. When, at last, the officer retired, Mayhorn succeeded in hooking the boots and making off with them. Next morning, however, he began to grow ill at ease, lest the officer, missing his boots, should institute a search, discover the boots in his possession,

and deal summarily with him.... He, therefore, carried the boots to another part of the island, and sold them to one of the rebel sentinels for twenty dollars....

Meantime, the bereaved officer missed his dear boots, and took active measures to recover them, in the shape of offering twenty dollars reward. Mayhorn heard of it and, seeking out the officer, he said: "Will you give me the reward if I tell you who has your boots?"

"Yes, certainly; why not?"

"I thought because I was a Yankee—"

"Oh, that makes no sort of difference; tell me who has my boots...and here are twenty dollars;" and the officer produced a twenty-dollar Confederate note.

"Well," said Mayhorn, "I will point out the fellow who has your boots, but I don't want him to know who informed on him.... He would kill me if—"

"Very well; he shall not see you. Come with me and point him out, and here is your money."

The unfortunate sentinel was on post at the time, and wearing the stolen boots, large as life.

"Yonder he is! He has them on!" exclaimed Mayhorn, as he led the officer to a point from which the sentinel could be seen.

"So he has!... The barefaced scoundrel...here, take your money—Oh, I'll fix him!... To steal my—and from an officer...."

"It's too bad," said Mayhorn, sympathizingly; and he thrust his twenty-dollar bill into his pocket, and sought a position from which he could see the—as he called it—*fun*.

The rebel officer approached the sentinel, who was walking his beat displaying his boots to the best advantage—his pantaloons thrust within the tops.

"You burglar!" exclaimed the officer, savagely....

"What!" and the rebel sentinel expanded his optics to an incredible size.... "What have *I* done?"

"What have you done! Varlet, look at those boots!"

The sentinel surveyed his boots with evident pleasure; he began to think that the officer was jesting with him. Supposing this to be a piece of unpardonable impudence and reckless defiance, the officer grew violent.

"You infernal rascal! OFF WITH THOSE BOOTS!" he vociferated.

The sentinel now perceived that the officer was in earnest; and he asked:

"What do you mean, anyhow?"

"What do I mean! You d___d thief!... Those boots are mine! You stole 'em; you know you did!"

"They're my boots; I bought 'em."

"You lie! You didn't!"

"I did; I bought 'em off a Yankee."

"You lying scoundrel! I'll—CORPORAL OF THE GUARD!..."

"Corporal," said the officer, "bring another man here, and put him in this one's place. He has stolen my boots, and he must be arrested...."

"I didn't steal the boots," persisted the hapless sentinel....

"Not a word, or I'll punch a hole right through you, you miserable scamp."[27]

As the adventurous—some would suggest suicidal—Mayhorn was among those Union prisoners who were exchanged, it may be concluded that neither the wrongfully accused sentinel, nor the outraged officer, managed to deduce that the brazen Yankee had outwitted both of them and gained 40 dollars in the bargain. Unfortunately, Mayhorn's Confederate bills would prove useless along "Robbers' Row," as the sutlers' area at Harrison's Landing was called.

Adam Bright commented on the lowly status of the Southern currency, and on the return of the Union prisoners, in a letter to his uncle:

> Harrison Landing Virginia
> August 8th 1862

Dear Uncle

Yours of the 30th received and read with interest. I am glad to hear that you are blessed with good health and an abundant harvest.... This is the warmest country I ever saw. During the heat of the day the sweat just pours out of me laying in the shade. The nights are cool and pleasant. The movements of the army are generally made at night now....

We are expecting anything to take place any minute. All our sick were sent away this morning and we have three days rations in our haversacks so you may expect to hear some interesting news before long.

All the prisoners taken out of our division returned from Richmond yesterday evening. They had rather a hard time. All they got to eat was one fourth ration of sour bread and a small piece of stinking fresh beef without salt each day. Salt is eighty dollars per barrel.... Flour is the only cheap thing they have. It is only 18 dollars per barrel.

They will give seven dollars of confederate money for one of our five dollar treasury notes and will pay a premium for all our Northern bank notes....

I suppose recruiting is going on quite brisk by this time. I like the plan the government is pursuing. If they won't enlist right away I say draft them. And a young man that is at home and can come and has to be drafted I can never think anything of. He has very little patriotism and it would do me good to see him put in seven days like we did some time ago. And then to see how they blow in some of the letters they write....

But I guess it is time for me to stop. My love and best respects to you all. Write soon and let me know how the recruiting is going on.

> Your Affectionate Nephew
> Add[28]

General McCall and General Reynolds were exchanged on August 13: "When it became known among the regiments that Generals McCall and Reynolds had arrived at the landing, the troops immediately assembled at the headquarters of the division to receive their beloved commanders. General McCall briefly addressed the men, thanking them for the hearty reception they had given him, and expressed the hope that he would soon be able again to lead them to battle and to victory."[29] Unfortunately, McCall's age and the poor state of his health combined to preclude him from resuming command. He therefore resigned his commission and returned to his farm near West Chester, Pennsylvania. General Reynolds, as the ranking officer in the division, assumed command of the Pennsylvania Reserves.

Changes occurred in the command structure at the regimental level as well. Colonel Hays, who commanded the 8th Regiment during the Seven Days Battles, resigned his commission due to the severity of the injuries he sustained at Glendale. Lieutenant Colonel Oliphant, who would have succeeded to the command, had become seriously ill himself and was later honorably discharged on disability.[30] Major Silas Baily of Greene County was next in line, but he had been badly wounded at Gaines's Mill. Consequently, Captain William Lemon of Company H assumed command of the 8th Regiment during its stay at Harrison's Landing.

It was Captain Lemon who, in response to a request from General Truman Seymour to "list [those] non-commissioned officers and men belonging to [the 8th] regiment who...are deserving of more than a mere passing notice for their bravery, coolness and strict attention to duty while on the Field of Battle," named Corporal Isaac Moore and selected him to return to Fayette County on recruiting service.[31] Moore left for Uniontown August 9, and his return was noted in the *Genius of Liberty* in its August 21 edition: "Corporal Isaac A. Moore, of Co. G...8th Pennsylvania Regiment, is in town recruiting for his company. This is one of the oldest and finest companies in the service."[32] As Moore went about the business of recruiting in Fayette County, his comrades in the 8th Reserves pulled up stakes at Harrison's Landing. Together with the rest of McClellan's Army of the Potomac, they were headed for Major General John Pope's Army of Virginia and a date with destiny at an old battlefield.

George A. McCall in the uniform of a major general of Pennsylvania volunteers.
National Archives

Isaac A. Moore in the uniform of a Union corporal.

Author's Collection

"We Have Had a Pretty Hard Time of It"

The Debacle at Second Bull Run

Shortly after Corporal Moore left for Fayette County, the Pennsylvania Reserves began to evacuate Harrison's Landing. With Robert E. Lee having checked McClellan on the Peninsula, General in Chief Henry Halleck ordered the Federal commander to withdraw from Harrison's Landing and join Major General John Pope's newly constituted Army of Virginia north of Richmond. Pope's troops were strung out from Fredericksburg to the Blue Ridge, well positioned either to cut the rebel capital's communications with the vital Shenandoah Valley or to march on Richmond itself. McClellan's failure on the Peninsula, however, had thrown Pope over onto the defensive. He would have to content himself with protecting Washington and Maryland until the Army of the Potomac could reach him. McClellan, however, was in no rush to reinforce Pope. It was not until 10 days after being ordered to evacuate Harrison's Landing that he put his army in motion.

Late in the evening of August 15, the soldiers of the 8th Regiment boarded a steamship at Harrison's Landing and headed down the James River: "About noon [on August 16] we arrived at Hampton Roads. Here we saw all that was visible of the wreck of the [USS] *Cumberland* [destroyed March 8 by the CSS *Virginia* in a naval action off Hampton Roads]...three masts, with the wonted rigging, protruding in a slanting manner twenty or thirty feet from the water."[1]

Later that afternoon, the steamship *New Brunswick,* carrying the 8th Reserves, rounded the point at Fort Monroe and entered Chesapeake Bay, making for the landing at Aquia Creek on the Potomac River: "[A]bout ten o'clock we arrived at Aquia Creek Landing, and there disembarked. This done, a rush was made on all the sutlers and storekeepers in the vicinity; and we purchased all the cakes, pies, apples, cheese, lemonade, and whiskey which they chanced to have on hand."[2] The 8th Regiment moved by rail to Falmouth Station where they camped for the night. Sergeant Hill and his messmates promptly set about finding some dinner, and their efforts were rewarded when they spied a flock of sheep and managed to capture one: "George Wagner, being a butcher, removed the hide of the animal in a business-like way, and we hid it. He then cut the sheep up into seven pieces; and half an hour after, we entered camp each carrying the one-seventh part of a sheep. The result was that we had mutton three times a day for twenty-four hours."[3]

While at Falmouth, Hill inspected the area occupied by his regiment the previous May when the Pennsylvania Reserves had advanced to Fredericksburg with McDowell:

> Two months had wrought a great change; I could scarcely recognize our old camp-ground. It was overgrown with weeds and grass; and thick bushes had sprung up and covered the spot where our tent had stood. 'Twas very quiet and lonely now in that pine wood. A bird here and there might be seen hopping from branch to branch, uttering, ever and anon, some little note that sounded too mournful for a song. Only here and there the sun penetrated the thick foliage. The scene was one of solitude.
>
> My mind reverted to the time, but a few months gone, when that green grove was a scene of life and mirth—when the roll of the drum and the bugle notes floated gaily...among those green pines. I fancied I could still hear our brass band playing some favorite air at guard-mount or at dress-parade. Where now was that life-inspiring band? Gone! I thought of the many merry voices, now hushed forever, that once rang out in joyous peals of laughter, at some amusing little scene of camp-life—at some trick or prank of Gaskill, perhaps;... They were gone now;... they would answer to roll-call no more;... the word "killed" or "missing" was written opposite the names of many on the roll-book. I thought of many of our brave comrades, once so full of careless glee, whose forms now lay mouldering away in front of Richmond! I thought of many who, two months before, full of eager anticipations of glory, marched with us from that camp-ground, to return to it no more forever![4]

The Pennsylvania Reserves soon pushed on, joining John Pope's Army of Virginia the night of August 22. The first of McClellan's troops to reach Pope, they were attached to Major General Irvin McDowell's III Corps. Robert E. Lee, of course, had not remained idle during the 20 days it took McClellan to get to Pope. Having earlier dispatched Stonewall Jackson to Gordonsville to counter the Federals, Lee joined him there August 15, intent upon suppressing Pope before McClellan could join him. The Union commander, in turn, withdrew behind the Rappahannock on August 19. Five days later, the Pennsylvania Reserves marched into Rappahannock Station, only to find that Pope, with Longstreet in front of him and Jackson threatening his right flank, had begun a general withdrawal. The Army of Virginia and the newly arrived Pennsylvania Reserves fell back to Warrenton and awaited Lee's next move.

> On arriving at Warrenton we went into camp on a beautiful lawn which lay round about a fine brick residence. The house belonged to a gentleman...who

was serving at the time as quartermaster of the rebel army under General Lee. His family had fled upon the approach of the Yankees, leaving everything about the premises. Upon hearing that there was a fine library among other things in the house, I concluded that I would go in and draw a book or two, as the rules in regard to returning them were not over rigid.... But unawares I walked into a room where General George E. [*sic*] Meade [now commanding the first brigade of Reynolds's division][5] was giving some of the soldiers whom he had caught in the act of destroying the furniture Hail Columbia with variations, saying, "If you had the d___d rebel who owns the property here, I would not care a d——n how soon you hung him, but don't wantonly destroy property." Then much to my gratification he added, "If any of you boys want a book to read, take it and go, but don't break up the furniture." So I walked into the library where the book-cases had been overturned and their contents scattered in wild confusion over the floor, and proceeded to select my book. I made choice of a fine copy of Shakespeare, and going to the barn got a nice pole of leaf tobacco. I returned to camp and stemming my tobacco, made it into a twist, which, together with my book, I placed in my haversack.[6]

At his headquarters in Warrenton, General Pope learned that Stonewall Jackson had swung around his right flank, passed through Thoroughfare Gap, and raided Bristoe Station the night of August 26. The hungry Southerners descended upon the Federal depot at Manassas Junction the following day, feasting on the immense stores of foodstuffs gathered there and burning everything they could not carry off. Neglecting scattered reports that Robert E. Lee and James Longstreet were themselves nearing Thoroughfare Gap with five divisions of hard-marching Confederates, Pope promptly started 50,000 troops for Manassas Junction, intending, as he told General McDowell, to trap Jackson there and "bag the whole crowd."[7] John Reynolds's Pennsylvania Reserves, astride the Warrenton Turnpike with McDowell's corps west of Gainesville, headed east on the pike. At Pageland Lane, west of Groveton, they would turn south and descend upon Manassas Junction from the north, thereby eliminating any possibility of the rebels escaping in that direction.

There was one glaring problem with Pope's plan to bag Jackson: it depended upon the rebel general remaining idle at Manassas Junction, passively awaiting the arrival of a vastly superior force. In reality, however, while Pope and his lieutenants consumed the better part of 12 hours organizing the details of the Federal march, Stonewall Jackson's "foot cavalry" were busy conducting a march of their own. Throughout the night of August 27, Jackson's men tramped north toward the old Bull Run battlefield. By the following morning, they had crossed the Warrenton Pike and taken cover in woods along the grade of an unfinished rail line.

With Jackson's rebels hiding in the woods north of the pike and Reynolds's Pennsylvanians marching east along it, the chance of an encounter grew greater with each passing mile. As Meade's first brigade (comprised of the 3rd, 4th, 7th, 8th, and 13th Reserves) approached Groveton, the inevitable occurred. George Darby described what happened:

> The next morning, August 28th, 1862...when we reached Gainesville the Johnnies opened upon us with a battery of artillery and the second Battle of Bull Run was on. The column was halted which left Companies G [the Fayette Guards] and B of our regiment in range of the rebel fire, and as we stood in line I was scraped by a shell which exploded after passing me, and killed Sergeant W. H. Leithhead and J. M. Wells, of Company G, and one private in Company B. It also took an arm off of W. H. Doud, of Company G, and a leg off of the adjutant of the regiment, at the same time killing his horse. My clothing, even to my shirt, on my left side, was carried away by it as was also my bayonet and haversack, Shakespeare, tobacco and all. I was painfully wounded, although not dangerously....[8]

Federal artillery soon silenced the rebel battery, and the soldiers of the first brigade, who had deployed in line of battle, resumed their march toward Manassas. As Meade's soldiers grappled with the Confederate battery near Groveton, the first Federal troops reached Manassas Junction. There, the men of Kearny's division found hundreds of smoldering boxcars, but no Stonewall Jackson. They captured a few Confederate stragglers rummaging through the debris and questioned them concerning Jackson's whereabouts. The prisoners told their captors that the rebel commander had marched toward Centreville. When this information reached John Pope, he ordered Irvin McDowell to pursue the Southerners who, he imagined, must surely be retreating. Before the order even reached McDowell, however, Pope countermanded it. Giving momentary attention to the possibility that Lee and Longstreet might, indeed, be marching to join Jackson, Pope now directed McDowell to hold his troops near Gainesville to counter any attempt by the Southern commanders to do so and overwhelm the Federals. Incredibly, the Union commander then changed his mind yet again and reinstated his order to pursue the rebels fleeing in the direction of Centreville.

Throughout that confusing afternoon, the Pennsylvania Reserves pressed on toward Manassas Junction. About 5 o'clock, however, Pope ordered them to turn north toward the Warrenton Pike to join in the pursuit of Jackson. As they neared the old Bull Run battlefield, they heard the sound of artillery fire: "When we heard the thunder of this conflict, we were near Bethlehem Church [about three miles south of Groveton].... We had already marched many long and weary hours, but, tired and exhausted, we pressed on until the musket firing became distinct, the flashes seen and the mingled voices of the combatants heard. Darkness put an end to the fight [a vicious stand-up shootout between Jackson's men and King's division of McDowell's corps on the Brawner farm near Groveton]. After marching eighteen hours and twenty-four miles, many without anything to eat, we stretched our weary limbs upon the grass to sleep."[9]

The second battle of Bull Run got under way in earnest early on August 29. Having finally found Jackson—not near Centreville as he had supposed, but lurking north of the Warrenton Pike near Groveton—Pope promptly ordered Franz Sigel's I Corps to attack him. Supported on their right flank by Heintzelman's corps and on their left by the Pennsylvania Reserves, Sigel's men moved out. As the attack got under way, Robert Schenck, commanding Sigel's left division, asked General Reynolds to send a battery across the pike to drive off Confederate artillery that threatened the Federals' advance. Reynolds sent Cooper's battery, supported by Meade's brigade, and a firefight with Early's Virginians ensued.

As the Pennsylvanians battled the rebels along the Warrenton Pike, an ominous development occurred—the one that John Pope had virtually willed out of all his calculations. Robert E. Lee and James Longstreet had fought their way past a small Union force at Thoroughfare Gap the night of August 28 and, with John Bell Hood's Texas brigade in the vanguard, now marched to the sound of the guns. Late in the morning Hood's men deployed in line of battle south of the pike with their left resting on the road. As they advanced eastward, the Texans, Georgians, and South Carolinians relieved Early's Virginians and pressed on, endangering Reynolds's left flank. The Pennsylvanians quickly changed front to meet the advancing rebels but in short order were forced to fall back. Reynolds sent word to General Pope that he had encountered a significant Confederate force in his front and on his left, but Pope, preoccupied with Jackson's "retreating" rebels, ignored the warning.

About three o'clock in the afternoon, Pope ordered General Reynolds to "threaten [Jackson's] right and rear" in support of an attack then being made upon the center of Jackson's line by troops of Hooker's division. The Reserves "proceeded to do [so] under a heavy fire of artillery from the ridge to the left of the pike. Generals Seymour and Jackson led their brigades in advance, but notwithstanding all the steadiness and courage shown by the men they were compelled to fall back before the heavy fire of artillery and musketry which met them both on the front and left flank.... King's division engaged the enemy along the pike on our right, and the action was continued with it until dark by Meade's brigade."[10] Yet again, General Reynolds sent an aide to John Pope's headquarters with word of the ominous Confederate presence on the Union left flank. And yet again, the Federal commander failed to grasp the significance of the news, telling the officer who bore it to him: "You are excited, young man; the people you see are General Porter's command taking position on the right of the enemy."[11]

That evening as the fighting finally subsided along Sigel's front, the Pennsylvanians cast about for something, anything to eat: "We *were* hungry. The last rations we had received were two days' rations issued to us on the previous Tuesday night near Warrenton. It was now beginning to be Friday night [August 29], and we were entirely without anything in the eating line."[12]

Just before dark on August 29, General Longstreet mounted a reconnaissance in force eastward along the Warrenton Turnpike. At about the same time, General Pope, still believing that the Confederates were retreating down the pike to the west, ordered Irvin McDowell to pursue the "fleeing" rebels. McDowell tapped John P. Hatch's division of New Yorkers for the task. As Hatch's men neared Groveton, they stumbled into Hood's division. The Southerners most definitely were not retreating, and they tore into Hatch's Federals with a vengeance. By the time nightfall put an end to the firefight, the fields surrounding the crossroads were littered with dead and wounded New Yorkers. The Pennsylvania Reserves could hear the sounds of Hatch's clash with Hood from their bivouac south of Groveton: "After the battle ceased, [we] were withdrawn to the position [we] occupied the night before, and, hungry and wearied, [we] lay down upon [our] arms to sleep. But, unfortunately for us, some boys belonging to the 'Coffee Brigade' kindled small fires to boil their much-coveted beverage, by which the enemy discovered our bivouac, and opened at long range, with solid shot, by which several were killed or wounded. The boys, however, were too tired to pay much attention to this."[13]

As dawn broke on August 30, John Pope persisted in his single-minded belief that the Confederates were retreating to the west. Despite Reynolds's clear warning of the preceding afternoon that substantial rebel forces were arrayed south of the Warrenton Pike and Hatch's disastrous "pursuit" of Jackson later that evening, Pope prepared to deliver what he supposed would be the coup de grâce to Stonewall's "trapped" rebels. Unbeknownst to the preoccupied Union commander, however, it was his army, not Jackson's, that found itself in an extremely precarious position that Saturday morning. The Federals were caught in a gaping maw formed by Jackson's 24,000 Southerners posted along the unfinished railroad cut north of the Warrenton Pike and Longstreet's five divisions, by then fully deployed south of the pike just west of Groveton. As the day unfolded, a confident Robert E. Lee patiently awaited John Pope's next move. The slightest misstep by the Federal chieftain could trigger a massive Confederate assault threatening the very survival of his army. Sadly for the thousands of Union soldiers who would become casualties that day, that misstep was not long in coming—and John Reynolds's Pennsylvania Reserves were destined to end up in the thick of the resulting battle.

Early in the morning as Pope busied himself preparing yet another attack on Jackson's "retreating" rebels—this time by Porter's V Corps—General Reynolds, acting on his own initiative, moved west again, feeling for the enemy. As they neared the Groveton crossroads, Meade's brigade began taking fire from some of

Hood's men concealed in the houses there. Deploying additional skirmishers to deal with the rebel resistance at the crossroads, Reynolds led his Pennsylvanians westward across a small valley where a terrible sight greeted them: "[As we] descended into the valley...I looked across to the hill opposite, and saw a sight which I shall never forget. The whole face of the hill was literally covered with our dead. The fighting on the previous day had been, at this point, very desperate; and so thick did the dead lie, that one might have stepped from one to another for several hundred yards. They were all our own men—the rebels, I suppose, having removed theirs. As we ascended the hill, we had to walk with care to keep from stepping on some of them; and the battery that accompanied us could not ascend at all without running over some of the poor fellows."[14] The dead men that Sergeant Hill saw were Hatch's unfortunate New Yorkers who had run into Hood's Texans the night before.

As the Reserves engaged the rebel skirmishers in the vicinity of Groveton, John Reynolds scouted ahead on horseback to ascertain for himself the nature of the Confederate force in his front: "Becoming convinced that the enemy were not in retreat, but were posted in force on our left flank, I pushed through the skirmishers to the edge of the woods on the left, gaining sight of the open ground beyond, and advancing myself into the open ground, I found a line of skirmishers of the enemy nearly parallel to the line of skirmishers covering my left flank, with cavalry formed behind them, perfectly stationary, evidently masking a column of the enemy formed for attack on my left flank when our line should be sufficiently advanced. The skirmishers opened fire upon me, and I was obliged to run the gauntlet of a heavy fire to gain the rear of my division."[15] It was now abundantly clear to Reynolds that, as he had conjectured the day before, he faced a substantial rebel force on the Federal left flank. It was equally clear that the Southerners were not retreating but, rather, were massing for an attack that would place that flank in imminent danger of being turned. Reynolds immediately rode to John Pope's headquarters to apprise him of the perilous development. Pope's reaction was one of apparent disbelief. Irvin McDowell, however, was concerned enough by what he heard to ride back to Groveton with Reynolds to see for himself. Confirming Reynolds's information, McDowell ordered him to fall back to Chinn Ridge and deploy his division there to resist any attempt by the Confederates to turn the Union flank.

At about two o'clock, Reynolds started the Reserves back toward Chinn Ridge. An hour later, Porter's corps attacked Jackson north of the Warrenton Pike. After a series of piecemeal advances, all of which were ultimately repulsed following bloody fighting, Porter's assault finally petered out, and thousands of Federals streamed to the rear. General McDowell, observing the action from Chinn Ridge, then made a fateful decision. He ordered Reynolds's troops off the ridge and sent them north to support what he perceived to be a faltering Union center. As the Pennsylvania Reserves headed for the Warrenton Pike, they left behind them on Chinn Ridge just one battery and four regiments—the 1,200 Ohioans of Nathaniel McLean's brigade—to defend the Federal left flank against the five Confederate divisions massed south of Groveton. It was the moment that Robert E. Lee had been waiting for.

James Longstreet unleashed nearly 25,000 rebel troops and pointed them at Henry Hill, the key to the Federal position. If the Southerners could take it, they stood a very good chance of cutting off Pope's line of retreat and destroying his already battered army. Only G. K. Warren's brigade near Groveton and the pitifully small band of Ohioans atop Chinn Ridge stood between Longstreet's men and victory. Irvin McDowell, now recognizing the gravity of his error in sending the Pennsylvania Reserves to Porter's assistance, desperately sought to recall them. He managed to stop Colonel Martin Hardin's third brigade before it reached the pike and placed it, together with Captain Mark Kerns's battery, on a small knoll midway between Chinn Ridge and Groveton just as Hood's Texas brigade smashed through Warren's hapless New Yorkers. The Pennsylvanians fought a desperate delaying action on the knoll in which Colonel Hardin was seriously wounded and Captain Kerns was killed.

Although Hardin and Kerns had momentarily slowed the Confederate advance, Colonel McLean knew that his position along the top of Chinn Ridge was where the crisis would occur. He deployed his regiments and awaited the inevitable. It came soon enough. Hood's and Evans's brigades stormed up the ridge, only to be stopped by Federal battery fire and repeated musket volleys. James Kemper's Virginians came on next, and they wrecked McLean's left flank, nearly driving the beleaguered Ohioans from the ridge.

McLean's heroics on Chinn Ridge gave John Pope and Irvin McDowell 30 precious minutes to find and dispatch additional troops to his relief and, more importantly, to the defense of Henry Hill. McDowell quickly gathered some 7,000 additional troops and hurled them into the maelstrom atop the ridge. Drawn from Ricketts' division and Sigel's I Corps, the Yankees arrived just as McLean's line collapsed. Fierce fighting erupted anew as the surging Southerners struggled to drive the Federal reinforcements from the high ground. By six o'clock sheer weight of numbers told, and the Confederates stood victorious on top of Chinn Ridge. Their victory had cost them dearly, however, not only in terms of casualties, but also in time lost. As the last Federal defenders retreated down the northeastern side of the ridge, there was but one hour of daylight left—and Henry Hill still lay ahead.

While McDowell sought desperately to stem the Confederate tide on Chinn Ridge, John Pope sought with equal desperation to patch together a defensive line on Henry Hill, the scene of the shocking Union defeat one year earlier. Henry Hill represented the last possible line of defense on the Union army's battered left flank,

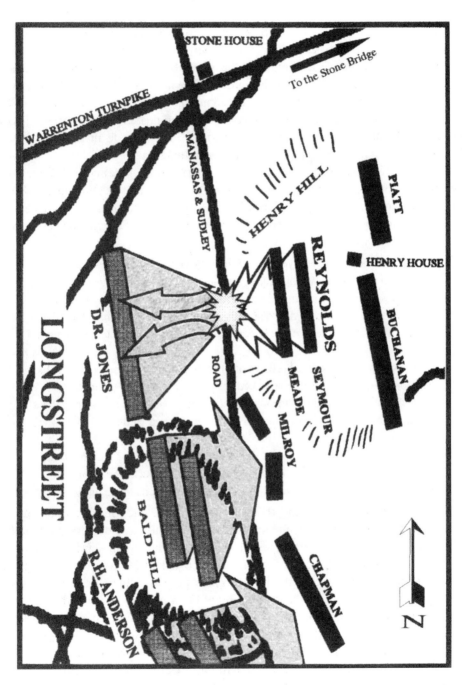

The Battle of Second Bull Run, August 30, 1862. The charge of the Pennsylvania Reserves at Henry Hill.

and John Pope knew it. If the Confederates broke through at that point, the left flank would collapse, and Longstreet could interpose his five divisions between the Union army and its only line of retreat—the Stone Bridge over Bull Run. The Union commander first secured the two brigades of Reynolds's Pennsylvania Reserves that McDowell had sent north of the pike earlier in the day. George Meade and Truman Seymour hurried their men to Henry Hill and posted them near the ruins of the Henry House. Meade's brigade formed in line of battle in the front, with Seymour's brigade forming a second line just behind it.

With Reynolds's men posted on the western slope of Henry Hill, Pope hurried the two brigades of Sykes's regulars, Milroy's brigade of Ohioans and West Virginians, and three batteries of artillery into position to bolster the makeshift line. The Pennsylvania Reserves fixed bayonets and waited. Sergeant Hill described the scene:

> Each brigade was deployed in line, ours [Meade's, which included the 8th Regiment] in front.... Each brigade comprised a line about as long as a regiment ought to; so many had fallen out on account of hunger and fatigue, while many had been killed or wounded.... The regiment consisted of about a hundred and twenty; the brigade of about five hundred; the division of less than two thousand [*sic*].[16]
>
> The smoke and dust had become so dense that the sun was but dimly visible; and objects could not be distinguished at the distance of eighty yards....
>
> A cheer—it sounded like the wailings of an approaching storm—rose above the din of battle; it came from the woods a few hundred yards in front; it was a rebel cheer.
>
> "They're coming!" exclaimed the captain of the battery; "they're coming, boys! Nothing but case shot—bring nothing but case shot!"[17] he shouted to the men who were carrying the ammunition from the caissons to the guns.[18]

The "approaching storm" that Hill heard were the Georgians of Henry Benning's brigade. They were making for the stone house at the intersection of the Warrenton Pike and the Manassas-Sudley Road. If they could seize the intersection, they would cut off all the Union forces posted to the west of it and place Pope's entire army in grave peril. The Georgians' path took them directly across the Pennsylvania Reserves' front, and John Reynolds was quick to seize the opportunity. As the Confederate tide rolled on toward the intersection, Reynolds, "driving his spurs into his horse's side, shouted his order: 'Forward, Reserves!'... [H]is troops, inoculated with his enthusiasm, swept forward and downward. The two lines met. Outnumbered, the Reserves fought with bulldog tenacity.... Still, The First and Second Regiments seemed about to give way beneath the tremendous pressure, when General Reynolds, 'observing that the flagstaff of the Second Regiment had been pierced by a bullet and broken, seized the flag from the color-bearer, and dashing to the right rode twice up and down his entire division line, waving the flag about his head and cheering on his men.'"[19]

Hill described what happened next: "With a mad shout that arose far above the thunder of the artillery, we rushed forward—General Reynolds leading the charge. Bullets were poured upon us from the wood in swarms. Still we rushed on. There is a wild excitement about a charge...which induces men to face death without a thought of fear. How fast our poor fellows fell during that charge! My wonder was that any of us could pass unscathed through that leaden storm. I could actually hear the savage bullets striking and crashing among the bones of men around me. We could not see the rebels—the smoke was so dense; but *we knew they were there.* We charged across a road, and right into the wood.... We charged to the very ranks of the rebels, when they turned and fled."[20]

The Federal line on Henry Hill had held.[21] In his report of the action, General Meade stated: "It is due to the Pennsylvania Reserves to say that this charge...was made at a most critical period of the day. The enemy had repulsed the attack made by...[other Federal troops] on our right flank and had himself assumed the offensive on our left flank. His infantry had emerged from the woods, had already secured one of our batteries and was advancing to the Henry House ridge, which, if he had succeeded in gaining, might have materially altered the fortune of the day."[22]

The Federal armies under John Pope's command lost 14,462 officers and men killed, wounded, and missing between August 16 and September 2. The vast majority of those losses occurred on August 29 and August 30. The Pennsylvania Reserves lost 66 men killed, 300 wounded, and 211 missing. Casualties in the 8th Regiment totaled 5 soldiers killed, 21 wounded, and 32 missing.

While Robert E. Lee and his lieutenants had clearly won the Battle of Second Bull Run for the Confederacy, the valiant charge of the Pennsylvania Reserves late in the day on August 30 proved critical in preserving the Federals' line of retreat. The Union army, though battered and driven from the field, would live to fight another day. As night fell, John Reynolds's weary Pennsylvanians withdrew across Bull Run and trudged down the Warrenton Turnpike toward Centreville:

> When we arrived to within two or three miles of Centreville, we halted for the night. We were in no kind of order; and the commanders of the regiments were allowed to use their own will and judgment with their commands. Captain Lemon, therefore, concluded to halt and rest for the night.... He requested me to go over into a field, and see whether I could find a suitable place to lie. I soon found a "suitable place," and reported to him. We then left the road, entered the field, and marched to the spot, when Captain Lemon informed us that we were at liberty to lie down and rest for the night.
>
> "Charley," said I, addressing Charley Brawley, "this is the thirtieth day of the month."

"Well," said Charley, who thought this a very singular...remark.

"Do you remember this night two months ago?" I asked.

"Oh, yes—the night of the battle of—"

"Exactly; do you remember who you slept with that night?"

"Oh, yes—I slept with you."

"Then suppose, just for the sake of coincidence, that we—"

"I was just going to propose that myself—why, it's beginning to rain, as I am a sinner."

And it *was* beginning to rain. We lay down together, arranged our tent blankets so as to shelter us as much as possible, and proceeded to go to sleep.

As my eyes closed, I thought of those now lying upon the battle-field cold in death, and of those dying from their wounds, crying perhaps for water to slake their burning thirst. I felt that I had great reason to be thankful that I was still spared. Why it was so I could not tell; for well I knew that many better men than I, and exposed to no greater danger than I had been, had fallen, while I was still allowed to come out of the battle without a scratch.[23]

In the days following the Battle of Second Bull Run, General Pope would be relieved of command, and President Abraham Lincoln would turn once again to George B. McClellan. Lincoln placed McClellan in charge of the defenses of Washington and then returned him to command of the Army of the Potomac (into which much of Pope's battered Army of Virginia was integrated). In Washington, the politicians and generals maneuvered to put the best face possible on what clearly had turned into a debacle. At the same time, in Centreville, the common soldiers who fought at Bull Run mourned their fallen comrades and caught up on their correspondence.

Cordello Collins wrote to his mother, telling her that "[w]e have had hard times lately. For about 2 weeks we have had to march every day and had 3 fights.... Last thirsday Friday and Saturday all day hard. We had 1 days ration of food to last the 3 days. I was the nearest dun out then that I ever was. I could hardly stand a lone but I had to keep a going."[24]

At the same time that Collins penned those words to his mother, Tom Springer, then a corporal in the Fayette Guards, wrote to his father in Uniontown. Portions of the letter were reprinted in the *Genius of Liberty* under the heading "From the Eighth Regiment":

We have been permitted to read a letter written by Thomas W. Springer, of company G, 8th Penna. Reserves, from Arlington Heights, Sept 3rd, to his father, Mr. D. M. Springer, of this place, from which we get the following information: "We have been so situated that we could neither receive, nor send the mail since the 23rd of August.... On the 21st, at 11 o'clock at night we started and marched till 3 o'clock the next morning, when we laid down and slept till daylight—started again and marched twenty five miles, nearly to Rappahannock Station, next day to near Warrenton and laid two days. On the 28th marched in the direction of Manassas, and run into a masked battery—a shell exploded right in the centre of our company killing three and wounding six. 'Will' Leithead was killed at this time, he was sitting down and the shell hit right in his lap tearing him all to pieces.[25] 'Jim' Wells was also killed at this time.... On the 29th we moved on to the attack at 8 o'clock a.m.—we tried to flank them but they drove us back, we were reinforced—moved again to the attack, drove the rebels from their position and held it all night. On the 30th we attacked and drove the rebels from their position and occupied it, the fighting continued nearly all day. About 4 o'clock, p.m., they turned our left flank and we had to retire—retreated to Centreville and stayed there till the evening of the 31st, when we went on picket for the night, were relieved on the 1st and marched back to Fairfax Court House where we stayed all night. On the 2nd we marched to Munson's Hill and stayed all night. To-day (3rd) we marched here, (Arlington Heights,) so you see we have had a pretty hard time of it."[26]

Springer was no stranger to hard times, and, unfortunately, there were more to come. Less than two weeks after writing to his father, the young corporal and his comrades in the 8th Reserves would be marching again—this time northward into Maryland.[27]

"Die Like Men; Don't Run Like Dogs!"

The Maryland Campaign

Robert E. Lee wrecked John Pope's Army of Virginia—and his career—at the Battle of Second Bull Run. However, the victory, as welcome as it was, presented Lee with a dilemma—what to do next. He could not assail the defenses of Washington into which the shattered Federals had retreated. They were simply too strong. Any withdrawal in the direction of Richmond was out of the question, as it would simply encourage the Union army to regroup and march southward once again. And if he wished to retain the strategic initiative so recently gained, he could not afford to sit idle astride Bull Run.

Lee resolved his dilemma by deciding to advance into Maryland. Such a move would draw the Federal army away from northern Virginia, already ravaged by a year of war, and the farms and fields of the border state would provide much-needed food and forage for the long-suffering Confederate army. Moreover, Lee believed that the majority of Marylanders were pro-Southern in their sympathies. He felt that a successful advance across the Potomac might well persuade Maryland to join the Confederacy. Indeed, in writing to Jefferson Davis he made this very point: "The present seems to be the most propitious time since the commencement of the war for the Confederate Army to enter Maryland. The two grand armies of the United States that have been operating in Virginia [Pope's Army of Virginia and McClellan's Army of the Potomac], though now united, are much weakened and demoralized. Their new levies, of which I understand 60,000 men have already been posted in Washington, are not yet organized, and will take some time to prepare for the field. If it is ever desired to give material aid to Maryland and afford her an opportunity of throwing off the oppression to which she is now subject, this would seem to be the most favorable."[1]

Most of all, however, the Southern commander wanted to draw the Federal army out of the defenses of Washington and engage it in a decisive battle. In an interview following the war, Lee said: "I went into Maryland to give battle, and could I have kept General McClellan in ignorance of my position and plans a day or two longer, I would have fought and crushed him."[2]

The vanguard of the rebel army crossed the Potomac River at White's Ford early in the morning September 4, 1862. One soldier noted that the sunrise "'caused the rippled surface to sparkle with the brilliance of a sea of silver studded with diamonds set in dancing beads of burnished gold....' Bands played 'Maryland, My Maryland' and the men were cheerful, splashing through the waist-deep water, yipping the Rebel Yell."[3]

Word of the invasion soon reached Washington, and General McClellan, acting with unaccustomed speed, quickly placed his army in motion. Among the troops marching to meet the rebels were the Pennsylvania Reserves, reassigned to the Army of the Potomac after the disaster at Bull Run and newly commanded by Brigadier General George G. Meade. Meade had taken the reins of the Reserves when John Reynolds was ordered to Harrisburg to take command of the Pennsylvania Emergency Militia. Attached to General Hooker's I Corps, the Reserves headed north late in the evening of September 6 and reached Leesborough, some ten miles into Maryland, the following day. The next evening, Leo Faller, a private in the 7th Regiment, wrote to his parents in Carlisle, expressing concern that Lee's army might enter Pennsylvania:

> Camp near Leesborough Md
> September 8th 1862

Dear parents

Mr Cockley arrived at the Regiment on Satuarday and gave us a letter from hom[e]. We were very glad to hear from you and that you were all well.... I suppose you will be somewhat surprised to find that we are in Maryland.... There is a large force of Rebels reported somewhere about here and I guess we will have to go on the hunt of them and try and drive them out of the State.

I hope the Rebels will never get into Pennsylvania for they would lay the Country as bare as a Desert and Pennsylvania would become like Virginia. Now is the time for every one who has a Single Spark of Patriotism in him to Volunteer for if the Rebels ever get into Pennsylvania, Cumberland County will be among the first to feel the Horrors of War and they will make Pennsylvanians Suffer with a vengeance for the Rebels are terribly down on us for they think the troops from the [good] Old Keystone State fight them harder than any other state troops....

We were in the two [day] battle of Friday and Saturday [Second Bull Run] but our Division suffered very little in killed. There was none killed in our Regiment and only about twenty wounded. My head is well now, the Ball only cutting the scalp for about an inch long and then it passed out at the crown. I tell you it was a narrow escape but a miss is as good as a mile and I have to thank providence that it was no worse. Our Regiment was making a charge when it happened.

There was a piece published in the Philadelphia Press blaming the Pennsylvania Reserves with Cowardice and said that we deserted Gen Reynolds. Gen Reynolds was better pleased with us at Bull Run than ever, and he said that he would sooner fight with our Division than any he ever saw. There is some one jealous of the Reserves and they are trying to injure us by slandering us but let them go. I guess they cant do us much harm but it is almost enough to discourage men who have been marched until they were almost dead and then go into Action and fight for two days....

There is a report here this morning that the Rebels are in Gettysburg if that is the case I wish they would send us there to fight them for I don't want to see them stay in Pennsylvania.... Give my love to Uncle Bens and Uncle Henrys folks and to...all inquiring friends. We are both well. Write soon.

No More at present

From your Affectionate Son
Leo W. Faller[4]

Faller's regiment, together with the 3rd, 4th, and 8th Regiments, made up the second brigade of the Pennsylvania Reserves. They crossed the Monocacy River September 13 and marched into Frederick, Maryland, early the following morning. Sergeant Hill recalled the reception that the thirsty Federals enjoyed as they entered the county seat: "[W]e passed through Frederick, where the number of flags and white handkerchiefs waved at us from doors and windows was truly gratifying. At almost every door stood some bewitching creature with a pail of clear, cold, sparkling water; while others stood with glasses in their hands inviting us to drink. They talked pleasantly with us, and manifested every indication of preferring us to the rebels. I can't for the life of me tell what made me so thirsty that morning; for I must have stopped a dozen times for a drink of water; and each time it chanced...I was helped to a glass by a beauty."[5]

Pressing on, the Pennsylvanians crossed Catoctin Mountain and headed toward the village of Middletown: "From [the summit of Catoctin Mountain] the scenery is magnificent. In our rear lies the valley of the Monocacy, with Frederick resting on its breast; and in front stretches that of the Catoctin, with the South Mountains beyond. Down this beautiful valley winds the broad creek that gives it name, and in which is situated Middletown. Long lines of troops and ammunition wagons were moving across it, towards the mountains, from whose sides issued puffs of white smoke and came the booming of cannon."[6]

When the Federals reached Middletown, they received a welcome no less generous than that accorded them in Frederick. Samuel Waters, of the 6th Regiment, described what he saw—and heard—as his unit marched through the town: "The Union flags was displayed out of nearly every window, the people seemed to be very much rejoiced at us driving the rebels before us and getting the cleare of them. One man in partikler cauld them stinken lousey filthy sons of bitches."[7]

The good citizens of Middletown did not limit their acknowledgment of the Federal troops merely to patriotic displays. As Sergeant Major Woodward noted: "Never was a more cordial welcome given to troops than was given to us. Bread, cakes, milk, water, fruit and tobacco, were freely given by the good people who crowded the doors and windows and lined the pavements, and flags and handkerchiefs were waved and flowers thrown as we passed. We felt then, for the first time during the war, we were fighting among friends."[8]

Before the day was out, Woodward and his comrades would, indeed, be fighting. "Friends," however, would be few and far between. Those puffs of smoke emanating from the hills west of Middletown were harbingers of the Battle of South Mountain, an engagement largely overshadowed by the cataclysmic struggle that would take place at Sharpsburg three days later.

That a battle was fought at South Mountain at all was the result of one of the most unusual incidents to take place during the war. In order to protect his supply lines through the Shenandoah Valley during his movement into Maryland, General Lee decided to divide his army, sending six divisions to capture the Federal garrison at Harpers Ferry, Virginia, while the rest of his army advanced into Maryland. The directions for this operation were set out in "Special Orders No. 191," copies of which were distributed to the several division commanders assigned to carry it out. However, one copy of the order was lost, apparently through the carelessness of a Confederate courier. Several Union soldiers found the lost order late in the morning of September 13 in a meadow near Monocacy Junction. They turned it over to their company commander who quickly forwarded it to General McClellan. Delighted at this stroke of good fortune, McClellan exclaimed, "Here is a paper...with which if I cannot beat Bobby Lee, I will be willing to go home."[9]

Thus privy to his counterpart's plans, the Young Napoleon determined to cross South Mountain and crush Lee's divided army before he could concentrate it. True to form, however, he vacillated for nearly seven hours before ordering an assault on the three main gaps through the mountain. This delay gave Lee, who had become aware of the Federal advance through Middletown, time to throw a small force forward to defend the gaps while he attempted to gather his scattered divisions. Lee's orders to the South Mountain defenders were simple and direct: "The gap[s] must be held at all hazards until the operations at Harper's Ferry are finished."[10] From the Confederate perspective, the Battle of South Mountain would be all about trading lives for time. The "trading" began the next morning and continued unabated throughout the day.

Late in the afternoon of September 14, General Hooker ordered General Meade to deploy his Pennsylvania Reserves north of the National Road in an attempt to turn the Confederate left flank at Turner's Gap. Sergeant Hill described the movement:

About four o'clock [our division] began to advance. We toiled up the steep ascent in front of us, when we discovered that a valley lay yet between us and the main ascent of South Mountain. While passing through a corn-field upon the hill, the enemy's artillery again opened upon us with solid shot. Down the hill we went—across the small valley—up the steep ascent of the mountain. A few hundred yards from the base of the mountain was a stone-fence. Below this, the ground was clear; above, the face of the mountain was covered with trees and rocks. When within fifty yards of the stone-fence, a murderous fire of musketry was opened upon us by the rebels, who lay concealed behind it, and swarms of bullets whistled about our ears. With a wild shout, we dashed forward...while volley after volley was poured upon us; but we heeded it not; we rushed madly on. The rebels...taken aback by our recklessness and disregard of their bullets, began to give way. We reached the stone-fence, and sprang over. The rebels reformed among the rocks and fought with remarkable obstinacy....

We pressed the rebels closely. They stood awhile, loading and firing, but at last began to waver. Directly in front of the right of [the 8th] regiment, they gave way; and several companies from the right—[the Brownsville Grays] among them—pressed forward, becoming detached from the regiment. We soon found ourselves thirty or forty paces ahead of the regiment, having gained the flank of the Seventeenth South Carolina. We were within twenty or thirty steps of them, directly on their left, and they did not see us; then we mowed them down. Poor fellows! I almost pitied them, to see them sink down by dozens at every discharge! I remember taking deliberate aim at a tall South Carolinian, who was standing with his side to me loading his gun. I fired, and he fell into a crevice between two rocks. Step by step we drove the rebels up the steep side of the mountain. By moving a little to the left, I reached the spot where I had seen the rebel fall. On my arrival thither, he arose to a sitting posture.... I inquired whether he was wounded, and he...nodded assent. The blood was flowing from a wound in the neck. He also pointed to a wound in the arm. The same bullet had made both wounds; for at the time I fired, he was in the act of ramming a bullet home— his arm extended vertically. He arose to his feet.... I informed him that...he was a prisoner; and I sent him to the rear....[11]

Hill was not the only Fayette County soldier to capture a rebel on South Mountain: "[Joseph Sturgis] captured a prisoner, who proved to be a major [*sic*] of a South Carolina regiment, and a son of the governor of that state. Joe, after

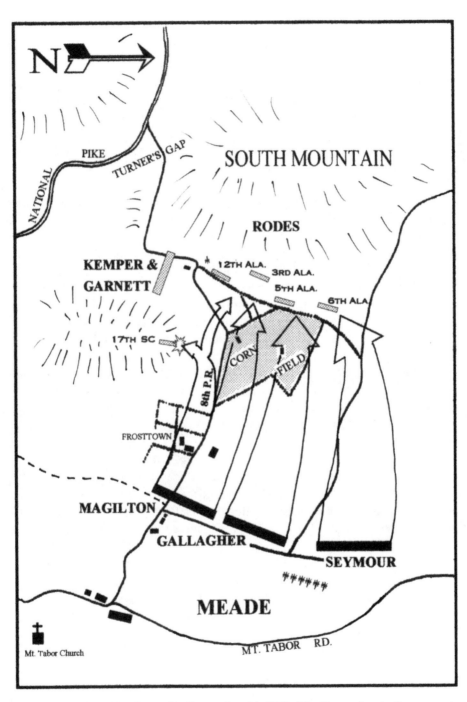

The Battle of South Mountain, September 14, 1862. The Pennsylvania Reserves attack the Confederate left flank at Turner's Gap.

receiving the glove of the rebel major as a pledge that he and his companion would remain where they were, started in pursuit of the fleeing enemy. He had only gone a short distance, however, when the major's companion treacherously fired upon him, but missed. The rebel then started on a wild run down the mountain and David Richie, who came up at this time, took a shot at him, supposedly wounding him in the arm; the rebel, however, made his escape. On Joe's return the major [*sic*] denounced the act of his companion and said he had fired without his sanction or knowledge."[12]

Joe Sturgis's prisoner proved to be Lieutenant Colonel R. Stark Means, the son of South Carolina governor John H. Means. Governor Means had organized the 17th South Carolina and served as its colonel until he was shot at the Battle of Second Bull Run. Lieutenant Colonel F. W. McMaster took over the regiment September 1 when the mortally wounded governor died and recounted the fatal wounding of the governor's son at the Battle of South Mountain: "September 14, about 4 o'clock...the brigade took position on the slope of a mountain on the east side of the turnpike. Soon after we had halted, the enemy advanced upon us in overwhelming numbers. After fighting for about an hour, and after the other regiments of the brigade had broken and retired, and we were about being flanked by the enemy, I ordered my regiment to retire, firing. After we began the retreat, we were so unfortunate as to lose our gallant lieutenant-colonel (R. S. Means), who was shot through the thigh. I detailed four men to bear him off, but he magnanimously refused to allow them to make the effort, as the enemy was in a short distance of him and still advancing."[13]

Like Means, many of the prisoners taken by the 8th Regiment were wounded. Franklin Holsinger of Company F recalled coming to the aid of one Southern soldier he encountered: "I took the blanket from my knapsack and wrapped it about a poor rebel lad who had his ankle broken by a minie, and who was suffering terribly from the cold upon the mountain. I suffered considerably myself from the loss of my blanket, yet I had no regrets when I remembered the thanks of the poor, misguided boy so badly injured."[14]

Meanwhile, the outnumbered Confederates fought on valiantly, contesting every foot of ground given up. On the Union side, the ground gained by Hill and the Brownsville Grays came at a bitter cost: "Our boys had just reached me, when Dave Malone was struck in the head by a bullet, and he fell back, quivering and gasping for breath. He soon expired. After the battle he was buried in that wild, lonely mountain—where he fell."[15]

Meade's Pennsylvanians finally took the high ground north of Turner's Gap late in the day. At the same time, elements of the Federal IX Corps were pushing toward Turner's Gap, having fought their way northward from Fox's Gap to the south. Nightfall put an end to the fighting, however, before the two Federal forces could coordinate a final assault on the gap.

The 8th Regiment lost 50 men on South Mountain: 15 killed, 34 wounded, and 1 missing. George Darby reflected on his company's part in the day's work and on the grim sights that greeted him and his comrades as they overran the rebel defenses: "The enemy's dead...were mostly killed by shots through the head, as they were behind rocks and stone fences and could not be seen until they raised up to shoot. Our loss was very small as the rebels in shooting down the mountain fired high and the most of their missiles passed harmlessly overhead. One of the saddest incidents it was my lot to observe...was that of a strapping Confederate soldier who had taken refuge from the storm of battle with ten or twelve others, behind a rock, all of whom had been killed but this one, and he had lost both eyes, and was being led off by two of my comrades...and what seemed remarkable was that all those that had occupied the shelter of the rock had been killed by bullets through the head."[16]

One such rebel was found by a Maryland farmer who visited South Mountain after the battle ended: "[T]he morning after the battle...my father found the body of a fair-haired, beardless boy about eighteen years old. A minie ball had struck him in the center of his forehead. In the breast pocket of his coat there was a letter from his sister in Georgia, in which she urged him to 'hurry up and whip the Yankees and come home.' That poor girl, I presume, never knew just how her brother met his death."[17]

When the fighting died down after dark, the Confederates barely held on to Turner's Gap—a position they would abandon before the next day's dawn. Union forces managed to take Crampton's Gap late in the day, but halted there rather than pursuing the rebels further. The fight on South Mountain was perceived initially as a great success for Union arms. Indeed, General McClellan telegraphed Washington: "It has been a glorious victory."[18] At a cost of 2,300 casualties, however, Robert E. Lee had achieved the one critical objective for which he fought—time.

The Army of the Potomac, flush with what seemed to them to be a clear-cut victory over Lee's Army of Northern Virginia, continued their advance the next morning: "It was ten o'clock when [the Pennsylvania Reserves] moved. As we descended the western slope of South Mountain, a wide valley of many square miles lay extended to our view. Here and there a village could be seen—Boonsboro among the rest. The sound of artillery could be heard, and bright flashes and puffs of white smoke were seen beyond Boonsboro. The advance of the column had already come up with the rebels, and were now feeling for them with shell; though it scarcely seemed like *feeling for them*, after all."[19]

George McClellan and his lieutenants assumed that Lee was retreating toward the fords over the Potomac in an effort to reach Virginia and put the river between a battered Southern army and their pursuers. By the afternoon of September 15, however, it became apparent that Lee had halted his troops on the northern side of the Potomac, near the village of Sharpsburg. Indeed, Federal scouts saw rebel forces arrayed in line of battle on the far side of Antietam Creek. After a brief reconnaissance, McClellan, cautious as ever, concluded that it was too late in the day to commence an attack. He believed he had good reason to proceed cautiously. Harpers Ferry had fallen to the rebels early that morning, and he reasoned that Stonewall Jackson and the six Confederate divisions that had been engaged there might well be marching for Sharpsburg at that very moment. In point of fact, at that very moment, Lee was engaging in a daring bluff. Well aware of his opponent's cautious nature, the Southern commander had deployed the scarcely 18,000 men then available to him to face down an advancing Federal army nearly four times as large. While Jackson was indeed marching toward Sharpsburg, the vanguard of his exhausted troops would not reach Lee until midday on September 16. McClellan had squandered another priceless opportunity to destroy the Army of Northern Virginia before it could concentrate.

Even nature appeared to be conspiring against the Union commander as a thick ground fog settled over the woods and hollows around Sharpsburg the follow-ing morning, shielding the rebels' positions: "Next morning [September 16] a dense fog hung over us and obscured everything from view. It was obvious that nothing would be done till the fog should disappear. The white veil hung heavily over us till near noon; then it began to move away. Still it was cloudy, and rain was even expected. The artillery fighting was resumed, and continued till near three o'clock. Then we began to move. We marched out the road, crossed Antietam Creek, marched three-quarters of a mile, and halted for half an hour. All was still. That silence more dreadful than the battle of which it is ominous now reigned."[20]

The dreadful silence that Sergeant Hill remarked upon was soon rent by the roar of cannon fire. A sharp artillery duel erupted on the left of the rebel line as Lee sought to beat back the I Corps' advance. Bates Alexander, a sergeant with the 7th Pennsylvania Reserves, recalled the scene vividly in an article he wrote for his hometown newspaper, the *Hummelstown Sun*:

> A powerful Confederate battery opened...somewhere beyond and to the right of the Dunker church.... We replied with a battery of small iron cannon...but they were too light for the enemy's guns, though our gunners did their ablest. During the cannonade an artillery sergeant's head was cut off by a missile from the enemy. They were slamming into our fellows wildly, when Gen. Meade came riding from the right, through the iron storm, holding his hat on as though in a heavy rain storm, and called..."For God's sake take that battery out of there...." We lay flat on our faces and wished the short grass out of the way that we might get closer to the ground. Some of the cannon shot seemed to fly but two feet above and this together with the fragments of shells crashing, howling and whirl-ing through the timber caused one to wonder if we would ever get out of there alive.[21]

The fighting tailed off at nightfall, and the soldiers from both armies slept fitfully, dreading what was to come with the morning sun. One soldier recalled that "'time flew with slow wings' that night; 'conjuring up the hosts who are to blaze [away] at you...is not pleasant.'"[22]

Dawn came early to the Maryland countryside the morning of September 17, and the Pennsylvania Reserves were up and ready for action before six o'clock: "I knew that we were going into battle," Sergeant Hill noted. "[T]hat it would prove to be a desperate one, I had no doubt. I felt that Lee was about to make a last desperate effort to maintain the foothold he had gained on the Maryland shore; and as McClellan was equally determined to dislodge him, the conflict promised to be a terrible one. I examined my cartridge-box, and found it all right; it contained forty rounds. I examined my cap-box, and found *it* all right; it contained about half a pint of caps. Then I thought of the thirst under which a man labors in battle, and I looked to my canteen; to my chagrin, I found it *empty*."[23] One of Hill's comrades gave him some water, and the two men waited, along with the rest of their company in the North Woods. Some six hundred yards to the south lay a 30-acre cornfield owned by a farmer named Miller. Three hours later, it would resemble a charnel house and would be referred to ever after simply as "the Cornfield."

The battle began just after daybreak when General Hooker ordered Doubleday's and Ricketts's divisions forward. Doubleday's brigades advanced southward along the Hagerstown Pike, while Ricketts's men headed for the Miller cornfield and the East Woods where Seymour's brigade of Pennsylvania Reserves had passed a sleepless night. Lawton's and Jones's divisions of Jackson's corps opposed them. The fighting raged back and forth as both sides fed more men into the struggle. About seven o'clock, Hooker ordered General Meade's remaining two brigades—Anderson's and Magilton's—into action to counter Brigadier General John Bell Hood's division then advancing toward the Miller cornfield. Albert Magilton's second brigade, consisting of the 3rd, 4th, 7th, and 8th Regiments, moved forward to support Seymour's brigade. It had come under heavy fire in the East Woods. "As we neared the grove—it was at the far corner of the [corn]field—a regiment of rebels, who had lain concealed among the tall corn, arose and poured upon us the most withering volley we had ever felt," Hill recalled. "Another and another followed, and a continuous rattle rent the air. We could not stop to reply—we could but hurry on. The slaughter was fearful; I never saw men fall so fast; I was obliged to step over them at every step. I saw Lieutenant Moth fall senseless to the ground—stunned by a spent ball. Poor Page fell dead; John Woodward, too, fell to the earth—a bullet buried in his brain. Putty Stewart, Jim Hasson, John Swearer, Dave Cease, Juggie, and a number of others fell wounded."[24]

Franklin Holsinger was caught in the middle of this maelstrom and recalled what happened to him in an article published after the war. Given the devastating

nature of the attack, he may be forgiven for mistaking the identity of the Southerners involved: "[W] hen surprised by the Sixth Georgia Regiment [*sic*: actually the
6th North Carolina] lying immediately behind the fence at the celebrated cornfield,[25] allowing our regiment to approach within thirty feet, and then pouring a
volley that decimated our ranks fully one-half, the regiment was demoralized. I was
worse—I was stampeded. I did not expect to stop this side of the Pennsylvania line.
I met a tall, thin, young soldier, very boyish in manner, but cool as a cucumber, his
hat off, which he was lustily swinging, who yelled: 'Rally, boys, rally! Die like
men; don't run like dogs!'"[26]

The 8th Regiment, although badly shot up, held its ground. The men served as
an inspiration to their comrades in the other regiments and earned a well-deserved
accolade from Colonel Magilton, their brigade commander, in his report of the
action: "[T] he Second Brigade...was ordered to the front and deployed, then moved
by the left flank, under a dreadful fire which caused the center and right of the
brigade to give way; but rallying immedi-
ately, afterward advanced to the front, and
drove the enemy after an obstinate resistance.... I have to speak particularly of the
gallant conduct of Major Baily and his regiment (the Eighth).[27] It was this regiment that
stood its grounds manfully, and served as the
rally point for the rest of the brigade that at
one time had broken."[28]

The carnage in the cornfield was such
that Hill, the Brownsville Grays' third sergeant, soon became the company's ranking
officer on the field. He quickly realized, however, that his men "did not stand in need of
much commanding just then. They were doing very well—selecting their own positions,
and firing at any rebels who presented the
most tempting mark."[29] Hill moved his men
into a position from which they could open a
flanking fire on the Confederate line and
"observed, not thirty yards from me, two
stout rebels assisting a wounded comrade
from the field.... I could have killed one of
them; their backs were presented toward me
very temptingly.... I hesitated. Could I shoot
one of the men who were bearing him away

**Colonel Silas M. Baily was wounded
at the Battle of Gaines's Mill and again
at Fredericksburg. He recovered from
his Gaines's Mill wound in time to lead
the 8th Reserves at South Mountain
and Antietam. In May 1865 he was
brevetted brigadier general of volunteers.**

Library of Congress

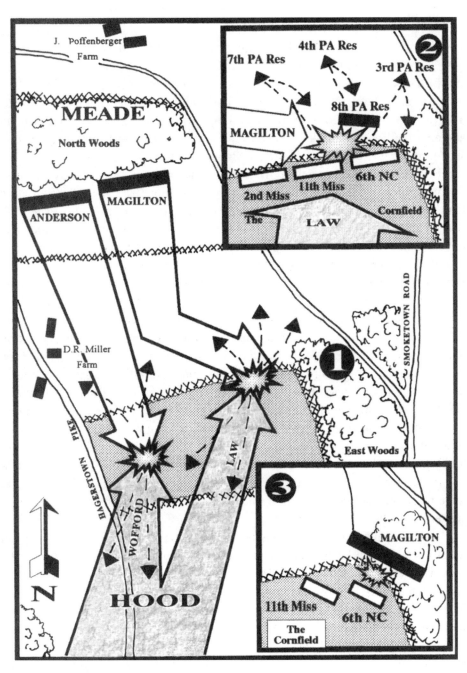

The Battle of Antietam, September 17, 1862. The Pennsylvania Reserves engage Hood's division in the Cornfield.

and allow him again to fall to the earth? I could not. I sought another mark; and seeing a rebel in the act of loading his gun just at the edge of the corn-field I fired at him."[30] Incredibly, in the person of Ashbel Hill, a spark of humanity still flickered amidst the death and destruction being wrought in farmer Miller's cornfield.

Moments later, the new company commander switched his attention, and his aim, to a Confederate color bearer who was waving a battle flag vigorously in an attempt to rally his comrades: "I had fired a dozen rounds at the rebel flag, when I suddenly became conscious of a most singular and unpleasant feeling in my left leg. I was in the act of ramming down a ball at the time, and I would have finished, but my left foot, of its own accord, raised from the ground, a benumbing sensation ran through my leg, and I felt the hot blood streaming down my thigh. The truth flashed upon me—*I was wounded.* I could not yet tell where the ball had struck me, but on looking down I perceived, by a small round hole in my pantaloons, that I was shot in the thigh about three inches below the hip joint. It was plain that the bone was broken; the contracting of the muscles had shortened the limb, and raised the foot from the ground."[31]

The North Carolinians who shot down Sergeant Hill were in a foul mood even before they ran into the Pennsylvanians. General Hood ordered them into action while they were in the midst of cooking their breakfasts in the woods behind the Dunker Church. The hungry rebels of Law's and Wofford's brigades launched a devastating counterattack that shattered the Union troops then in the Cornfield. George Darby witnessed the attack and recalled its ferocity: "The fire at this point was so terrific that every thing was swept before it, except, here and there, a panel of fence. Here I saw a very strange sight. Some Union soldier in his excitement in loading his rifle had neglected to withdraw his ramrod, and in its flight it had struck and passed through the head of a rebel soldier and pinioned him to the fence, and there he stood stark dead."[32] Hood's angry veterans charged on through the corn, scattering the Federals before them.

As the Southerners reached the north end of the cornfield, however, they ran into Anderson's third brigade posted behind a fence with their rifles resting on the rails. The Pennsylvanians shot the 1st Texas to pieces, gunning down no fewer than eight color bearers: "Among the Confederate troops...in the corn field was the Eighth [*sic*: actually the 1st] Texas.[33] This regiment had a large silk battle flag bearing the lone star, and I noticed that although there was a most destructive fire...directed against it, it still continued to wave, but...the Yankee fire had become so fierce...that no man could live in it, and the color bearer had driven the staff into the ground.... The staff was literally riddled by bullets, but the flag continued to wave. At length one of the boys...charged alone across the open space into the corn field, seized the lone star flag and bore it safely back in triumph to his company."[34]

As the battle raged around them, two of Sergeant Hill's comrades helped to carry him to safety:

Supporting my whole weight between them, [Charley Brawley and Will Hoffman] moved slowly toward the rear. My left leg hung powerless, my foot dragged on the ground, and I felt the shattered pieces of bone grinding together. The pain thus caused was so acute that I grew deathly sick, everything faded from my sight, and sense left me....

Just in rear of [a strip of woods] stood a number of ambulances ready to convey wounded men from the field. I was placed in one—*a one horse one*—another sufferer was placed beside me, and the jumping, jostling...vehicle moved off.

The ambulance now began to go over the ridges of [a] corn-field, and it made such a succession of starts and knocked me about so alarmingly, that I really wondered that the wounded limb stayed on at all. My companion groaned in agony. At last the vehicle came to a stand-still, and we were lifted out and laid down in front of a barn. Many wounded were lying in and around the barn. Someone very near me uttered a deep, agonizing...groan; and turning my head in the direction, I beheld Juggie lying prostrate upon the ground—pale as death, and his clothes sprinkled here and there with blood.[35]

Troops engaged in ambulance drill. It was in a wagon such as this that Ashbel Hill was taken from the battlefield at Antietam to the field hospital where his left leg was amputated.

As Hill made his way to a Union field hospital, the fighting in the Cornfield finally began to die down. In little more than two hours, Joseph Hooker's I Corps had sustained some 2,600 casualties, nearly a third of those engaged. The toll was even worse on the Confederate side, with total casualties of nearly 3,000. When General Hood was asked where his division was, he replied: "Dead on the field."[36]

During the fierce fighting along the northern border of the Cornfield, the Pennsylvania Reserves alone lost 573 men killed, wounded, and missing. In Major Baily's "gallant" 8th Regiment, 12 men were killed, and 44 were wounded. Among those Pennsylvanians who fell was Leo Faller of the 7th Regiment. In August, he'd been spared by "providence" near a stream in Virginia; in September he was deserted by it near a cornfield in Maryland.

Around ten o'clock in the morning, the exhausted survivors of the Pennsylvania Reserves were sent to the rear, where they ate their first meal in 22 hours, refilled their cartridge boxes, and searched for their missing comrades. The battle would rage throughout the remainder of the day—one that would gain grim renown as the single bloodiest day in American military history. By nightfall, the combined casualties on both sides would total nearly 23,000, and "Bloody Lane" and "Burnside's Bridge" would join "The Cornfield" in the sorrowful lexicon of the Civil War.

Tragically, the enormous loss of life occasioned by the meeting of the armies at Sharpsburg did not produce a clear-cut result—neither side could claim to have achieved a decisive victory. While McClellan, at least, had forced his adversary to withdraw across the Potomac into the friendlier confines of Virginia's Shenandoah Valley, he failed in his stated purpose of destroying "Bobby Lee's" army. Lee, though greatly outnumbered and with his enemy privy to his plans, nonetheless fought superbly from a tactical perspective, inflicting a greater number of casualties on his enemy than he had sustained himself, and preserving his army to fight another day. But he had failed as well. He was unable to realize any of his strategic goals: Maryland remained firmly committed to the Union; and the opportunity to achieve the crushing victory he sought on Northern soil was lost just as surely as was Special Orders No. 191. The war would go on.

After the battle ended, Private Cordello Collins of the Bucktails returned to the cornfield where he had fought in the morning. He described the battle's appalling detritus in a letter to his parents: "Oh Dear parents...day before yesterday we came across a part of the battle field where the dead laid so thick a man could step from one to a nother without eny trouble at all. Some places they laid a cross each other and they was swelled so they looked more like some kind of wild brutes than men and black as nigars. Oh how horable it did look. Some shot in the head in the body. Some both lages of lost up and some mangel in the most horabel maner that can be thought. They was mostly secesh."[37]

Private Darby also returned to the battlefield. He was stunned by the extent of the violence visited upon D. R. Miller's farmstead:

> Just back of the cornfield everything was in evidence of the destructiveness of our fire. I observed a rebel cannon which had been struck by a shot from one of our guns which had carried away its muzzle, while wrecked caissons, dead men and horses were heaped in wild confusion over the blood-stained ground. In passing a nearby house, I noticed a dog in the yard. He was in a kneeling position, as if smelling at a rat-hole, but upon closer examination he was found to be stone dead, having been struck by a stray bullet. A visit to the farm yard revealed that the farm stock, horses, cattle and hogs, had all shared the fate of the dog, and it was indeed pathetic to see their wide staring eyes, as though they had died in amazement at the horrid confusion about them. I noticed one horse in particular with its head turned; with its wide eyes fixed upon its flank, where it had received the fatal wound, as if it would inquire the cause of the suffering.
>
> On entering the barn, the floors and mows were full of dead men. The grim reaper Death had gathered his human sheaves and garnered them where once had been stored the golden grain. The stable of the barn was in the basement. There, too, stalls and mangers were filled to repletion with the bodies of men who but a few brief hours before were filled with life and its varied ambitions.[38]

The scene was no less heartbreaking behind the Federal lines where the wounded Sergeant Hill found himself. He had been transported to a small school-house that had been taken over by Union surgeons and put to use as a field hospital: "Within this little building, the work of amputation was going on. It was a kind of field hospital. The surgeon-in-charge came out after half an hour, and I asked him what he thought of my wound. He examined it, and very coolly and indifferently said: 'I'll have to take that leg off for you after a while, but I haven't time just now—there are so many cases on hand.... It was near evening when my turn came. I had lain during the whole afternoon without the school-house, listening to the horrible screams which came from within, and occasionally, to kill time, gazing upon a heap of men's arms and legs which lay piled up against the side of the house."[39] Hill's left leg was added to the pile later that same night. He would spend the next 13 weeks in a crude field hospital not far from the battlefield recovering from the ordeal. He was discharged on disability December 20, 1862, and made his way home to Fayette County where he began to write his memoir, ultimately published as *Our Boys*.

Union surgeons weren't the only ones treating their comrades who had been wounded during the day's fighting. A number of Confederate doctors were working equally diligently to treat the hundreds of Southern soldiers left on the field. Darby recounted the details of one amputation he witnessed and the effect that it had upon a civilian bystander:

After the Battle of Antietam our command went into camp in an orchard near a brick house which stood on an elevation, and just below it, in the valley, gushed one of the largest flowing springs it was ever my good fortune to see. As Gaskell was pitching his tent in the orchard, in making the necessary excavation, he unearthed an arm, and grasping the hand as he might that of a living comrade, exclaimed, "Hello, old fellow, how do you do, how is it down there anyhow?" and then calmly proceeded with his work. A short distance below the spring were some buildings which the rebels were occupying as hospitals.[40] Out in the open air was an operating table where amputating was being performed. Arms and legs by the cart load had been dissevered, some of which had been buried, and it was one of those which Gaskell had disturbed while engaged in pitching his tent.

There were large numbers of sightseers and relic hunters visiting the battle field at this time, and some gruesome sights they saw, I can assure you. As I was going to the spring for water on one occasion, the surgeon was preparing to amputate a leg, and as I halted to observe the operation, a civilian who had come to see the sights, was also standing near, and as the rebel surgeon with his sleeves rolled up, like a butcher in the shambles, displayed his shining scalpel, and with one sweeping stroke, severed the muscles to the bone, around the entire circumference of the limb. At this sight down went the civilian in a dead faint; he revived, but with an expression of horror upon his face which I shall never forget, exclaimed, "My God, this is terrible...."[41]

There were other terrible sights to be seen in the days following the battle. One that proved particularly tragic involved a young relic hunter, one of the many who poured over the battlefield in the days following the fighting. George Darby was the witness on this occasion also: "One day a young man with his family, consisting of his wife and one child, a bright little girl, drove onto the field, which was thickly strewn with the debris of battle, and wishing to carry off some memento of his visit to the scene of the recent carnage, he gathered up two or three unexploded conical shells, not dreaming that there was danger lurking there, placed them in his wagon and drove away. But, alas! [He] had not gone far when the jostling of the vehicle over the rough ground brought the shells into contact, and a fearful explosion followed, which resulted in the death of the three persons, and the annihilation of the team and wagon."[42]

In the days following the battle, Robert E. Lee's battered army withdrew into the Shenandoah Valley. Despite the carnage at Sharpsburg, however, morale among the Southern veterans remained high, as evidenced by the following exchange pertaining to the loss by the 1st Texas of its flag during the fighting in the Cornfield: "[A] long, lean private of the Sixth North Carolina...administered a retort...to a

Colonel Silas M. Baily, *seated, right center,* **and the officers of the 8th Pennsylvania Reserves.**

Ronn Palm's Museum of Civil War Images, Gettysburg, Pa., Private Collection

would be wag of the First Texas. The regiments were passing each other, two or three days after the battle, and the representative of the Lone Star State, with more wit than discretion, sang out to the Sixth: 'Halloa, Fellers! Have you got a good supply of tar on your heels this morning?' "Yes," answered the long, lean man pleasantly, but too pointedly to be misunderstood; 'and it's a real pity you'uns didn't come over and borrow a little the other day; it mout have saved that flag o' you'n."[43]

McClellan's Army of the Potomac went into camp near Sharpsburg. There, the soldiers who had survived the holocaust of September 17 rested, regrouped, and did what soldiers have done since time immemorial—they wrote letters to friends and loved ones at home. One soldier noted in a letter to a friend that "[t]he boys think that Governor Curtin will try and have the Reserves taken back to Pennsylvania to recruit, and there is much speculation in camp over the rumor. Well I do think we have seen harder service than any other division in the army and if the exigencies of the service will permit, we ought to get a little rest."[44] Young John Strathern seconded that assessment in a letter to his father:

Headquarters, 8th Regt. P.R.V.C.
Near Sharpsburg, Md.
September 21st 1862

Dear Father,

Yours of the 9th instant was received yesterday....

There has been a very severe Battle here. The Reserve suffered badly in the fight. Thomas James was killed and Henry Struble. John James is wounded and Andrew Baker of our Company, that you know.

As far as I can see, the Government has determined not to interfere with slavery in any of the loyal states, but I see that they are not at all disposed to use the Army as slave catcher. Lincoln['s] motto appears to be, "Save the Union. If slavery aids the rebellion it will have to go by the board, but the Union must be preserved."

I am glad to hear that James [one of John's brothers] has not enlisted. For my part, I would not advise him to come. I do not think he could stand it. We have had some hard times and hard marches, but we have this consolation, that Jeff's men are something smaller since he crossed the Potomac. The spot where the Pennsylvania Reserve...met the Rebels can be plainly seen. The Rebels lie dead, just as they were formed in line of battle. That Brigade was totally annihilated. I passed over the field, and from all that I can see, there are three dead Rebels to one Union man. This is no exaggeration. I assure you they did the wounding, and we the killing. The carnage was fearful. May such work soon cease....

I am glad to hear that the work of the Lord is prospering in Braddock's Fields. Give my best respects to all...inquiring friends.

Your son,
John Strathern[45]

On October 2, President Lincoln arrived from Washington to inspect the army and consult with its commanding general. He stayed with the army for four days, reviewing troops, inspecting the battlefields, and visiting wounded soldiers. Private Strathern was in line when the president reviewed the troops:

On Thursday, we were reviewed by the President and General McClellan. Our Regiment was so small that [he] inquired if, "that was a full Regiment?" General Meade replied that that was all that was left of a thousand men. Abe paid particular attention to our colors. They are fearfully torn; a shell having passed through them, and a host of rifle bullets. The Rebels were badly beat in these battles....

I am glad to see that the President has concluded to emancipate the slaves. This is what I call getting at the root of the matter. It is power that [the Rebels] are fighting for, and this is what has given them power in times past. It is slave labor that feeds their Army. He tills the soil while his master is fighting for Jeff [Davis] and his impr[isonment].

I wonder to see some men so very a[fraid] of meddling [with] the time hallowed institution. Some men calling themselves "loyal" would rather see the Union go to wreck, than that this blackest of stains should be wiped from our national character. Such men's loyalty is exceedingly doubtful, I think, and if they dared to speak their sentiments, these sympathies are with the South.[46]

While the war would drag on for another two and a half years, the Battle of Antietam nonetheless constituted a true turning point in one critical sense—one that young John Strathern touched on in his letter to his father: Robert E. Lee's failure to achieve the major victory he sought on Northern soil emboldened Abraham Lincoln to proclaim officially his position on the abolition of slavery. Henceforth, the North would fight not only to preserve the Union, but also to emancipate the slaves. The issuance of a preliminary Emancipation Proclamation on September 22, 1862, stilled for all time those voices in London and Paris that had been calling for intervention on the side of the South. Lincoln's observation the preceding January had proved prescient: "I cannot imagine that any European power would dare to recognize and aid the Southern Confederacy...if it became clear that the Confederacy stands for slavery and the Union for freedom."[47]

Robert E. Lee understood that reasoning as well as anyone. Early in the war he had concluded that "[w]e must make up our minds to fight our battles ourselves."[48] He had fought his last battle against George B. McClellan, however. On November 7, 1862, President Lincoln, unwilling to abide McClellan's caution and inactivity any longer, relieved "the Young Napoleon." In his place, Lincoln appointed Major General Ambrose E. Burnside to command the Army of the Potomac. Burnside had not sought the appointment; nor did he believe himself qualified for it. This forthright assessment of his own limitations would be proved tragically accurate little more than one month later at Fredericksburg, Virginia, on the cold, bitter slopes of Marye's Heights.

"We Passed Through a Terrible Fight"

The Battle of Fredericksburg

After lingering near Sharpsburg for more than a month following the Battle of Antietam, George McClellan finally stirred, beginning a half-hearted pursuit of the Army of Northern Virginia in late October. Jacob Heffelfinger welcomed the movement. He was determined to bring the "traitors" to heel. Crossing the Potomac with his 7th Regiment on October 30, he wrote: "Once more we will try Virginia soil. May we never come back until every traitor is whipped."[1]

McClellan's effort, as welcome as it may have been to the men in the ranks, came too late to appease Abraham Lincoln. The president relieved him early in November, entrusting the Army of the Potomac to his senior subordinate, Major General Ambrose Burnside. Lincoln's action did not sit well with the army. Sergeant Heffelfinger's letter to his sister reflected the common soldiers' esteem for McClellan:

> Camp of the 7th Reg. P.R.C.
> Brooks Station, Stafford Co., Va.
> Nov. 24th 1862

Dear Sister Jennie:

Yours of the 18th inst. came to hand last evening. I received Father's letter on the 13th inst. And the "handy jack"[2] arrived the day following. Its utility has already been proven [with] the replacing of some lost buttons. Accept my thanks....

On the 10th inst. We received the parting address of, and were reviewed by, Maj. Gen. McClellan. The address was received by the men in what appeared to be an ominous silence, which seemed to say, "If he has not been successful, who can do better?" When the General made his appearance the enthusiasm was unequalled by any thing I have ever seen in the army. There were no military formalities, but cheer after cheer went up from each regiment, not cheers ordered for the occasion, but cheers which made you feel that there was soul in them. The air was black with hundreds of caps, which men tore off, and threw high in the air, so great was the excitement. Twice since I have been in the service I have shed tears; once, on the evening of the battle of Gaines Mill, and next, at this review.... To see the enthusiasm of men composing the old regiments, whose numbers sadly thinned by battle and disease, told too plainly how faithfully they had done their duty, to witness at what pride they had dropped their soiled and bullet ridden flags, flinging their folds into the very face of their loved general, to notice the deep emotion so plainly traceable in his manly countenance, and then to think that he was about to leave us, touched a chord too tender, and the tears came.... McClellan is deeply, sincerely imbedded in the affections of the army, and the army has certainly been faithful to him....

> My love to all at home,
> Your aff. Bro.
> Jac. Heffelfinger[3]

While McClellan undoubtedly had his share of detractors among the rank and file in the army, the vast majority of the common soldiers in the Army of the Potomac would have followed their beloved general through the gates of hell in the autumn of 1862. George McClellan, though, had no intention of leading them there—nor, for that matter, anywhere else that would endanger an "army not now in condition to undertake another campaign nor to bring on another battle...."[4] The Union commander reluctantly ordered a desultory movement across the Potomac River in late October, most likely anticipating a brief, inconclusive campaign, followed by a rapid repair to winter quarters. McClellan's successor, however, did not have the luxury of whiling away the winter preparing and honing plans for a grand spring campaign. Ambrose Burnside was under the gun. Lincoln expected results, and he expected them quickly. Burnside therefore decided to launch yet another assault against Richmond, this time by way of Fredericksburg. He reasoned that a feint against Culpeper would fix Longstreet's corps in place long enough for the Union army to reach Fredericksburg before Lee could get there in force to oppose it. Once in control of the heights behind Fredericksburg, Burnside could advance against Richmond along the line of the Richmond, Fredericksburg & Potomac Railroad. Running from the Confederate capital through Fredericksburg to Aquia Landing on the Potomac, the railroad would serve as the Union army's line of communication.

As Burnside and his generals plotted strategy, the men in the ranks plotted ways to keep warm. It was cold in northern Virginia that November, and the Union soldiers "derived great enjoyment from sitting about our fires...telling stories...singing or card playing by fire light in early evening."[5] Isaac Moore had his share of stories to tell, having returned from recruiting service at the beginning of November. He also had a new stripe on his frock coat, having been promoted to sergeant September 1. Firewood in the quantities required to keep those enjoyable evening campfires burning was hard to come by. Burnside's men solved this problem as soldiers have always done—by "appropriating" the nearest available material suitable for the task at hand. Unfortunately for the hard-pressed farmers in the area, that often meant the fences lining their fields.

Bates Alexander recounted a humorous incident involving the 8th Regiment and the endangered fences of northern Virginia: "When 'twas supposed we would soon halt for the night many [of the soldiers] would seize [fence] rails carrying them sometimes a mile or more. One evening at a halt, the officers of the Eighth Regiment, which marched next to us, were trying to form their men in line...but the sight was something ridiculous, as nearly every man had a fence rail on his shoulder. Finally the Col[onel] gave some command not in the books as every rail was promptly stood on end supported by its man, when the Seventh called, 'Hurrah for the fence rail brigade.'"[6]

By the third week of November, the Pennsylvania Reserves had availed themselves of fence rails as far south as Brooke's Station, some five miles northeast of Fredericksburg—and that wasn't all: "The boys [were] short of meat, and the fields around us...[were] one vast butcher shop. In every direction, squads...[could] be seen killing cows, sheep, and hogs."[7] The Pennsylvanians camped at Brooke's Station for two weeks and during that time the 2nd and 8th Regiments made their headquarters in the home of an ardent secessionist named Schooler. There, the fortunate officers of the two regiments enjoyed a campfire of a much more gracious nature than those they had become accustomed to on their recent march:

> The field and staff [officers] of our regiment and the Eighth, made Mr. S[chooler]'s house [their] headquarters, where, in despite of circumstances, they were soon on most sociable terms with the family. This is a matter most easily accomplished if rightly managed, all that is necessary being to show a due respect to their feelings and sentiments, and to get [on] the right side of the old lady. Before we had been in the house long, some of the officers were busily engaged in assisting in the household affairs, cutting wood, cleaning the clock, white washing the parlor chimney, and chasing the sheep back into the pen. In fact we made ourselves at home and generally useful, and only one incident occurred to mar our pleasure, and that was, at precisely eight o'clock P.M., the old gentleman bid us good night, and with his family retired. This was equally annoying to the young ladies as it was to us, and was a serious evil that required remedying. Many were the plans of operations devised during the ensuing week, but our picket turn came before any was matured. To turn the clock back was a stale trick that probably the old gentleman had had played upon him before, and something new must be devised. But "fortune favors the brave" and luckily the old gentleman was slightly indisposed. Of course he applied to our most estimable surgeon for relief, and then it was that a bright idea entered the doctor's head. After due examination a couple of opium pills were administered, with a

Isaac A. Moore in the uniform of a Union sergeant. He was promoted to that rank September 1, 1862. The photograph was taken while Moore was in Uniontown, Pennsylvania, on recruiting duty in the fall of 1862.

Courtesy Roger Moore

Soldiers of the 44th Massachusetts Militia taking fence rails to use as firewood in Martin County, North Carolina. Similar scenes were enacted by the Pennsylvania Reserves throughout Northern Virginia.

North Carolina Collection, University of North Carolina at Chapel Hill

good glass of old Cognac to rinse them down. About seven o'clock the old gentleman commenced nodding, and soon afterwards showed decided symptoms of drowsiness.... [A]t last with eyes half closed and unable hardly to speak, he retired much to the satisfaction of all.

Mr. S[chooler] had three daughters, the oldest possessing an excellent education and most fascinating manners, she being the lady of the family, and the others were almost her reverse, though all possessed honest and warm hearts. They told us frankly they were secessionists at heart, and that they had two brothers in the Confederate army, but situated as they were, they had no objection to entertaining Union officers whose duty placed them upon their property. They conversed freely about the war, sung "My Maryland," "The Bonny Blue Flag," "Dixie," and other Confederate songs for us. The mother showed us many times the daguerrotype of her darling "Charlie," a boy of sixteen, who belonged to the Forty-Seventh Virginian infantry, whom we promised, if we caught, to spank and send home to her.[8]

The wily Federal officers might have been censured for displaying less than gentlemanly conduct, but the "old gentleman" suffered nothing worse than a restful night's sleep, and a good time was had by all. Of course, the Union army's officer corps did not enjoy a monopoly on mischievous behavior. Indeed, the men in the ranks were masters at employing the *ruse de guerre*. George Darby recounted an amusing episode involving one such enlisted man who, despite his best efforts on the occasion in question, proved less than successful:

Cyrus Eislie was easily the most wily, crafty and successful bummer and forager in Company G, if not in the entire [8th] regiment.... On the outskirts of Fredericksburg, while Eislie was looking around for something to "accumulate," he discovered near a house an old goose setting on a nest of eggs.... Sneaking up he grabbed the goose by the neck and started on a dead run for camp. Just at this time a lusty negro wench made her appearance at the door and seeing Eislie and the goose scooting across the field, stopped long enough to yell, "Massa, Massa. White man done steal de old goose," and then started in a hot chase after Eislie with "Massa" a close second. The wench kept yelling, "Sojer, sojer, fotch back dat goose; fotch back dat goose; dar goes de last goose on de plantation and how's I gwine to hatch dem aigs widout a goose." Owing to the resistance of the goose with its powerful wings to being towed along in this manner, Eislie soon discovered his pursuers were rapidly overtaking him and that the outcries of the wench had been heard by a mounted patrol that also joined in the chase. Eislie was therefore compelled to release the goose and he narrowly escaped capture by jumping a nearby fence and taking to the bushes...."[9]

Such pleasant diversions as entertaining secessionist ladies and chasing secessionist geese soon gave way to the grim realities of war. During the second week of December, the army took up positions directly across the Rappahannock River from Fredericksburg. General Burnside had hoped to cross the Rappahannock and gain the high ground behind the town before Lee could concentrate his forces there. However, the pontoons required to bridge the river arrived late, and Burnside lost the element of surprise, as well as the superiority of numbers that he hoped to enjoy. By the time the pontoons finally arrived, Longstreet's corps occupied the ridge beyond the town, and William Barksdale's Mississippi brigade, reinforced by a Florida regiment, had taken up positions in the buildings along the southern bank of the river. Federal engineers began laying their pontoon bridges before dawn on December 11, but Barksdale's sharpshooters quickly opened fire on them. Throughout the morning, the Confederates repulsed nine separate attempts to span the river. Unable to get his army across the Rappahannock as long as the rebel snipers remained in place, Burnside ordered the buildings along the waterfront shelled. The ensuing two-hour barrage not only wrecked the buildings in which Barksdale's men were hiding, but also devastated much of the town:

> One hundred and forty three guns were brought to bear upon the city, a large portion of which opened fire. The sight was a magnificent one, and towards dark it became grand. The city was on fire in several places, the flames and smoke ascending high into the air, while shells were seen bursting in every quarter. Great care was taken by the cannoneers to avoid injuring the churches, but the other prominent buildings received due attention. An officer rode up to a battery, and, saluting the lieutenant, said: "Lieutenant, do you observe that high building to the right of the white steeple? That is the Shakespeare Hotel, and the proprietor and his ladies are particular friends of mine; do me the favor of sending my compliments to them." A gun was trained upon the building, and soon a shell went crashing through the walls. "Thank you, Lieutenant, for your kindness; you have enabled me to pay a debt of gratitude I have owed them since May last," and off rode the facetious officer.[10]

The ladies of Fredericksburg—indeed all the inhabitants of the doomed town who endured the bombardment—never forgot those terrifying hours. One woman, Jane Beale, recalled the shelling in her diary:

> 'Martha' our chamber maid came in and said..."Miss Jane the Yankees are coming, they have got two pontoons nearly across the river." [B]efore we were half dressed the heavy guns of the enemy began to pour their shot and shell upon our ill-fated town, and we hastily...rushed into our Basement for safety.... I remembered 'Julian' my sick boy and turned back to seek him. I met him with his youngest brother, half dressed...and tried to help him, but I was trembling so violently that I believe I was more indebted to him for assistance than he was to me. [Our] Pastor Mr. Lacy was still with us, and commenced...repeating 'the

27th Psalm' as we all knew it we heartily responded to each verse as the words "Tho an host should encamp against me, my heart shall not fear" were upon our lips, we startled from our seats by the crashing of glass and splintering of timber close beside us.... [P]oor 'Lucy' lay on some straw put down on the damp floor, almost paralyzed with terror, while Helen G. sought refuge close under the wall on the side from whence the shots seemed to come.... [B]rother John told us that the town was on fire in many places, a whole row of buildings on Main St were already burnt, and as my house had a shingled roof I thought we would soon be driven from it by fire also.... [T]he sound of 173 guns echoed in our ears, the shrieking of those shells, like a host of angry fiends rushing through the air, the crashing of the balls through the roof and upper stories of the house, I shall never forget to the day of my death, the agony and terror of the next four hours, is burnt in on my memory as with hot iron, I could not Pray, but only cry for mercy.[11]

Unbelievably, the massive Federal barrage failed to drive the Confederate sharpshooters from the waterfront. Not until several Union units poled across the river in pontoons and engaged the Southerners in house-to-house fighting were they finally driven out. Throughout the night and into the following morning, the rest of Major General Edwin V. Sumner's Right Grand Division soldiers made their way over the hard-won pontoon bridges and occupied the town.

While Sumner's men secured Fredericksburg proper, Major General William B. Franklin's Left Grand Division, made up of William F. "Baldy" Smith's VI Corps and John Reynolds's I Corps, crossed the Rappahannock about three miles below the town. Once across, Franklin and his corps commanders spent the remainder of December 12 preparing for a massive assault against the Confederate right flank, held by Stonewall Jackson. The Federals planned to throw some 40,000 troops against Jackson's position along the heights in front of them. Burnside appeared to approve the plan during an afternoon inspection of Franklin's position. The Union commander believed that Robert E. Lee would have no choice but to reinforce Jackson by drawing troops away from Longstreet on Marye's Heights behind the town and hastening them to the threatened right flank. Burnside would then hurl his remaining forces against Longstreet's weakened position and force the rebels to abandon the Fredericksburg line altogether.

Anxious to get the attack under way, Franklin, Reynolds, and Smith waited at Franklin's headquarters for the order that would unleash two full Union corps against the Confederate position on Prospect Hill. They waited in vain. General Burnside's order did not arrive until 7:30 the following morning. When it finally did reach Franklin, it was not at all what he expected. Rather than employing all of the forces at his command, the Left Grand Division commander was directed to "send out at once a division at least...to seize, if possible, the height near Captain Hamilton's

[Prospect Hill]...taking care to keep it well-supported and its line of retreat open."[12] Franklin, not a gambler in the best of times, felt constrained by the vague and cautious nature of the order and chose to interpret it strictly. He directed Reynolds to select one division from the I Corps to spearhead the now-diminished assault. Reynolds chose his old command, the Pennsylvania Reserves, now under George Meade, and ordered his other two I Corps divisions, under Gibbon and Doubleday, to be prepared to support the Pennsylvanians' effort.

About noon on December 13, following a Federal artillery barrage aimed at silencing the rebel batteries planted on Prospect Hill, Meade's veterans stepped off: "As we passed our batteries between the guns, a good looking young gunner smilingly said...'[B]oys, we have done our duty, now go and do yours.' But he soon found their work not yet ended, for at the sight of our advancing column [the Confederate artillery] blazed away. As we returned no fire from our line while thus advancing, we must imagine the Confederate boys almost dancing with delight at the fun they were having at our cost. This, together with their shot and exploding shell howling by, and our own batteries thundering in our rear, sending their shots over our heads as we advanced...caused us to think of our oft-repeated expression on different fields that 'hell itself had broke loose again.'"[13]

It was apparent that the Southern batteries had survived the Union barrage— and that the rebel gunners had prepared their fields of fire with great care. Henry Flick, a private in the 1st Regiment, described the ground the Pennsylvanians had to cover in order to reach the crest of the hill: "[T]he Confederates had the high ground and could see everything we did; we marched in line of battle. They had driven stakes in the ground and when we came to them their artillery had range on them and opened fire on us. Then we were given orders to lie down."[14] The Union artillerymen quickly brought their guns forward and resumed their bombardment of the rebel batteries. This time they were successful, and Meade's Pennsylvanians launched themselves against the Confederate line once again:

"We were now under way in this ever-to-be-remembered charge, one of our most terrible pieces of work; 'twas even worse than standing in front of the famous corn field at Antietam, as we lost over three times the number [of casualties] here," Bates Alexander recalled. Although the Southern artillery had been silenced, the massed muskets of Stonewall Jackson's corps now opened up on the advancing Federals: "We were now well into the enemy's warm fire on this December day; the men inclined their heads somewhat as though moving against a driving rain. The familiar 'chock,' 'chock' of balls stricking [*sic*] the line was heard constantly to right and left while men tumbled out of line in quick succession...." Alexander himself was struck: "The sharp thud of a spent ball on my front below the belt caused me to quickly look and feel for a hole in [my] overcoat, but no hole this time, though 'twas no false alarm as I felt it thump against me with some force. I

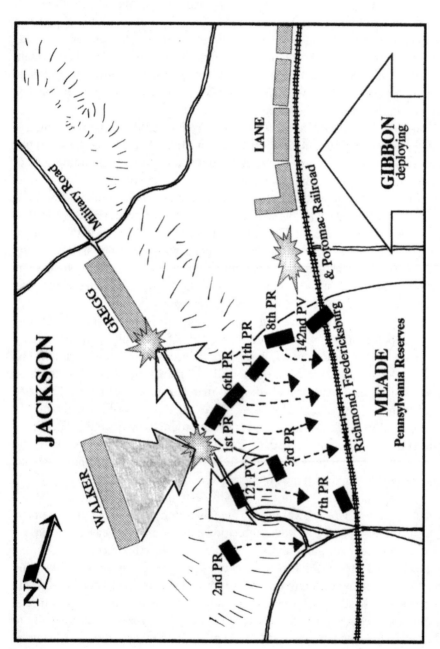

The Battle of Fredericksburg, December 13, 1862. The Pennsylvania Reserves assault Stonewall Jackson's line on Prospect Hill.

had heard of men having been shot through without feeling pain for an instant, and didn't know but that—well I was pleased it ended as it did."[15]

Meade's first brigade led the charge up the hill, crossing a railroad track that ran along its base—the second brigade right on their heels. As the untested 142nd Pennsylvania, recently attached to the second brigade, crossed the track, they were blasted by a volley from Lane's brigade of North Carolinians, concealed off to their right. The rookies broke immediately and ran for cover. "The experienced 8th Reserves stormed past the stunned 142nd Pennsylvania and crossed the railroad tracks farther south. Exposing their right flank to the hidden Confederates, the 8th Regiment staggered under a sudden and tremendous fire.... The veteran Reserves intuitively wheeled around and returned the fire. Lane's Rebel brigade yielded a portion of the railroad to re-fuse its flank and face the 8th Reserves head on."[16] While the 8th Regiment was slugging it out with Lane's Tar Heels on the right flank of Prospect Hill, several of Meade's other hard-charging regiments actually broke through the Confederate front line at the crest, and penetrated deep into their defenses. Bates Alexander remembered seeing a rebel soldier there "who had been firing from...the crotch or fork of a dogwood tree just high enough to allow him to take aim while kneeling. He must have had a glorious time and smiled while 'working his gun' as we advanced. But the poor young soldier had been struck by a ball or small fragment of shell just above the right eye, he lay on his back with legs stiff bent under. It seemed as though a bucket full of blood had run out of his head." As Alexander pressed on he encountered a "tall sandy haired Georgian [lying] on his back gasping. Halting a few seconds I looked down upon his pale face and blue lips. His musket lay by his side.... This was the first sight on the field of battle that touched my heart. From some cause I felt for this dying enemy and was almost sorry that it became a necessity for us to go to war."[17]

Momentarily victorious atop Prospect Hill, the Pennsylvania Reserves could have achieved a signal victory had they been supported properly. Despite a late start, John Gibbon's division did manage to advance on Meade's right as far as the railroad track. Gibbon's men encountered stiff resistance there and became embroiled in a series of charges and countercharges that ended any hope they entertained of effectively supporting Meade's advance. Abner Doubleday's division, harried by rebel artillery posted in woods south of the high ground, had their hands full protecting the Federals' left flank and never did get into the fight for Prospect Hill. General Meade, desperate to maintain his hold on the crest in the face of a fierce Confederate counterattack, pleaded for reinforcements, but no help was forthcoming. Just then, the 1st and 6th Reserves atop the hill were hit hard by Walker's brigade, ordered into the breach by Jubal Early to help stem the Yankee tide.

Meade's outnumbered veterans, many out of ammunition, finally broke and fled back down Prospect Hill, with the resurgent rebels breathing down their necks. In their haste, the Pennsylvanians were forced to leave many of their wounded comrades on the slopes. Jacob Heffelfinger, shot through the legs during the advance, was one of them: "All that we gained at so fearful a cost is lost," he managed to scribble in his diary. "I am still lying where I fell. The rebels have advanced a line over me, so that I am a prisoner.... Death has been doing fearful work to-day."[18]

In his report filed after the battle, General Meade defended his soldiers' conduct: "While I deeply regret the inability of the division, after having successfully penetrated the enemy's line, to remain and hold what had been secured, at the same time I deem their withdrawal a matter of necessity. With one brigade commander killed [Colonel Conrad F. Jackson], another wounded [Colonel William Sinclair], nearly half their number *hors du combat*, with regiments separated from brigades, and companies from regiments, and all the confusion and disaster incidental to the advance of an extended line through woods and other obstructions, assailed by a heavy fire, not only in front but on both flanks, the best troops would be justified in withdrawing without loss of honor."[19]

In testimony before the Committee on the Conduct of the War, Meade was unsparing in his assessment of the impact of General Franklin's failure to support him:

> My division succeeded in driving the enemy from all his advanced works, breaking through his lines, and occupied the heights he had occupied; piercing his lines entirely, and getting into the presence of his reserves. The division on my right [Gibbon's], which I had understood was to have advanced simultaneously with my own, did not advance until I was driven back. It advanced until it came within short range of the enemy, when it halted. The officers could not get the men forward to a charge, and the division was held at bay some twenty or thirty minutes, during which time my division had gone forward. That delay enabled the enemy to concentrate his forces and to attack me in front and on both flanks. I had penetrated so far that I had no support on either flank, and therefore was forced to fall back;... I think if we had been supported by an advance of the whole line, there is every reason to believe we would have held our ground. The effect of this would have been to have produced the evacuation of the other line of the enemy's works in rear of Fredericksburg.[20]

Of course, the other line of the Southern works was not evacuated, and it was against that impregnable line that Burnside tragically hurled division after division in the series of senseless assaults for which the Battle of Fredericksburg is so widely remembered. The disastrous attacks on Marye's Heights cost the Union army more than 9,300 men killed, wounded, and missing. Another 3,309 soldiers became casualties in the struggle for Prospect Hill on Lee's right flank. George Meade's Pennsylvania Reserves suffered the lion's share of these losses, with 175 officers and men killed, 1,241 wounded, and 437 missing, a casualty rate of nearly 50 percent of the division's initial strength on the day of some 3,800 officers and men.[21] Total Confederate losses on the day amounted to fewer than 5,400 men.

In the 8th Regiment, which went into the battle with 18 officers and 325 men, 2 officers and 22 men were killed, 11 officers and 87 men were wounded, and 22 soldiers were reported missing.[22] One 8th Regiment soldier fortunate enough to have survived the fight lamented "[w]e were mowed down like grass upon the field."[23] A measure of the ferocity of the fighting may be gained from the report filed after the battle by Captain George Gallupe, the highest ranking officer left in the regiment: "[O]ur officers and men behaved with great gallantry, driving the enemy across the Rail Road to the top of the hill immediately beyond, but for want of sufficient support we were obliged to give way on account of their overwhelming numbers. Whilst advancing, Major S. M. Baily commanding the regiment was severely injured by the falling of his horse upon him. At this time the command devolved upon Capt. R. E. Johnston who was wounded while fighting the enemy at the Rail Road disabling him, the next-in-command being Capt. Geo. S. Gallupe, he took charge of the regiment, which command he now retains."[24] In addition to Baily and Johnston, Gallupe listed Captains Lemon, Eichelberger, Dawson, Kent, and five lieutenants as having been wounded.

Robert E. Lee offered perhaps the best summary of the extent of the Federal debacle at Fredericksburg in his battle report: "The attack on the 13th [of December] had been so easily repulsed and by so small a part of our army, that it was not supposed the enemy would limit his efforts to an attempt which, in view of the magnitude of his preparations and the extent of his force, seemed to be comparatively insignificant."[25] Lee overestimated the perseverance of his opponent, however: Ambrose Burnside had had enough, and the Army of the Potomac did not renew its attack on December 14. Evan Woodward, the historian of the 3rd Pennsylvania Reserves, recalled how that regiment spent the day:

> During the day there was considerable artillery and infantry skirmishing, and we were several times called into line to meet the enemy. It being Sunday, about two o'clock the excellent and beloved Chaplain of the Third, the beloved Rev. Mr. Pomeroy, determined to hold religious worship. Surrounded by a few friends, with uncovered heads they raised their voices in a sweet hymn as they advanced in front of the line to a clear space. Soon around them was collected a large concourse of attentive listeners. He spoke of the justness and righteousness of the cause we were engaged in, of the duty of all citizens to defend their country, as the child defends its mother, of courage in battle, of mercy to the wounded, of fortitude in suffering, of love and kindness to comrades. But he exhorted them, above all precious gifts and treasures, to seek the blood of Jesus for salvation. When he spoke of our fallen comrades, of the gloom it would cast over the cottage homes of Pennsylvania, he moved all hearts to sadness, and when he

raised his eyes to heaven in humble prayer, heeding not the exploding shells of the foe, we thought what entire confidence that pure man placed in the protection of our God. While thus engaged in worship, the call to arms was sounded.[26]

During the night of December 15, the Army of the Potomac retreated, slipping quietly back across the Rappahannock. The 8th Reserves crossed the river near midnight and headed north toward Belle Plain.

News of the Federal disaster at Fredericksburg reached Uniontown shortly after the battle, but the first detailed information concerning the Fayette Guards did not appear until January 3, 1863, when the *Genius of Liberty* printed a portion of a letter from Lieutenant Jesse Ramsey:

> We have been permitted to make the following extracts from a letter written on the 20th ult. by Lieut. Jesse B. Ramsey, of Co. G, 8th Pennsylvania Regiment, who was in the fight at Fredericksburg: "It was a terrible battle for those engaged, the loss in the [Pennsylvania Reserves] will show about one-third of our number being killed and wounded. The Eighth Regiment went into the fight with 18 officers and 325 men, and lost 13 officers killed and wounded, and 146 men killed, wounded and missing, nearly one-half the men and more than two-thirds of the officers. We not only had to stand the fire of the enemy from the front, but a cross fire both from the right and the left, which told with terrible effect on our lines; this we stood for two hours and a half, driving the enemy from their position on the hill in the woods and completely silencing their battery, and had we been supported as we were to have been we could have held the hill and captured their battery, but our support failed to come up and the enemy being in mass in such overwhelming numbers, both on our right and left, and the ground being such that our batteries could not be moved to a position to bear on the enemies line, we were forced to yield the ground we had gained and fall back under the most galling fire ever experienced by any troops. We fell back from a hill covered with timber and across a level open plain for one fourth of a mile, and the whole body of the enemy fired on us from the hillside as long as their shot could reach us. So you can see that we passed through a terrible fight, the consequences of which should fall heavy on the officers that refused or neglected to come to our support....
>
> Killed—Private Geo. Walker, Connellsville
>
> Wounded—Capt. H. C. Dawson, slightly; Lieut. H. H. McQuilken, badly; Sergt. M. V. B. Hazen, slightly; Sergt. A. Rholand, West Newton, badly; Corp. William Mitchell, West Newton, badly; Private James Ashcraft, in arm.
>
> Missing—Private George Ashcraft; Corp. Henry Lark; do. J. C. Darnell, Morgantown; Private D. F. Darr, West Newton.[27]

The Fayette Guards had passed through a "terrible fight," indeed. Yet again, the Army of the Potomac had been savaged to no good purpose. Ambrose Burnside had proved no better than Irvin McDowell, John Pope, or George McClellan at commanding troops in the field. And what of those troops—the men in the ranks who had survived the slaughter on the slopes of Marye's Heights and the Confederate counterattack on the crest of Prospect Hill? Surely, as those battle-weary veterans trudged northward through the bitter Virginia snow, their thoughts must have turned to winter quarters and a few months' respite from the horror of a seemingly endless war.

"Burnside's Stuck in the Mud"

Winter Quarters and the Mud March

The blessed prospect of winter quarters was very much on Bates Alexander's mind as he crossed the Rappahannock that cold, bitter night of December 15. The 7th Regiment private contrasted the chill of that mournful night with the warmth of his "house" at Belle Plain (where the Pennsylvania Reserves' winter quarters were set up) in an article that he wrote for his hometown newspaper after the war:

> After recrossing the Rappahannock we were halted for a few hours a little distance from the river, in a corn stubble field. Twas now so cold the ground froze under us as we lay upon it. Elias Wike of Cornwall, and another bedfellow of mine, being unable to sleep because of the extreme cold, walked about part of the night, when I rolled in the blankets and slept O.K. Fuel was scarce so we had but little fire. At a small house, near by, about which was some fencing, a plucky little woman came out with a club, calling "git away from this fence you d____d Yankees." A guard was stationed to watch the fence, which 'tis presumed he did...while the fence lasted, but as usual by morning there was a vacancy where the fence once stood, so the little woman had no further use for her club. Soon thereafter we encamped near Belle Plain Landing on the Potomac. Here we built winter quarters. Some messes built log huts, but most of the boys dug a three or four foot cellar, setting the tent over it, then dug fire places at the rear end of the cellars and built stick chimneys over a hole in the ground communicating with the fire place and away from the canvas. Occasionally a tent would be partially destroyed by a fire from the chimney.... The four in our tent...took turns together at going into the forest for hickory saplings for fuel. On cold evenings we have sat in our "house" and sweat. The thieving qualities of the soldiery among themselves never ran very high so that little of our fuel was stolen and this by the Philadelphians. Here we often stood out in the crisp morning air listening to the pretty bugles of the artillery and cavalry calling the troopers to form line for roll call.[1]

Thus did the soldiers of the Pennsylvania Reserves pass the time as Christmas—their second in the field—approached. On Christmas day the troops were mustered to receive an order issued by their commander, General Meade. In bittersweet language, Meade apprised the Reserves of his promotion to command of the V Corps and reflected poignantly upon his time as their commander:

> Headquarters Third Division
> December 25, 1862
>
> *General Order No. 101.*
>
> In announcing the above order, which separates the commanding general from the division, he takes occasion to express to the officers and men that, notwithstanding his just pride at being promoted to a higher command, he experiences a deep feeling of regret at parting from them with whom he has so long associated, and to whose services he here acknowledges his indebtedness for whatever of reputation he may have acquired.
>
> The commanding general will never cease to remember that he belonged to the Reserve Corps; he will watch with eagerness for the deeds of fame which he feels sure they will enact under the command of his successors, and though sadly reduced in numbers from the casualties of battle, yet he knows the Reserves will always be ready and prompt to uphold the honor and glory of their State.
>
> By command of
> Major-General Meade[2]

The soldiers of the Pennsylvania Reserves, who had followed Meade since his days as a brigade commander on the Peninsula during the Seven Days Battles, were sorry to see him go. Private Levi Richards, a teamster who served on General Meade's staff, undoubtedly spoke for many in the division when he wrote to his former commander in January 1863:

> To relieve my mind of things that I wish to make known to you, I will take this opportunity. As I am a Private soilder in the P. R. and as one soilder will express himself more readily than to an Officer I think I can tell you the feeling of this Division towards you. Since the battle for the Peninsula I have never heard but two men that had anything to say against you and one of them was an officer. They all as a Division loved you as a commander. They all appeared glad to hear of your Promotion but parted with you with Regret.... They all told the same tale and that was officers and men were used alike.
>
> And as for myself I consider you have used me as [would] a father...although strict yet no more so than I think it requires to make good soilders and I am satisfied if a man does his duty with you it is all that is required and as I have been with you for almost one year to my knowledge you have never given me a

Major General George Gordon Meade. Prior to assuming command of the Army of the Potomac in June 1863, Meade commanded the Pennsylvania Reserves, most notably at the Battles of South Mountain, Antietam, and Fredericksburg (Prospect Hill).

cross word or misused me in any way it was with great regret that I left you and your staff. This is not written for any benefit that I wish to gain only that I wish you to know the feelings of the Reserves as far as I know and also the feelings of myself towards you.[3]

Two days after General Meade took his leave of the Pennsylvania Reserves, Adam Bright wrote to his uncle regarding the Reserves' misfortune at Fredericksburg:

> Camp near Bell Plain
> December 27th 1862

Dear Uncle

Shortly after I wrote you we received marching orders and as you are aware crossed the river at Fredericksburg but unfortunately after losing about one half our noble old Reserve we had to cross back. Worst was we had to leave our wounded laying on the field and it was freezing cold for several days.

I was in the fight and come out all right, and the rest of your friends are safe. Henry Snively had a wound in his head, but the last I heard of him he was able to join his company....

Had we been supported we could have taken the Hights but our Division is too small now to fight the whole rebel army. When we came out [in the spring of 1861] we had 10,000 men; now we number about 1,700. The Division is now commanded by a Colonel and the Brigades by Lieutenant Colonels.[4] You can see that the Pennsylvania Reserves best days are over. We opened all the battles on the Peninsula and have opened every one since. Before the Battle of Fredericksburg the Generals had a council of war and selected the two best Divisions to open the ball. Our Division opened on the left and was the only one during the whole engagement to take any of their earthworks. Not being supported of course we were unable to hold them.

We have been very busy since we came here putting up winter quarters. We have a tolerable good shanty 16 feet long by 10 wide roofed with gum blankets....

We spent Christmas very poorly. My Christmas dinner was 3 dry crackers and a piece of fat Pork. We have been on about half rations for the last 2 months. A mess of 5 of us have spent ten dollars in that time to buy provision. I never like to complain but our rations have been 10 small crackers and a small piece of Beef or Pork and a little coffee and sugar for a day....

If convenient send me a little butter and a can of applebutter. If you have any apples put me in two or three, for I have not seen an apple for a year. Send me some cand fruit and anything that is good to eat and send me a plug of tobacco and a hundred tobys....

Give my love to Aunt and the children. I remain as ever your affectionate Nephew.

> A.S. Bright[5]

Many of the Reserves were absent from winter quarters the day General Meade's farewell order was read, having been wounded at Fredericksburg or worse. One of them, John Strathern, had been shot on the slopes of Prospect Hill and sent to Alexandria for treatment of his wounds. He wrote to his father from the hospital there one week after the battle:

> Mansion House Hospital
> Alexandria, Virginia
> December 20th 1862

Dear Father

I wrote to you when I expressed the money to you. I was wounded two days after and as we were to be moved to a General Hospital, I thought I would wait until I found out where I was going to be before I wrote.

I received two flesh wounds in the action of the 13th before Fredericksburg, but of which I think will soon be well. They are both in the left leg. It is just one week today since I was wounded. My wounds are doing well.

We were marched up [Prospect Hill] on a concealed foe under an engulfing fire. Our ranks were fearfully thinned by it. We lost just one-half our number.

I must close for present, as I am very tired.

> Your son,
> John Strathern[6]

Jacob Heffelfinger lay in Libby Prison in Richmond, recuperating from his wounds. He kept up his diary there, and his entry for the last day of the year was bleak: "The sun has risen for the last time in the year 1862. I am writing on the last page of my diary. How short, and few, the days appear since I wrote on the first. A year of bloody work for poor bleeding America, and how dark the future yet appears.... God help and save us, is the involuntary expression of our hearts."[7]

God did appear to be looking after John Strathern, as he seemed to be recovering from the wounds he received at Fredericksburg. He took a sudden turn for the worse in early January, however, and died January 8, 1863. It was little consolation to his family that he had been promoted to the rank of corporal some three months earlier following the bloodbath at Antietam. Lyman C. Howard wrote to Strathern's brother, apprising him of the tragic news: "Since morning, your brother has breathed his last. He died very suddenly. There was not one of us that thought his end was so nigh. He was taken only three days ago with the fever. He is no more."[8]

Poor Corporal Strathern, at least, would be spared the agony of what came to be known as the "Burnside stick-in-the-mud." In late January 1863, Ambrose Burnside, attempting to polish a reputation badly tarnished by the disaster at Fredericksburg, sought to regain the initiative against Lee's Army of Northern Virginia. He ordered a rare winter offensive, intending to outflank the Confederates who were still entrenched on the heights behind Fredericksburg. As Burnside

A typical scene in winter quarters. The Pennsylvania Reserves built "cabins" such as these throughout northern Virginia.

Union soldiers relaxing in winter quarters. Note the mud and barrel chimney at the rear of the nearest cabin.

envisioned it, Union forces would recross the Rappahannock some ten miles above the town and attack the left flank of the Southern line, rolling it up and gaining possession of the high ground. From the outset, the forces of nature conspired against the maneuver and ultimately doomed it to ignominious failure. George Darby recalled the failed Union effort in his book, *Incidents and Adventures in Rebeldom*:

> Every soldier who participated in the tiresome, enervating and distressing march known as the "Burnside stick-in-the-mud" will remember its hardship, exposure and suffering until his dying day. From start to finish the windows of heaven were wide open and a cold rain incessantly, day and night, beat upon the heads of the devoted soldiers. The roadway was speedily converted into a quagmire in which the wagons were buried up to their beds and the mules dropped down in their harness and suffocated in the mud. The troops floundered along both sides of the quagmire in mud from ankle to knee deep, their destination being the fords of the Rappahannock, and their design, to flank the rebels out of Fredericksburg. Owing to the severity of the weather the movement was a complete failure. The order was countermanded before the objective point was reached and the troops were returned to their old camps. The rebels were informed of this fiasco and on the picket [line] jeered and taunted our men over this miserable failure.[9]

Bates Alexander also recalled the infamous march in the series of articles he wrote for the *Hummelstown Sun*:

> Major Lyman read the order [to march to the Rappahannock] to the regiment as he sat on his horse and held his tobacco pipe in hand. We filed out to our place in line...as the column moved ahead at common time, on the way to see if General Lee was at Marye's Mansion. Rain began to fall heavily. Some of the more intelligent and thoughtful boys concluded the river would be so high that we should be unable to cross to present ourselves before Jackson's men again. The roads soon became a mass of mud, wide and deep. Once at a temporary halt, [the] Adjutant...read to us the stereotyped order something like the following: "Soldiers You have fought and won on many fields, &c. Now, the Commanding General hopes you will fight as bravely as heretofore, and that victory may perch upon your banners." During the reading he raised an elbow that his gum blanket might shield the paper from the rain. Such a thing as an umbrella was unknown to the service, except occasionally among the Chaplains. We lay in a woods by the roadside near the river, with only green wood for fuel which emitted much smoke and little flame, causing heavy volleys of profanity on all sides.... Finally we returned to camp.... 'Twas a terrible move and known throughout the army as the Burnside stick-in-the-mud.[10]

After slogging back to his company's camp, Adam Bright wrote to his uncle of the army's plight as it attempted to move up the Rappahannock, and of the Confederates' jocular response:

Camp near Bell Plain Virginia
January 27th 1863

Dear Uncle

Well we have had another grand move of the Army of the Potomac, and as you are aware another grand failure. On the morning of the 20th, fully equipped with sixty rounds of cartridges and 4 days rations, we started for the scene of action.

We marched all day.... We crossed hills and hollows and marched through pine woods so thick we could not see a foot before us. But night came on and compelled us to stop and I was not sorry for I was so tired I could scarcely stand. Shortly after we stopped it commenced raining and blowing, but we went to work and built a little fire and made some coffee. After drinking our coffee and eating a few hard tack we selected a prominent place on the ground and lay down for the night.

When I awoke the next morning I discovered to my surprise that I was lying in about half a foot of water and I was as stiff as an old horse and it still continued to rain. But in a few minutes we had taken the line of march again. After marching about three miles through mud up to the (you know where) we halted where we remained for two days and two nights (the rain pouring down all the time) when we were ordered to return to our old camp.

It was impossible for us to keep the road on our way back, for the road was full of wagons and artillery in mud to the axle. Some places mules would be in the mud so deep we could see nothing but their head and ears. Every wagon had from 16 to 20 mules or horses on it and almost every one was stuck fast in the mud.

The rebs on the other side of the river had signboards up with large letters on them. "Burnsides stuck in the mud" was the one I had the pleasure of looking at. But this was not the case for Burnsides was in his good quarters while we were sticking in the mud.

After we returned to camp I was sick for 2 or 3 days. I thought I was taking the fever again, but it wore off and I am almost as well as ever. But another move like the last one would almost induce me to desert, for I don't believe a man was ever born to be made a hog of.

The only good news I have heard for some time is that Burnsides has been relieved of the command. But I don't believe it. It is too good to be true....

But I must close. My love to you all. Write soon.

Add[11]

For Sergeant Isaac Moore of the Fayette Guards the "Mud March" undoubtedly evoked bitter memories of a similar experience that befell him the previous spring. In March 1862, the Pennsylvania Reserves had been ordered from Hunter's Mill,

Virginia, to Alexandria. As the march got under way, "[t]he rain continued to pour down steadily.... The mud became deep, and the marching...laborious; a cold wind was blowing; our clothes became saturated; our shoes were filled with mud.... The rain...increased and was now pouring down in torrents."[12] Moore, already suffering from rheumatism, fared especially poorly on the march, as noted by his messmate, James Eberhart: "I know of [Sergeant Moore] having Rheumatism or what he called it to be on march from Hunters Mills to Alexandria Va. A very hard rainy day and night that he had to bandage up his ankle and foot with a Bandana handkerchief. So the boys made fun of him. And when we reached camp at Alexandria he limped around for several days...."[13]

Jacob Heffelfinger, of course, missed out on Ambrose Burnside's "stick-in-the-mud" altogether, spending the early part of January 1863 in Libby Prison. He was exchanged January 8 and sent to the U.S. General Hospital in Annapolis for further treatment of his wounds. He wrote his sister Jennie shortly after he got there. One can imagine her relief upon learning that her brother was finally safe within the Union lines:

> U. S. General Hospital
> Annapolis, Md. Jan 19th 1863
>
> Dear Sister Jennie:
>
> I received Father's letter...with contents, all safe. I was glad to know that you had received my Richmond letter, but sorry that you had been kept in suspense so long, by its delay. I was pained to know that you all had been given cause for unnecessary distress, by the false rumors of my having been mortally wounded, having died on the field, &c. Anyone who saw me lying where I fell, would no doubt have thought me to be mortally wounded, as I was wholly disabled.... It is my own fault, that I was not taken off the field, as there is always plenty of a certain class of sulkers, who do not like to be seen running away from danger, and are eager to help a wounded man in order that they themselves may get to the rear. The proper way, and the only way to rightly take care of the dead and wounded, is to gain the victory. Thus, by refusing to be carried off by anyone whose duty it was to be in the front, fighting, I was made prisoner, for when our men were driven out of the woods, each one had enough to do to take care of himself, and, although Capt. King, and a number of Co. H passed very near me when leaving the woods, I did not call their attention to me....
>
> I have no reason to complain of the treatment I receive here, but still it is lonely, in short, it is a hospital. No furloughs, is the rule at this hospital.... The general way of getting furloughs here is to have a suit of citizens clothes sent from home. But I don't *sneak* home.... *Is Mother well?* My love to all at hand....
>
> Your aff. bro.
> Jac. Heffelfinger
> You can't write too often. J.H.[14]

As the bitter winter of 1862–63 covered the blood-soaked soil of Virginia with a blanket of white, the Pennsylvania Reserves took stock. John Strathern was dead. So were Andrew Lewis and Leo Faller. Joseph McQuaide was killed August 30 at Bull Run. John Urban had been wounded and taken prisoner at Glendale; Jacob Heffelfinger, at Fredericksburg. John Willoughby was captured there, too. Ashbel Hill, seriously wounded at Antietam, had been discharged on disability, as had Albert Rake. And they weren't alone. Thousands of young men from the farms and towns of the Keystone State had been killed or wounded in the fighting in Virginia and Maryland.

Still, the veterans of the Seven Days Battles, of Antietam and Fredericksburg, marched on. Isaac Moore, though hobbled by long exposure to the elements, still answered "Present" at each muster of the Fayette Guards. So, too, did his friends, George Darby, Thomas Springer, and James Eberhart. But the Pennsylvania Reserve Volunteer Corps would not "open the ball" again, as they had on the Peninsula, at Antietam and at Prospect Hill. A year's service on the front lines had reduced the Reserves to a pale shadow of the proud division that President Lincoln had reviewed at Tennallytown in September of 1861. Where nearly 15,000 hearty recruits had cheered the president on that fine autumn afternoon, fewer than 3,000 gaunt, battle-weary veterans were mustered to bid farewell to General Meade 16 months later. It was time to rest and recruit.

"Who Stole Baer's Duck?"

Guarding the Orange & Alexandria Railroad

The Pennsylvania Reserves lay in winter quarters near Belle Plain, Virginia, through the remainder of December. For many of the soldiers of the 8th Regiment, December 25 marked their second Christmas spent far from home and family. Indeed, New Year's Day 1863 heralded the advent of the third year of a war that few people had believed likely to last more than three months. January passed away quietly, with Major General "Fighting Joe" Hooker assuming overall command of the Army of the Potomac in place of the forlorn Ambrose Burnside. Hooker spent his first weeks as commander reorganizing the army, and it was during this time that the Pennsylvania Reserves, or rather what was left of them, were taken out of the front line and reassigned to the defenses of Washington. The longed-for news reached the men on February 5, 1863:

> [A]bout dark on the 5th of February, Colonel Sickel[1] received a telegram from General Doubleday, who, for a short time, commanded the division, stating that in consideration of the arduous and gallant services of the Reserves, they were to be withdrawn to Washington, to rest and recruit. The news was sent to each regiment and created the liveliest joy. In despite of the cold rain the camp-fires were soon brightly burning, around which the boys gathered and talked of the good times coming until late at night. The next morning, before reveille beat, all were up, and soon after breakfast everything was packed ready to move. About three that afternoon the order to march came. Falling in, and bidding farewell to our old camp...we took up our march for Bell Plain. Although the distance was not four miles, on account of the bad roads we did not reach there until after dark, but the boys plunged through the mud with light hearts, for in every breast was the secret hope of seeing home for a little while.[2]

From Belle Plain, the Reserves were transported by boat up the Potomac River to Alexandria, Virginia, where they were stationed along the line of the Orange & Alexandria Railroad. Among the wizened veterans who took up their new positions in and around Alexandria was the irrepressible James Gaskill. Ten months of battle, hardship, and privation had not dimmed his penchant for hilarity. George Darby preserved one of Gaskill's many "Alexandria Escapades" for posterity in his book, *Incidents and Adventures in Rebeldom*:

> At the Battle of Fredericksburg our command was so nearly annihilated that it was ordered back to Alexandria, Va., to be recruited and re-organized. During this time we did patrol duty in that city. The government had established a con-traband camp at that point in which was kept several thousand negroes; it also happened that Nixson's circus had gone into winter quarters there, and Gaskell, true to his instincts managed to steal a clown's fantastic suit which was deco-rated with horns, fringes and bells. One evening he dressed himself in this outfit and put in a sudden appearance in the negro camp performing acrobatic feats. The terrified negroes thinking the devil himself had dropped down among them, men, women and children fled precipitately through the street, scattering in ev-ery direction. Gaskell, for this trick, was confined for a time in the slave pen. The negroes were employed by the government to perform labor on the fortifi-cations, and many of them were so frightened that they never returned to their work again.[3]

With the constant movement inherent in campaigning finally behind them, many of the soldiers began to receive letters and packages from home on a more regular basis. News of family and friends was always welcome of course, but John Faller (whose brother Leo had been killed at Antietam) left no doubt that victuals from home were the most anticipated items when the mail call sounded in the 7th Regiment's camp: "Yesterday when I was eating my dinner, the wagon came in with the express and what do you think, my box was among them. I got it to my tent and after dinner I opened it. Everything was very nice but the crock of peach butter was broken but we gathered it up and put it in a tin cup. Yesterday we drew fresh beef and a nice shin bone and today we have it on the stove cooking and we are going to have noodle soup for dinner. We put the pickles in vinegar & they are first rate. We had sausage for supper last night and we drew eight loves of bread and we intend living nice as long as the things last."[4]

Richard Crutchfield, the contraband adopted by George Darby and his messmates when they embarked for the Peninsula (and dubbed "Coon" by them), served his erstwhile employers faithfully throughout the campaigns that followed and accompanied them to Alexandria. There, in addition to cooking for them, he provided them—albeit often inadvertently—with many moments of levity:

> One summer day, as we were doing guard duty at Burke Station along the line of the Orange & Alexandria railroad,[5] hearing the peculiar song of a grass-hopper on the opposite side of the roadbed, I called Coon's attention to the

Soldiers of the Pennsylvania Reserves warmed themselves in similar fashion while doing picket duty along the line of the Orange & Alexandria Railroad.

singing of the grasshopper, as I wished to hear the quaint remarks which he would make upon the subject. I said, "Coon! What is that noise over there?" "Dat am a hoppergrass, Masser Darby," said Coon. "Well," said I, "Go and catch it for me!" "Oh, Masser Darby! Gin I dun get ober dar, he dun fly." "Now Coon," said I, "You can't make me believe any such stuff as that. You say he is a hoppergrass, now, but if you go over after him he will be a dun-fly. Now I never heard of such a thing as a grasshopper turning into a dun-fly." "Oh! I doan mean dat, Marser Darby," said Coon, "I des mean that he dun flew; he done gwine away, he dun git out ob dat ar place fo' I dun get dar." "O, I understand you now," said I, "You mean that he will fly away before you could reach him." "Now you is shoutin', honey!" exclaimed Coon, "Dat is perzackly what dis niggar am tryin' to depress upon yo' mine." It was this strange vernacular of the negro, and his attempts to use words, of which he had not the remotest notion as to significance, that made him a constant source of amusement to the northern soldier.[6]

Darby and his messmates ultimately attempted to repay Crutchfield for his many services to them by sponsoring his education, but their efforts came to naught: "On our command's being sent to Alexandria, Coon, having developed great aptitude for learning, we clubbed together and offered to send him North to school, but he respectfully declined our generous offer. He was afraid of the cold of our climate, and chose rather to remain in the South. Soon after this, in the vicissitudes of camp life, Coon became separated from us, and as I learned, entered the government service as a teamster, and that was the last I ever knew of poor, comic Coon."[7]

Although "Coon" had gone missing, one missing soldier had returned. Jacob Heffelfinger, who had been wounded and taken prisoner at Fredericksburg, was exchanged in January and recovered from his wounds in an army hospital at Annapolis. He wrote to his sister on April 17 of his return to his regiment: "At last I am safe among the boys.... I remained in Washington until yesterday when I came here [Camp Metcalf, Virginia] via Alexandria. The regiment came here on Tuesday morning for general duty at the convalescent and stragglers camps. We have a very good quarters—do not know whether we will stay here for some length of time or not.... An order has been received, requiring us to be ready to go to Washington. I found the boys all well, and in good spirits."[8]

It would not be long before those "good spirits" were dashed. In June, Robert E. Lee and his Army of Northern Virginia, emboldened by a brilliant victory over "Fighting Joe" Hooker's Federals at Chancellorsville, commenced their momentous invasion of Pennsylvania that culminated in the Battle of Gettysburg. News of the Confederate movement across the Potomac and into the Keystone State quickly made its way to the camps of the Pennsylvania Reserves. Many of the Reserves' field officers petitioned their superiors to have their regiments attached to the Army of the Potomac so that they might take part in the defense of their home state. The officers of the 2nd Regiment forwarded the following petition to Colonel William McCandless, their brigade commander:

> We, the undersigned, officers of the Second Regiment P. R. C., having learned that our native state has been invaded by a rebel force, respectfully ask that you will, if it be in your power, have us ordered within the borders of our state for her defense.
>
> Under McCall, Reynolds, Meade, Seymour and yourself we have more than once met and fought the enemy where he was at home; now we wish to meet him again when he threatens our homes, our families and our firesides. Could our wish in this be realized, we feel that we could do some service to the state that sent us to the field, and not diminish, if we could not increase, the luster that already attaches to our name.[9]

Both General Reynolds and General Meade applied to the War Department to have the Reserves attached to their respective commands. On June 25, the Department issued an order assigning Colonel McCandless's first brigade and Colonel Joseph Fisher's third brigade to Meade's V Corps. The two brigades—under Brigadier General Samuel W. Crawford, the commander of the Pennsylvania Reserves since May—made up the third division of the V Corps. Breaking camp that same day, the elated veterans rushed northward to rejoin their comrades in the Army of the Potomac. Many of the men worried for the safety of their families, as their homes and farms lay in the path of the invading rebels. John Faller wrote a hurried letter to his sister as his regiment prepared to march northward to meet the invaders:

Camp of 7th Regt P. R.

Alexandria Va

Thursday June 25th 1863

Dear Sister

I received your very welcome letter yesterday and was glad to hear you were all well and safe. I am happy to hear that the rebels have not molested you yet and I don't think they will.... I suppose they have possession of [Carlisle] by this time and I hope and trust they won't interfere with the women and children.

Yesterday we received orders to be ready to march at a moments notice. We drew small shelter tents and three days rations and had everything in readiness to move. But as yet we have not moved and I cannot say whether we will go now or not. I heard this evening that the first and third Brigades of our Division were ordered off and we were to remain here but I cannot say how true it is. We may go and again we may not....

The boys all feel highly indignant at the people of Pennsylvania in not responding more promptly to the call of the Governor.[10] I think it will serve some of them right if they get their things taken from them. They have an idea that they have nothing at stake and they don't care about risking their lives in this holy cause. Such men are not fit to be called Americans.... Tomorrow the 26th of June is the anniversary of our first battle which occurred along the dismal swamp of the Chicahominy. We have seen many a hard day since then and maybe we will see some more before the affair is over. Give my love to all the dear ones at home and all the neighbors and friends and every person else—Write soon

No more at present

> I remain your
> Affectionate brother
> John[11]

The rumor that John Faller had heard the evening of June 25 proved to be true. While the first and third brigades marched homeward to help repulse the Confederate invaders, he and his comrades in the second brigade—the 3rd, 4th, 7th, and 8th Regiments—were ordered to remain behind to help man the defenses of Washington and guard the line of the Orange & Alexandria Railroad. It was a bitter pill to swallow for the men of those regiments. As Jacob Heffelfinger noted in his diary, "While I write, no doubt my home is within the rebel lines. One year ago this evening, I lay a wounded prisoner of war on the battle-field of Gaines Mill. Then we were near Richmond, now we are back within the defenses of Washington, and our homes are invaded by traitors. Such are the uncertain chances of war. To God alone can we look for help."[12] That night, Heffelfinger led a company of 7th Regiment pickets to an outpost on the Alexandria and Leesburg Pike. A raid by rebel cavalry was expected in the area.

Meanwhile, the men of the first and third brigades caught up with the Army of the Potomac June 28 at Frederick, Maryland. There, they learned that President Lincoln had relieved General Hooker and appointed their former division commander, George G. Meade, to lead the army. By June 30, the Reserves had reached Union Mills, Maryland, where the contents of the following circular, issued by General Meade earlier that day, were made known to them:

> The commanding general requests that previous to the engagement, *soon expected with the enemy,* corps and all other commanding officers address their troops, explaining to them the immense issues involved in the struggle. The enemy is now on our soil. The whole country looks anxiously to this army to deliver it from the presence of the foe. Our failure to do so will leave us no such welcome as the swelling of millions of hearts with pride and joy at our success would give to every soldier of the army. Homes, firesides, and domestic altars are involved. The army has fought well heretofore. It is believed that it will fight more desperately and bravely than ever, if it is addressed in fitting terms. Corps and other commanders are authorized to order the instant death of any soldier who fails to do his duty at this hour.[13]

Crawford's footsore veterans crossed the Mason-Dixon Line and entered Pennsylvania the next day. Of their return to their native soil, Evan Woodward wrote: "That day was one of the happiest of our lives, and every heart beat warm with the thought, we would soon press the soil of our mother state, in whose defense we were marching. The brigade bands and regimental drum corps poured forth their soul-inspiring airs from morning till night, and light was the tread of our feet to their notes."[14]

The Reserves reached the V Corps assembly area east of Gettysburg around noon on July 2. It was there they learned that Major General John F. Reynolds, their commander at Second Bull Run, had been killed the previous morning while resisting the Confederate advance west of town. Lee's Southerners had won the day, driving the Union I and XI Corps back through Gettysburg to Cemetery Hill. The Federals rallied there and established a defensive line that ran south along Cemetery Ridge to the Round Tops.

About four o'clock in the afternoon of July 2, General Meade moved the V Corps, now under George Sykes, toward the left of the Union line to support the Union III Corps on the Federal left flank. The III Corps commander, Major General Daniel Sickles, was to have posted his divisions in line along Cemetery Ridge with his right joining the left of Hancock's II Corps. Sickles, however, had imprudently advanced his troops nearly three-quarters of a mile beyond Cemetery Ridge, posting several brigades along the Emmitsburg Road near a peach orchard, with the remainder angled back through a wheat field toward a rock outcrop known as Devil's Den. The new III Corps line lay scarcely half a mile from the Confederate positions on Seminary Ridge. When General Meade learned of Sickles's troop dispositions, he immediately recognized that their position was untenable and ordered Sykes's V Corps forward into line along Cemetery Ridge with orders to "hold [the Federal left flank] at all hazards."[15]

The V Corps had barely taken its place in the line when eight brigades from Lafayette McLaws' and Hood's divisions of Longstreet's corps tore into Sickles's hapless III Corps. Hood slammed into Sickles's left flank between Devil's Den and the Wheatfield, while

Major General John F. Reynolds commanded the Pennsylvania Reserves during the critical fighting on Henry House Hill August 30, 1862. He later rose to command of the Union I Corps and was killed July 1, 1863, at Gettysburg.

National Archives

McLaws struck the apex of the Union line in the Peach Orchard from both sides at once. Sickles's troops fought desperately, but the vicious Confederate advance drove them out of the Peach Orchard and back through the Wheatfield. Overwhelmed, the Federals finally broke and ran for the safety of the Union line, hotly pursued by the rampaging Southerners.

As the remnants of the III Corps passed through the V Corps' front along Cemetery Ridge, General Sykes ordered a countercharge. As J. R. Sypher put it in his *History of the Pennsylvania Reserve Corps*: "The crisis had been reached, the enemy must be driven back, or the National army must abandon its line...."[16] Colonel McCandless, commanding the first brigade of Crawford's division, ordered his troops to open fire on the advancing rebels, and his men responded by hitting them with two volleys at close range. Union artillery added to the carnage, blasting the Southerners with double canister. "At this point, General Crawford rode onto the stage. Seizing the flag of the 1st Reserves, one of whose color-bearers had fallen, Crawford placed himself at the front of...[McCandless's brigade] and shouted 'Forward, Reserves....' [F]orward they went down the slope with a loud cheer 'peculiar to the Reserves....'"[17] The Southerners were driven back, and the imperiled Union line was preserved.

Together with Vincent's and Weed's brigades, whose heroics on Little Round Top prevented the Confederates from gaining that vital position, Samuel Crawford's Pennsylvanians had done their part to stem the Southern tide on the Federal left flank. Robert E. Lee would have to wait one more day to strike the blow that he hoped would yield a decisive Confederate victory. On July 3, the Southern commander hurled a massive assault against the center of the Union line in what would come to be called the "High Water Mark of the Confederacy." The repulse of that gallant, but doomed, charge put an end to the Battle of Gettysburg, and prompted General Meade to issue the following order:

> The Commanding General, in behalf of the country, thanks the Army of the Potomac for the glorious result of the recent operations.
>
> An enemy superior in numbers and flushed with the pride of a successful invasion, attempted to overcome and destroy this Army. Utterly baffled and defeated, he has now withdrawn from the contest. The privations and fatigue the Army has endured, and the heroic courage and gallantry it had displayed will be matters of history to be remembered.
>
> Our task is not yet accomplished, and the Commanding General looks to the Army for greater efforts to drive from our soil every vestige of the presence of the invader.
>
> It is right and proper that we should, on all suitable occasions, return our grateful thanks to the Almighty Disposer of events, that in the goodness of His Providence, He has thought fit to give victory to the cause of the just.
>
> By command of Major General Meade[18]

While the soldiers of the Army of the Potomac covered themselves with glory at Gettysburg, the same could not be said for certain of those Pennsylvania citizens whose homes lay in the path of the invading rebels. An irate Jacob Heffelfinger wrote to his sister in Mechanicsburg, Pennsylvania, shortly after Lee's defeat at Gettysburg, heaping scorn upon the citizens of his hometown for the manner in which they conducted themselves when the Army of Northern Virginia appeared on their doorstep: "So, Mechanicsburg received the rebels in more style than any other town.... Bread and meat asked for, and chicken potpies, cakes, pies and straw- berries and cream given. You cut the bread for the poor fellows didn't you?... Quite thoughtful of their health! Your burgess delivered the flag to them; very accommo- dating, I must confess. Enclosed you will find a photograph of the flag of the 7th Reg. P.R.V.C. You can show it to the brave men of Mechanicsburg.... Its history is inscribed on the back. We are proud of it. Wish we could feel proud of the conduct of the citizens of Mechanicsburg. Quite encouraging for soldiers to hear of men carrying rations to rebels, who might have carried muskets if not to fight, to pre- serve the good name of the town at least."[19]

The news of the decisive Union victory at Gettysburg resounded throughout the defenses of Washington and gave the soldiers of the Pennsylvania Reserves' second brigade cause for great joy. So too did the fact that casualties among their comrades in the first and third brigades had been relatively light.[20] In many cases, however, that joy was tempered by the fact that those soldiers held back in and around Alexandria had not been permitted to take part in the defense of their native state. Writing from Alexandria to his sister, Jacob Heffelfinger noted that "The 1st and 3rd Brigades...have been with the Army of the Potomac in the Maryland and Pennsylvania campaign. I see that they did nobly in the battle of Gettysburg. We do not share their glory, but in order that they may be spared from here, we have been performing double labor. For two weeks at one time I did not sleep in camp. We were out under arms every night. Lee has escaped across the Potomac, and we too, may soon have hot work. Who from Mechanicsburg shouldered a musket, during the time of the invasion."[21]

Joy of another kind was to be found in occasional off-duty sojourns into Alex- andria. These afforded the hard-working soldiers of the second brigade an opportu- nity to relax and take in the sights. Even Jacob Heffelfinger's mood surely would have brightened had he observed the following scene described by George Darby:

> [I]n Alexandria one day I saw a crowd gathering at the corner of King and
> Henry Streets and approached to see what was going on. A showman had rented
> a room and had on exhibition a large Anaconda and a blowhard posted at the
> door was enlarging on the wonderful sights within, something after the follow-
> ing manner: "Here's the greatest living Anaconda in the world, twenty-seven
> feet, two inches long and weighing one hundred pounds. Caught in the wilds of

Central Africa by three black natives. By the kind treatment of his master he has become perfectly docile. You can stick your finger in his mouth and he will not bite you. Step this way, ladies and gentlemen, and see this great living curiosity for the small sum of ten cents." Directly Gaskell approached the showman and an animated conversation took place between the two.... Gaskell wanted to perform with the big snake but the showman refused. Gaskell remarked that he would bust up his old fraud of a show and...began to cry in mockery of the showman "Here's the only living Anna Conder. She was caught running wild in the lowlands of old Virginia.... By the kind treatment of her captors she has become perfectly docile. You can kiss her...lips and she will not bite you. Step this way, ladies and gentlemen and...without price see the great 'Burnside Stick-in-the-Mud,' after which Anna may easily be seen in the audience...." [I]n a very short time he had an immense motley crowd of whites and negroes collected around him that completely blocked both streets. The showman was left without a single patron and he finally came to [Gaskill] and gave him two dollars and a half to go away.[22]

Sojourns to the nation's capital were not uncommon. Soldiers often visited the War Department and the Capitol, where they listened to politicians debate the great issues of the day. And they attended musical recitals and plays. Lieutenant Heffelfinger, who frequently attended Ford's Theatre, commented on one play in particular: "Saw J. W. Booth play Richard III tonight. He sustains his part well."[23] In April of 1865, the Shakespearian actor would play a much darker role in a drama that would change the course of American history.

When not taking in the sights in Alexandria or Washington, many of the soldiers spent their free time singing and playing musical instruments. The following lyrics, set to the well-known tune *When Johnnie Comes marching Home*, illustrate the wry humor that leavened the very real horrors of a war that seemed to have no end:

> In eighteen hundred and sixty-one
> Skewbaul. Skewbaul.
> In eighteen hundred and sixty-one
> Skewbaul says I.
> In eighteen hundred and sixty-one
> This cruel war was begun
> And we'll all drink stone blind, Johnny fill up the bowl sir
>
> We met a misfortune at Bull Run
> Skewbaul. Skewbaul.
> We met a misfortune at Bull Run
> Skewbaul says I
> We met a misfortune at Bull Run

And all skedaddled for Washington.
And we'll all drink stone blind, Johnny fill up the bowl sir.

The Marshall house it is the spot
Skewbaul. Skewbaul.
The Marshall house it is the spot
Skewbaul says I.
The Marshall house it is the spot
Where Colonel Ellsworth he was shot.[24]
And we'll all drink stone blind, Johnny fill up the bowl sir.

The slave pen it's as cold as ice
Skewbaul. Skewbaul.
The slave pen it's as cold as ice
Skewbaul says I.
The slave pen it's as cold as ice.
Get up in the morning full of lice.
And we'll all drink stone blind, Johnny fill up the bowl sir.[25]

Of course, sightseeing and merrymaking did not occupy all of the Pennsylvania Reserves' off-duty time. Large numbers of soldiers attended Sunday church services in Alexandria. One Sunday, Lieutenant Heffelfinger took a stroll through a soldiers' cemetery: "Over eleven hundred soldiers are there interred.... The graves are arranged side by side in long rows...with military exactness. Each grave has a neat white head-board on which is inscribed the name, Co. & Reg. of the dead soldier. A large number are simply marked...*unknown dead*. Sad words. Sad commentary on this hellish rebellion, unknown but not unmourned."[26]

Many soldiers passed the time engaging in spirited debate concerning the merits of the war and the positions taken with respect to it by the various political parties. Martin V. B. Hazen, of the 8th Regiment, wrote to the editors of his hometown newspaper from the regiment's camp near Alexandria, lamenting the state of the Democratic party in Fayette County:

Eighth Regt. P.R.V.C.
Camp Davies, Va., March 31st 1863

To the Editors of the [Brownsville] Clipper

Dear Sir: Having a little leisure, I concluded to pen you a few lines, not on the conduct of the war, but on the conduct of some of my old party friends in your town and vicinity. The question may well be asked, how we here in the army know everything about what is done by persons in your county?... The *Genius of Liberty*, that old Democratic paper which was in my father's house from the time I first knew how to read, and from which I got all my training in politics...[and which] find[s] [its] way to the Eighth Regt., publishes the proceedings of Democratic meetings held in...your county. Well, Mr. Editor, on reading the resolutions passed at several of those meetings, I was at a loss to know really whether I belong to the Democratic party or not. Having been taught obedience to the laws, a veneration for the "Stars & Stripes," and in a crisis like the present one, a sacrifice of everything, to be the duty of a good Democrat— I say I was at a loss to know where I stood. If a cheerful obedience to the laws, giving money and means, and taking up arms to preserve the "Union" is democracy, I am a Democrat. But on the other hand, if meeting in little township cliques and supporting a numbskull committee, to bring before the meeting resolutions gotten up by some <u>Traitor</u>...denouncing the administration and all its measures to crush the rebellion is democracy, I am not one of that kind, nor will you find any of that kind in the army. Why is it that those in rebellion against the government never receive any condemnation by the Editor of the *Genius*, or by those holding these traitor meetings in your county? This has been the inquiry of every Democrat here...and I will here say, that if the Democratic party in the north persist in the course indicated in the resolutions passed in these scandalous meetings, and in the editorials of certain papers, they will not be endorsed by the democratic soldiers in the army, as we look upon them as more dangerous to our cause than the rebels that meet us on the field of battle.... I am not much of a writer, but you have my sentiments which I believe are the sentiments of every good soldier in our Regiment, whatever his politics.

> Yours truly
> Martin V. B. Hazen
> Co. G; 8th Regt., P.R.V.C.[27]

Arguing politics, of course, just like fighting rebels, was best accomplished on a full stomach, and the Alexandria countryside afforded ample opportunities for the men of the Pennsylvania Reserves to supplement their camp fare with some of Virginia's finest game. As George Darby put it: "Wild game was abundant in the woods of Fairfax County...as it had not been disturbed much since the opening of hostilities;... Men had been too busy in hunting men to waste their energies on smaller game, hence game birds, turkeys, deer, foxes, rabbits and squirrels, had multiplied exceedingly, but the fellow who had the hardihood to take to the woods in quest of game was quite sure to become himself the quarry before the hunt was ended."[28]

One of those hardy fellows was E. D. Baer, a member of the Fayette Guards. Baer, who fancied himself a crack shot, was not bashful about boasting to his friends of his prowess with firearms. He finally got his comeuppance at the hands of his comrades after one too many boasts:

> About three miles above our camp was a small...bayou, that put into the land from the Potomac, which was much frequented by wild ducks, as were the swamps

bordering the river. Several of the comrades had made ineffectual efforts to shoot them with their army rifles but the Springfield was a complete failure for duck killing....

Baer, who was much given to self laudation and praise, went to the bayou early one morning, stealthily approached the shore, and seeing several ducks, fired and by accident killed one of them. He returned to camp with his prize, triumphant and greatly elated over his success, and after plucking and nicely dressing it, he placed it in a mess pan ready for cooking and then proceeded to the camp fire where a number of the comrades were congregated and began to blow about the accuracy of his aim and his expertness as a hunter. After allowing him to blow for a while one of the men said it was probably a wooden decoy duck he had shot as he had seen a number of them down there.... This riled Baer and he declared that all the other men who had been down there after ducks were chumps and pot-hunters that could not hit a barn door with a rifle, and therefore they were jealous of him, but he continued, "I'm going to have duck for breakfast in the morning and you fellows can stand around with watering mouths and get a smell while you see me eat it." Richie said, "Baer, if I was you I would not blow so much about that duck. Somebody might pick its bones for you before morning." "Oh," said Baer, "I'm not a bit afraid of that. I would like to see the man in this company that is smart enough to steal that duck." Richie said no more and Baer, after placing his precious mess pan at his head, went to bed and to sleep. Marching orders for the next day were issued late that night and Richie was detailed to cook the meat and have it ready for issue to the men in the morning. About midnight Richie went to the back of Baer's tent and silently raising the canvas reached in and abstracted the duck which was placed upon the fire, cooked to a turn and devoured by himself and [a] comrade. The bones, after being trimmed, were returned to the mess pan and it was replaced at Baer's head without disturbing his slumbers. Baer upon discovering the loss of his duck, raised a howl that was pitched in an altogether different tone and tune to the song of fulsome self-praise he had been singing the previous evening, but as the laugh was on him and Richie was decidedly handy with his fists, Baer had to stand the jibes of the entire company. On the march and for days afterward in camp he would be greeted with "Who stole Baer's duck?" "Who eat Baer's duck?" and "Baer done swaller dat duck whole, I see de fedders on his upper lip," and "Baer, wy doan yo' pick dat duck meat outen yo' teef?"[29]

Fruits, too, were abundant in the countryside surrounding Alexandria, and many were new to the boys from Pennsylvania:

One of the most peculiar and distinctive wild fruits of this section...is the persimmon. They grow in great abundance in most of the Southern states, and are very toothsome, especially in the late autumn and winter, when they fall from the trees.... I have gathered them from the snow...and they were delicious, having passed through a candying process in their own sweet juices.... [T]he persimmon tree becomes a snare and a delusion to the rabbit, where in winter he resorts to feast upon the fallen fruit and thus he falls an easy prey to the negroes, who are well aware of his weakness for the succulent fruit. The persimmon is utilized to some extent also in the manufacture of an intoxicant known to the natives as persimmon beer.... The fruit is first mixed with wheat bran or middlings, dampened, made into large cakes, or pones, and baked in a Dutch oven, and when desired for use, the pones are placed in a keg or other tight vessel and cold water poured over them, and as soon as fermentation takes place, the beverage is ready for use.[30]

When out on patrol or performing escort duty along the railroad, the soldiers of the 8th Regiment exercised their ingenuity to insure that they could enjoy a hot meal at midday:

At the station at which we were doing service...we had very comfortable quarters, but as we were obliged to escort to the woods and guard the men composing the timber contingent, we were at first unable to get a warm meal at dinner, but at length we hit upon a scheme which enabled us to overcome this difficulty, and it worked like a charm.... Holes about two feet deep and sufficiently large in circumference to nicely admit a camp kettle, were dug in the clay soil, then the first thing upon arising in the morning a rousing fire was started in and over these holes, and the result would be that by the time we had our breakfasts, the holes in the ground would be hot, so we would insert our camp kettles, (all of which were provided with metallic covers), into the holes...first having filled the kettles with beans, having a liberal chunk of pickled mess pork smothered in their midst, then we covered the kettles over, with the hot embers left from the morning fire, and on coming in at noon time, there would be our pork and beans, done to a turn, and these supplemented by hot coffee and hardtack, made a meal fit for a king.[31]

While the Pennsylvanians certainly enjoyed the myriad opportunities to secure fresh game and fruit afforded by the northern Virginia countryside, the majority of their daily rations came from the army commissary. Bread, of course, being a daily necessity, was supplied by a government-run bakery:

[The bakery in Alexandria] was the largest...in the world. It converted into bread five hundred barrels of flour daily. The bread was baked in sheets of sixteen loaves.... [O]ne loaf of soft bread, or in lieu thereof twelve ounces of hardtack was the daily allowance for each man.... One hundred thousand loaves were sent daily from this bakery to Culpepper for General Grant's army, and large gangs of negroes were constantly employed in carrying these sheets of bread and packing them in the [railroad] cars, and although the distance was sixty miles to Culpepper, the bread reached them still warm from the ovens. While lying in barracks near Alexandria, a company mess was organized and our excess rations were placed in a general fund with which to purchase extras for our tables. A negro cook was employed, and as he was an expert in piscatorial matters, and as all kinds of fish were plentiful and cheap, the baked shad and sturgeon which often graced our tables would have caused the mouth of an epicure to water.[32]

As 1863 passed away and Christmas day approached, the hard-working bakers of the Alexandria commissary might have been forgiven for expecting a word or two of thanks from their well-fed customers in the Fayette Guards. The wily veterans of Company G had other, less noble, thoughts on their minds, however:

> As the Yuletide drew near the bakers secured a fine lot of turkeys which were dressed and placed in the pans ready for roasting for their contemplated Christmas dinner, but "The best-laid plans of mice and men gang aft aglee," and it is safe to say that the bakers dined, on that Christmas day, without turkey, as some of our wide awake boys had seen their way clear to confiscate the birds. And so it turned out that what was the bakers' loss was the soldiers' gain. But the bakers...lodged complaint with the colonel, and he of course ordered an immediate search of the quarters. Lieutenant Ramsey, of our company, being officer of the day we were promptly informed that an investigation was on, also we were given to understand the dreadful consequences of being found guilty of the offence charged. But somehow the officer of the day on this occasion was a trifle slow in getting around to our quarters, but he finally arrived, and made the investigation, but not a turkey bone was discovered in or about our quarters, although there was a lingering suspicion of an odor which might have been mistaken as arising from roast turkey. However, it would have been impossible to have convinced any of the boys of our mess that we did not have turkey for dinner that day.[33]

The boys of the 8th Regiment who survived the brutal campaigning of 1864 would doubtless recall that Christmas feast in Alexandria with great longing. In the spring of that eventful year, Abraham Lincoln finally found the fighting general he had been looking for in Ulysses S. Grant. Grant assumed command of all Union field armies on March 9, 1864, and lost no time in joining George Meade's Army of the Potomac in the field. He immediately set about reorganizing it and placing it in motion. On April 29, 1864, the Pennsylvania Reserves broke camp and headed south. On May 4, after five days of hard marching, they crossed the Rapidan River and bivouacked for the night on a farmstead belonging to a man by the name of Lacy. It lay in the heart of a densely wooded area known simply as "The Wilderness."

"We Sorrowfully Laid Him to Rest"

The Wilderness to Bethesda Church

On taking command of all Federal forces in the field, Ulysses S. Grant's orders to George Meade, commanding the Army of the Potomac, were simple and direct: "Lee's army will be your objective point.... Wherever Lee goes, there will you go also."[1] There would be no more cries of "On to Richmond" for Meade's veterans. Now they would seek out and engage the Army of Northern Virginia in a battle to the death. "To get possession of Lee's army was the first great object," Grant wrote. "With the capture of his army Richmond would necessarily follow."[2]

Robert E. Lee's veterans had spent the winter behind strong entrenchments near Orange Court House, just across the Rapidan River from Culpeper. Grant's strategy was to turn the Confederates' right flank, thus forcing Lee to come out of his lines and fight or retreat toward Richmond. On the night of May 3, 1864, the Army of the Potomac was set in motion, and the Pennsylvania Reserves, now commanded by Brigadier General Samuel W. Crawford, took up their place in the line of march. The Reserves made up the third division of Major General Gouverneur Warren's V Corps. The 8th Regiment was now assigned to Colonel Fisher's third brigade, along with the 5th, 10th, and 12th Regiments. Crawford's division reached the Rapidan at 9:30 in the morning, crossed it, and pressed on.

Andrew Jackson Elliott, a corporal in Company A of the 8th Regiment, kept a daily diary during the opening days of what came to be known as Grant's "Overland Campaign." His terse entries for the days encompassing the Battles of the Wilderness and Spotsylvania illustrate the extent to which grand strategy and tactics were utterly foreign to the common foot soldier. Elliott's purview, and that of his comrades, was limited to those events occurring within the immediate range of his senses.

5/4/64 Brok up camp at 12 a. m. and started toward the enemy. The whole army appears to be on the move. Our Div. crossed the Rapidan at 9 1/2 o'clock. We rested about 2 hours and took diner then pushed on. We marched about 25 miles to day and went into camp about 4 P.M. near Hobsons church. I feel pretty tired. Com[mitted] myself to God & laid down & slept.[3]

After crossing the Rapidan, Warren's troops advanced to the junction of the Germanna Plank Road and the Orange Turnpike where they halted to allow their supply train to catch up with them. They camped for the night on the Lacy farm near the old Wilderness Tavern: "Some of the veterans remembered later that a sad silence seemed to settle over the army that night in bivouac. The haunting cry of the whippoorwill echoed through the deep shadows. Occasionally someone stumbled over the bones of the unburied dead from the Chancellorsville battle just over a year before, sapping the morale of the new men in the blue ranks. Around the campfires in the stillness of the woods the veterans were unusually quiet, haunted by memories or premonitions."[4] Corporal Elliott was a veteran himself. He had been wounded at the Battle of Antietam and had seen enough in his time with the 8th Regiment to know that, all too soon, the whippoorwills' cries would be replaced by the cries of wounded comrades.

5/5/64 We was routed up at 4. At 5 we [moved] to our position in the line on the left of the 5 corps. Our co. [A] was thrown out to skirmish. At 1 the Div was flanked. We had to get out the best way we could and lost some wounded and prisoners. The Div was rallied and threw up breast works and remained in them all night. I com[mitted] my all to God and slept some in the R Pits.[5]

The V Corps, with Crawford's Pennsylvania Reserves leading the way, resumed their march south through the Wilderness just after dawn on May 5. Well before then, Robert E. Lee, having been informed of Meade's crossing of the Rapidan, had started all three of his corps eastward to intercept the Federals' advance. If the Southerners could strike the Union army during its transit of the Wilderness, they stood a good chance of defeating it. It would be Glendale all over again, but this time the victory would belong to Lee's ragged veterans.

By noon, elements of Lieutenant General Richard Ewell's Second Corps had caught Crawford's division in an isolated position near Chewning's farm where, earlier in the day, soldiers from the 1st Regiment had come within two hundred yards of General Lee himself: "The Pennsylvanians, who soon realized they were in a bad fix, fired wildly into the Georgians. The Confederates overlapped the company and struck Crawford's division from the flank and the rear. Colonel Samuel M. Jackson of the 11th Reserves pulled his regiment and the 2nd Reserves from the division's second line to meet the attack and give the rest of the division time to withdraw. The two regiments charged...and opened the road to Lacy's. With the 7th Reserves posted as the rear guard, the entire division escaped northward."[6] Robert McBride, a corporal in the 11th Reserves, recalled these critical moments in a book he wrote after the war: "Hurried orders were received; the line moved by the right flank, double quick. The Seventh Regiment deployed and vanished into the woods, forward, and the Eleventh followed in line of battle. Moving on through the thick underbrush, the enemy was quickly encountered. Their first volley was deadly. A ball struck Boss. M'Cullough in the forehead. He fell dead, a portion of his shattered brain lodging on the arm of John Stanley, a boy of seventeen, who had come to us during the Spring. John shuddered, shook it from the sleeve of his blouse, raised his gun and began firing.... To crown all, the woods took fire, and soon the only problem...was to withdraw as quickly and safely as possible."[7]

It had been a very close call. Fierce fighting raged elsewhere along the lines of the contending armies but, despite mounting casualties, neither side gained a decisive advantage. Late in the afternoon, as noted by McBride, the struggle turned nightmarish when dry tinder caught fire. Many of the wounded soldiers on both sides were burned to death as the blaze spread through the forest. Come the next morning, Andrew Elliott would find himself in the thick of things again.

5/6/64 Left the R P about 4 and took a pos[ition] to the right of where we were yes[terday] on the ex[treme] front. Our co[mpany] was out as ski[rmishers]. Som of them was out all day. The Regt threw up pits & held them until rel[ieved] at 6. Then we marched to the rear and the right of the 6 corps gave away. We were sent up to support them. Came back to where we started about 12 M. I feel that I canot praise God enough for His Goodness and mercy towards me.[8]

Severe fighting flared anew along both the right and left flanks of the Union line shortly after dawn on May 6. Crawford's division, being posted in the center, was little involved (other than for occasional sharp skirmishing with the rebels entrenched opposite them) until shortly after six o'clock in the afternoon. At that time, Confederate troops under Brigadier General John B. Gordon assailed the extreme right flank of the Union line and shattered two brigades of Sedgwick's VI Corps, capturing two Union generals in the process. This imperiled the right wing of the Army of the Potomac and, had it been crushed, the army's line of retreat across the Rapidan would have been blocked. The Pennsylvanians, who had just moved back to the Lacy farm, were rushed to Sedgwick's support, leaving their half-finished suppers behind. General Warren, the V Corps commander, noted in his journal that "[l]ate in the evening the enemy turned General Sedgwick's right very unexpectedly, and threw most of his command into confusion. I sent General Crawford at double quick, and the line was restored by him."[9]

The action on Sedgwick's right was the last in what became known as the Battle of the Wilderness. U. S. Grant had hoped to get Meade's Army of the Potomac through the Wilderness without a fight, while Robert E. Lee had hoped to trap Meade there and destroy him. Neither man got his wish. Instead, some two hundred thousand men engaged each other in an appalling struggle that produced nearly

18,000 casualties on the Union side and 11,000 on the Southern side. When it was over, and the smoke had cleared, the lines of both armies stood essentially where they had when the conflict began.

5/7/64 At 5 Div moved from where we lay last night. We was in the res[erve] line to day and was not...engaged. The day was warm. I feel pretty tired. I feel that God is still good to me. My trust is still in him. After dark started toward Spot[sylvania] C. H. and marched all night. The enemy appears to be falling back.[10]

In one sense, the fiery struggle in the Wilderness had changed nothing—on the night of May 6, both armies occupied virtually the same lines as those they had occupied on the morning of May 5. In another sense, however, those two days in that flaming cauldron changed everything. For the first time, a Union commander, bloodied by the hard-fighting Army of Northern Virginia, did not retreat, but maintained contact with his adversary and pressed on. Grant was cut from different cloth than the other Union commanders who had gone up against Robert E. Lee. A young reporter for the *New York Tribune* who had accompanied the Army of the Potomac into the Wilderness returned to Washington with a message for the president from the new commander in chief: "'Something from Grant for me?' Lincoln said. [The reporter] swallowed and spoke quickly. 'He told me I was to tell you, Mr. President, that there would be no turning back.'"[11] And, indeed, there was not.

On the evening of May 7, the Army of the Potomac pulled out of the Wilderness and marched through the night toward a strategic crossroads at the tiny village of Spotsylvania Court House. Grant's purpose in heading there was two-fold: "first, I did not want Lee to get back to Richmond in time to crush [Union General] Butler [who had occupied City Point on the James River] before I could get there; second, I wanted to get between [Lee's] army and Richmond if possible; and, if not, to draw him into the open field."[12] Grant would not have long to wait. Neither would Corporal Elliott.

5/8/64 Caught up with the enemy at 9 and got engaged with them. Before we stoped made sev[eral] charges. Did not accomplish much. Was engaged all day. In the evening a gen[eral] charge was made. 5 of the co. was wounded. May God save us from another such scene on the Holy Sab[bath] day.[13]

By the afternoon of May 7, Robert E. Lee had begun to suspect that Grant was not retreating toward Fredericksburg (as Lee had thought he might), but, rather, was heading for Spotsylvania. Consequently, he ordered General Longstreet to start his men toward that place as quickly as possible. The race was on! If Grant got to the crossroads before Lee, he would succeed in placing the Army of the Potomac between Lee's army and the Confederate capital at Richmond. Lee would have no recourse then but to give battle. If, on the other hand, Lee could get to Spotsylvania before Grant, he could protect his line of communication with Richmond and force Grant to attack him.

Pressing on through the night, the leading contingents of Longstreet's corps, under Major General Richard H. Anderson, reached the Spotsylvania area early in the morning of May 8, moments ahead of the approaching Federals. They went into battle immediately, fighting for control of Laurel Hill, a small rise that dominated the road on which the Army of the Potomac was strung out as it neared Spotsylvania. More troops from both sides were fed into the fighting as they arrived on the field. Warren's V Corps tried several times during the day to take the hill, but failed. Finally, in the evening, a combined force from the V and VI Corps made one last attempt. Crawford's Pennsylvania Reserves were at the forefront of this effort. One Pennsylvanian recalled that it was "'half-past six o'clock in the evening when 'a great shout rolled along the line and the columns of attack moved forward.' 'The men fought forward and upward desperately,' added another.'"[14] Despite heroic efforts, the assault was beaten back, and the Confederates ended the day as the masters of Laurel Hill.

The race for Spotsylvania was over, and Robert E. Lee had won. Grant would not get between Lee and Richmond. Nor would he force Lee into the final, decisive engagement he sought. Indeed, on the morning of May 9, Lee wrote to Jefferson Davis, advising him that "[w]e have succeeded so far in keeping on the front flank of [Grant's] army, and impeding its progress, without a general engagement, which I will not bring on unless a favorable opportunity offers, or as a last resort...."[15]

The Fayette Guards lost one of their own during the fighting on May 8, a young soldier who arguably should not even have been there. George Darby recalled the sad scene—just one of hundreds played out on that critical day:

> While the death of a comrade always brought sadness to the hearts of those who survived, yet there seemed something inexpressibly sad in the death of one, who having endured the privations and hardships of the soldier life, until after the expiration of his term of enlistment, [was killed] when his heart and mind were full of the joyful anticipation of the home-going.... Among my messmates was one, a genial, great-hearted, brave young man whose name was John Sisler. Death had deprived him of both fatherly and motherly care; for at a very early age he was left an orphan. He had found a home and had been carefully reared by a family near Uniontown, Pa., by the name of Parshall. At Robinson's Farm, May 8th, 1864, where the field was skirted by a dense piece of woodland...we had improvised a line of rifle pits from which our skirmishers would sally...to feel the strength and position of the enemy.... [N]ot far from our rifle pits, [stood] an oak, growing among the pines, which forked at about four or five feet from the ground, forming two trunks.... In the rear of our position was an old field.... [A] Rebel sharpshooter had located himself in a pine tree and from his perch among the branches amused himself by picking off such officers and men as had occasion to pass through the field. John Sisler and David Richie...were detailed

to go out and kill him if possible. Accordingly they slipped over to the timber and Sisler took shelter behind the oak tree...and while looking through the forks of the tree was discovered by the rebel, who fired, his bullet striking Sisler squarely between the eyes, killing him instantly. Richie, however, discovered where the rebel was located, and shot at him, but his gun was not of sufficient range to reach him, so he came back and reported the fact, whereupon two of the Buck Tails were dispatched with their Spencers to do the job, and they soon brought Johnnie Reb to terms by shooting him dead from his roost in the pine. We secured Sisler's body and digging a grave in the rear of our battle line; we sorrowfully laid him to rest, marking his lowly grave with a cracker box lid. Sisler was killed about two weeks after his term of enlistment had expired, but as the companies composing the regiment had entered the command at different dates, the time had been averaged, which resulted in retaining our company, to which Sisler belonged, a few days longer than we were justly entitled to serve....[16]

Grant and Lee spent the better part of May 9 adjusting their lines and entrenching. Two days of fierce fighting in the Wilderness, followed by a night march and heavy fighting around Laurel Hill the preceding day had left both armies too exhausted to engage in anything other than the occasional skirmish. The most notable event of that Monday was the killing of the popular Union VI Corps commander, Major General John Sedgwick, by a Confederate sniper. Corporal Elliott noted in his diary that "I got some rest today and feel pretty well." He would be glad of that come the morrow.

5/10/64 Our Regt is in the R. P. At 9 went out to sup[port] the skir[mish] line. Found the enemy in force and fell back to R. P. A Div of the 2nd corps came in and took positions in front of us. At 3 our Div formed in line for a charge. At 6½ the whole line charged on the enemy works & was repulsed. I committed myself to God and laid down and slept some.[17]

By May 10, the Army of Northern Virginia was so well entrenched behind reinforced breastworks that a frontal assault against them would have been suicidal. Nonetheless, that is exactly what Grant and Meade ordered. Warren's V Corps and Hancock's II Corps were directed to launch "'an attack on the enemy in your front...at 5 P.M. this day.'" The result was predictable: "'The lines struggled stubbornly through the woods, cheering and undaunted, but only to meet a terrible repulse.'" Another soldier remembered that "'[g]rape and canister ploughed through our ranks. Both color-bearers were shot down.... No army on earth could capture the works with such odds against it, but we charged once more....'" That second assault proved as futile as the first.[18]

Finally, about seven o'clock in the evening the Federals made one last, supreme effort. As their lines were being dressed, "General Crawford...came walking along the front, accompanied by several of his staff. He was gesticulating in an excited manner...and exclaimed in a tone of intense anguish...'I tell you this is sheer madness, and can only end in wanton slaughter and certain repulse.'" According to General Hancock, the II Corps commander, that is precisely what happened: "The troops encountered the same obstacles which had forced them to retire when they had assaulted this point at 5 P.M. They were again repulsed with considerable loss." One soldier who lived through the maelstrom said that "[t]he troops had witnessed the failure of Warren's men to take the ridge and the terrible slaughter which resulted, and moved forward with a great deal of reluctance, for they all felt it to be a hopeless undertaking and that they were like sheep being led to the slaughter."[19]

Elsewhere on the battlefield, troops of the Union VI Corps assaulted a salient in the Confederate lines defended by the Georgians of George Doles's brigade. Despite some initial success, this attack was beaten back when anticipated reinforcements failed to materialize. It was the last fighting of the day. Near midnight, as the last of the Union wounded were being removed, "a Confederate band moved up...on the line and played 'Nearer my God to thee.' The sound of this beautiful piece of music had scarcely died away when a Yankee band over the line gave us the 'Dead March.' This was followed by the Confederate band playing 'Bonnie Blue Flag.' As the last notes were wafted out on the crisp night-air a grand old-style rebel yell went up. The Yankee band then played 'The Star Spangled Banner,' and...it seemed by the response yell, that every man in the Army of the Potomac was awake and listening to the music. The Confederate band then rendered 'Home, Sweet Home,' when a united yell went up in concert from the men on both sides."[20]

While both armies spent the better part of May 11 sending their wounded and prisoners to the rear and reordering their lines, senior Federal commanders planned a second major assault against the Confederate line, at a point known as the "Mule Shoe" salient, for first light on May 12.

5/12/64 At 3 AM moved toward the left. The enemy attacked us in the R P and was repulsed. Remained in the RP until 5 then moved towards the ex left and took a position in the RP. We do not appear to be gaining much on them. It is raining and has been all day. Thank God my life has still be spared. I feel that I am not worthy of the least of all these blessings.[21]

Dawn came reluctantly that morning. The air was damp, and fog shrouded the ground. Finally, at 4:35 a.m. troops of the Federal II Corps charged the apex of the Mule Shoe and crashed through the Confederate breastworks. The Union soldiers initially seized most of the Confederate works in vicious hand-to-hand fighting, but repeated counterattacks by the beleaguered Southerners drove the Federals back. The fighting in the Mule Shoe raged without respite for some seventeen hours, largely in and around a breach in the Confederate defenses that came to be known as the Bloody Angle. Of this unprecedented confrontation one historian would write: "Along those two hundred yards of mutually held trenches, men now killed each other with zealous abandon. In a war that had birthed its share of bloody angles, this day and the morning of the next at Spotsylvania would give birth to the bloodiest of them all."[22]

While planning the May 12 attack on the Mule Shoe salient, Grant had ordered the V Corps to threaten the Confederate left flank in order to prevent the transfer of troops from that position to reinforce the rebels at the salient. Thus, General Warren ordered an artillery bombardment of the line in his front shortly after daylight and eventually committed his infantry to yet another frontal assault on Laurel Hill. The attack was a failure, and Warren later reported that he had sustained heavy losses in the attempt. Nonetheless, his men could count themselves lucky that they had spent May 12 on the Confederate left flank and not in the "Pandora's box of hate and killing lust" that was the Bloody Angle.[23] The day had cost the Army of the Potomac more than 6,800 casualties.

May 13 was largely given over to caring for the wounded and catching up on correspondence. John Willoughby, by now a first lieutenant in the 5th Reserves, wrote to his friend James Simpson, expressing his hope that the "grand end" might be within sight:

> Field of Battle
> May 13th, 1864

Dear Simpson,

This is the morning of the 9th days fighting. So far am unscathed. Today General Meade issued a congratulating address. The presents so far are 19 guns, 22 colors, 8,000 prisoners. The work "he says" is not over. Reinforcements are expected. Our loss is heavy.... That of the enemy no doubt is as great. How we dig—Talk of McClellan digging; we lay him in the shade. Both armies after an hour's halt are entrenched. The trenches are charged, at times with success, then otherwise. The privations endured have been great. But the hope that this campaign will be the means of obtaining the grand end sought for, will lead us to endure even greater hardships. The old Reserves have been engaged seven days; the casualties will amount to over a thousand to the present date.

In this Regiment we have 50 some killed, wounded and missing. Been extremely fortunate. In Co. G we have 4 killed and 4 wounded....

In making a charge on Sunday I stuck in a Swamp; the whizzing of the minnies helped me through. I am sorry to chronicle the death of Col. Dare which happened on a skirmish line on the 7th, picked off of a sharp shooter. I was talking to him when he received the wound.

The 7th Res. were captured almost entire. Many of our dead and wounded that were left in the woods [in the Battle of the Wilderness] were burned. The fighting has all taken place in woods, mostly scrub pines. This evening we lay in the front works. A new line of works are being erected.

May 14, 1864

Last night we moved to the left of the line. March all night through mud and water.

Evening—7 o'clock

I am back to the trains for a change of clothing. Reinforcements are going forward. I think the grand struggle will take place tomorrow or the day after. We lay near Spottsylvania Court House. I must close for a night's rest. At dawn I go [to the] front to participate in the final effort.

Remember me to all Yours

J. A. W.[24]

In addition to letter writing, soldiers on both sides took advantage of the lull in the fighting to bury their dead. One burial in particular bore ominous consequences for the Southern cause. Late in the afternoon at Hollywood Cemetery in Richmond, Major General Jeb Stuart was laid to rest. The "Bold Dragoon" had been mortally wounded in a clash with Sheridan's horse soldiers at Yellow Tavern two days earlier. Of his lamented cavalry commander, Robert E. Lee said, "I can scarcely think of him without weeping."[25]

In the evening, Warren's V Corps was moved from the extreme right to the left of the Union line in anticipation of another Union attempt to turn Lee's right flank. It would be another night march for the weary veterans of the Pennsylvania Reserves.

5/14/64 After a severe nights march arrived on the left of the a[rmy] at an early hour and took a position in front of the enemy. About 4 took a position in line of battle. A battle took place to our left. The enemy was repulsed. We were shelled. Had no person hurt. Both armies appear to be in line about one mile apart. I com[mitted] my all to God and laid down. Did not sleep much.[26]

There was little action on May 14 involving the Pennsylvania Reserves. For the men of the 8th Regiment, the day was one of anxious waiting—after three years of marching and fighting, the regiment's term of service was nearing its end.

5/15/64 Got orders that our time had expired and turned over the recruits and vets to the 12 Regt. Left the line of battle and marched to the rear. Our papers are not right. We have to wait. It rained today. The armys are drawn up in line of battle about half a mile apart.[27]

The great day was finally at hand. On Sunday morning, May 15, 1864, the 8th Regiment, having completed its three-year's service, was taken out of the line and relieved from duty. One day later, some 75 soldiers, a tattered remnant of the proud regiment that had mustered 1,000 men at Camp Tennally in the autumn of 1861, left for Fredericksburg.[28] From there, the jubilant veterans went on to Washington and thence to their respective homes throughout the Keystone State. The return of the 8th Regiment, and, particularly, of the Fayette Guards, was noted in Uniontown's *Genius of Liberty*: "The Eighth Regiment of Pennsylvania Reserves was mustered out of service and paid off at Pittsburgh, this week. This regiment has done noble service—has been in the hardest battles, and on every occasion has distinguished itself as the bravest among the brave. Company G was from this place and was originally known as the Oliphant Company [the Fayette Guards]. Their loss has been terribly severe, and the joy at meeting the few gallant survivors who have returned, is marred and mingled with regret and sorrow for those who have gone out from among us to return no more. A few from this company have reenlisted, and only ten were mustered out of service."[29]

In fact, 235 soldiers from the old 8th Regiment, including 31 of the Fayette Guards, had reenlisted.[30] On May 15, when the 8th Reserves were taken out of the line, these men were transferred to the Pennsylvania Reserves' 12th Regiment by order of General Crawford. Among the veterans of Company G who reenlisted were Third Sergeant Isaac Moore, Fourth Sergeant James Eberhart, and Fifth Sergeant Thomas Springer. Private George Darby signed up to keep on fighting too, and it would not be long until he found himself back on the firing line.

Following a final, failed attempt to pierce the Confederate defenses at the Harrison House on May 18, General Grant swung the Army of the Potomac south toward the North Anna River. He hoped to entice Lee out of his entrenchments and catch him in the open between the several corps of the Union army. Warren's V Corps crossed the North Anna May 23 and established a bridgehead on the south side. Toward sunset, the

A soldier displays the first state colors of the 8th Pennsylvania Reserves at their muster out.

National Archives

Confederates attacked the Union line, intent upon pushing the Yankees back into the river. The Pennsylvania Reserves, anchoring Warren's left, were in open ground when "[t]he enemy opened about thirty pieces of artillery on the division. As the division had not had time to entrench, the men were under about as warm artillery fire as they ever had [been]...."[31] Warren's men held, however, and darkness brought the contest to an end.

Unable to gain any advantage on the North Anna, and with his corps south of the river threatened by Robert E. Lee's clever positioning of his defenses, Grant pulled back and, in yet another attempt to gain Lee's right flank, headed southeast, following the northern bank of the Pamunkey River. The Federal infantry crossed the Pamunkey on May 28, hoping to steal a march on their antagonists, but Lee, as might have been expected, countered Grant's move by quickly shifting his lines to the east. By the following morning, the two armies stood deadlocked once again, staring at each other from opposite banks of Totopotomoy Creek.

Anxious to confirm the exact disposition of Lee's principal forces, Grant sent Hancock's corps and part of the V Corps (including Crawford's Pennsylvania Reserves) across the Totopotomoy to seek out the main Confederate line. While probing south of the creek on May 30, the Pennsylvanians ran into elements of Jubal Early's Second Corps near Bethesda Church. Colonel Hardin's first brigade was in the vanguard as Crawford's men headed west along Old Church Road. Robert McBride described what happened as he and his comrades in the 11th Regiment unexpectedly ran into a swarm of Confederates: "[We] advance[d] some distance. 'Someone has blundered.' [We] have no support on either wing. [We] are flanked, and, after a brief struggle are driven back. Some noble men were lost here.... At the woods [we] rally. A fence is torn down, and with this and whatever is nearest at hand a breastwork is hastily improvised."[32]

Chased by Confederate troops who smelled a rout, the surprised soldiers of Hardin's brigade fell back on a defensive position that General Warren had organized along Shady Grove Road. George Darby, with the Reserves' 12th Regiment since May 15, was on that line and described the Confederate attack:

We reached Bethesda Church on May the 30th and on this day the time of enlistment for the whole division expired, it having been averaged to fall on this date, as some of the regiments had been mustered into service sooner than others. We formed line of battle behind a rail fence which ran along side of a dense woods; to our left was a farm house, in front of which was planted a battery of artillery; in our immediate front was a cleared field in which stood two negro cabins, and beyond the cabins the field was skirted by a heavy pine forest which our battery at the house was vigorously shelling. We had torn down the fence and piled up the rails, and with picks and shovels were busily engaged in throwing earth over them to make rifle pits, when suddenly we heard the rebel yell.

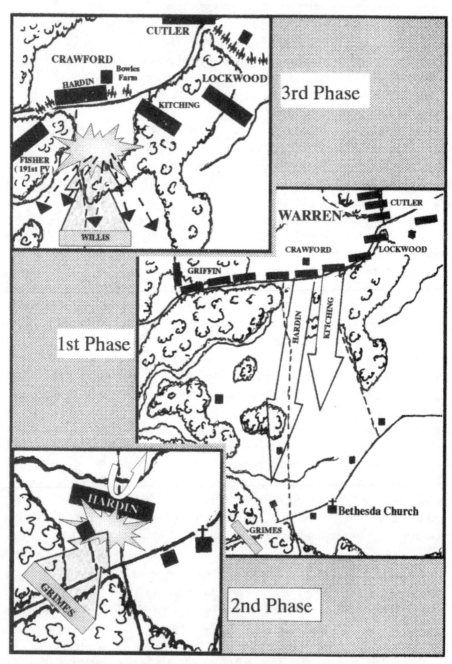

3rd Phase

CUTLER
CRAWFORD
Bowles Farm
HARDIN
LOCKWOOD
KITCHING
FISHER
(191st PV)
WILLIS

WARREN
CUTLER
CRAWFORD
LOCKWOOD
GRIFFIN
HARDIN
KITCHING

1st Phase

HARDIN
GRIMES

Bethesda Church
GRIMES

2nd Phase

The Battle of Bethesda Church, May 30, 1864. The Pennsylvania Reserves engage elements of the Confederate Second Corps on the last day of their term of service.

On looking to the front we saw a Virginia brigade...coming at full charge out of the pine woods, and they were making for our battery double quick. We dropped our spades and grasping our rifles we poured a most deadly cross fire at close range into their ranks, while the battery rained double shotted grape and canister into them, and in less time than it takes to tell it, the rebel brigade was almost annihilated, a very few only making their escape back to the woods. As I was firing across the top of the pit, a piece of a human jaw containing five teeth struck and stuck upright in a rail just in front of me. I suppose the rebel to whom it had belonged had been hit by a cannon shot and his head dashed to pieces....[33]

The brigade that George Darby mentioned was Pegram's brigade, led by Colonel Edward Willis, who was killed during the charge. Lieutenant Colonel C. B. Christian of the 49th Virginia survived the carnage despite being badly wounded; he recalled the valor of the ill-fated brigade in an article that appeared in the *Southern Historical Society Papers* in 1905: "As soon as the brigade was well into the open fields the enemy opened with the heaviest and most murderous fire I had ever seen with grape, canister and musketry. Our veterans of a hundred fights knew at a glance that they were marching up to die, rather than to waver. Our line melted away as if by magic—every brigade, staff and field officer was cut down...in an incredibly short time."[34]

In anticipation of the battle, Christian had to select a new color bearer, the regiment having lost nine in the fighting since the Wilderness: "I went down the line to select another. I came to a tall, lanky, beardless boy, from Amherst, with a 'red cap' on...[and] said 'Orendorf, will you carry the colors?' He replied, 'Yes, Colonel, I will carry them. They killed my brother the other day; now damn them let them kill me too.' " In the attack that followed, Orendorf made it to "within twenty feet of the muzzle of the enemy's guns and waved his flag defiantly in their faces. They must have hesitated to kill him in admiration of his bravery. [F]inally a heavy gun was trailed on him not twenty yards distant. His little 'red cap' flew up ten feet, one arm went up one way, the other another—fragments of his flesh were dashed in our faces. They had 'killed him, too.' "[35]

Robert McBride reached the safety of the Union rifle pits just as Willis's Virginians began their doomed charge:

Now the enemy is seen advancing. Line after line comes swinging out. Shells come screaming over. One explodes in front of Company D. Its fragments sever the flagstaff close to Jim Shaffer's head, rip open Mike Coleman's cap, Tear off Culp's arm near the shoulder. Another bursts in the [farm] house, and sets it on fire. A woman, bearing a baby in one arm and leading by the hand a little child, comes out of the house, still unharmed. Frightened and bewildered, she is passing along the rear of the line instead of hastening away from it. A kind-hearted soldier directs her toward a place of safety. But now the rebel lines are within rifle range. Volley after volley is poured into them, and their ranks melt before the terrible fire. In our front they falter; but toward the right they see a chance for victory. They will swing around our flank, and crush us as they did but an hour before. With exultant yells, their left comes sweeping on, wheeling to envelop our right. But now there bursts from the underbrush a blast as if from the pit, crashing, tearing, grinding, enfilading their lines, leaving in its track a swath of dead and dying. This is decisive, and the battle is won.[36]

J. R. Sypher, the author of a contemporary (and somewhat romanticized) history of the Pennsylvania Reserves, offered the following summary of the engagement:

> Upon the line held by the Pennsylvania Reserves the assaults were more numerous and more determined...but the valor of the heroes who had survived their time of service, was equal to the emergency.... This was the last day of their term of service. The battle field was within six miles of Beaver Dam creek, where less than two years before, they had won a great victory over a superior foe—the end being thus brought near to the beginning in point of territory, the brave two thousand that remained of the ten thousand that fought at Mechanicsville, resolved that the end of the service of the Reserve Corps should be as glorious as its beginning was patriotic. To a succession of brilliant achievements from Dranesville to Gettysburg, without a blemish to mar the story of their greatness, without a defeat to tarnish their unsullied banners...the battle of Bethesda Church is a most proper ending.[37]

To veterans like Isaac Moore, James Eberhart, and Thomas Springer the irony of the Pennsylvania Reserves' last battle being fought within an hour's march of their first must have been overwhelming. One can only imagine their emotions as they bid a final farewell to their comrades who were heading home at last. Robert McBride described the scene in his book, *In the Ranks*: "Mingled feelings of joy and sadness were in the hearts of all, as good-byes were spoken, and they marched away. The war-worn veterans, who now turned their footsteps homeward, and those who stood there, watching their going that day, knew too well how certainly these 'good-byes' might be 'farewells.' I think I saw tears in a certain brave colonel's eyes; and perhaps strong hands were clasped with a little more than usual fervor, as friend looked into the face of friend...."[38]

That colonel with the tears in his eyes just might have been Thomas Chamberlin, a lieutenant colonel in the Bucktail brigade, who witnessed the Reserves' leave-taking: "Without special orders or previous understanding, the other troops of the corps fell into line and presented arms as these veterans of many campaigns, full of scars and honors, marched past; and as the notes of 'Home Again' from the band of the Reserve, rang in their ears, the cheeks of hundreds of veterans who remained were moistened by tears of which they had no reason to be ashamed."[39]

Part Three

Among the Famished Brave

My brave lad sleeps in his faded coat of blue.
In a lonely grave unknown lies the heart that beat so true.
He sank faint and hungry among the famished brave,
And they laid him sad and lonely within his nameless grave.

He cried, "Give me water and just a little crumb,
And my mother she will bless you for all the years to come.
Please tell my sweet sister so gentle, good, and true
That I'll meet her up in heaven in my faded coat of blue."

Long, long years have passed, and though he comes no more,
Yet my heart will startling beat with each footfall at my door.
I gaze o'er the hill where he waved his last adieu,
But no gallant lad I see in his faded coat of blue.

No more the bugle calls the weary one.
Rest, noble spirit, in thy grave unknown.
I'll find you and know you among the good and true
When a robe of white is given for the faded coat of blue.

"The Faded Coat of Blue" (1865)
Words and Music: J. H. McNaughton

"I Guess I'll Ride That Horse Again Now!"

Cold Harbor to the Weldon Railroad

Brigadier General Samuel W. Crawford said his good-byes to the Pennsylvania Reserves on June 1, 1864. As had George McCall, John Reynolds, and George Meade before him, General Crawford issued a formal farewell to his troops. On this occasion, however, it was not the Pennsylvanians' commander who was moving on but, rather, the rank and file who were departing the field, their term of service honorably concluded. For Crawford, who had led the Reserves since June 3, 1863, and had been with them at Gettysburg and throughout the Overland campaign, the parting was bittersweet:

SOLDIERS OF THE PENNSYLVANIA RESERVES—To-day the connection which has so long existed between us is to be severed forever.

I have no power to express to you the feelings of gratitude and affection that I bear to you, nor the deep regret with which I now part from you.

As a Division you have ever been faithful and devoted soldiers, and you have nobly sustained me in the many trying scenes through which we have passed, with an unwavering fidelity. The record of your service terminates gloriously, and "the Wilderness," "Spotsylvania Court-House," and "Bethesda Church," have been added to the long list of battles and of triumphs that have marked your career.

Go home to the great State that sent you forth three years to battle for her honor and to strike for her in the great cause of the country, take back your soiled and war-torn banners, your thinned and shattered ranks, and let them tell how you have performed your trust. Take back those banners sacred from the glorious associations that surround them, sacred with the memories of our fallen comrades who gave their lives to defend them, and give them again into the keeping of the State forever.

The duties of the hour prevent me from accompanying you, but my heart will follow you long after you return, and it shall ever be my pride that I was once your commander, and that side by side we fought and suffered through campaigns which will stand unexampled in history.

Farewell,

S. W. Crawford[1]

The duties of the hour to which Crawford referred involved, of course, the continuing prosecution of the war against Robert E. Lee's Army of Northern Virginia. Crawford stayed on as commander of the third division in Warren's V Corps, a position that enabled him to maintain the connection he spoke of in his farewell order with the 2,231 officers and men who had reenlisted out of the old Pennsylvania Reserve Regiments.[2] These veterans were reorganized into the 190th and 191st Pennsylvania Veteran Volunteers.[3]

Sergeants Moore, Eberhart, and Springer, along with Private Darby and 27 other veterans from Company G of the old 8th Reserves, were assigned to Company G of the new 191st Pennsylvania. The 191st and its sister regiment, the 190th, made up the third brigade of Crawford's division. It was led by an officer who began the war as a private and ended it as a brevet brigadier general. James Carle, a printer by trade,

Major General Samuel Crawford commanded the Pennsylvania Reserves from June 3, 1863, through June 1, 1864. He led the Reserves' first and third brigades into the Wheatfield at Gettysburg July 2, 1863, in a counterattack that rolled back the Confederate thrust against the Federal left flank.

National Archives

enlisted in the 6th Pennsylvania Reserves in April 1861. Prior to the war, he had spent five years in the regular army, mustering out as a sergeant. When his comrades in the Tioga Invincibles found out about Carle's prior service, they promptly elected him captain of their company. Despite losing a hand at Antietam, Carle took command of the regiment in March 1863. He also served for a time as provost marshal for the division under General Crawford.

Carle was commissioned a colonel June 6, 1864, and took command of the third brigade on that date. Three days earlier, the Pennsylvanians, and the V Corps to which they belonged, had played but an inconsequential part in the massive Union assault on the Confederate works at Cold Harbor—a fiasco that cost the

Colonel James Carle assumed command of the 190th and 191st Pennsylvania Infantry Regiments June 6, 1864, and led them during the fighting along the Weldon Railroad. He was captured August 19, 1864, at Globe Tavern.
Courtesy Kevin Carle

Army of the Potomac some 3,500 casualties in little more than half an hour. Fortunately for the Reserves, casualty totals among the V Corps divisions were relatively low. Of the doomed Union advance against the impregnable rebel breastworks, Ulysses S. Grant later said, "I have always regretted that the last assault at Cold Harbor was ever made.... [N]o advantage whatsoever was gained to compensate for the heavy loss we sustained."[4]

Sobered by the disaster at Cold Harbor, Grant abandoned any further efforts at a frontal assault and attempted, yet again, to sidle around the Confederate right flank. This time, however, the Federals didn't stop moving until they had crossed to the south side of the James River. Grant's new goal was the isolation of Richmond from its sources of supply to the south. The key was Petersburg, a rail center located some eighteen miles south of the Confederate capital. Following several unsuccessful attempts to take it by storm, the Union army dug in and laid siege to the beleaguered city.

The Confederate defenses around Petersburg were among the most extensive erected by either side during the war. The Federals, too, constructed entrenchments, redoubts, and forts on a scale hitherto unseen. In some places, the Union and Confederate lines were so close that, over time, an unusual camaraderie developed between the common soldiers manning the opposing works. These were men who had seen too much war—men who had no desire to keep on killing when the end of the war seemed to be within sight.[5] George Darby recalled one such scene in his book, *Incidents and Adventures in Rebeldom*:

> The opposing lines were in such close proximity on some parts of the field, that a conversation with the enemy could be carried on in an ordinary tone of voice, and we finally arranged a truce, the conditions of which were, that in case either side received orders to reopen hostilities, a signal shot must be fired in the air, as a fair warning to the other side. And to the honor of both parties, be it said this stipulation was faithfully carried out. This arrangement was made between the men without the consent or knowledge of the officers. We finally became

upon so good terms with each other that traffic sprang up between us. The barter was usually coffee and tobacco. Of the former we frequently had superabundance, and of the latter they usually had an excess, so the conditions of trade were favorable, and under this treaty we became quite neighborly, so much so indeed, that sitting on top of our rifle pits, we would read aloud from our Northern papers for Johnnie's edification, and Johnnie would reciprocate in kind...and to hear the criticism that would follow the reading of an article, by those of adverse side, would furnish lots of amusement for the boys.[6]

These pleasant diversions from the brutal business of war continued until the Pennsylvanians, relieved for a time from duty on that part of the line, returned to their encampment. It was not long, however, before they were back in the thick of things. In mid-June, James Carle led the third brigade in a successful assault against a line of rebel breastworks south of Petersburg. In reporting the action to the V Corps commander, General Crawford noted, "Colonel Carle...by a gallant effort succeeded in capturing the Thirty-Ninth Regiment North Carolina troops, the commanding officer of which surrendered to Colonel Carle, himself, regiment, and colors."[7] It was a performance that would earn Carle a well-deserved commission as a brevet brigadier general.

On July 26, 1864, Colonel William Hartshorne succeeded Carle as commander of the third brigade, Carle assuming command of the 191st Pennsylvania. Shortly thereafter, he led his Keystone State veterans back into action. General Grant had set the V Corps the task of interdicting the Weldon Railroad, which lay about three miles west of the left flank of the Union siege line. The railroad carried supplies stockpiled at Weldon, North Carolina, north through Petersburg to Richmond. As Grant himself noted: "This road was very important to the enemy. The limits from which his supplies had been drawn were already very much contracted, and I knew that he must fight desperately to protect it."[8] George Darby and his comrades in the 191st Pennsylvania were in the forefront of the action when the V Corps hit the railroad: "As the enemy held the Weldon railroad, we were marched to Yellow Tavern [Globe Tavern] to seize and destroy the road at that point. Here on the 18th of August, 1864, we advanced upon the enemy's works under a terrific fire from their field batteries, and in the midst of a rain storm, with heaven's artillery let loose upon us, it seemed as though the wrath of God was conspiring with the fury of man, in wreaking vengeance upon our devoted heads. We drove the enemy from their position at the railroad through a piece of woods, and into their line of works, and there succeeded in holding them at bay while the railroad was being destroyed."[9]

Silas Crocker, a private in Company E of the 191st Pennsylvania recounted the regiment's movements in an article he wrote for the *National Tribune* in the years following the war: "[L]ate in the afternoon [of August 18, while the rest of the division was tearing up railroad track] our whole brigade was deployed as skirmishers and ordered to advance in the direction of Petersburg till we found the enemy, then hold the position. My regiment deployed to the right of the railroad, and after advancing some distance our right joined the left of [Edward] Bragg's Brigade, which formed a continuous skirmish line from our old position on the main line of the army, covering our operations here. We soon found the rebel outposts, but instead of halting were pushed on, driving them in till we developed enough force of rebels to stand us off and we had to stop. We dressed our line, collected in groups of three, and at once constructed small rifle pits to shelter ourselves from the fire of the enemy...."[10]

George Darby was posted on the skirmish line near Private Crocker: "Our position...being very exposed...I succeeded in scooping out a small pit, into which I crawled, but from which I was soon forced...as the downpour of rain continued. I then secured a position behind a nearby tree. While standing behind my tree I saw...a man who was evidently a cannoneer. I aimed, and shot; he fell, and I am glad that that is all I know about the transaction. I do not of course know how all old soldiers feel about such matters, but while it is probable that no soldier who was in several engagements, and did his duty...but caused the death of one or more of his fellow beings, and while he might have been, and probably was entirely justifiable in so doing, yet there is an aversion I believe in every old soldier's heart, to knowing that he killed anybody."[11]

Darby and Crocker held their positions through the night and into the afternoon of the next day. Private Crocker described what happened then:

> Some time in the afternoon [of August 19] word was passed along our line that we would be relieved at 4 o'clock, and that we would move directly to the rear when our relief should come. We were posted in thick woods and could not see men very far, so when at what I believed to be about time for our relief I heard quite a racket, as of men marching and shouting in the bushes over on my right. I slung my knapsack and prepared to "limber to the rear," glad of the chance to get needed rest. I had not slept a wink the previous night, and was completely worn out with the 30 hours of steady marching and watching. By the time I was ready to move the tumult had reached my post, and looking around at the supposed relief my surprise may be imagined when I saw that they were clad in gray, and I was greeted with—"Throw down your gun and fall in here!" I "caught on" without waiting for a second invitation, and believing especially just then that "discretion was the better part of valor," did as directed. Nearly the whole [third brigade] line was relieved in the same manner, we having no chance to either fight or run.[12]

Sergeant Springer of Company G of the 191st Pennsylvania was equally startled by the unexpected appearance of rebels in their rear:

At about this time we dispatched Comrade Springer to the rear on a double mission, as our ammunition was nearly exhausted, and we were anxious for a cup of coffee. This little unimportant incident was the beginning of the most desperate and soul-harrowing dilemma we as soldiers were ever fated to be caught in. Springer came rushing back in a few moments with blanched face to inform us that we were completely surrounded, that the enemy was in our rear, and for every man to look out for himself. On hearing this we very naturally started back by the way we had come. I now think if we had taken an oblique direction, to our left, we might have flanked the rebel line and escaped, but that was not to be for we soon encountered a line of rebel skirmishers whom we captured and disarmed. Among our captives was a mounted officer to whom one of our men said, as he threateningly raised his gun, "Get down off that horse, you rebel son of a b___h! Or I'll blow your brains out," and the reb dismounted without parley. "Now make off there," says Yank, "I'll do the riding act myself," and we started on with our prisoners, thinking we were taking them into our lines, when suddenly we ran into a rebel brigade which was drawn up in line of battle. The tables were turned, the officer so recently dismounted looked up at the man on his horse, and said, "I guess I'll ride that horse again now!" "I guess you will," said the man, and jumping nimbly down, he dashed his gun against a tree, and the rest of us imitated his example, thus making our arms useless to the enemy.... The officer whom we had so unceremoniously dismounted, proved to be the rebel General [William] Mahone, and it was [one of] his brigade[s] which now stood so much in our way of escape."[13]

After surviving three years of campaigning with the Pennsylvania Reserves, the veteran volunteers of the 190th and the 191st Regiments had finally fallen victim to a misapprehended order. Early on August 19, General Warren had ordered Bragg's brigade of Lysander Cutler's division to Crawford's right flank. Bragg was to support Crawford and establish a connection with the IX Corps, then manning the extreme left of Grant's siege line below Petersburg. Writing after the engagement, General Warren noted: "General Bragg did not execute [this order] as directed, but took up another line a mile or more to the rear. I at once directed...Bragg to correct his line and sent the best officers of my staff to assist."[14]

Tragically for the Pennsylvanians, before Bragg could reposition his line a scratch force of Confederates under William Mahone burst through his skirmishers, wheeled to the right and swept down on the rear of Crawford's division. The unsuspecting soldiers of the two Pennsylvania regiments never had a chance. They only lost 5 men killed and 18 wounded, but 624 men were captured—among them Colonel Hartshorne and Colonel Carle. Late in the day, Mahone's rebels were repulsed, and the V Corps' line astride the railroad was restored. That was small

Confederate Brigadier General William Mahone led the attack against the Federal position at Globe Tavern that resulted in the capture of the 190th and 191st Pennsylvania Infantry Regiments.
National Archives

consolation, however, to the unfortunate Pennsylvanians who, at that very moment, were being marched to Richmond and an uncertain future as prisoners of war.

Writing of the disaster that had befallen Crawford's veterans, Robert McBride noted, "[a] few men escaped by taking the suicidal risk of running through a gap in the rebel lines. Mike Coleman, Captain Birkman and a few others escaped in this way. Mike told me he heard men call 'Halt! Halt!' on every side; but he looked neither to the right nor left and went ahead."[15]

Few men were as lucky as Mike Coleman on that calamitous day. One who was, gained his freedom, but lost his knapsack in the process. A young rebel private, pursuing the fleeing Federal, scooped up the heavy knapsack he had dropped in his haste to escape. After the fighting ended, the North Carolinian "opened [the] knapsack to see what was in it, and, among other things, I found a large packet of letters. I began to read them, but soon learned what they were. It was beneath the dignity of a Southern soldier to read letters a loving wife had sent to her soldier husband, so I destroyed them."[16]

It didn't take long for news of the Pennsylvanians' misfortune at Globe Tavern to reach Uniontown. On August 25, the following dispatch appeared in the *Genius of Liberty*:

From Army of Potomac
Our Forces Surprised
The Union Loss About 3,000
HEADQUARTERS ARMY OF THE POTOMAC

August 21, 1864

Our losses at the Weldon Railroad on Friday afternoon were greater than heretofore reported. The number of prisoners taken by the rebels is now put down at 1,500. It seems that our troops were surprised, many of them being in shelter tents at the time, trying to escape the heavy rain that had been falling several hours previous. The rebels appeared about noon on the right of the road in front of the Third Division, Fifth Corps, but this was evidently a feint or for the purpose of feeling our lines.

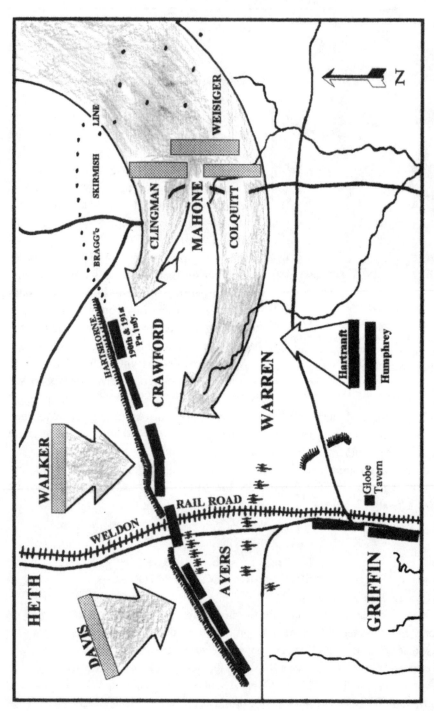

The Battle of Globe Tavern, August 19, 1864. The 190th and 191st Pennsylvania are captured during fighting along the Weldon Railroad.

About three o'clock p.m. they charged in heavy force between the 5th and 6th [*sic*: IX] corps, succeeding in turning the flank of the former, capturing a large number of prisoners. This part of our line was forced back some distance, when the 9th corps, which had been relieved the night previous by a part of the 2nd corps, came on to the field and opened fire, checking the advance of the rebels, and taking a few prisoners.

A heavy column of rebels at the same time charged on the left of our line, west of the railroad, held by the Second Division, General [Romeyn] Ayers, which they broke, and here they also took 500 or 600 prisoners, of the regular brigade, which was commanded by General [Joseph] Hayes, who is believed to be a prisoner as he cannot be found. Our whole line was thus forced back with heavy loss in killed and wounded. The rebels, however, suffered worse than we in this particular, their men lying thick all over the field.

Before dark our men were reformed, and being reinforced a desperate charge made to recover our lost ground, which was successfully accomplished, so that at night we held the line which had been taken from us in the afternoon. The entire number of prisoners captured by us is about 230, and some stands of colors. Our loss is estimated at over three thousand.

Nothing but skirmishing took place along the line today, both parties being busy entrenching themselves. A battle is looked for at any moment, as the enemy seems determined to regain possession of the [rail]road, while we are determined to hold it.[17]

More fighting did take place along the Weldon Railroad in the days following the disaster that befell Crawford's Pennsylvanians on August 19. On August 21, the battle that everyone was looking for broke out as the Confederates made one last, desperate effort to roust the Federals from their lodgment astride the railroad. The Southerners were repulsed, suffering heavy casualties in the process, and, as Ulysses S. Grant noted in his memoir, "the Weldon Railroad never went out of our possession from the 18th of August to the close of the war."[18]

The siege of Petersburg ground on and, in time, would lead to the surrender of the Army of Northern Virginia at Appomattox Court House April 9, 1865. On that auspicious day, against all odds, soldiers of the 190th and 191st Pennsylvania would be present to witness the final act. Those few lucky souls who eluded capture on August 19, 1864, were reunited with their comrades who had been absent on convalescent leave, furloughs, or detached duty when the debacle at Globe Tavern occurred. These men—some 550 in all—were attached to the third brigade of Ayres' division. Retaining their regimental designations, these veterans fought through to the end of the war, taking part in the Battles of Peeble's Farm in September 1864, Boydton Plank Road in October 1864, and Hatcher's Run in February 1865. They also participated in the Appomattox campaign that culminated in Robert E. Lee's surrender of the Army of Northern Virginia on April 9, 1865. On that Palm Sunday morning, the third brigade veterans were in action once again, with the Bucktails leading the way. As the Pennsylvanians advanced against a rebel battery, "over the brow of a hill in front came a horseman, then another, and another. The first bore a white flag. 'Cease firing!' 'Cease firing!' was the order, and the rider, bearing it, passed down through our line. 'They've surrendered!' 'they've surrendered!' was repeated from man to man, until the whole army knew the glad tidings, and cheer after cheer rent the air. The glad hour, for which we had been battling for four long years had come."[19]

But for Sergeants Isaac Moore, James Eberhart, and Thomas Springer there was no "glad hour," no opportunity to share in the glory of the final victory. Their war ended August 19, 1864, when they, and nearly 2,700 of their comrades, were captured at Globe Tavern. They would spend the next six months in a succession of Confederate military prisons, and many of them would not survive.

"Today I Am Twenty Years Old"

The Prison Diary of Sergeant Thomas W. Springer[1]

On the eve of what came to be known as the Battle of Globe Tavern, Sergeant Thomas Springer sharpened a pencil and made his first entry in a small, pocket-sized diary: "Received orders to march at 4 a.m." Three years of marching and fighting had brought Springer and his comrades in the 191st Pennsylvania to the Union siege works south of Petersburg. On August 18, 1864, the Pennsylvanians marched westward with Gouverneur Warren's V Corps to the Weldon Railroad, one of the last open supply lines into Confederate-held Petersburg. The Battle of Globe Tavern the following day, and the fate that befell Springer and the other veterans of the 191st Pennsylvania there, formed the subject of the preceding chapter.

In this chapter and the next, Sergeant Springer and his friend and brother sergeant, James Eberhart, speak to us in their own words of the bitter days that were their lot as prisoners of war. Typhoid fever stilled young Thomas Springer's voice forever on November 29, 1864, but James Eberhart continued to make daily entries in his own diary through to his parole and return to Union lines in March of 1865. Together, these two diaries present a gripping and poignant account of life and death in Confederate military prisons during the waning days of the Civil War.

In these two chapters, supplemental material that would otherwise appear in endnotes is indicated by one or more asterisks within the text of the daily diary entries and is presented immediately following the relevant diary entry. Similarly, selected entries from James Eberhart's diary are included in this chapter whenever they describe the day's events in greater detail or add information relevant to the day in question not presented by Springer. Such entries are indicated by the name "Eberhart" followed by a date, both in bold type within brackets. In a number of instances, the entries for a given day by each of the diarists appear to be quite similar. While there is no apparent explanation for this, it is possible that the two, who were messmates, composed their daily entries jointly, with each one then adding details that were of particular significance to him.

As with the supplemental Eberhart diary entries, excerpts from George Darby's book are included in this chapter where they afford additional detail regarding the day's events or present information not related by Springer or Eberhart.

Silas W. Crocker, a private in Company E of the 191st Pennsylvania, was imprisoned with the rest of his comrades and was fortunate to survive the ordeal. In 1900 he authored a multi-part article in the *National Tribune* relating his experiences in the various prisons where the soldiers of his regiment were held. In this chapter and the next, excerpts from Crocker's article are included where relevant to provide additional insight into the conditions the prisoners faced during their six months of captivity.

Diary from Aug 18th 1864

Thursday Aug 18th

Received orders to march at 4 a.m. Took up our line of march about 5, direction south. Struck the Rail Road at 12 m. Halted in an open field. About 1 p.m. our batteries commenced firing. We were drawn up in line. Deployed 600 skirmishers and advanced through very thick woods until they opened fire on us. The line advanced and fell back several times and finally took a position near the edge of the wood in sight of Rebel Rifle Pits. Rained all day.

Friday Aug 19

Nothing transpired during the night. About 2 p.m. the Rebs tried to advance. The whole line opened out. And they fell back to their pits. About 5 p.m. we received orders from the Maj to fall back. The line fell back about 1/4 mile and found we were surrounded. As near as we can judge the whole line was taken prisoners. We were marched out to the right on a double quick. We formed in line about 300 and marched through Petersburg and camped on low ground for the night. Rained all day. About 48 of our Com. and nearly all of the Regt.

[Eberhart-8/19] *All quiet during the night untill about 2 am [sic]. The Rebs tried to advance. The whole line opened on them and drove them back to thier Rifle pits & Remained all day in the same position untill about 3 pm. The Colonel said we would be Relieved about dark & at 4 one of the boys went back to make some coffee & had his fire made & pot on & came a Running back & told us the woods was full of Rebels in the Rear of us. So we soon found it was true & our officer told us to get back & stop at the breast works at the edge of the woods. We started & came on two line[s] of battle of Rebs. We took some prisoners from their skirmishers that had been sent to pick us up & got a general & went on and came up to thier Battle line & had to surrender. They marched us to the right and Rear on a double quick. As our batteries was a shelling the wood we went in fearfully & glad to get out of it. Got out in an open field & found all of our officers our general & some 4 or 5* hundred prisoners. It rained about all day. I put on my rubber blanket a going out & a Rebel came behind me & caught hold of one corner & jerked. Its string broke & he run, but I could not follow him. Had on a new hat got from home by mail a few days before. A Rebel tried to steal that but I was too quick for him. They march us back to thier Breast work at Petersburg & stoped a while. An officer came to me & said I had a nice hat. I told him yes. He wanted to trade. I thought I might want it before I would get out. He told me that they would take it from me at Richmond & he would give me 2 dollars in our money & 15 in his & his hat all the money he had. So I traded with him. They marched us to [P]etersburg near the Canal & Camped all night. In the night 4 of [us] were a laying togeather & had 2 blankets over & 2 under us. A Rebel came in & tried to steal a blanket & Dave Ritchey was on the outside & he got up and knocked the Johnny down. He went out a howling & got his gun & wanted to come in and kill the Yank. The Rebel officer came & took him away. So we had a quiet night. 48 men & 2 officers of our company were taken.

Saturday Aug 20 1864

Rained pretty much all night. About 9 a.m. our names were taken and every-thing but our haversacks.* Two more squads came in this morning Altogether about 2000. About 2 pm we all marched to the Depot about 3 miles from Petersburg. We arrived at the station about 4 p.m. (20 miles from R). We got on open cars. Started at 4 1/2. Commenced raining and rained until we arrived in Richmond. We got to Richmond about 6 1/2 and was taken to a Prison on Cary Street.** The room was 100 by 40. We only had one hundred in here tonight.

* Private Silas Crocker elaborated on the confiscation of the prisoners' be-longings: "Next Morning we went...on an island in the Appomattox River where our personal property was thoroughly inspected and every article, such as blankets, shelter tents, etc. having the United States brand on it [was] confiscated as contra-band of war." *National Tribune*, August 9, 1900.

**"On arriving there we were confined in a large brick building, known as Pemberton. It stood on Cary Street, above, and nearly opposite Libby Prison. While confined in this building John McClosky...threw a Spencer rifle cartridge which he wished to be rid of out the window. It struck the window and exploded. This occur-rence caused a great stir among the Johnnies and they at once rushed a number of soldiers and several officers into the building to punish the Yank who had tried to blow up the guard. The Buck Tail explained that having no further use for the cartridge, he had simply thrown it away; however, this explanation was not ac-cepted and the man was brutally bucked and gagged." Darby, *Incidents and Adven-tures*, 102–4.

Sunday Aug 21st 64

Wakened at daylight. About 9 1/2 am the other squad came in. The room pretty well crowded. At 10 a.m. we were taken to Liby just across the Street.* We got *in the upper story. The room just about the size of the other. About 300 in here. One of Bulters [sic] nigers in the same room with us.** He is a Sergeant and has charge of the room. They gave us something to eat. Corn Bread & Boiled Beef. After dinner our names were taken and the room swept up. We number all told in this room 299. After our names were taken they gave us Corn Bread & Bean Soup. Then we were drawn up in line and went through another Searching. They took our haversacks. Left us nothing but our personal effects. We were put into another room. As soon as they were done we were marched out through Richmond to Belle Island.*** Divided into squads of 50. Sergt Moore has charge of our squad (No 40). we arrived here about 8 p.m. Lay down to sleep.*

* "After the [McClosky] incident we were moved across to Libby and confined on the second floor of that infamously historical building, and the notorious Dick Turner, and his pal John Ross, put in an appearance, ostensibly for the purpose of taking charge for safe keeping of the effects of the prisoners of war, but really for the purpose of robbery in a wholesale way. 'Now,' said Turner...'all those of you who voluntarily give up their money and valuables to us, the same will be safely kept and returned to you on your leaving the prison, and the clerk will now take your names, make a schedule, carefully describing everything so left with him, but everybody will be searched, and all property not handed over to the clerk will be immediately confiscated.' The first division of Turner's speech was a lie, pure and simple, as that prince of thieves...and his robber gang, never returned...anything

Libby Prison in Richmond, Virginia. Thomas Springer, Isaac Moore, George Darby and their comrades were taken here following their capture at Globe Tavern.

they had stolen from the prisoners of war. However, the latter portion of the speech...we found to be literally true, for they did search every one of us, and they did confiscate everything that the search developed, lead pencils, combs, pocket knives, jewelry, watches and money; everything, in fact, but our scant clothing was taken." Darby, *Incidents and Adventures*, 104.

** This is believed to refer to Major General Benjamin F. Butler of Massachusetts, one of the Union's "political generals," who was a staunch abolitionist. Early in the war, Butler was the first to declare runaway slaves "contraband of war." His military administration of captured New Orleans earned him the sobriquet "Beast Butler," largely for his infamous order declaring female resisters to be "regarded and held liable to be treated as [women] of the town plying [their] avocation." Jefferson Davis issued a proclamation declaring Butler to be an "outlaw." In August 1864, United States Colored Troops under Butler began digging the Dutch Gap Canal on the James River. The diary reference is probably to one of these soldiers who had the misfortune to be captured.

*** "Shortly after Dick Turner's robbery had been enacted at Libby, we were transferred to Belle Island, which is situated in the James River, above the city of Richmond, Va. The Tredegar Iron Works, now busily at work turning out rebel war material, occupied the upper end of the island while our prison camp, several acres in extent, and surrounded by rifle pits, was located at the lower, or western end of the island. The entrance gate, the cook house and the guards' quarters were on the Richmond side of the island, while an alleyway skirted with tight board fence on either side led to the river on the Manchester side. Through this alley the prisoners passed in getting water from the river. From the alley round to the cook house the river made a sharp bend.... Lying between the prison pen and the Tredegar Iron mills, was a hill, upon the brow of which was placed a battery whose guns were trained upon our camp. Then across the river, on the Richmond hills, was another battery, with its guns trained in the same suggestive manner. We were supplied with a few old rotten rags of canvas for shelter...." Darby, *Incidents and Adventures*, 105.

Monday Aug 22nd

Up at daylight. Built a little fire and after blowing about one hour got a tin of coffee made. About 10 am they commenced putting up tents. Two squads in one row or 10 men in one tent. 1 p.m. they issued one day's ration 1/2 loaf corn bread and 1 bucket Soup. At 5 p.m. commenced raining. Rained about two hours. We all layed down on the wet ground in a row and spooned. Very hot until 5 p.m.

Tuesday Aug 23rd

Slept pretty considering the dampness of the ground. Sky cloudy. Sun came out and very hot all day. At 10 a.m. they issued our meal. 1/4 loaf Corn Bread & fat

Belle Isle, an island in the James River opposite Richmond, served as a temporary prison for the soldiers captured during the fighting on the Weldon Railroad.

These makeshift graves on Belle Isle serve as a stark reminder of the toll that disease took among the Union prisoners held there.

pork. In the afternoon another squad came in. Altogether on the island 3140 or 63 squads. At 5 p.m. they gave us two buckets of Rice Soup & Bread. Still putting up tents.

Wednesday Aug 24th

Sun came out very hot and very good prospect of being extraordinary hot today. Got our regular meal at 10 a.m. About 3 p.m. another squad of Yanks were brought in and swells the number up to about 3500 on the island. at 4 1/2 got our other meal. 2 Buckets Bean soup & Corn Bread. The day wore away as usual.

Thursday Aug 25

Got up at 7 and took our regular wash at the river.* Nothing of note transpired during [the day]. Issued one days ration at 1 p.m. At dark it commenced to cloud up and soon we had a good shower. It rained for about 1/2 hour. Made the ground very wet so that we could not sleep.

* "Regular washes," and the lack of all but the most rudimentary sanitary facilities, soon combined to contaminate the water near the shore. Private Crocker recounted how he and his comrades dealt with the situation: "When we reached [Belle Isle] the drinking water was obtained from four shallow wells inside the pen, but these soon went dry...and we were forced to get our water from the river. Plain river water is a beverage in only limited demand...and when polluted from the camp, as this became because of the...insufficient and terribly unhealthy arrangements, would remain untasted if the consumer had choice. But we had to drink this water or none.... We managed by the use of Yankee ingenuity to overcome some of the evil effects.... Some of us had tin coffee cups with bails; others had boots, from the legs of which strings were made which enabled us, by throwing the cup far out from the edges of the stream and then pulling it in quickly, to get a tolerably fair sample of river water. I was lucky as to have a quart cup, and by loaning it to those having a string was always able to drink as good water as the market afforded." *National Tribune*, August 16, 1900.

Friday Aug 26th

Did not sleep very well last night on account of the rain. We were all put out in the green outside of the Guard. Marched back single file and counted.* They posted a paper on the gate that no rations would be issued until the man was found that struck Sergt Mark yesterday while he was selling bread in camp. Four shots were fired last night. They killed one and wounded one of our men. 3 p.m. no rations yet and no prospect of getting any. At 6 p.m. they commenced drawing tents. And soon our squad (40) had a Sibley and were putting them up when they sung out for the Sergts to come & draw rations. Put our tent up ready to sleep in. Another man shot this afternoon by one of the Guards. 25 men in a tent.

* "To continue the account and description of our camp on Belle Isle. The space between the water and the bend in the river...down to the water's edge was utilized for the purpose of counting the prisoners. We were turned into this space as often as every other day, and as we were marched back into camp, we were counted off by the rebs. This ground was, when first set apart as a corral for us, well set with grass, but the starving men soon had pulled the last spear of it, and ate it up, root and branch, until that ground was as bare as the rock of Gibraltar." Darby, *Incidents and Adventures*, 107.

Saturday Aug 27th

We were wakened up a little after daylight & taken out & counted over again. Cloudy & cool, signs of rain. Rained nearly all last night. At 10 a.m. they issued us one meal. Wrote a letter home this afternoon. This is our ninth (9) day of imprisonment. At 3 p.m. they issued soup & Bread. In the evening the Rebs planted two cannon on the hill overlooking our camp. They are looking for a raid. A train of cars passed over the bridge into Richmond loaded with Yanks. The cars loaded with them supposed to be about 1000 or 1200.

Sunday Aug 28th

We were turned out again at sun up and counted over. Thus far I believe only three are missing. There are a great many rumors in camp in regard to exchange and Parole, but I think there is no truth in any of them. Sun shining beautiful but not hot. A strong wind blowing makes it cool. Between 10 & 11 a.m. they gave us our regular meal. Today they hoisted the stars and bars by our camp. Its a white rag with a red field in the corner & bars (blue) across the red field thirteen (13) stars in the blue bars. At 4 p.m. we got our soup & Corn Bread. Bread selling at $5.00 a loaf. I made an effort to get some bread but did not succeed. The day passed away pleasantly.*

* Private Crocker heard these rumors too: "Rumors of an agreement to resume exchange began to circulate among us early in my prison experience. I was always willing, even anxious, to believe [them].... [S]everal times the day was set when the new exchange would begin. The failure to start us toward City Point on these stated days made it more certain to my mind that we surely would go next time." *National Tribune*, August 16, 1900.

Early in the war, Union and Confederate representatives negotiated an arrangement for the exchange of prisoners of war. Known as the Dix-Hill Cartel, the agreement, signed in July of 1862, provided that "all prisoners were to be discharged on parole and exchanged at a strict ratio—general for general, private for private, 60 privates for one general. The cartel eventually collapsed [in May of 1863] over the knotty problem of exchanging former slaves, captured while serving in the Union armies.... Another obstacle to any agreement was the fear that paroled soldiers would be returned to the front. In 1864 [General U. S.] Grant wrote: 'Every man we hold, when released on parole or otherwise, becomes an active soldier against us at once either directly or indirectly. If we commence a system of exchanges which liberates all prisoners taken, we will have to fight on until the whole South is exterminated.' This meant, of course, that Northern boys would continue to languish in Rebel prisons. It was one more harsh reality which a North inured to horrors would have to accept." Bruce Catton, *The American Heritage Picture History of the Civil War* (New York: American Heritage Pub. Co., 1960), 500.

Monday Aug 29th

Marched out by squads this morning and was counted. Rained very hard in the night last night. Sun shining and the prospect of a hot day. At 8 a.m. the citizens guarding us were relieved (to go hom) by regular soldiers (Heavy Artilery) just from Petersburg (18th Va). At 12 m. we got our meal. At 2 p.m. another squad of Yanks came into the camp and swells the number to 5,900 or 59 squads. 100 each. These last men were taken at Reams Station, Weldon R.R. At 4 p.m. we drawed grub. Squad 39 & 40 were consolidated Made it the 20 squad. Sergt Moore in charge. Camp is very much crowded.*

* Private Crocker noted: "Toward the close of August our number was increased by the arrival of 8,000 Second Corps men captured at Reams Station [on the Weldon Railroad], and now all the space in the pen was occupied till we had scarcely room to lie down.... A few squads of prisoners who were there when we arrived had been supplied with tents, which sheltered them from the sun in the day and the cold dew at night, but the great mass of us had no relief from either...." *National Tribune*, August 16, 1900.

Tuesday Aug 30th

Tolerable cold in the nights & early in the mornings. They did not turn us out to count us this morning. Prospects of a hot day. 10 a.m. drew rations (21 loaves). Nothing of interest until 4 p.m. Drew rations (21) and only two buckets of soup instead of four.* Slight shower of rain at 4 p.m. Nothing of any interest during the rest of the day. After we had retired some one in a tent close by raised a big noise. They had a fight. One man got hurt considerable. There was a fire in Richmond sometime before 12 oclock. The Guard says the Central Depot & two blocks were burned down.

* Throughout his diary, when Thomas Springer writes about the drawing of rations, the loaves of bread and the buckets of soup or meat he mentions must suffice to feed an entire squad (typically one hundred men). Darby describes such rations in individual terms: "For breakfast we had a piece of cornbread about two inches square, or one slice of wheat bread (usually sour) and one pint of coffee (so-called) made from parched rye. For dinner we had absolutely nothing. For supper we were served the same amount of bread...and either a pint of rye coffee or instead thereof a pint of pea soup, or one tablespoon of boiled rice, or two ounces of rotten bacon or beef.... [I]f you got coffee you did not get soup, and if you got soup you did not get rice, and if you got rice you did not get meat. They never made the unpardonable mistake of serving any two of the articles named at any one meal. The peas used in making soup were of a variety known in the South as 'Nigger peas' and were invariably bug-eaten. The soup was flavored with a bit of the kind of pork of which I have spoken; it was necessary to skim the bugs off before the soup could be swallowed, as they rose to the surface in great quantities. In regard to the bacon furnished, if the human mind can conceive of anything really loathsome, that bacon would stand for its representative; if a bit of the rind were lifted it would reveal a squirming mass of maggots and worms, or if it were cooked, there they would lie in grim and greasy rows, rigid in death. The beef supply consisted of shin bones and heads from which the tongues were invariably extracted, and the eyes left in, and sometimes the cud would be found sticking between the jaws. When the meat was served an ox eye was a full ration of meat for one prisoner, and the poor starved men would trim and gnaw them until they had the appearance of large glass marbles." Darby, *Incidents and Adventures*, 112–13.

Wednesday Aug 31st

It is getting to be so cold during the nights that we cannot sleep without blan-kets. And does not get warm in the morning before 8 o clock a.m. Bread trade going on brisk behind our tent $1.00 per loaf Greenbacks. Apples 2 for $1.00. At 10 1/2 a.m. drew meat & bread (22). Saw in the Richmond Papers that the Commissioners of exchange meets today. At 4 p.m. we got 2 buckets of soup & bread (21). Very warm during the day. There was some artilery firing beyond Richmond but could not tell what it was.

[Eberhart-8/31] It is getting to be so cold at night that we cannot sleep with-out blankets, (and we have none at all). And does not warm up in the morning before 8 am. Bread trade a going on brisk behind our tent. $1.00 per loaf. Green-backs. apples 2 for 1.00 At 10 1/2 drew meat & bread 22 loaves. Saw in a Richmond paper the Commissioners of Exchange meets today. At 4 pm we got 2 buckets of Soup and Bread 21 loaves for 100 men. Very warm during the day. There was some artilery firing beyond Richmond. Very heavy—could not tell what it was. Wrote a couple of letters home one to Miss Gillmore but they say all are burnt & are not sent at all. Tried to wash one of my shirts at the River but it was worse after I got done than when I commenced. Water so muddy & no soap. So I have given up of ever trying to wash clothes. Traded one shirt off for 4 lbs of Tobaco a pie & a loaf of bread. I divided the tobaco among the boys.

Thursday Sept 1st

Up early on account of getting cold. Saw a Richmond paper and it stated that the commissioners met. The Confederate Commissioner Ould* proposed an *exchange man for man officer for officer, but the commissioner on our side had no instructions from the Government whatsoever. At 12 p.m. drew our meat & bread (21) At 4 p.m. Soup (2) & Bread (24). The day was exceedingly hot. The bells rung in Richmond & a big smoke could be seen from Camp. Another fire. Let our tent down and fixed it to make it warmer. Report say the evening paper said we were to be exchanged immediately.*

* Robert Ould acted as the Confederate Agent for Exchange throughout the war and was charged with implementing the cartel covering the exchange of prisoners of war. Some measure of the man may be gained through the following quote: "[I]f the exigencies of our army require the use of trains for the transportation of corn, pay no regard to the Yankee prisoners. I would rather they should starve than our own people suffer...." Robert E. Denney, *Civil War Prisons & Escapes* (New York: Sterling Publishing Company, 1993), 94 (hereafter cited as *Civil War Prisons*), quoting a letter from Ould to A. C. Myers of the Confederate War Department.

Friday Sept 2nd*

Slept tolerable well last night. I was up sometime in the night and the Bells were ringing in the city. A big light could be seen. Supposed to be another large fire. Very pleasant and cool in the morning until 9 a.m. Bread fell to three (3) loaves for $1 greenback. Pies 2.50 in script. At 11 a.m. drew Meat & Bread (23). Layed around until 4 p.m. when we drew Soup & Bread (23) & (2). Exceeding hot during the after part of the day. Darby made arrangements with a man named Davis for Bread. He brought one loaf of Corn Bread and a small piece of Pork just at dark. He is to bring one every night for 4 nights.

* On this date, one member of the 191st Pennsylvania who was fortunate enough to have missed the action on August 19 wrote the following letter home (reprinted in the *Genius of Liberty* on September 15, 1864):

HEADQUARTERS CO. G 191st PA. VOL.

Near Weldon Railroad

September 2nd, 1864

DEAR GRANDPARENTS: I have just rejoined what is left of my old company, some nine or ten in number, only four of these are from Uniontown, viz: Henry Bunting, John Collins, Isaac Jaquette and Henry Whaley, all of whom I found well, the balance are now supposed to be boarding at the "Hotel De Libby," Richmond, Va., viz: Sergts. Martin V B Hazen, Isaac A. Moore, James W. Everhart [*sic*], Thomas W. Springer—Corpls. James C Darnell, Rawley H Jolliff, John L Francis. Privates, James W Axton, Jacob Clark, George W Darby, Frederic Danbert, Jeremiah B Jones, John Malone, James Malone, Isaac N Mitchell, James H Rholand, David Ritchie, John R Rutter, Llewellyn Vaughn, Barth Warman, and Thomas Rhodetack, also 1st Lieut. S E Bryant, Commanding Company, and Wm E Ackey, acting second Lieutenant.

The manner in which our men were captured seems to have been this: The evening of the 18th our corps (5th) advanced near the Weldon Railroad acting as an advance guard, while Kautz and Gregg's division of cavalry destroyed the Railroad by tearing up the iron and burning the ties, towards the morning of the 18th the enemy was found to be massing his force in our immediate front, soon all hands were working at throwing up earthworks for protection; in a short time our skirmishers were engaged; in a few moments more the enemy threw a very heavy column upon our right, and forced back a portion of the line, and swinging in our immediate rear, and effectually cutting off our retreat, thus capturing some seven hundred of our Brigade, including some fifty enlisted men and one Commissioned officer of our company. As far as I could learn none of our company were either killed or wounded.

Yours affectionately,
JOS. W. STURGIS

Saturday Sept 3rd

Slept better last night than any night for some time. It was not so cold. When I got up it was cloudy and looked like rain. About 7 o clock a.m. it commenced to rain. The fire bells rang again in Richmond last night. This is my birthday—today I am 20 years old. At 11 a.m. we drew meat & bread (21). It cleared off and only rained about one hour. 25 of our men went to Richmond to work for the Gov.* At 4 pm drew soup (2) & Bread (22 1/2). The day turned out a very pleasant one. At dark Davis brought another loaf. Made a new place for a sink** and to get water.

* See the notes following the diary entries for September 13 and November 5.
** Terminology of the Civil War period for a latrine.

[Eberhart-9/3] *Slept better last night—not so cold. When I got up was cloudy and look like Rain. About 10 am it commenced to Rain. The fire bells are a Ringing again in Richmond. At 11 am we drew Bread & Meat—21 loaves. It Rained about an hour & cleared off fine. 25 of our men went to Richmond to work for the government. At 4 pm drew Soup 2 buckets and 21 loaves. Davis brot the bread at dark. Made a new place for a sink & to get water. Sergt Hazen got a Black bug in his ear in the night and he could not get it out. I thought he would go crazy. Two men held him down & filled his ear with water and in a short time the bug drowned and came out.*

Sunday Sept 4th

Cloudy and sultry, rained during the night. We were turned out & counted this morning. Cool & appearances of rain. Traded my Pocket Book off this morning for 5 Apples & 3 Peaches.* At 10 a.m. we drew Meat & Bread (23). Cleared out and became very hot. Traded my hat and got one loaf of Bread. Heard that Zed Springer was a prisoner in Richmond.** At 4 p.m. drew Soup (2) & Bread (23). Darby traded

16

Saturday Sept 3rd

Slept better last night than any
night for some time. it was
not so cold. When I got up it
was cloudy and looked like
rain. About 4 oclock A.m. it
Commenced to rain. The fire
bells rang again in Richmond
last night. This is my birth
day. Today I am 20 years old
At 11 A.m. we drew meat & Bread(2)
it cleared off and only rained
about one hour. 25 of our men went
to Richmond to work for the Gov
At 4 8 m Drew Soup(2) & Bread (2½) The
day turned out a very pleasant one
At dark Davis brought another loaf
Made a new place for a sink
and to get water

In this entry from his diary, Thomas Springer notes that September 3, 1864, was
his 20th birthday.

his hat and got four (4) loaves of Bread. He gave us one half loaf apiece. At dark Davis brought a small piece of corn Bread & meat. Prayer Meeting in Camp, Attendance pretty large.

* Private Crocker described the trading process: "Most of the trades between prisoners and guards were made at one certain guard post near the end of the lane running to the river, and just where the board stockade and earthwork joined, and here it happened that there was quite a space between the bottom of the lumber and the ground, and one night while a crowd of prisoners were dickering with a guard he laid his overcoat down at his feet so near this opening that my friend...succeeded in pulling it through to our side and carried it safely to our quarters. It was one of Uncle Sam's blue coats, and we felt that we were only reclaiming what belonged to some of our own men and didn't consider it stealing. This 'draw' was a godsend to our mess, and during the following Winter aided materially in saving our lives." *National Tribune*, August 16, 1900.

**Lieutenant Zadoc B. Springer, an officer in Company K of the 116th Pennsylvania (part of the famed Irish brigade), was a native of Uniontown, Pennsylvania, and was a second cousin of Thomas W. Springer. He was mustered into service April 7, 1864, was wounded June 3, 1864, at Cold Harbor and was captured at the Battle of Reams Station, Virginia, August 25, 1864, six days after Thomas Springer's capture at Globe Tavern. Reams Station was a stop on the Weldon Railroad several miles south of Globe Tavern.

Monday Sept 5th

Clear and appearances of a hot day. Heard that Atlanta was evacuated. It was published in their morning paper. At 11 a.m. we drew bread (24) but only half rations of meat. The day exceedingly hot. About the hotest we have had yet. The day passed away slowly. The Richmond papers stated that Atlanta was evacuated on the 1st Sept and Hardee's Corps had been driven from their position with the loss of 9 guns. At 4 p.m. we drew soup (2) & Bread (25). Mitchel & I bought a loaf of bread. After dark it commenced to rain rained very hard.

Tuesday Sept 6th

Cloudy & cool. Slight sprinkling of rain. Turned out and counted. I was up sometime in the night. A large light could be seen in the City and bells ringing. Supposed to be another fire. Sick call immediately after we were counted. Our squad are all in pretty good health. Only one man gone to the hospital yet. At 2 p.m. we drew the day's ration of bread (45) & meat. At 3 p.m. we drew soup (2). Continued raining at intervals all day In the evening it got very cold. Fixed up the tent and made it pretty comfortable. Sergts drew an extra ration today. No news.

Wednesday Sept 7th

Rained all night. Sun came out this morning in all his glory. We are going to have a hot day. Sick call at 8 a.m. One man sick in our tent (Malon Lynch). 2 men

*sick in the squad. At 12 m. drew meat & Bread (24). About 1 p.m. the bells began to
ring in the city. And a large smoke could be seen. Another large fire. At 4 p.m. drew
soup (2) & Bread (23). The rest of the day passed off quietly. In the evening saw a
Richmond paper. No News. Except the notice of the death of John Morgan.* And
several pieces on McClellan's nomination.*

* Confederate Brigadier General John Hunt Morgan operated in the Western
Theatre during most of the war, staging daring raids into Kentucky, Ohio, and Indiana. He was captured in Ohio in July 1863, and was imprisoned in Columbus, but
escaped with a number of his men in November of that year. He subsequently assumed command of the Department of Southwest Virginia and was killed September 4, 1864, at Greenville, Tennessee.

Thursday Sept 8th

*Very cold last night and early this morning. Sun up turned out to count us and
to police Camp. Sick call at 9 a.m. Kept us out nearly all day. Very hot. While we
were out I washed my shirt, socks and handkerchief. At 1 p.m. they commenced
going in. It took 2 hours for them all to get in. At 3 p.m. they issued meat & Bread
(1 day's ration)(17). At 4 p.m. it commenced raining. 4 1/2 issued soup (2). I sold
my Gold Ring for $4.00. I bought 6 apples (.25) and one loaf bread (.25) traded the
Wheat Bread for 1 day's ration of Corn Bread. Rained all night. Eberhart slept in
our tent. Quit chewing tobaco.*

Friday Sept 9th

*Turned out again this morning for the purpose of fixing camp, arranging
tents &c. Sick call 9 a.m. Issued rations at 11 a.m. Soft bread (23 1/2) instead of
Corn Bread. At 4 p.m. they commenced to go in by squads. Calling the role &
taking the names. Each squad got its rations as they went in. Bread (24) & Rice
Soup (2). The squads were all filled to 100 men. The thing was mixed up. We did not
get our tents. While we were out 12 men tried to escape by swimming to a little
island. They were found out and brought back but were not punished.* The men did
not all get in until long after dark.*

* George Darby recalled this incident differently: "In the course of the day
there were seven brave fellows who had determined to make a break for freedom,
so, watching until the guard was well around the bend on his beat again, when
silently they dropped into the water, and swimming to the isle twenty feet away,
they drew themselves up amongst the willows without having been discovered by
the guard. Their design was to lie concealed till night came on, then to swim the
river and so make their escape. But the rebs in some way discovered them, and they
were brought back, and made to ride the wooden horse as a punishment. As some of
my readers may not be familiar with this strain of horses, I will briefly describe a
wooden horse. It is a trestle such as carpenters use to rest lumber on which they
wish to saw, only that the wooden horse trestle is longer of leg than that used by the

carpenter.... [N]ow as to the fellow who has to ride the horse, I will tell you how they fix him. They take the offender and set him astride of the trestle, tie his hands behind his back, a tent pin is driven into the ground on either side of the horse, a tent rope is fastened to each of the ankles of the rider, then made fast to the tent pins which are then driven tightly into the ground, and while the rider's feet cannot touch the ground, he is stretched down so closely that he is in no danger of becoming unhorsed, and his hands being fastened behind him he cannot protect himself from the swarms of gnats and flies which attack his face and neck; and being totally unable to shift his position, the torture becomes unbearable, and the victim often faints away. I saw two of the recaptured prisoners faint, when I walked away from the brutal scene...." Darby, *Incidents and Adventures*, 108.

Saturday Sept 10th

Up at daylight—cloudy & cool. Did not turn out this morning until 10 a.m. Cleared off and became very warm (sick call at 9 a.m. 4 sick). At 10 a.m. they issued rations of Soft Bread (24) & meat. Lay around all day. At 3 p.m. we got in and was ordered to get tents wherever we could. We took a row next to 19 but was ordered out. We then went to our old Sibleys. At 4 1/2 p.m. they issued soft bread (23) & rice soup (2). After we had eaten our supper they fixed it up. About the tents, we got our old tents. After dark commenced raining.

Sunday Sept 11th

Rained all night—Turned out at Sun up. They did not keep us long. They commenced going in as soon as they got out. At 11 a.m. we drew Bread (soft-25) & meat. Cloudy. At 1 p.m. commenced raining. Turned out the Squad and had roll call. Rained about one hour. At 3 p.m. drew soft Bread (25) & Bean Soup (2). Give my soup to Jerry. I could not eat my soup or Bread. Had the Diarea very bad and had no appetite.

Monday Sept 12th

Slept very little last night on account of the Diarea and Pain in the Stomach. Up early. Turned out at 7 a.m. Prospect of a hot day. Sick call at 9 a.m. 2 men sick in the Squad. 25 day of captivity. At 10 a.m. commenced clouding up. Slight sprinkling of rain & a heavy wind. At 10 1/2 a.m. drew soft Bread (24 1/2) & meat. Got into camp about 12 m. Did not rain any of any account but continued cloudy and windy. At 4 p.m. drew Bean Soup (2) & Soft Bread (24). Built a fire & boiled my soup & Bread together. And made a pretty good supper. A sudden change in the weather. Very cold.

Tuesday Sept 13th

Extremely cold during the night. And early this morning. Sick call at 9 a.m. 2 men sick in the Squad. At 10 1/2 a.m. drew bread (24 1/2) and A Ration of Meat.

The meat has been cut down from 1/3 to 1/4 lb. Nothing of any note until 4 p.m. when we drew soup (4) & bread (24). 79 men went to Richmond today but no one knows what for. Report says 6 took the oath. The Sergts of Squads met & appointed a committee to get up a petition to the Authorities to Parole us. The Sergts to sign it.*

* By the summer of 1863, the fighting in the various theaters of the war had taken a substantial toll upon the Confederate pool of manpower. That pool was further diminished in dramatic fashion by the Battle of Gettysburg and the surrenders at Vicksburg and Port Hudson. Thus, in July of 1863, "[t]he Confederate government...adopted a policy of recruiting Union prisoners, military and civilian alike, to take an oath of neutrality. This permitted their release from prison and their employment as craftsmen and artisans in desperately needed skills in Southern manufacture. In general, these prisoners conducted themselves well in their parole." Denney, *Civil War Prisons,* 110. See also the note following the diary entry for November 5.

Wednesday Sept 14th

Slept pretty last night as it was not as cold as night before. Sick call at 9 a.m. 3 men sick. At 10 a.m. drew meat & Bread (24). Nothing of any note until 3 p.m. Drew soup (2) & Bread (24). The day was cool and pleasant. And the evening warm. Staid out and walked around about 8 oclock. In the evening heavy cannonading could be heard. It appears to be close. And many are the speculations as to where it is.

Thursday Sept 15th

Passed a very pleasant night last night. Up at 7 a.m. Old Sol out in all his glory and prospect of a hot day. The diarea has nearly stoped on me and I feel a great deal better this morning. Sick call at 9 a.m. 3 men sick. At 10 1/2 a.m. drew soft Bread (23) & meat-shoulder. Some says the paper states that Gen. Lee had evacuated Petersburg. At 12 m. we turned out and the squads filled to 100 men. At 4 p.m. they issued soup (2) & Bread (23 1/2). The Bread was miserable very sour. Roll call in the morning. All present.

Friday Sept 16th 1864

Slept very well. Up at 3 1/2 this morning and the Bells were ringing and making a big fuss in the City. Supposes to be another large fire. Sick call at 9 a.m. At 11 a.m. drew soft Bread (23 1/2) & meat, a tolerable good ration. At 2 p.m. we had roll call. The day warm & very pleasant. At 4 p.m. drew soft Bread (24) and soup (2) After eating supper we drew (2) Buckets of extra soup. This is the 29th day of captivity. In the evening it got very cool. And after dark it was very chilly. Retired about 8 p.m. The 18th Va. was relieved tonight by the militia.

Saturday Sept 17th 1864

Up at Sun up. Passed the night tolerable well although it was very chilly. The Bells rang furiously in the City last night. Heavy dew this morning. At 7 a.m. we were turned out. Sick call at 9 a.m. At 10 1/2 I drew the rations. Dick sick (24). We got a good bucket of meat today, but the Bread was sour. At 11 they commenced going in. All in at 1 p.m. At 4 p.m. I drew the rations Soft Bread (24 1/2) & Bean Soup (2). After supper I went after the Sergts extra ration, but did not get it. Only 16 squads drew. Cool and pleasant in the evening. At 8 p.m. we all retired.

Sunday Sept 18th 1864

Nothing transpired during the night. Up at 6 a.m. Cloudy & cool. Turned out at 7 a.m. At 8 a.m. they commenced going in by squads. Cleared off and the sun came out hot. Sick call at 9 a.m. 4 men sick in the squad. Between 10 & 11 a.m. drew soft Bread (24) & meat. When we went in we were put in old tents, did not get our Sibleys. After dinner I took a sleep. Wakened up at 3 p.m. Clouded up & was raining. Drew Bean Soup (2) & soft Bread at 4 p.m. Give my soup to Rawley and Darby. Stoped raining at dark. All retired at 8 p.m.

Monday Sept 19th 1864

All quiet during the night. Up at sun up. Turned out at 7 a.m. Started in at 8 a.m. I took the sick out at 9 a.m. Six men sick in the squad. At 10 a.m. the Drum sounded the grub call. Soft Bread (25) and meat. Traded my soup with Dick for 1/2 ration of meat. Nothing of any importance until 3 pm when the Drum sounded the supper call. Soft Bread (24 1/2) and Bean soup (2). Toasted my bread. I feel better this evening than I have for some time. the diarea has nearly stoped on me. Retired at 8 p.m.

Tuesday Sept 20th 1864

All quiet during the night (very cold). Did not sleep much. Up at sun-rise. Turned out at 7 a.m. The Camp was policed & limed and the sink cleaned out. All in at 9 a.m. Sick call at 9 a.m. 5 men sick in the Squad. At 11 a.m. Drum sounded the Dinner call. Soft Bread (24) and fresh Beef (2) instead of Bacon. Very hot during the middle of the day. Nothing of any note until 4 1/2 p.m. The Drum sounded the Supper call. Soft Bread (24) and four Buckets of Bean Soup. Traded my soup with Eberhart for his ration of meat.

Wednesday Sept 21st 1864

Bells made a great fuss in the City last night. No light could be seen. Could not make out what it was for. Slept tolerable well. Up at 7 a.m. Morning foggy and cool. Turned out at 7 1/2 a.m. Sick call at 9 a.m. All in Camp at 10. At 11 1/2 a.m. the Drum sounded the Breakfast call. Soft Bread (24) the best we have drew yet &

fresh beef (1). At 1 p.m. they [gave us] one Bucket of meat extra. Made coffee out of the crust of Bread. At 4 p.m. Drew soft Bread (24 1/2). The same kind we drew this morning & Bean Soup (2). Made Coffee again this evening. Evening clear & warm.

Thursday Sept 22nd 1864

Rained very near all night. I was up at 3 a.m. Stoped raining at daylight. Turned out at 7 a.m. Camp Policed. Drained &c. Heavy Cannonading heard in the direction of Deep Bottom. Morning cloudy & sultry. Sick call at 9 a.m. All in Camp at 10 a.m. At 11 a.m. the Drum sounded the Breakfast call. I drew the Rations Soft Bread (25) and fresh meat (1). At 1 p.m. drew another Bucket of meat. At 4 p.m. Drum beat supper call. Soft Bread (25) and bean soup. Traded my soup for meat with Eberhart. Made coffee out of a crust of Bread. Continued cloudy & cool all day.

Friday Sept 23rd 1864

Up at 7 a.m. Turned out immediately. Morning cloudy and sprinkling rain. Sick call at 9 a.m. All in Camp at nine a.m. At 11 a.m. the Drum sounded the Breakfast call. Soft Bread (24 1/2) & fresh beef (1). Stoped raining at 12 m. At 1 p.m. they issued the extra meat (1). Continued cloudy during the rest of the day. At 4 p.m. the Drum sounded the Supper call. Bread (24 1/2) and 4 Buckets of Bean soup. Warmed my soup and made a cup of coffee for Jerry. Cleared off late in the evening & sun set beautiful. All retired at 8 p.m.

Saturday Sept 24th 1864

All quiet during the night. Slept well. Up at 7 a.m. And turned out immediately. Morning cloudy and sultry. Commenced raining at 8 a.m. All in Camp at the sick call 9 a.m. Jim Malone of our company sent to the General Hospital.* Stoped raining at 10 1/2. At 11 a.m. the Drum beat the Breakfast call. I drew the Rations. Soft Bread (24) and one bucket of meat. At 1 p.m. they issued another bucket of meat. Nothing of interest until 3 p.m. when the Drum sounded the supper call. Soft Bread (24) and Rice Soup (2). Rained and blowed very hard in the evening. Very cool.

* Private Crocker commented on the daily sick call and some prisoners' efforts to utilize it to their advantage: "The sick were removed from the pen soon as the doctors pronounced them dangerously ill, and I believe were placed in hospitals in the city. Each morning there was 'sick call,' and the rebel doctors examined all who came to the gate, and sent away such as they pleased to hospital and obliged the others to wait till they got worse. We understood that there was an occasional exchange of the sick, and this induced some of our boys to try to 'play off' sick on the doctors, hoping thereby to secure an early exchange, but it was 'no go.' A Yankee, to gain admission to the hospital, must be 'sure enough' sick." *National Tribune*, August 16, 1900.

Sunday Sept 25th 1864

Very cold during the night. Did not sleep well. Morning clear and very cool. Not a cloud to be seen. Turned out at 7 a.m. All in Camp at 9 a.m. Sick call at 9 a.m. One man Griffith of the Squad sent to the General Hospital. At 11 a.m. the Drum sounded the Breakfast call. Soft Bread (28 1/4) and one Bucket of Beef. At 12 m. we drew another Bucket of Beef. Continued windy & cool all day. At 3 p.m. drew soup (4) & Soft Bread (24 1/4). Loafed around all evening. Evening clear and very cool. All retired at 8 p.m. Darby hooked 2 tent blankets.

Monday Sept 26th 1864

Slept tolerable well considering the coldness of the weather. Up at 7 a.m. and turned out right away. Morning very clear and tolerable cool. All in camp at 9 a.m. Cannonading heard in the direction of Petersburg. Sick call at 9 a.m. 6 men sick in the Squad. Two sent to the Gen'l Hospital. Ross and Lemley. The day clear and warm. The grub was not issued until 1 p.m. on account of the Bread not getting here in time. We drew soft Bread (25 1/2) & fresh Beef (2) the first had a liver in it At 5 p.m. the Drum sounded the soup call. Soft Bread (25) & Bean Soup (2). 2 men sent to us to fill up the squad. All retired at 8 p.m.

Tuesday Sept 27th 1864

All quiet during the night. Slept very well but it was pretty cold. Up at 7 and turned out immediately. Old Sol came up in all his glory and made it very pleasant. The sickness of the Camp is pretty large but the mortality is very small. A great many is sent to the General Hospital. The No. of men in Camp when we first came was 5791. It has come down to 4724. Sick call at 9 a.m. Cannonading heard in direction of Petersburg. All in at 9 a.m. 2 men sent to Gen. Hos. Bulford, McGarvey. At 11 1/2 drew soft Bread (25) & fresh beef (2) at 4 p.m. drew bread (25) but did not get the soup until 6 p.m. Boiled my soup. The day pleasant cool & windy. 2 men sent to fill up the squad.

Wednesday Sept 28th 1864

All Quiet during the night. Slept very well. Up before sun up and washed. Morning warm and pleasant. Turned out at 6 1/2 a.m. All in Camp at 8 1/2. At 9 a.m. the sick call beat. Lynch-of our company sent to the Gen. Hos. At 11 1/2 the Drum beat the Breakfast call. Drew soft Bread (24 1/2) and one Bucket of fresh beef. At 1 p.m. I drew the extra meat. At 3 p.m. they issued the Bread (24 1/2). Commenced raining shortly after and rained until we got our soup (4) 5 1/2 p.m. Boiled the soup. Someone stole my tin cup. Richey and Darnell tried to escape, but was discovered this evening. Somebody informed on them. They dug a hole in the ground and covered themselves up.*

* George Darby describes this escape attempt in detail: "[One day] when we were turned out for another count, I observed the imprint of a man in the sand, and like Robinson Crusoe on discovering a footprint in the sand, I was startled. It instantly suggested to my mind a method of escape and quickly obliterating the telltale imprint, I walked up to the rear of the cook house, where I had observed an old Sibley tent pole to be lying for a week or more and I had been cudgeling my brain for a chance to secure and use it. Now here was the chance, and the use would come later. I laid hold of it, and after a little struggle I succeeded in wrenching off one of the three iron feet and rolling it up in my shelter tent I carried it into camp. I immediately called a council of war among my messmates, and submitted my plans, which received their approval, and were as follows: The next time we were turned out for a count, a compact ring or circle was to be formed by us, so that the guard could not see what was going on within, thus screened we were to dig a cave in the sand, of sufficient size to accommodate two men, (for digging we used the iron foot I had secured from the tent pole). The men were to be covered up in the sand, and to remain until sometime the following night, when being outside the guard they could swim the river and make their escape, and at the next count off two more, and so on. On our next outing we dug our hole according to our plans and specifications and selecting Comrades David Richie and Calvin Darnell, they being small men, we buried them up, leaving holes for air which we concealed by placing some dead grass over them. The next time the hole was to be enlarged, and Isaac Moore [known as "Dick" Moore in Thomas Springer's diary] and myself, two of the larger men in the mess were to have our inning. With what anxiety we watched that spot of ground that afternoon. Imagine our alarm when late in the day we saw some pigs rooting around near where our boys were buried. Those infernal swine, they kept poking around there until one of them stepped into one of the breathing holes. Richie caught him by the foot. I saw the pig jerking to get loose, and as there were two rebels engaged in fishing only a short distance away, I was fearful lest they would observe it, and enter upon an investigation of the cause of the strange action of the hog, but they did not seem to see it at all and Richey let go of the pig's foot, and he walked off as if nothing had happened. I have often wondered why the rebs kept those pigs in the enclosure about the cook house, but after debating the subject to some extent we reached the conclusion that it was to garnish our soup with a pork flavor, as we have ofttimes detected them with their snouts in our soup buckets before the soup was served to us. However, I was never so fortunate as to find a scrap of meat of any kind in my soup, while in Belle Isle. But I conclude that you also are becoming anxious about the comrades we left buried in the sand some hours since. Well as the rebel officer of the guard that evening was making his rounds, a soldier belonging to a New York command called him up to the fence and informed him in regard to Richey and Darnell, and pointed out to him as nearly as he could, where they were in hiding. The officer drew his sword and proceeded to make search after the hiding prisoners. He pierced the ground all about them but failing to find them sent word to Major Turner at Richmond, who had charge of all prisoners of war in and about Richmond. Now, while this Turner was no relation to Dick, of Libby, they were as near of kin in villainies, as two peas in a pod. The Major came over to the island armed with an old pepper-box revolver. He had twelve or fifteen soldiers with him. These he set to work jabbing around in the sand, until one of them stuck Richie in the head, which caused him to cry out, then they set about digging them out of their hiding place. As soon as poor Richie was out of the hole the valorless Major presented his revolver at his head and endeavored to shoot him but the weapon refused to respond, and after snapping it for a while, threw it into the river in disgust. He then ordered that the prisoners be kept in the hole where they were found for two days and nights, without food or water, and after placing a guard over them, the chivalrous Southerner returned to his post at Richmond, where he no doubt gave to his associates in crime a glowing account of his deeds of valor done that day against two unarmed and half-starved prisoners of war." Darby, *Incidents and Adventures*, 108–12.

Thursday Sept 29th 1864

Up at 7 and turned out but not as early as usual. Richey & Darnell were still in the hole when we went out this morning. Dick [Moore] gave them something to eat.* Sick call at 9. They tore down the old tents that we stayed in and commenced putting up better ones. They put up 4 rows of tents and quit. At 2 p.m. they commenced to go in. All in at 3. Then they issued the day's ration of Bread (48) and (2) buckets of meat. At 4 p.m. drew soup (2). After eating soup they gave us tents and we soon put them up. 9 tents to 100 men Cannonading very heavy all day. Richey and Darnell were put in camp.

* Darby continues his account of the attempted escape: "On our being turned out again for count the next day we threw them some small bits of bread which we had saved for the purpose from our own meagre rations, but we could not give them any water. After remaining in the hole for the prescribed length of time, they were allowed to rejoin the mess. The man who informed the guard of the plot of these boys to escape was found out by one of our men, and we were about to organize a court martial for his trial, when we were all shipped to Salisbury, where I learned he afterward died of starvation." Darby, *Incidents and Adventures*, 112.

Friday Sept 30th 1864

Slept very well in our new tents as the night was not very cold. The wind blew all night. Up early and turned out at 7 a.m. Late last evening they planted 2 guns on the hill opposite the Camp. 2 men of the Squad sent to the Gen. Hos. yesterday. Morgan & Phillips. Sick call at 9 a.m. At 10 the Drum sounded the Breakfast call. Bread (28) and fresh beef. Rained slightly during the forenoon. In the afternoon 7

Squads of new men from Libby came in. Found one man among them that we knew. Bill Davis 1st Va. Cav. At 3 p.m. they issued Bread (25). Rained a little in the afternoon. At 4 p.m. they issued the soup. Built a fire and boiled it. Evening cool & cloudy. Very heavy firing all day.

Saturday Oct 1st* [44]

The night was very cold. But we slept pretty well. Up before daylight and stole a tin bucket. The morning cloudy and very cold. Turned out at 7. At 8 a.m. a northeast commenced blowing and soon it commenced to rain. a cold drisly rain. All in camp at 9 a.m. when the sick call beat. They did not sound the Grub call until 2 p.m. They issued one meal of Corn Bread (20) and one of soft Bread (25) and fresh beef (2). Continued raining all day. The sound of the cannonading seemed to be nearer. It was very plain. Musketry could also plainly be heard. At 4 p.m. they issued Bean Soup (4) (extra). Darby & I put our meal Bread and soup together & Boiled it and made my Bucket full 1/2 Gallon. A first rate meal. Continued raining all day at intervals. And made it very disagreeable. All retired at 8 p.m.

* On this date, Thomas Springer began to record the total number of days of captivity.

Sunday Oct 2nd [45]

Rained at intervals all night. After dark it got to be a little warmer. A man shot last night. We slept very well. At 7 a.m. turned out. The Camp policed &c. Morning cloudy & cool. Appearances of rain. All in Camp at 8 1/2 a.m. Sick call at 9 a.m. At 10 a.m. the Drum sounded the Breakfast. We drew 20 loaves of Corn and 5 of soft Bread and one Bucket of meat. It did not rain. The sun came out in the afternoon and made it very pleasant and dried up the mud. At 5 p.m. we drew our Rations. Corn Bread (21) and fresh Beef (1). The largest ration we have ever drawn yet. A new Q. Master was put in today. At sun down we drew our Bean soup. With the fresh beef we draw 1 quart of salt every day since we commenced drawing.

Monday Oct 3rd [46]

Up before the Drums beat and washed. Morning cloudy, sultry and appearances of rain. Turned out at 7 a.m. One man killed and one wounded last night. At 8 a.m. commenced going in camp. All in at 9 a.m. Drum beat the sick call at 9 a.m. At 10 a.m. the Drum sounded the Breakfast call. I drew the rations. Corn Bread (28) and one Bucket of beef 1 quart of salt. At 12 m. we drew a small ration of Beeff. About 300 more prisoners came in at 1 p.m. 5,600 all told. Commenced raining about 2 p.m. Quit a little before dark. At 4 p.m. the Drum sounded the supper call. Bread (25) and bean Soup. Built a fire and boiled my soup & Bread. Evening cloudy & cool. Retired at tattoo-7 p.m.

Tuesday Oct 4th [47]

Up at daylight—Drums beat the Reveille at 6 a.m. Morning very foggy. Turned out at 7 a.m. Did not go in till very late. Sick call at 9 a.m. Sent 1100 men away today with 3 days Rations.* Eberhart took charge of the squad today. Myers & Cooper of our Co went in with the squad that left. At 3 p.m. the squads were filled up. And 3 1/2 we drew Rations Corn Bread (28) 1 Bucket of fresh beef. 1 quart of salt. At 4 p.m. drew Rations Corn Bread (25) Bean soup (4) extra Warm Corn Bread. Boiled my soup at evening.

* Rumors of an imminent exchange persisted among the prisoners, and Private Crocker's hopes soared in early October when "the commanders of the five highest numbered squads...were ordered to get their men ready to move at daylight the next morning. In a few minutes the wildest scene of excitement and enthusiasm imaginable prevailed among us. Men threw up their caps, laughed, cried, hugged and kissed one another, shouted themselves hoarse, and all seemed to forget past suffering in the supreme joy of the moment. Our hopes of exchange were now to be reality, and in imagination I fancied myself already on my way home.... [A Confederate officer] came into the pen that night and told a crowd of us standing near the gate that he was to take charge of the 5,000 who would start in the morning, and that 5,000 more would go in the evening, and so on...till all were exchanged.... At last [my] turn came, and as I marched out of the pen I earnestly said good-by Belle Island, and mentally promised myself that the rebels would never capture me again.... We marched over the Long Bridge and turned toward Manchester, where I had alighted from the cars on my arrival.... I did not 'smell a mice' until we were ordered to board a train...'headed South.' I was thunderstruck, and said to one of the guards who was hurrying us into the cars that this was certainly wrong; that we didn't want to go that way to be exchanged! His answer, 'How are you exchanged?' hurt me worse than any words I had ever heard...." *National Tribune*, August 16, 1900.

Wednesday Oct 5th [48]

5 Squads (500) men sent away this morning at 3 a.m. with two (2) day rations. This makes 1600 sent away. Destination supposed to be N[or]th Carolina. Up at Reveille and turned out at sun-up. Morning clear and pleasant. Commenced going in at 9 a.m. All in Camp at 10 a.m. At 11 I drew the Rations. Corn Bread (25) one Bucket of meat. One quart of salt. Very hot during the middle of the day. At 2 p.m. 500 more men were sent away with 2 days rations. They are up to 17th squad. At 4 p.m. drew Corn Bread 25 and soup (2). Evening very pleasant.

Thursday Oct 6th [49]

We were wakened up this morning. And drew 2 days ration of Corn Bread (100) and one days ration of meat and one quart of salt. At 5 a.m. we marched out of camp (Nine (9) squads, 900) down the Rail Road to Manchester and stoped there. Very warm during the forenoon. About 1 p.m. it clouded up and slightly sprinkled rain but none of any account. About 4 p.m. another squad came from the Island (about 400) and shiped aboard of the Cars immediately. We did not get aboard until nearly dark. We got aboard about 5 1/2 p.m. 65 men were put in a car. We got off about dark.

Friday Oct 7th [50]

Run all night. Richmond & Danville Rail Road. Ten (10) men of our company escaped from our car. Sergt Moore, Corpl. J. C. Darnell, Corpl. J. L. Francis. Prvs. G. W. Darby, I. N. Mitchel, D. Richey, D. Elgin, W. H. Link, J. W. Axton & Barth. Warman.* We arrived in Danville about 10 a.m. and changed cars and run all day. Arrived in Greensboro about 12 m. And was marched about 1/2 mile and camped 50 miles from Salsbury.

* George Darby describes his part in this episode: "On the 6th day of October, 1864, one thousand three hundred prisoners, after being provided with what the rebels informed us were three days' rations, but which by the way were all consumed at one meal by most of the men, and I distinctly remember what an exertion of will power it cost me to save even a small piece of cornbread from my allowance; we were loaded into box cars and started for another rebel starvation hell, located at Salisbury, N.C. Sixty-five men were crowded into each car which rendered it impossible for us either to sit or lie down, so we were obliged to stand like cattle in a stock train; the doors on the right hand side of the cars were locked, while those on the left were open, with two guards stationed in each, and a number of guards also rode on the deck of each car. The cars were old rotten looking things, and when the train once got under headway it rattled and banged in a way to drown all other sounds, so I set about kicking at the front end of the car in which I was riding, and I soon succeeded in breaking a hole through it large enough to crawl out of if the opportunity came. So giving one-half of my dog tent to my comrade, Isaac Mitchell, I told him that the first stop the train made I proposed to make a break for liberty and he said, 'I will follow you.' The first stop which the train made was for wood. This was twenty-three miles from Richmond. So out I crawled, onto the bumpers, and down to the ground between the cars and out onto the side where the guards were standing in the doors. I started boldly along side the train toward the engine. One of the guards in the car next to the one I had escaped from as I passed, cried, 'Halt, who goes dar?' Without stopping I turned my head and said, 'Who the devil are you talking to!' and I passed without further challenge, it being so dark they could not distinguish the color of my clothing." Darby, *Incidents and Adventures*, 116–17.

Saturday Oct 8th [51]

The night was very cold and was spent in walking around to keep warm. About 11 a.m. we marched back to the Depot and shiped for Salsbury. We got on top of the cars. Started about 12 m. 1st Station passed Jamestown (10), 2nd passed High Point—15 miles, 3rd, Thomasville—20 miles, 4th, Lexington (33), 5th, Woltsburg—44 miles, 6th, Salisbury—51 miles from Greensboro. Arrived at sundown. We were on the W. & N. C. Rail Road 286 miles from Richmond to Salisbury. When we arrived at Salisbury we were nearly frozen, having been on the cars 7 hours. We were formed into line and marched out to the camp about 1/4 mile from town and counted off in squads of 100 men. Ours was the 10 squad 5 Division. The camp is a very pleasant one. One half is shaded by tall oak. And a row of brick buildings through the middle. The officers' quarters are log huts just in the rear.* When we started we had two days rations. They were up last night. We have had no rations issued to us. Or nothing to eat except what we bought on the road. The Guards with us treated us very mean. Stopping all the Pedlers and buying all their goods. And selling them to us for four times their worth. Jolliff sold his watch for $100. I borrowed $5.00 from him. The women along the road treated us very kindly, waving their kerchiefs &c. Men are scarce. At three houses I counted 18 women and not a man to be seen. The crops along the road appear to be pretty good. When we were dismissed I made my bucket full of Wheat Coffee. With that & the Hard tack, one Pie (sweet potato) and one large sweet cake we made a pretty good supper. Jerry laid down and soon we were along side of him but it was to cold to sleep. 286 miles from Richmond to Salisbury.

* Frank King, sergeant major of the 190th Pennsylvania, was captured at Globe Tavern and was among the last of the prisoners to be released. He maintained a record of his imprisonment from which he subsequently compiled a manuscript volume. In that volume, King described the prison at Salisbury in the following manner: "With the dawn of day, I was able to take a survey of the premises, which, as near as I can calculate, contained eight acres, and was surrounded by a tight board fence, eight feet high. The sentinels walked on elevated platforms outside the fence, but were not furnished with sentry-boxes like other prisons. The inside space was not square, being much wider on the north end than on the south. At the northern corners, spaces were left open in the fence, at each of which was a piece of artillery as a defense in case of an uprising or rebellion among the prisoners. At the south end was a large gate, wide enough for the ingress or egress of wagons, which were loaded either with wood or water to come in, or dead 'Yanks' to go out. On the west side was a small door, the same one by which our entrance was made, and through which all new-comers came. On the east, nothing but the bare fence, crowned with the rusty firelocks, and the no less rusty wearers of the 'Butternut,' was visible. So much for the boundaries—now for the internal arrangements. The small

This lithograph depicts the Confederate military prison at Salisbury, North Carolina. The Union troops captured at Globe Tavern were sent there October 6, 1864.

door on the western side, opened into what was termed the 'grove,' or 'square,' a large space, thinly sprinkled with big trees, (oak) and surrounded on the four sides with buildings and fence. Starting from the fence, on the north was a brick building, unused, but afterwards turned into a little bakery, a space, and then a row of brick buildings, three in number, with about two rods intervening between each, the first being used as barracks, (afterwards hospitals,) and the last the 'dead house.' The south side was formed by a one-story wooden building, which was the main, or (as familiarly known,) No. 1 hospital; then a three-story brick building, which was a barrack for the citizen prisoners, the main factory building, tenanted principally by the Yankee deserters, and the big bakery, from which rations were issued. The fence formed the western side. In the centre of the grove was a covered well. There was a row of one-story wooden buildings, four in number, at the northern extremity of the enclosure, which were occupied by the commissioned officers captured from our army. They were divided from us by a 'dead line,' (a small trench,) and a line of guard posts. All communication between them and us was forbidden. There was a well near the big gate, one some distance in rear of the buildings east of the 'square,' and one behind the Citizens' building which were in use at the time I arrived. Others were in course of construction, and were finished sometime afterwards. In the well behind the Citizens' building, the dead body of a negro had been thrown, previous to our coming, and we did not find it out until our frequent applications for water made the well almost dry, and thereby exposed the body to our gaze. It was taken up and carried off, but I had no relish for water from that well again." Samuel P. Bates, *History of Pennsylvania Volunteers, 1861–5* (Harrisburg, Pa.: B. Singerly, State Printer, 1871), 5:282 (hereafter cited as *History of the Pa. Volunteers*).

Sunday Oct 9th [52]

Passed the night pretty much the same as last night. I laid down and slept until I got cold. Then I would take a turn around the Camp to warm up. Morning clear & cool. At 8 a.m. all the squads fell in and was counted by Quarter Master. Then we drew rations. Bread 1 days ration (50) 2 Buckets of Beef. Just about twice as much as we drew on the Isle. About 3 p.m. 400 more came in camp. I suppose there is 6,000 here now. At 3 1/2 we drew soup. 4 Buckets Rice Soup. It was not worth anything. Evening cool & at 8 I layed down.

Monday Oct 10th 1864 [53]

The night was very cold but I managed to get some sleep. But I nearly froze myself. Morning clear & very cool. Made Jerry some tea out of bark. At 8 a.m. the Drums beat and all fell in and was counted off for rations. Drew nothing but soft Bread (50). Toasted some for Jerry in the hospital.* Sun came out and made it very comfortable. Slept all morning. In one corner of the yard is the Main Building—

Cotton Factory. In it they had confined their Deserters. They were taken away today. At 4 p.m. drew 1 pint of Rice soup. Directly after our soup Jolliff, Eberhart, Rutter & myself got in the Building. 3 stories high & capable of holding 300 on a floor. We slept on the 3rd floor Evening clear & cool.

* "To call the filthy pens where the sick soldiers were confined, 'hospitals,' is a strange perversion of the English language. A better term would be 'slaughter-houses'—and in fact that was the term applied to them by the inmates of the Salisbury prison. Long, low structures, averaging twenty-five by seventy feet, some of brick and others of logs, they were unattractive without and unspeakably horrible within. The sick and dying prisoners lay in rows on the rough, cold floors; no beds or bedding—rows of ghastly, starving faces—skeletons in rags. To see that spectacle once was to see it forever. The wasted forms, the sad, pleading eyes of those sufferers, the sobs of sorrow and the wails of despair, the awful hack! hack! hack!—such scenes and sounds can never be forgotten. The nurses could not even procure water enough to wash the hands and faces of those sick and dying men, and there they lay in the filth that proceeded from their own bodies. The air in these enclosures was stifling, and one would have thought would be sufficient to poison all sources of life within." Darby, *Incidents and Adventures,* 204–5, quoting C. H. Golden.

Tuesday Oct 11th [54]

Slept very well. Better than I have any night yet. I got up at 3 a.m. to get water (it is very scarce) but the Guard would not let anyone out until 7 a.m. I burned my bread and laid down again. At 7 we got out. Knox Campbell got the water. I made a pot of coffee. I saw Lt. Springer this morning. At 9 a.m. fell in and was counted off by the Q.M. At 10 a.m. they issued bread & nothing else (50). Very hot all day. At 1 p.m. they commenced issuing soup but it did not reach us. We had to do without. We drew a pretty good ration of wood.* Report says they are going to Parole us. This is the hardest hole we was ever in. No water and only one-half loaf Bread. Got a shave today. Made a Bucket of coffee. Evening clear, cool & chilly.

* Private Crocker described the effect that burning the wood had upon the men: "Our supply of wood was very small. It was issued daily, and each squad was allowed as much as two of its members could carry from the railroad into the stockade.... It was mostly of green sap-pine timber, which would hardly burn at all, and emitted a sticky black smoke that would not wash off, and our hands and faces soon became coated with it and our long, uncombed hair was matted and stuck together with it till, clad in our ragged garments, we resembled anything rather than intelligent human beings." *National Tribune,* August 23, 1900.

Wednesday Oct 12th [55]

Did not sleep very well last night. Rather to cold. Morning clear and warm after the sun came out. At 8 a.m. the Drum sounded the fall-in call. Counted off by the Quarter Master. About 10 a.m. we drew Bread (50) and nothing else. Day passed off quietly. Quite warm. Drew 2 sticks of wood. Jolliff bought a blanket (25) & 2 Potato Pies (5).

Thursday Oct 13th [56]

Slept pretty well under the blanket. Did not get up until the Drum beat the fall in call. Counted off. At 11 a.m. drew our rations. Hard Bread (4 1/2) & one pint of rice soup. Quite warm during the day. At 4 p.m. was counted off by the Quarter Master. Evening cool. I took the dumb ague at 4 p.m.* Drew a small ration of wood.

* "Ague" was a nonspecific term commonly used to refer to the chills and violent shivering associated with malarial, typhoid, and other types of fevers. This seemingly innocuous entry represents the first mention by Thomas Springer of what ultimately became a mortal struggle against typhoid fever. Typically, the disease was caused by contaminated food or drinking water, and was prevalent in over-crowded prison camps where sanitary conditions generally were appalling. A "shake" was the soldiers' vernacular for the tremors caused by the chills and fever that were symptomatic of the illness.

One Union surgeon described the symptoms common to these fevers as fol-lows: "The fevers by which the men were attacked shortly after their arrival, were, in many cases, of the most malignant type, and in some cases the patients never reacted perfectly, but sank on the first chill. Men were brought into the hospital with what would be regarded as epileptic fits, but what, in reality, was the coast fever. These would froth at the mouth, have some convulsions, and, for a time, be perfectly demented. The chief complaints made by them were of severe headache, and of a burning skin, when in reality the surface was cold and covered with a clammy sweat. When reaction took place, the skin became excessively hot, the eyes bloodshot, the pulse bounding and corded. When the fever broke up the heavy sweat was of a most disagreeable odor. The only hope for the patient was in the exhibition of free doses of quinine." Robert E. Denney, *Civil War Medicine* (New York: Sterling Publishing Company, Inc., 1994), 56. As of 1865, the mortality rate from typhoid fever reached 56% of those who were stricken by it.

Friday Oct 14th [57]

Up nearly all night. At daylight I made Jerry a tin of coffee. At 8 a.m. I made him a tin of beef tea. Someone stole Eberharts cup last night. Commenced drawing rations at 7 a.m. At 11 a.m. we drew warm Bread (50) and a large ration of Beef. At 4 p.m. drew rice soup. All passed off quiet Counted off at 4 p.m. Had a shake at 4 p.m.

Saturday Oct 15th [58]

Slept tolerable well last night. All quiet during the night. At 11 a.m. we drew Warm Bread and 1/2 pint of molasses. At 1 p.m. drew rice soup. Quiet warm during the day. Counted off at 4 p.m. Drew wood x12 m. Had a shake at 4 p.m.

[Eberhart-10/15] *Slept tolorably well last night. All quiet during the night. At 11 Drew warm bread. 1/2 Pt of molases. Quite warm during the day. We would get out in the Sun and take our Shirts off to hunt the grey back and then our pants next.* Could not do any washing. Hard job to get enough to wash your face. Counted off at 4 pm & Drew wood.*

* "Greybacks" was the vernacular for body lice. "'There is not a man in the army, officer or private that does not have from a Battalion to a Brigade of Body lice on him' wrote an Alabamian in 1863.... Both body lice, which roamed over the anatomy at large, and crab lice, which confined their attacks to hirsute areas, are mentioned—but the former, being the more numerous, came in for a lion's share of comment. They were dubbed with a great variety of grimly jocular names, such as 'graybacks,' 'rebels,' zouaves,' 'tigers,' and 'Bragg's body-guard.'"

"Military terms extended also to methods of extermination. Killing lice was referred to as 'fighting under the black flag'; throwing away an infested shirt was spoken of as 'giving the vermin a parole,' and evading them by turning a garment wrong side out was called 'executing a flank movement.'"

"Naturally there were many fantastic stories circulated about these unwelcome creatures. Several [soldiers] testified to catching lice with the letters C.S. (Confederate States) inscribed on their backs; one asserted that he saw a grayback adorned with the insignia I.W. (In for the War). Another claimed: 'I pulled off a Shirt last night and threw it down; this morning I saw it moving first one way and then another; I thought at first that there was a rat under it but upon inspection found that it was the lice racing about hunting for a Soldier.'"

"An Alabama [soldier] whose wife had suggested bringing two children to visit the camp wrote with a degree of seriousness advising against the proposal. 'If you was here the Boddy lice would eat up booth of the children in one knight in spite of all we could doo; you dont hav any idea what sort of a animal they are.'"

"But to Private Shield of the Virginia Light Artillery must be credited the most striking comment on record. One night as he prepared to retire he assumed a prayerful pose and recited:

'Now I lay me down to sleep,
While gray-backs oe'r my body creep;
If I should die before I wake,
I pray the Lord their jaws to break.'"

All quoted material from Bell Irvin Wiley, *The Life of Johnny Reb* (Baton Rouge, La.: Louisiana State University Press, 1943), 250–51.

Sunday Oct 16th [59]

All quiet during the night. Day very warm. At 11 a.m. drew Bread & molasses. At 12 m. drew soup. One of our Officers was shot by the Guard today. The cause I did [not] learn. Mortality of the camp when we first came here was small. It has increased every day. It will average now about 12 a day. Drew wood in the evening. Eberhart's Tin Cup was stolen.

Monday Oct 17th [60]

Up at 3 a.m. Morning clear & cold. The night was very cold. Warm after the sun came out. At 9 a.m. drew our rations. Soft Bread (50) & molasses (1). At 11 1/2 we drew rice soup. Gave it to Eberhart. At 1 p.m. had a shake. Drew wood. Counted off at 5.

Tuesday Oct 18th [61]

Staid up until 12 oclock. Got a pretty good nap from that till morning. Someone stole our bread last night. At 11 a.m. drew our rations. Soft Bread & molasses. The day was cloudy and the sun did not come out much. At 1 p.m. drew our rice soup. At 3 p.m. drew wood. Shake at 4. Doc gave me a dose of quinine. Counted at 4 p.m.

Wednesday Oct 19th [62]

Up at 3 a.m. Quite cool. At 9 I went to the doctors and got a dose of quinine. At 12 m. drew Bread (48) meat & Rice Soup. Rawley got into the Hospital. 552 more prisoners came in this afternoon. Dick Moore Dan Elgin & Link were among them.* The officers were sent off this afternoon at 5 p.m. Had no shake today.

* See the note following the diary entry for October 7. Moore, Elgin and Link were among the ten Union prisoners from Company G who managed to escape from the train carrying them to Salisbury. All ten were ultimately recaptured. See Chapter Sixteen for George Darby's account of their eventual fates.

Thursday Oct 20th [63]

Very cold during the night. Did not sleep very much. At 9 a.m. drew Soft Bread & molasses. And at 1 p.m. drew Rice soup. Very hot during the day and cool in the evening. At 4 p.m. we were counted off by the Quarter Master. 5 p.m. drew our ration of wood. One man shot sometime in the night last night. For some cause or other. 10 men went out at the sink. 3 of them were caught. I suppose the rest got away. They say that 20 men left today. One guard went with them. No shake today.

Friday Oct 21st [64]

Very cold last night. Slept by turns by the fire. Made Rawley some coffee & toast. At 9 a.m. we drew our Bread and molasses. I traded molasses for meat. Nothing of any note during the day. At 3 p.m. we drew Rice Soup. At 4 p.m. drew wood. Evening clear & cool. Sickness in camp is increasing every day and the

mortality is also increasing. They haul them out every day by the wagon loads. No*
shake today.

* Frank King described the burial of the dead: "The squad [of prisoners] already referred to as having made the ditch around the entire camp was not disbanded.... They were retained and kept at work digging trenches in which to bury the dead. The mortality was fearful, the deaths increasing daily from the first of October, when we went there, until about the middle of January, 1865, when they had reached about the number of fifty a day. Forty deaths in one day was a common occurrence, and one team and wagon was kept busily employed in carrying the bodies from the dead-house to the place of interment. During our first week at Salisbury coffins were furnished, which did seem to the living like one degree towards humanity; but at the end of that time, we discovered that the same coffins, five in number, were used every day. When it was found out that we knew their secret, the practice was discontinued, and the bodies were carried out piled on the wagon like logs of wood." Bates, *History of the Pa. Volunteers*, 5:285.

Saturday Oct 22nd [65]

Very cold. And slept by turns. Kept the fire up all night. Burned all the wood we had saved. Made Rawley some coffee & toast. At 8 a.m. drew our Ration of Bread & molasses. Morning cloudy and cool. The sun did not come out but was cool all day. At 12 m. we drew our Rice Soup. Bought a pint of Rice. Cooked one

This photograph depicts trench burials outside the Confederate prison at Andersonville. Some four thousand Union prisoners of war were buried in similar fashion at Salisbury.

National Archives

*half of it. Evening very cool & cloudy. After dark the wind fell. Drew a small ration
of wood.*

Sunday Oct 23rd [66]

*Slept better last night although it was a great deal colder than the nights
before. At 7 a.m. we drew our rations of Bread and molasses, our division being
first this morning. Warm during the day. Drew soup at 2 p.m. also wood. Evening
cloudy & cool.*

*[Eberhart-10/23] Slept better last night although it was colder than usual
the night before. At 7 Drew Bread & Molases our Division being first to draw.
Warm during the day. Draw Soup at 2 pm & wood in evening. A Minister and a lady
Came in to Camp today and held a short service. Was glad to hear them.*

Monday Oct 24th [67]

*Morning cloudy & cool. At 9 a.m. commenced drawing Rations. We drew
Flour instead of Bread. Nearly all the camp drew Flour. Sprinkled rain but cleared
off by 12 m. In the afternoon they issued 2 tents to the squad. Clouded up and
rained a little then cleared off. We put up our tent a Sibley. Drew Rice Soup. Also
wood.*

Tuesday Oct 25th [68]

*Slept very well. Although the tent was crowded full. Morning clear & pleas-
ant. At 9 a.m. we drew flour & molasses. Eberhart & I mixed ours up & baked 6
cakes before the fire. And made drop dumplings in our soup.*

*[Eberhart-10/25] Slept very well considering the crowded tent. Morning clear
& pleasant. At 9 Drew Flour & Molases. Tom Springer & I mixed ours togeather &
Baked some Cake & made drop dumplings. Picked up a Bone in the camp and
pounded it up & boiled it for the marrow.* For our dumpling soup.*

* Frank King recalled the satisfaction a bone could provide: "I remember...when
our rations were cut off, that some others and myself, for want of more substantial
sustenance, burnt pieces of bone, eating the crisp, and repeating the operation until
the bones were pretty nearly demolished. When fortunate enough to draw a ration
of meat that was part bone, we would get a great deal of nourishment from it. By
breaking a bone into small pieces, with a knife and a stone, and boiling it, we could
make quite a decent soup. Until I was a prisoner it was always a wonder to me what
satisfaction a dog could possibly derive from gnawing a bone; but from that time
my wonder ceased." Bates, *History of the Pa. Volunteers*, 5:287.

Wednesday Oct 26th [69]

*All quiet during the night. Morning clear & pleasant. The day passed away
slowly. We did not draw our rations until 4 p.m. Flour molasses & Rice soup. One
barrel of Flour to 200 men no salt. Made a bucket of drop dumplings in the soup.*

Thursday Oct 27th [70]

Morning cloudy and sprinkling rain. Made a bucket of dumplings. Meadwell of our Company died last night. Average 100 per week. All of them or the most of them die from Diarea and Disentery. They haul them out in a wagon every day. No Coffin. Heisley of our Co. died this morning. Continued raining at intervals pretty hard all day. 590 more Prisoners from Richmond Captured in the Valley 19th Oct. came in this afternoon.* At 8 p.m. we drew Bread Hot from the Oven. Nothing else. Drew Rice Soup.

* Private Crocker described the evil that could befall new prisoners: "The new prisoners were victims of much brutality at the hands of a gang of men who belonged principally to the Mississippi Marine Brigade, who behaved much like the 'Raiders' of Andersonville. We called these men 'Muggers' here, and they were a terror to all the honest prisoners; but the newcomers were the worst sufferers at their hands as the Richmond robbers had stripped the older prisoners so bare that now they furnished mighty 'poor picking....' These fellows murdered a negro prisoner, and threw him in our well, and we used the water for some time after. We found the water tasted badly, and finally discovered the dead body, and, as we had no means of removing it, abandoned the well." *National Tribune*, August 23, 1900.

Friday Oct 28th [71]

Rained nearly all night. Up at sun up. The sun came out beautiful. The camp is very muddy and disagreeable. I went into the dead house this morning.* I counted 22 died during the night. Keys of Company H died today. They hauled out 27. At 10 a.m. we drew a good Ration of Beef & Mutton. I got mutton. Also Eberhart's Ration of Beef. At 1 p.m. drew Rice Soup. Eberhart got mine. The day wore away. It was very pleasant. But we drew no Bread. Counted at 4 p.m.

* "In Salisbury prison, besides buildings called hospitals, was a brick building about forty feet long by twenty feet wide, with a fire place in it and a dirt floor. This was called the dead house, where all the dead were deposited during the day and night.... [T]he dead were taken to the dead house with their clothes they had on, and many of them had money sewed up in those old clothes or rags; sometimes jewelry and other valuables were found. The clothing was removed, except the drawers, if they had any, and these poor bodies of our once near and dear comrades were handled in their nude state and loaded into an old fashioned wagon and hauled outside to be placed in the trenches by our other dead." Darby, *Incidents and Adventures*, 209–10, quoting C. H. Golden.

Saturday Oct 29th [72]

Up at daylight. Morning pleasant but quite cool. No Flour or Bread yet at 10 a.m. (13 Dead) At 11 a.m. we drew a Ration of Beef. At 1 p.m. Drew one pint of Rice soup. At 3 p.m. Drew another Ration of soup. Half Ration rather. At 4 p.m. the

Flour came and the Bakers went to work. No Bread issued, except to the Hospital and working squad. Counted at 5 p.m.

Sunday Oct 30th [73]

Up early and washed Rawley. He gave me Bread & meat enough for break-fast. Got his pants washed and skirmished his clothes.* Then I went up to see Jerry. When I came back the squad had drawn Bread & Rice Soup. Made arrangements to set up with Jerry. He is very low. Dick [Moore] took the first part of the night.

* "Skirmishing" was one name given by the prisoners to the never-ending process of attempting to rid their clothing of lice (or "greybacks" as the prisoners called them) and other vermin. See the note following the entries for October 15. For Private Crocker, skirmishing for greybacks was part of his daily routine: "I would search my ragged garments and kill all I could find daily, but would hardly get dressed again till the 'varmints' would be galloping over me in apparently undiminished numbers. Sometimes we would hold our shirts over the fire and, giving the garment a quick shake, hundreds of the 'critters' would fall. At times the noise of their bursting bodies resembled that made by throwing a handful of salt on hot coals." *National Tribune*, August 30, 1900.

Monday Oct 31st [74]

I wakened up at 1 a.m. and went to the Hospital. Staid there until daylight. Drew Bread at 8 a.m. and soup at 12 m. Jerry died this afternoon at 2 p.m.* Our Division moved up in line today. Put up our tent by the Hospital. Drew wood. Counted at 4 p.m. Had a shake of the ague this afternoon.

* At the time of his enlistment, Jeremiah B. Jones was a member of the International Order of Odd Fellows. He was remembered by his brother members in the following Resolution, reprinted in *The Genius of Liberty* dated March 9, 1865:

A Tribute of Respect to the
Fallen Hero
Hall Gallatin Lodge No. 517
I.O.O.F. SMITHFIELD PENNA.

March 1, 1865

WHEREAS, It has pleased the Almighty in the conduct of His Providence, to remove by the hand of death, our beloved and true-hearted brother, Jere B. Jones, who being fired by patriotism was among the first in our locality to enlist under the banner of our common Country, and rush forward to the field of sanguinary conflict, and if needs be, offer up his life on his country's alter.

He attached himself to Co. G, 8th Regt. Penna. Res. Corps. The bare allusion to his Corps is associated in our mind with the seven days of terrible struggle in front of Richmond. Who that has read can doubt that the Penna. Reserves (be it to their honor said, and let the historians' pen so put it down) saved our young and noble army. The subject of our sketch fell at the battle of Mechanicsville, pierced with two balls, one of which entered his shoulder, and passing out at the breast, inflicting a wound considered by his comrades mortal, however, he being of a vigorous constitution survived it, though honorably discharged from the service. As his wounds improved, he felt that his country still needed his services, and impelled by love to it, he once more tendered those services, enlisting in his old Company and Regiment. He fought well through the battles of the Wilderness, and once more up to Richmond. In the battle of Weldon Railroad he was taken prisoner, was confined awhile at Richmond, from thence sent to Saulsbury, N.C. Suffering from diarrhoea, without proper nourishment or medical aid, he gradually sunk, and on the 31st of October last, saying to his companions—"Write to my mother and tell her I died a true-hearted soldier," he closed his eyes in death. Therefore

RESOLVED, That we deeply deplore the early death of our brother, who was a true Odd Fellow, as well as a brave soldier. Therefore

RESOLVED, That we express our deepest sympathy towards his widowed mother, his sisters and brothers, commending all to the care of Him, whose love is ever manifested toward his creatures, and His power exercised for their benefit, Therefore

RESOLVED, that the usual badge of mourning be worn by the members of this lodge for thirty days and a copy of the above be presented to his mother, and that our County papers be respectfully requested to publish the same.

> J. L. Showalter
> B. L. Black
> L. W. Burchinal
> Ewing McCleary

Tuesday Nov 1st [75]

Up early and went down to see Rawley. Found him much better. Morning cool & pleasant. At 10 a.m. we drew Hard Tack 6 to a man. At 11 we drew soup. Eberhart got mine. Pleasant all day. Counted off at 5 p.m. Drew a good ration of wood.

Wednesday Nov 2nd [76]

When I got up this morning I found it raining. At 9 a.m. we drew a Ration of Beef. At 11 a.m. we drew Rice Soup. Rained steady all day. A cold drisling rain. The Tent smoked so that we could hardly stay in it. Just at dark we drew Flour and very mean Flour. Sour & musty. Dick, Eberhart & I made my Bucket full of Dumplings. We dried our canvas and retired.

[Eberhart-11/2] Got up this morning & found it raining. At 9 Drew a Ration of beef. At 10 drew Rice Soup. Rained steady all day. A Cold drisling Rain. The tent

smoked so we could hardly stay in it. Just at dark we Drew flour. And very mean flour Sour & Musty. Tom, Dick and I made a pot of dumplings. Dried our tent Canvas and retired. Very little to eat today—only Raw flour. N. Patterson died today, from Cookstown, Pa.

Thursday Nov 3rd [77]

Rained very little during the night. I slept very little on account of the smoke. Morning very cold & cloudy. Looks as if it was going to rain again. Camp very muddy & disagreeable. Made Rawley a cup of Beef Tea. Found him a great deal better this morning. At 11 a.m. we drew our Ration of Rice soup. The day was very disagreeable and drisling rain at intervals most of the day. At 12 I made Rawley another cup of soup. At 3 p.m. we drew our Ration of Hard Tack. They run 7 to a man. At dusk we made a Bucket of soup. After dark rained very hard for a while.

Friday Nov 4th [78]

Slept very well. Morning clear and cool. Sun came out. But not very warm. At 11 a.m. we drew Rice Soup. I eat mine. In the evening it clouded up and at dark rained pretty hard. After dark 700 more prisoners from Richmond came in. We have drew no Bread today. They cannot begin to feed what is here now.

Saturday Nov 5th [79]

Up at Reveille. Morning clear & cool. At 8 a.m. we drew a Ration of Beef. The sun came out and made it very pleasant. A great many are taking the Oath & volunteering for the Rebel Army.* They are to do Garrison duty. They went out this morning. The Working Squad are done digging the ditch around the camp. They are now diging drains through the camp. At 11 a.m. we drew our Ration of Rice soup. At 2 p.m. we drew Bread right from the Oven. Sergt of the Squad gave me a loaf for tearing my blanket. Drew wood. Green Pine.

* C. H. Golden described the taking of the oath as follows: "Once a week or oftener they would offer us liberty if we would take the oath to the so-called Confederacy, telling us that all they would require of the galvanized Yankees was to guard forts and build fortifications. This Captain Wirz No. 2 of Salisbury, would mount the stockade, or fence, along side of the guards and call the prisoners up close to the fence. The poor creatures, with sunken eyes, skinny and ghastly looking faces, would stagger up to hear what this babbler had to say. 'All you Yankee prisoners who want to take the oath to the Confederate States of America will please come up close to the small gate here, and go out into a good clean camp, and have plenty to eat.' Although food, clothing and life were offered them to betray their country, less than five percent accepted the offers; and it is but justice to them to say that some of these fled to the Union lines at the first opportunity that presented itself." Darby, *Incidents and Adventures*, 207, quoting C. H. Golden.

Sunday Nov 6th [80]

Up at Reveille. Morning clear & cool. Sun came out and made it very pleas-
ant. Benj. F. Fuller of our Co. "G" Died this morning. At 10 a.m. we drew our
Ration of Rice soup. At 12 they issued 1 Paunch to each Squad for tripe. It had
never been cleaned. Not even washed but the Boys took it and eat it. At 2 p.m. they
issued Corn Meal 1 Barrel to 200 men. 1 pint to the man. At 4 p.m. the Drum beat.
All fell in and marched under the trees and formed in regular Order. Division after
Division. After the counting was over we made a pot of mush and eat it. Then
Retired. Someone stole our salt. 10,000 sick & wounded exchanged today at Savanah.

Monday Nov 7th [81]

Clouded up after dark and rained some. 600 more Prisoners came in some-
time during the night last night. Captured on the 29th Oct. They report everything
favorable inside our lines. They had a General engagement on the 27th Oct. 1864.
Rawley is still getting better. Made a Pot of Mush & baked a small cake early this
morning. The day wore away slowly. At 3 p.m. I looked [after] Rawley's Clothes for
him. At 3 1/2 p.m. Drew our Rice Soup. At 5 p.m. we drew Corn Bread right from
the Oven. The loaves were larger than we got at Belle Isle, but it was not as good.
No salt in it. And baked to quick. Eat it all.

Tuesday Nov 8th [82]

Up at daylight and made a tin of Crust Coffee. Then took a turn around by the
Cook House. Found them issuing nothing. But they commenced issuing soup to the
1st Division a few moments after. Today is a memorable day to all the Prisoners.
The Presidential Election. There is a great deal of speculation as to who will be
elected. The weather is just like it always was on Election day.* Cloudy and drisling
rain all day. The Navy Officers that was here for a few days was sent away yester-
day. At 9 a.m. we drew soup. Nothing else in the cook House. After dark we drew
half Ration of soup. Did not go all the way around the Roll. Ague again today.

* William Barnes, a private in Company G of the 191st Pennsylvania, also
kept a diary during his incarceration at Salisbury. Of the election he noted: "This is
a wet day of The presidadent election and I am in prison and can not voat But I am
a Mclelan man." Charlotte Palmer, comp., *The Diary of a Civil War Soldier: Pri-*
vate William Barnes: A journal written during a Washington County man's con-
finement in three Confederate prisons: August 1864–January 1865 (Washington,
Pa.: The Washington County Historical Society, 2002), 12. William Barnes contracted typhoid fever in Salisbury and died on or about February 1, 1865.

Wednesday Nov 9th [83]

Rained a good deal during the night. Morning cloudy. But appearances of
clearing off. 30 Barrels of Corn Meal came in yesterday. And the Bakers went right
to work. They issued nothing yesterday but soup. They say we have a new Quarter

Master this morning. Probably we will get our Rations more regular. At 11 a.m. we drew our Ration of Bread. The Bread was half Flour & half Corn. At 1 p.m. we drew Soup. It was very good. Plenty of Rice in and Pork boiled with it. Evening cloudy & warm.

Thursday Nov 10th [84]

Rained a good deal during the night. Morning clear and a strong wind blowing. It dries the mud up very fast. We had no fire in the Tent last night. And we slept very well as the night was very warm. At 9 a.m. we drew Rice Soup. It was very good. Plenty of salt in it. At 10 we drew a Ration of Beef & Mutton. And shortly after we drew Bread. Warm Corn Bread. The day was very warm. I suppose the warmest we have had since we have been here. At 3 p.m. I had a severe shake. Lasted until 5 p.m. I got Rawley's pants washed for him. Made out the Descriptive List of the Squad for the Sergt today.

Friday Nov 11th [85]

Up at Reveille. Morning clear and very sharp. At 10 a.m. we drew our Ration of Corn Bread. The Bread was much better than we have been getting. Half Flour and baked well. At 12 m. we drew our Ration of Rice Soup. In the evening I went out and carried in a big stick of Pine. Aleck gave me a half loaf of Bread. Rawley is very low today.

Saturday Nov 12th [86]

The morning clear & very cool with a sharp wind blowing. At 9 a.m. we drew our Bread & Beef. Salt meat. Mutton & fresh Beef mixed. Our Ration was salt Beef. At 11 a.m. we drew good Rice Soup. At 2 p.m. I had a shake of the Ague. It lasted until 5 p.m.

Sunday Nov 13th [87]

Morning clear & very cold. At 8 we drew our Ration of Bread. At 9 a.m. we drew our Ration of Beef. Half of it was raw. At 10 a.m. we drew Rice Soup. The day was chilly and wore slowly away. In the afternoon I got a dose of quinine. Very dull all day. Borrowed $5. Dick.

Monday Nov 14th [88]

Morning cold. It froze some last night. At 8 a.m. we drew our Ration of Corn Bread. It was not half baked. And very small loaves. Yesterday we drew salt and part of the Camp drew Potatoes instead of meat. The men are dying off faster than ever. 185 last week. Average 20 per day. I spent the afternoon in the Hospital with Rawley. He was very low. We drew soup in the afternoon. Dick bought some Rice & Salt. My throat got very sore today.

Tuesday Nov 15th* [89]

Up very early. I went to the dead house. I found Rawley & John Malone both dead. At 11 a.m. we drew Rice & Cabbage soup. At 4 p.m. we drew warm Corn Bread. The day was pleasant but quite cool. Dick and I bought $5 worth of Sweet Potatoes. Cooked the bucket full. My breast got sore tonight.

* On this date, the mayor and commissioners of the town of Salisbury caused a petition to be forwarded to the Confederate secretary of war. The petition, which appears at Appendix A, described the deteriorating conditions in the prison caused by overcrowding and sought the relocation of at least one-half of the prisoners to another facility. The petitioners pointed out the inadequate supplies of water, wood, and food and concluded that "the site of the prison is a most ineligible one, wanting in every facility for the secure confinement and proper subsistence of [such] a large number of prisoners."

Wednesday Nov 16th [90]

My breast pained me all night. I did not sleep much. Very little. I did not go outside of tent today. The Doctor was up to see me. He gave me some cough medicine and two doses of quinine. The cough medicine relieved me a good deal. At 2 we drew Bread & soup. Gave my soup to Eberhart. Retired at 8 p.m.

Thursday Nov 17th [91]

Slept some little during the night. My cold was much relieved. Today was a splendid day but I did not get out except to go to the sink. At 11 a.m. we drew our Corn Bread. Gave my Bread to Eberhart. At 5 p.m. we drew soup. Felt a good deal better this evening. Traded some Bread for Tobaco. Bought a dollars worth of Sweet Potatoes. Got more medicine.

Friday Nov 18th [92]

Slept a good bit last night. Great deal better this morning. Still cough some. The pain has all left me. At 9 a.m we drew Bread & Meat. The day was very pleasant. I walked around a good deal. At 1 p.m. drew soup. Eberhart got mine. The day was very pleasant & I walked around a good deal. Got worse again this evening.

[Eberhart-11/18] *Slept pretty good last night. At 9 we drew Bread & Meat. The day was very pleasant. At 1 pm drew Soup, Rice and drew wood in the evening. Went out for T.J.S. [presumably Thomas W. Springer] as he is not at all well—poor boy. I am afraid he will not hold out untill the End. Who will "God only Knows."*

Saturday Nov 19th [93]

Coughed all night & did not sleep a wink. The pain came back in my Breast. The medicine run out just at dark. It rained some during the night. At 7 a.m. it commenced Raining & Rained until 8 a.m. It stoped for a while. We drew Bread a little after 8. Bought some Sweet Potatoes. Rained all day. In the afternoon we drew soup. Jim got mine. Jim Eberhart went out & got the Doctor to come to the Tent. He gave me some cough medicine and a sleeping Powder. The day was very disagreeable, staid in the Tent. Retired at 8 p.m.

[Eberhart-11/19] *Last night it Rained the Most of the night and stopped for a while about 8 am. Drew our Ration of Corn Bread. In the afternoon we drew Soup. Has been a very disagreeable day. Went and got a Doctor to Come and see Tom Springer. Gave him some medicine.* Will try and get him in one of the buildings as soon as he can.*

* Private Crocker wrote of the Confederate physicians' efforts to treat the prisoners: "For a long time the rebel doctors seemed to try to heal the sick and to provide shelter for the worst cases, but their stock of medicines was small, owing, as they said, to the stringency of the blockade at that time, and the variety as well as malignancy of the diseases to be treated made their efforts of little avail. The sick list grew so rapidly they could not give necessary attention to any, and the death rate soon became frightful." *National Tribune*, September 6, 1900.

Saturday Nov 20 [94]

[Eberhart/Springer] *Slept some little last night got up at 7 a.m. and drew our Ration of Corn Bread. Boiled the last of the potatoes morning cloudy cold & disagreeable.**

* Beginning with this entry on Saturday, November 20, 1864, the handwriting in Thomas Springer's diary changes noticeably, becoming heavier and darker. It is evident from the next day's entry that Thomas Springer has become so weak from illness and lack of food that he is no longer able to make daily entries in his diary and has asked a friend to undertake that task for him. That friend (and the author of the remaining entries in Thomas Springer's diary through November 29, 1864) was James Eberhart. With respect to Springer's other close friends, it is noted that Rawley Joliff died November 15, 1864 (see the diary entry for that date); Isaac "Dick" Moore is mentioned in the entry for November 28 as helping the writer (James Eberhart) move Springer to "the brick building." Eberhart and Moore, both sergeants like Springer, survived their imprisonment and mustered out with their company in June 1865. To reflect the fact that James Eberhart wrote the daily entries in Thomas Springer's diary from November 20 through November 29, those entries are identified by the notation "Eberhart/Springer" in bold type within brackets. Where relevant, daily entries from James Eberhart's diary (which he continued to keep during this time period) are also included.

Sunday Nov 21 [95]

[Eberhart/Springer] *Cold morning. Tom not as bright. Gave me his book to keep for him & asked me to bring them home—I promised to if I live to get out. Only*

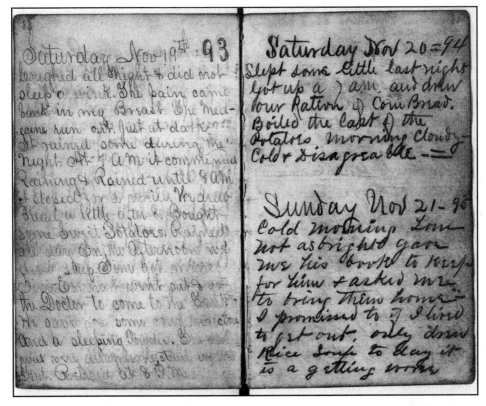

These two pages from Thomas Springer's diary reflect the change from his handwriting to that of James Eberhart.

Special Collections, University of Virginia Library

drew Rice soup today. It is a getting worse every day here. Nathan Patterson died today of our Co. G.

Monday Nov 22 [96]

[Eberhart/Springer] *Weather a little warmer but very muddy. Went out and carried in wood for Toms turn. Drew a Ration of flour & Rice Soup today.*

[Eberhart-11/22] *Weather a little warmer but very muddy. Went out & carried in wood for Tom. Drew a Ration of Flour & Rice Soup today. It is strange layed down last night feeling pretty good & got up this morning could not talk above a whisper. I had a cold but seem to be better of it.*

Tuesday Nov 23 [97]

[Eberhart/Springer] *Weather a little brighter. News came that Lincoln was elected. Great cheering through out the camp. No rations of any kind today. Tom not so well today.*

Wednesday Nov 24 [98]

[Eberhart/Springer] *A cold rain last night. Toward morning froze ice on the trees and some limbs broke off with the weight of ice. Got a letter from home. Said they had put in a lot of stamps & 50 cents. But no money & no stamps. No rations today again. Came in a recruiting. A good many of the boys go out. Sun melted the ice all away.*

[Eberhart-11/24] *A Cold Rain last night. Towards evening it froze Ice on the oak trees that it broke off big limbs. They would fall through the night. My the poor Men that has no Shelter of anny kind to night.* God, have mercy on them. I got a letter from home today. Glad to hear from them. If I was only with them now how thankfull I would bee. Says they had put in some stamps & 50 cent & would send me money if I could get it at all but no money or Stamp either but letter was welcome. No Rations to day again of any description.*

* Private Crocker described the shelter that he and his messmates constructed: "We began early in the Fall to construct a 'dugout' for our residence. This was a square hole down in the ground about four feet, then an excavation made in one side large enough to curl up in for our bedroom. We managed to get sticks enough for a roof over the door, which we covered with earth enough to keep out moderate rains, and by ditching managed to keep dry, except in long rainy spells, when water would ooze in and pieces of wet dirt fall from the ceiling of our bedroom, making it extremely disagreeable. We did our cooking 'upstairs,' and when we had company entertained in the open air." *National Tribune*, August 23, 1900.

Thursday Nov 25 [99]

[Eberhart/Springer] *A little warmer today. But very muddy. The mortality is fearfull here now from 40 to 50 a day. How long will we last? Got up at daybreak and went to the well and drawed water for tobacco. Sold the tobacco and bought a piece of bread from a Johnny. Got a ration of Rice soup and Bread today about 11 a.m. At noon when the relief came in a lot of us—our squad and one next to us— jumped on them and took their guns. Got 14 and got a few from the post inside. We tried to get out. The ones near the gates came a running towards us to see what was up instead of a taking the gates so we failed. They opened with 2 guns on us. The first was blank and the boys cheered & the next shots were scrapnell. We had 28 men killed and about 70 odd wounded. Tom Springer wanted me to get a mule if we got out and come for him. I told him I would do so but we did not get out. We were ordered to get in our holes and stay there.**

* Frank King described the uprising in detail: "During the month of November half rations were so frequent that it did seem as though the rebels intended to starve all of us to death. It got to be so serious a matter that some of the leading spirits resolved on a general outbreak. On the 25th of the month the guards were relieved by the militia of the State, principally old men and country farmers, a class of men that knew but little about the use of the musket. Intelligence reached us that the guard just relieved (young conscripts) had been ordered to the front. We hailed this as a good opportunity. It was resolved, therefore, that as soon as the inside guards were secured, that the ninth and tenth divisions, who lay nearest the big gates, should force them open with clubs and axes, a few of the latter articles being owned by the prisoners. The gates once forced, egress would be easy, and it would be short work to overpower the militia, most of whom, probably, had never fired a gun in their lives. When free from the prison we intended to make for Tennessee in as compact a body as possible. The plan was well laid, and all it wanted to insure success was patience and cool judgment on the part of a few, and a general understanding of the situation by all.... There was no want of courage and valor on the part of the prisoners, but the fool-hardiness and ill-timed action of the prime mover proved fatal to the enterprise. He, a Sergeant Major of Division, gave the signal a full hour and a half before the time agreed upon, and rashly, though bravely, commenced the assault with his own hands. 'Who's for Liberty and who for Death?' he cried, and immediately leveled a guard with a blow, and secured his musket. The entire guard inside the pen was overpowered within three minutes, and, with a tremendous cheer a rush was made for the gates; but here the fool-hardiness was apparent, as the two divisions relied on for the main stroke did not know their part, and the enterprise was nipped in the bud. It was soon discovered, too, that the conscripts had not left the place, and the sentinel's platforms fast filled up amid the discharge of grape and canister from the two pieces of artillery. Three-fourths, if not more of the prisoners, were unprepared for so sudden an assault, nevertheless, they rallied to the cheers of their comrades. But it was of no use; the rebels were fully armed and prepared at all points, many of our men were already killed or wounded, and still we were being fired upon; so we dispersed as quickly as possible, and in half an hour the camp was entirely quiet. I took refuge in a comrade's tent for about an hour, when I deemed it safe to return to my own quarters. On arriving there, I found that the tent had been in direct range of one of the guns, and that it was riddled with the charge of canister, having forty-two holes in the canvas. Fleming had been hit in the neck with a musket ball, and I learned that a rebel sergeant, with a file of soldiers, had been searching that and the neighboring tents for concealed arms. It seems that the authorities had an impression that we were fully armed and prepared for a pitched battle. They were never more mistaken; for it was only the feeble effort of a handful of men, made desperate by acts of inhuman barbarity. We had the satisfaction of knowing that we had pretty thoroughly frightened our brutal keepers.... I ought to mention that fifty of the prisoners were killed and wounded." Bates, *History of the Pa. Volunteers*, 5:285–86.

Friday Nov 26 [100]

[Eberhart/Springer] *Up early & went to the well and drew water for tobacco. Got quite a lot! The wells were about 20 feet deep and you had to have a
string & bucket or quart cup with a bail on it. The only way to get water in camp.
No Rations drawn today. Brot a Regt of 3 or 4 hundred in camp to get the guns.
Some were broke around the trees and some throwed down the wells. They hired
our men to go down the well for the guns. Gave them a loaf of bread for a gun.*

Saturday Nov 27 [101]

[Eberhart/Springer] *Weather a little warmer. Mud a drying up some—Drew
a Ration of Bread & Rice soup to day—had the Doctor to see Tom today. He said he
would get him one of the buildings as soon as a vacant place was [available]. More
recruiting to day—went out for wood for Rutter this eve.*

Sunday Nov 28 [102]

[Eberhart/Springer] *Sun coming out bright—bug some for myself & Tom.
Drew Bread & Soup this morning. Walked up to the grove and minister and a lady
came in camp and held a little Service. It was pleasant to see a lady once again &
to think of her a coming in such a hole as this. After noon the Doctor came about 4
and told me if I would bring my friend right a long he had a place for him in the
brick building. So Dick Moore helped me to get him in and he thanked us and gave
an ambrotype a piece of watch chain & a gold pen to bring home for him. I said I
would do so. I wanted to stay with him but he said no as I had enough to do to take
care of myself—stayed a while and he asked his savior to Relieve him of his pain. I
left him at dark.*

Monday 29 Nov [103 day]

[Eberhart/Springer] *Went in at daylight—to see him and he was a dying
then. Could not speak but seemed to know me. I stayed a while and got a lock of his
hair. And he was carried to the dead house. Drew Bread & Soup to day. Weather a
little warmer than has been for some time.*

*Thos W. Springer
Died Nov 29 about
6 a.m. or thereabouts*

[Eberhart-11/29] *Up at daylight and went in to see Tom & he was a dying &
could not speak but seemed to know me by his Eyes. I stayed a while & got a lock of
his hair & he was Carried to the dead house. Weather a little warmer today. Drew
Bread & Soup today. In evening got wood. Tom Springer died today—one of my
Messmates & Bro. Sergts.*

In this entry in Thomas Springer's diary, James Eberhart reflects upon Springer's worsening condition, noting that he and Isaac Moore carried Springer into the "brick Building" where a Confederate doctor attended him.

I could not Sing because
to as to by Tibe I rather
I knew the Hymn —
account of my voice
The Teacher Came about
it and told me to bring
my friend right along.
He had a place in them
in the Brik building so
I got Dick more and he
and got them in and he
(Hawks) me and gave
me an Ambrotype a piece
a match Plate to send and
begin with two Bords to
bring home for him. I
wanted to stay with him
but he said no as I had
Enough to take Care of
my self stay a till dark
and he asked two Dollars
to deliver them to the

raining left him at dark
Ford Vorges Come in the
morning life at daylight til
and wrote in to see how
and he was a dying and
Could not speak but
seamed to know me
by his eyes I stayed a
awhile I got a shock of
his hair I am he you
Carried to the Dead House
weather a little warmer
to day — drew Bread & Soap
to day — in Evening got wood,
Tom Springer died to day
Nov 29 1864 one of my
Messmates & Bro Sergts

In this entry from James Eberhart's diary, he notes the death of Thomas Springer, "one of my Messmates and Bro Sergts."

"Tis a Hard Christmas for Us"

The Prison Diary of Sergeant James W. Eberhart[1]

Following the death of his messmate, Sergeant James Eberhart continued to make daily entries in his own diary. These became progressively shorter as his health and strength failed him. By early January 1865, one- or two-line entries, covering several days at a time, became commonplace. Ultimately, Eberhart would write only sporadically. Death and rations (or the lack thereof) consumed the daily thoughts of Eberhart and his comrades at Salisbury, as he noted on New Year's Day: "Tis a cold Raw day & the boys are a going fast on a/c of Exposure and grub.... Nothing to eat today. Tis a good day to fast on." Indeed, sickness and food dominated Eberhart's diary entry for November 30, 1864, the day after Thomas Springer's death.

Tuesday Nov 30

Morning clear & cool. Went out Side today & help carry 1/2 bbl of Water from the Creek. Glad to get out Side of the pen. Had some Diorhea. Went to Doctors & got a pill. Near Noon Drew Corn Bread and Rice Soup. Drew wood in Evening.

Wendsday Dec 1* [day 105]

*Morning frosty, & clear & cool. The death rates have been very heavy the last week. Went to Doctors to get some pills for Diorhea.** I am accumulating them so if I get so I cannot walk, I will have some. Are a good pill to check it but he will only give you one at a time. Drew Raw flour and Rice Soup to day.*

* On this date, Eberhart began to annotate each daily entry to reflect the total number of days spent as captives.

** Eberhart was fortunate to be given medication for this dread condition that killed tens of thousands of soldiers during the war. Private Crocker noted that "[d]iarrhea prevailed to an alarming extent, and was very fatal." *National Tribune,* August 30, 1900.

Thursday Dec 2 [106]

Morning brighter. Has appearance of a fine day. 9 am got Bread corn, at 12 drew Soup. Dont get meat very often now. I exercise a good deal a walking around

Camp as I get Stiff if Set down. Some set on there hunkers all day before the little fire and get so stiff that they Cannot Straiten up. Have one man that way now that Cannot Straiten. We tried to get him up so to walk him around, but he yelled so and plead with us we let him alone—W Winkleman Died to day. I got his bible.

Friday Dec 3 [107]

Morning Cloudy & Cold appearance. Needs of rain. A man went past our Squad with a quarter of Mutton. One man remarked there goes Blood Money. He went to his quarters & after a while came back with 30 or 40 of his chums & wanted to fight so we all got out with Sticks Bricks & annything we could get our hands on for them ready for the fray. The gaurds on the fence said if we did not disperse that croud he would fire in to them and pulled up his gun. So they went to thier places again. Drew Bread & Soup to day.

Saturday Dec 4 [108]

Rained through the night last night. A cold Rain. Recruiting nearly every day. A great deal of Sickness in Camp. Drew Very dark Bread & it was sweet. Seemed to be made from Sorgum Seed Flour & it was sweet. Was not bad to eat if only we would get more of it. Drew Rice Soup at 2 pm. Drew wood this Evening. Went out for wood. Picked up too big a stick. Got the Rebel gaurd to help me on my shoulder & fell against the wood pile. So I had to get him to take it off my neck. He said, I guess Yank you will tote a smaller stick—so I did. Was too weak—

Sunday Dec 5 [109]

A bright morning. Went to the well & drew water for tobaco. Got quite a lot. Traded tobaco for some bread & made a quart of Crust Coffee. Drew a Ration of Bread and meat this 11 am & at 2 pm got Soup 1/2 pt to a man. Day passed off quiet. No Service in camp to day.

Monday-Dec 6 [110 day a prisoner]

Did not Sleep very good last night. Ground damp and have to lay on one side all night. It makes one Hip Bones very sore. I look at mine to see if they are coming through the Skin or not. Made a pad to put under my hips at night. Use my Shoes & hat for a pillow at night. Drew our Ration of Bread and Soup this morning. It dont last very long & then a long wait for the next meal. Drew wood this Evening & was Counted off.

Tuesday Dec 7 [111]

More rain through the night. Camp very muddy & disagreeable. Brot Some prisoners in from Andersonville. They look very hard. I thought they were negroes are so black from the pine smoke. Drew flour this Morning at 12. Got Soup. Days drag a long very slow. Got wood this evening.

Wendsday Dec 8 [112]

Up early & went to the well & drew water for tobacco or annything I can get. Got a part of Ration of Bread. From one, heard some one a crying murder in the night two or 3 times & then all was quiet. Heard there was a man killed for the paltry little Sum of money [he] had. At 11 drew Corn Bread & got Soup. Rice Soup but it is very thin and no Salt in it. I H Rholand died today.

Thursday Dec 9*

A bright and clear morning. Appearances of clearing up. Hope it may & dry up the mud. Some got a Ration of Corn Bread & Soup to day. F. Dunbert died to day.

* On this date, Eberhart neglected to note the number of days spent in captivity. He resumed the practice with the next day's entry, but mischaracterized the number. Thus, the annotations from December 10 through January 2 are "off" by one day.

Friday Dec 10 [113]

Morning Clear & Cold. Frosty this morning but Sun is a comming out bright. Got our Bread & Some meat beef this morning. Got Soup at 2 pm & drew wood this evening.

Saturday Dec 11 [114]

Up early & went to the well and got water. Made a cup of Crust Coffe. Got our Bread & soup this morning. They issued some clothing to us that the Goverment had Sent to us but the Rebs stole the most of it. I got a blouse and a blanket with annother man so we can be a little more comfortable now at night.

Dec 12 [115]

Slep late, and pretty good. Slept warmer. Drew Corn Bread about 10 am & beef. And drew Soup Rice about 2 pm. Was counted and got our Ration of wood.

Dec 13 [116 day]

Up early & went to the well and drew water for tobacco. Drew Soup & Corn Bread. Every thing quiet to day.*

* On this date, Confederate Brigadier General John H. Winder wrote to General Cooper, the adjutant and inspector general at Richmond, forwarding a report of his inspection of the Salisbury prison. He noted that "[t]he ratio of mortality at...Salisbury exceeds...that at Andersonville" and recommended that the prison property be sold and the proceeds be used to purchase another tract with adequate supplies of water and wood upon which a new prison could be constructed. General Winder's Report appears at Appendix B.

Dec 14 [117 day]

A cold raw day. Rained Some & So Cold. Nothing to eat today. Came in and wanted recruits. Boys are a getting discouraged with the treatment here. Am glad Darby Ritchey and the boys that escaped are not here.* *Hope they all got home save.*

* See the notes following the entries for October 7 and October 19, 1864, in the preceding chapter. Of the 10 escapees, Moore, Elgin, and Link were captured and returned to Salisbury. Darby, Darnell, Francis, Mitchell, Ritchey, and Warman were captured and returned to Richmond where they were imprisoned in Libby Prison. Axton "went to [the] enemy," according to an entry in Eberhart's diary.

Dec 15 [118 day]

Has moderated through the night and warmer but Very muddy & damp. Drew Ration of Rice Soup & Raw flour. So we had a time to bake it. Wood scarce today.

Dec 16 [119 day]

Up early & went & drew water for tobacco. Got quite a lot & gave the boys some that are sick & cant go. Got corn bread & soup to day. A man shot by the guards to day for coming too close to the line. A genuine murder.

Dec 17 [120 day]

I went out to day to Carry in Some wood for one of Boys as he was not able to go & the men are So Selfish if a man is a dying they think he must do his Share of his work. Drew Corn bread & Soup. A little more rain again.

Dec 18 [121 day]

Up early. Not Much Sleep last night. Cold & damp. Drew our Rations of Soup Bread & Some meat. The first for a week. Went out after wood to day. Everything quiet today.

Dec 19 [122 day]

Rested better last night. Sun out Bright & warm. Done some bugging to clean up what I can. Drew Rice Soup & Soft Bread.

Dec 20 [123 day]

Up early and went and drew water at the well for tobacco. Got a goodly portion. I share with some of the boys. Got our Ration of Rice Soup & Corn Bread. Weather warm & drying up. Counted off today.

Dec 21 [124 day]

Up bright & Early. Am not a feeling very well. Pain in my breast. It is a bright Sunny day. Got my bugging done. Drew our Rations of Corn Bread & Rice Soup but no Chris Kinkle for us this year. Oh if I only had what is left at my Mother's table how happy I could bee to night.

Dec 22 [125 day]

Annother day before us. How will it end? It is a little cloudy. Looks as it may rain. Have finished a bugging. Got a Ration of Corn Bread & Rice Soup. Sold 1/2 of my bread to buy some Salt. Went out after wood to day for Tute Rutter as he is not very well.

Dec 23 [126 day]

Up early and went to the well to draw water. Got a double handfull of chews of tobacco for my work. We drew our Ration of Corn Bread & Soup Rice. The Mortality seems to be increasing in the Camp. A Cold Rain to day. Got a piece of canvas from the bottom of the tent & wear it around my feet to keep my feet dry. Counted off today.

Dec 24 [127 day]

Up Early. And washed & took a walk around the Camp for Exercise. Got our Ration of Corn Bread & Rice Soup about 11 am. Bugged today in the tent. Held my clothes over the fire. Oh how they do crack.

Dec 25 [128 day]

Up early and had a good wash. Got my bugging done and cleaned up the best I could. A bright day. Oh if I was only home the good things I should of have today. Nothing would be too good for them to give to me—but alas it cannot be so. Nothing to Eat to day. Tis a hard Christmas for us. But we must keep up our spirits. God have Mercy on us. A Men. Done some trading of Buttons & a gold pen. Got a molases pie & 5 Sweet potatoes. So fared pretty well after all. G. Quinn Died to-day—of Co. "G" 191.

Dec 26 [129 day]

Up early. Drew some water for tobacco & got Enough to wash myself. Went out after wood to day on my own account. They gave us Soup & Corn Bread to. Oh how good it was. There was some 15 men escaped from the wood train yesterday. I hope they will get through all Safe. Fell in & was Counted off.

Dec 27 [130 day]

Had not a Very good night's Rest last night. My hips seem so sore as though the bones would come through the skin. We got soup & Corn bread a gain to day.

Dec 28 [131 day]

Rested better. Up Early and had a wash. Feel somewhat refreshed. Drew Rice Soup & Corn bread & some beef to day. How good it tasted. Took a good walk around Camp for Exercise. Am a feeling pretty fair. If I only had my Voice.

Dec 29 [132 day]

Up early and got water to wash with. Weather dark cold & raw. Was counted today. And got ration of Rice Soup & Corn Bread. I went out side to help to carry in water in afternoon. Glad to get out side of the pen.

Dec 30 [133 day]

Up early. Went to the well and drew water to wash with & a cup to drink. Fell in early and was counted off. Drew Soup today but nothing else all day. Bread did not go around. A great many of our boys are a complaining and death rate is high. How much longer are we to remain here?

Dec 31 [134 day]

Weather a little brighter than has been for some days past. Drew our ration of Bread & Soup today with some little Meat for a N-year gift I presume. Oh if we were only home. What a treat it would be for us.

Jan 1st 1865 [135]

Oh for a happ. New Year. Can this be one for us? God forbid. Tis a cold Raw day & the boys are a going fast on a/c of Exposure and grub. We had a Recruiting officer at gate.* Want Recruits. Nothing to eat today. Tis a good day to fast on.

* See the description of recruiting following the entry for November 5, 1864, in the preceding chapter.

Jan 2 [136 day]

A little better than yesterday. Got Corn Bread & Rice soup. 40 men hauled out from the dead House.

Jan 3

Same as yesterday. Drew Rations and feeling some better. Weather cool. Looks like Rain. 33 died today.

Jany 4 1865

A Cold Morning & Raining. Got our Ration of Bread & Rice Soup about 11 am.

Jany 5

Weather damp & Cold. Had a hard Rain yesterday and a wet bed last night to sleep on. Sun is a coming out. Hope it may be a bright day.

Jany 6

It has been a clear day with Sun Shine and warmer. Done some bugging today. Hope to sleep better. 28 hauled out today.

Jany 7

Up Early and got Water before Camp up. Ration Bred & R. Soup 39 hauled out today.

Jany 8–9–10

About the same. Weather nice. 80 hauled out the last three days.

11–12–13

Recruiting has been a going on. Missed Ration one day of the three. 97 died the 3 days.

14–15–16

The last 2 days we have had Rain and it is cold. Went out and carried in wood today for a comrad. 125 died these 4 days.

Jany 18–19–20*–21

Weather Cleared and fine. Got our Ration of Corn Bread & Soup pretty Regular the last few days. 140 has been hauled out Jany 23 to 31. We have missed our Ration one day this week. 250 has died this week. There wont be many of us left.

* On January 20, 1865, George Fritz of Port Perry, Pennsylvania, wrote a letter seeking information concerning his son and two of his comrades who were believed to have been captured at Weldon Railroad on August 19, 1864. This letter, poignant in its simplicity, illustrates the tragic burden that families at home often had to carry during the many months they waited for information regarding the fates of their loved ones:

Port Perry Jan 20/65

Gen. Hoffman

Dear Sir

Having been informed by the Provo Marshall of Pittsburgh that you could give information about prisoners captured by the Rebels I wish to know whether my son George S. Fritz along with two others John Rogers and Patrick Hurly were taken on the 19th of August on the Weldon Rail Road. They belonged to the 191st Regiment Co. G of the consolidated Reserves and had served in the 8th Pa. Reserves.

If you can give any information about them as to whether they were taken and where they are...and whether still alive you will confer a great favor on the Parents of the persons named and also receive their lasting gratitude. These boys served in the 8th Pa. Reserves Co. C. They had first served for 3 months and then reenlisted in the 8th and then were transferred to the 12th Reserves and from that were consolidated into the 191st and at the time they were captured on the 19th of August they had served within three day[s] of the end of there time.

Respectfully yours

Geo. Fritz

A handwritten note at the bottom of the original letter indicates that it was answered March 10, 1865, as follows: "No Record." In fact, George S. Fritz survived his imprisonment and was paroled March 10, 1865. He was honorably discharged from the army in June 1865 and returned to his home and family. Patrick

Hurley was not so fortunate. He died in the Salisbury prison October 31, 1864. John Rogers's fate is unknown. The Fritz letter is held at the National Archives and Records Administration, Washington, D.C., in Record Group 94, Records of the Adjutant General's Office, Muster Rolls of Volunteer Organizations, 8th Pennsylvania Infantry, Regimental papers.

Feby 1 to 8*

They have a been a bringing some men from Andersonville here. Have fared fairly well for Rations this week. **

* On February 1, 1865, the governor of North Carolina, Zebulon B. Vance, wrote to the Confederate secretary of war, expressing his concern and dismay over the conditions at Salisbury. He noted that if the prisoners were "willfully left to suffer when we can avoid it, it would not only be a blot upon our humanity, but would lay us open to a severe retaliation." Vance's letter, together with a similar one to General Bradley Johnson, appears at Appendix C.

** One reason that some of the surviving prisoners "faired fairly well" was that they engaged in a practice known as "flanking," as explained by Private Crocker: "Yankee ingenuity failed to supply the deficiency in the quantity of food furnished, but by sharp practice and the aid of the Squad Sergeants a few were able to get a double ration at times. Each day we had to get into line and be counted by a rebel officer. Rations were issued to the number counted each day, and some of the more active boys would manage to be counted in two different squads. This we called 'flanking', and [it] were indulged in successfully by several men I knew. Dubois [Crocker's messmate] was a lucky flanker. Many of the men were not able to stand in line to be counted, and sometimes the counter would number such ones in their quarters, and sometimes would take the word of the squad commander for the number sick and issue rations accordingly, but the rule was that every man must be seen by the counting officer." *National Tribune*, August 23, 1900.

9–16

Have more Rain & very disagreeable weather. Missed Rations 2 days this week.

17–21

*Weather has been nice. Got our Rations.**

* On February 17, 1865, Assistant Adjutant and Inspector General T. W. Hall forwarded a report of his inspection of the Salisbury Prison to General Cooper in Richmond. The report was quite detailed and was unsparing in its depiction of the shortcomings of the prison and the authorities charged with its administration. Hall concluded that the prisoners' suffering and the high incidence of mortality was due "(1) to the unfortunate location of the prison, which is wholly unsuitable for the

purpose [and] (2) to the want of administrative capacity, proper energy and effort on the part of the officers of the Quartermaster's Department, charged with the duty of supplying the prison." Hall's complete report, with endorsements, appears at Appendix D. Enclosure 1 to the report, being a diagram of the general plan of the prison, appears at Appendix E.

Feby 22*

G Washington birth day. Was called in line and Read a parole for us not to try & escape as they were a going to Exchange. What glad news. I drew Ration & Issued the same. 2 days to walk 50 miles to Greensboro. Let us out about 12. Walked untill dark and Camped in woods. We had plenty of wood & a good fire although it was a Raining. Rested fairly well.

* On this date some 2,800 gaunt Union prisoners of war—those who were still able to walk—began a 51-mile trek from Salisbury to Greensboro, North Carolina. The line of march extended for nearly three miles. Many of the men trudged along in twos or threes, supporting those of their comrades who were too weak to walk alone. Nearly 1,000 of the newly liberated prisoners never made it to Greensboro, falling out of line too weak to continue or dying along the way. The 1,800 haggard veterans who survived this final ordeal were herded onto rail cars at Greensboro and sent on to Wilmington where they reentered Union lines. For an account of this march see A. W. Mangum, "Salisbury Prison," *Histories of the Several Regiments and Battalions from North Carolina in the Great War 1861–65,* Vol. 4, ed. Walter Clark (Goldsboro, N.C.: Nash Brothers, 1901).

Feby 26

Arrived at Greensboro. All hungry. After dark they gave us Molassas & Corn Meal to eat. Slep in wood all night with a good fire.

Feby 28

Got on train in afternoon and arrived at Ralegh about 10 pm. Encamped in open field. Nothing to eat.

Mch 2nd

We all signed a parole and put us on the cars and took us to our lines near the Black River. Came in through the Colored troops. What a joyous deliverance when we once more saw old Glory. I never saw it more beautifull. The Colored troops fed us in their camp and then we went to Wilmington about 3 miles and got all we wanted to eat. Stayed one night and took a steamer for Anopolis Md.*

* Private Crocker described the emotions of the ragged survivors of Salisbury as they came into sight of the Union lines: "At about 3 o'clock in the afternoon of March 10...we came to the bank of the Nolechucky...and just across the river I saw

the Stars and Stripes proudly floating to the breeze. I had always loved that flag, but never till now did I fully realize its beauty and its meaning.... The terrible mental and physical strain to which I had been subjected so long now began to relax, and while I had not felt the least like giving up before, now that the need for firmness had passed I sank on the ground utterly exhausted. In a short time, however, we rallied again, and began congratulating each other on the happy termination of our perilous tramp, and had a regular camp-meeting jubilee for a few minutes. We hugged and kissed each other, laughed, cried, shook hands, danced and shouted in a perfect ecstasy of joy.... I felt now that my deliverance was indeed complete, and that I had really reached 'God's country' at last." *National Tribune*, September 20, 1900.

18 March 1865

I am home on furlough. Thanks be Mercifull God that brought me Home again.

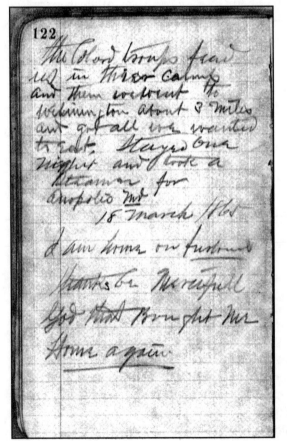

18 March 1865: the final entry in James Eberhart's diary.

Part Four

We Were Comrades Together

We were comrades together when the boys marched away;
In hard times we were faithful, and in good times we were gay;
And sometimes we were longing for the dear ones afar
We were comrades together in the days of the war.

We have march'd along together in the sun and the rain;
We've faced the fight together and together borne the pain!
And each one tells his story of the wound or the scar—
We were comrades together in the days of the war.

To the dear ones gone before us, here's a health, comrades all!
We shall soon go to meet them, at the last great bugle call!
Beneath the star of Liberty, the bright, shining star—
We're growing old together since the days of the war.

Don't you hear the bugle calling, comrades today?
Echoing still in mem'ry of the days pass'd away!
Rally round the camp-fire, from near and from far;
We were comrades together in the days of the war.

"We Were Comrades Together in the Days of War"
Words; Col. Joe Whitfield; Music: Collin Coe (1884)

"The Peace Their Valor Had Established"

The Survivors Come Home

On the same day that Sergeant James Eberhart penned those last, joyous lines in his diary, one of his comrades had occasion to write a much more melancholy letter. Second Lieutenant Joseph W. Sturgis, who had marched out of Uniontown with George Darby, Isaac Moore, and Thomas Springer in April of 1861, was among the fortunate few who avoided capture at Weldon Railroad. A printer by trade, he was one of the few original members of the Fayette Guards still on active duty as the war ground inexorably toward its climax at Wilmer McLean's farmstead near Appomattox Court House. On March 18, 1865, Sturgis wrote the following letter to the editor of *The American Standard* in Uniontown:

> Camp 191st P. V. (2d Regt. P. V. R.)
> Dinwiddie Co., Va., March 18, 1865

Mr. Editor:

Once again, after the lapse of months, do I presume to write a few lines for the general information of those of your readers who feel a deep interest, and their number is by no means small, in the "Old Penn'a Reserve Veterans."

My last was written just after the capture of our boys—51 in number, by the Confederate forces, in their attempt to retake the Weldon R. R., which you recollect proved a failure, although they succeeded in capturing quite a number of prisoners in August last.

Until lately we have never received any reliable information concerning them, although madam rumor has had them paroled, also many of them dead; this last rumor in regard to many of them having died, seems to have been, alas, too true.

Today I received a letter from one of our paroled prisoners, a member of Co. "G," formerly the "Fayette Guards" from Fayette County, and I am proud to say the *first* Company from the County to respond to Gov. Curtin's call for volunteers, to the effect that of the fifty-one prisoners captured, twenty-three have died during the months of Oct., Nov., and Dec., 1864, and Jan. and Feb., 1865.

Believing it will be interesting to their friends, I send you a list of those who have died, and also the dates:

Sergt. Thomas W. Springer, Nov. 29, 1864

Corpl. Rhowley H. Jolliff, Nov. 15, 1864

    "   Harvey Snyder, Jan. 12, 1865

    "   Perry Madara, Feb. 21, 1865

Private John Barmuth, Jan. 16, 1865

    "   William Barnes, Jan. 31, 1865

    "   Andrew Brown, Feb. 18, 1865

    "   Jacob Bolinger, Jan. 15, 1865

    "   Knox G. Campbell, Feb. 5, 1865

    "   Fred. Daubert, Dec. 9, 1864

    "   Benj. F. Fuller, Nov. 6, 1864

    "   Fred. A. Heisely, Oct. 27, 1864

    "   Patrick Hurley, Feb. 8, 1865

    "   Jeremiah B. Jones, Oct. 31, 1864

    "   James A. Meadwell, Oct. 27, 1864

    "   John Malone, Nov. 15, 1864

    "   Nathan Patterson, Nov. 21, 1864

    "   Geo. H. Quinn, Dec. 25, 1864

    "   John R. Rutter, Feb. 11, 1865

    "   John Ross, Feb. 7, 1865

    "   Thomas Rhoadaback, Feb. 5, 1865

    "   James H. Rholand, Dec. 8, 1864

All of Co. G who were captured except Privates George W. Darby, James W. Axton, Wm. H. H. Link and Alex. Davidson had been paroled and are now at Annapolis, Md., and will be furloughed to visit their respective homes as rapidly as possible. George W. Darby was retained in one of their hospitals at Richmond, as Ward Master, until all of our sick should be shipped off, and may now be at Annapolis also. The last three named were well when heard from, but were still in the South.

It is a sad thought to think that so many of our brave comrades have been so illy treated and so scantily fed, that they have died from such usage, from actual starvation. Had they fallen upon the battlefield it would have been quite different to all, but a death by lingering starvation, seems not a befitting death for a soldier, but they have fallen noble martyrs to their country's cause, peace to their moldering clay. I cannot help but drop a tear to their memory as I write, may God in his Almighty goodness preserve me from so terrible and sad a fate, is my earnest prayer. Alas for the boasted chivalry of the South. An unknown grave upon the bloody field of battle, with nothing but the summer breeze to sigh a requiem, over the nameless grave, or a sheet of snow is a soldier's choice, rather than a lingering death by starvation.

Our Regt. [the 191st] is still in 3rd Brigade, 2nd Division, 5th A. C.; we are now under "marching orders" and may break camp at any moment, and when we do go, I feel confident the "Little Corporal," as Gen. Warren is called, it being a name given him by his own Corps, will have a good account to give of our doings. He is the man in the right place, the Corps all seem to have the utmost confidence in him. There is a large revival of religion now in progress in our Camp, some forty or fifty have professed to have found peace in a dying Savior, much good has been done.

I have heard that a Soldiers' Cemetery has been purchased near Uniontown. Do you not think it would be an excellent idea, and a move in the right direction, to have a suitable "monument" erected to those who have fallen in defense of their Country, and have their names engraved thereon; *many more of us may yet fall*, and it would be a pleasing thought to know that our names would be thus cherished by a grateful community. Co. "G" would contribute handsomely to such an enterprise. Can you not "start the ball rolling?"

But I must close, as I am detailed for Picket; when duty calls, "it is ours to obey," so I must off and prepare. More anon. S.[1]

Lieutenant Sturgis's letter appeared on page one of the March 30, 1865, edition of *The American Standard*. The editor of the *Standard*, John F. Beazell, reflected upon the tragic news in an editorial that appeared in the same issue:

The melancholy intelligence has reached us of the death at the prison-camp near Saulsbury, N. C., of Thomas W. Springer, Rowley H. Jolliff, John R. Rutter and Jerry B. Jones, members of Company "G" of the old 8th Pa. Reserves. These young men joined this Company at its organization at Uniontown, early in April, 1861, and followed the fortunes of the Reserves through all the vicissitudes and dangers incident to the soldier's life; from the defenses of Washington to the Rappahannock under McDowell, thence to the Peninsula, thence to Manassas the second, to Antietam, back to the Rappahannock and Rapidan, and through the terrible Wilderness battles, they were present always at the post of danger, and bore themselves with the pride and spirit of faithful and loyal soldiers.

Jones was most dangerously wounded at Gaines Mill, he languished a long time in hospital, and was at length discharged, but to the surprise of all he finally recovered and with a patriotism unusual even in these times of self-sacrifice returned again to his old comrades.

The Regiment was discharged in May, 1864, but these youths determined to remain in the service "to see it out," as they said.

> *"The mountains that saw them descend to the war,*
> *Should view them as victors, or view them no more."*

They looked forward with delightful anticipation to the time when the last rebel should be disarmed, and the dear old flag that they had followed with intrepid hearts through the hurricane of a score of battles, should be acknowledged in every corner of the national territory, then would they return to the comforts of home and the endearments of friends; then, with their fellow soldiers who had gone with them through the war to its successful conclusion, veterans in reality, would they return amid the thanksgiving of a grateful people, to enjoy the rewards of toil and long suffering, and lie down in the peace their valor had established.

But alas they are now numbered with the multitude of those who have died that we might enjoy the beatitudes of life, and the glory of national greatness. For more than eighty years we have been drawing inspiration from that stock of noble examples and exalted public virtues called into life by the revolutionary struggle. But henceforth whoever may wish to instruct in those sentiments that cultivate the heart, or form the mind to honor, fortitude, or high resolve need look no further back than to this second period in the nation's history.

We will not dare to offer consolation to the friends of these gallant boys, but silently regret with them that it must be so, and thank them in behalf of our fellow citizens for the gifts they have bestowed upon our common country.

> *"The hero youth who dies in blooming years,*
> *In man's regret he lives, and woman's tears*
> *Dearer than in life, and fairer far*
> *For having perished in the front of war."*[2]

On a far happier note, a brief paragraph just to the right of Mr. Beazell's editorial announced the safe return of George Darby and Isaac Moore, two of the original Fayette Guards: "AT HOME—We are pleased to record the names of several of our 'soldier boys' now at home, who but recently were suffering the horrors of rebel prisons, viz: Capt. James A. Hayden, Lieuts. Z. B. Springer and Thos. Smith, privates George W. Darby and Isaac Moore. May they long live to enjoy their own personal liberty, and a regenerated nationality, which they have contributed to establishing."[3]

As Joseph Sturgis noted in his letter of March 18, 1865, George Darby had been detained as a "Ward Master" in a military hospital in Richmond, Virginia. The story of how he came to be serving in that capacity in the Confederate capital, when nearly all of his comrades who were captured in the Battle of the Weldon Railroad ended up in Salisbury, North Carolina, consumes several chapters of his book, *Incidents and Adventures in Rebeldom*. Suffice to say here that his eventual posting to

General Hospital No. 21 was the ultimate consequence of several failed escape attempts.

George Darby first plotted to escape while he was confined on Belle Isle in the James River near Richmond. That attempt was foiled when another prisoner told a guard about the secret hole in which Darby and his friend, Isaac Moore, intended to hide until, under cover of night, they could swim the river and make good their escape. Undeterred, Darby attempted to escape again, this time while he, along with hundreds of other prisoners, was being moved by train from Richmond to Salisbury. On this occasion, Darby jumped from the train while it was stopped for wood some twenty miles south of Richmond. He was successful in eluding the train guards, only to be accosted by a county sheriff while attempting to reach the Union lines. Darby tried to bluff his way out of his predicament: "I said I belonged to a North Carolina regiment, that my mother was sick, that I had been given a furlough to go see her, that I had lost the document, and a whole lot of lies which would have made the father of lies turn green with envy to have been able to imitate. But it was no go. That mullet-headed sheriff would not believe a word of the whole lot. He said I was no doubt an escaped Yankee, and he would be obliged to take me back and place me in jail at Amelia."[4]

In fact, the sheriff took Darby to the depot at Amelia Court House and turned him over to a Confederate officer who was taking a group of rebel deserters back to Richmond. In the days that followed, Darby attempted to escape on several occasions, but was recaptured in each instance and was eventually returned to Libby Prison in Richmond where a surprise awaited him:

> I was...confined on the ground floor in the west end of that building. I soon found that my fellow prisoners on that floor were all negro soldiers.... On the two floors above the negro quarters...white men were confined and as the prison keepers always took down the communicating stair at night I slept the first night among the negroes. The next morning I chanced to get under the...opening left for the stairs and I heard someone shout 'By G-d, if here ain't old Father Darby, (father was the nickname by which I was called in my company), and on looking up I beheld the smiling face of David Richie.... [Richie]...let down a blanket which I laid hold of and they soon landed me on a higher plane. On this floor I found as partners in distress...Isaac N. Mitchell, of Uniontown...Leslie Francis, of Perryopolis; David Richie, of New Haven; Calvin Darnell, of Grindstone, and Bartholomew Warman, of Dunbar, all of whom had escaped through the hole I had kicked in the end of the [railroad] car,[5] but like myself they had been retaken and returned to Libby several days before I was sent back to keep them company. After a hearty greeting, we related to each other our experiences and...all had the same sad sequence, in that we each and all failed to make good our escape to God's country, as the North was called by the boys in captivity. Darnell

and Warman had gotten fifty miles away before being captured. They were sighted by a planter who had a gang of negroes engaged in cutting a field of tobacco. He started the darkies in pursuit of them, armed with their tobacco knives, Warman was taken, but when Darnell's pursuer got close enough, Darnell, without stopping, turned his head and said, "Slack up! Slack up! D-mit, what do you want to take me for?" and the negro pretending to be winded, did slacken pace and allowed Darnell to run away from him. He now made his way to the rebel General Malone's [sic] line at Petersburg and was concealed by a negro for two days at Mahone's headquarters, but was retaken on attempting to run the lines. Mitchell, Richie and Francis made their way one hundred miles from Richmond and then had been run down by bloodhounds and recaptured. Darnell had been given a silver dollar by a negro, (the only money the poor fellow had). With this dollar he had bought the blanket with which they hoisted me to the second floor on the morning after my arrival at Libby.[6]

In November 1864, the commandant of Libby Prison selected George Darby to act as ward master of a new hospital that the Confederates were establishing in Richmond for wounded and sick Union prisoners of war. Darby was permitted to choose four fellow prisoners to serve as nurses. He picked his old comrades from the Fayette Guards, Mitchell, Darnell, Richie, and Warman. The hospital was set up on the upper two floors of a three-story tobacco warehouse that had been surrounded by a high board fence. Here Darby and his staff treated prisoners who suffered from "gunshot wounds...pneumonia, chronic diarrhoea, scurvey, diptheria, pleurisy, typhoid and remittant fevers." The medicines available to treat these conditions included "[a]qua pura, sheep's tallow for dressing amputations, Spanish fly and mustard for blisters or counter irritants, flaxseed for poultices, nitrate of silver as a caustic, opium and corn whiskey as stimulants, tincture and iodide of iron, and perhaps a few other drugs of like character."[7]

The ordeal of one prisoner illustrates the conditions in which Darby and his comrades had to labor—and the resiliency of the human spirit. Albert Morse, a Union sailor, had been wounded and captured at Plymouth, North Carolina. He was imprisoned in Charleston and later sent to Richmond. There, a Confederate doctor proposed to poultice the wound, which had become infected:

[Morse informed the doctor] in language more expressive than elegant, that he would submit to no such nonsense.... [T]he wound on the leg was a desperate one. The bone for the space of five inches in length, was bare of flesh, and to add to his discomfort, he had three frightful bedsores.... Yet not withstanding his sufferings, this man exhibited the most determined resolution and courage;... He would roundly curse and damn [the doctors] daily for refusing to amputate his leg. Gangrene finally set in and he was transferred to the gangrene ward and there submitted to the painful operation of having the affected flesh burned out with nitrate of silver. On being returned to my ward he said to the rebel doctor, "G-dd-mn you, why don't you cut that leg off? You think I'll die! But I'll show you that I'll never die in your damned old Southern Conthieveracy. I'm going to live to get home." The doctors still refused to take the limb off, and in spite of all our efforts to prevent it gangrene set in again. Then the doctors concluded to amputate.... Morse stood the operation like the hero he was, and we gave him the best care possible under the circumstances. Nevertheless, thirty days later the flesh had receded three inches from the end of the bone, leaving it protruding from the stump.... Sloughing...ensued, a piece of flesh as large as the palm of my hand dropping out from alongside the bone, and at the same time an artery gave way. Chancing to be near him at the time, I at once seized the artery and held it until the doctor...arrived.... [H]e ordered that...a tourniquet [be] applied, but it was found that the patient was too far reduced in strength to endure...[it], so for three days and nights we, by alternate reliefs, held the artery. By this time the process of coagulation had put him beyond danger from hemorrhages, and in a short time he had so far recovered as to be paroled, and the last I ever saw of the courageous-hearted Morse he was being borne upon a stretcher to the wharf to take passage on a vessel bound for God's country....[8]

In late January, 1865, a rare exchange of prisoners took place. Darby's patients, and then his four comrades, were paroled and the ward was closed. Darby was reassigned as a ward master in General Hospital No. 21. His ward was reserved "for the most desperate cases only." Among the patients there was a soldier from Company F of the former 8th Pennsylvania Reserves, Darby's old regiment. His name was John Barman, and he and Darby had known each other well. Despite their earlier acquaintance, Darby failed to recognize Barman due to his blackened and terrible condition. Surprisingly, while Darby was attending to Barman he called out Darby's name and told him who he was: "Grasping his wasted hand I sat down by him on the cot, while in the weak and trembling voice of a dying man, he told me of the horrible deaths of many of my comrades, as they had met their fate in the prison hell of Salisbury; as he mentioned the names of long-loved schoolfellows, messmates and fellow soldiers...it seemed to me my heart must break, and I gave way to a flood of tears....The news...concerning the fate of my poor comrades at Salisbury, was the first tidings I had received of them since my escape from the box car.... [P]oor Barman soon after responded to the last roll call, and was mustered out of the earthly ranks to join the great majority of our comrades on the eternal camping grounds above.[9]

George Darby continued to work in General Hospital 21 through the first part of March when he was exchanged:

On the 23d [*sic*] of March, 1865,[10] the auspicious moment came and Sawyer and myself were, with the few others remaining, paroled and I think we were the last squad of Federal prisoners to be exchanged.... Words are inadequate to express the happiness and joy we experienced...or with what glad exultation we marched down to the wharf and boarded the rebel flag-of-truce boat which was to bear us back to the sheltering folds of "Old Glory" once more....

Our boat backed away from her moorings, and we steamed away down the James to the outpost of the rebel lines, where we were met by a Union vessel to which we were transferred, and so at last we were beneath the starry folds of the banner of the free. Out of the depths of perdition. Out of the prison cell. "Out of the jaws of death; out of the mouth of hell."[11]

Darby was taken to Camp Parole in Annapolis, Maryland, where he was "stripped to the buff, given a bath and furnished with a new and complete outfit of clothing, and given two months' pay." While at Camp Parole, Darby chanced to meet his old comrade, James Eberhart: "We had not met each other since the day upon which we left the inferno at Belle Isle to be transferred to the hell at Salisbury. Eberhart was terribly reduced in flesh, was sick and weak and had entirely lost his voice. It is needless to say that our comradeship was resumed. We ate and slept in the same barrack. He had been paroled from Salisbury a month before I was at Richmond, but the rebels had sent him by the way of Raleigh, causing many delays, so that he was nearly a month in reaching Annapolis. He occupied a bunk directly over mine...and one night while in a trance, he fell out of bed and was stunned by the fall, and on being carried out into the air and revived his voice suddenly returned to him as good as ever."[12]

Darby left Annapolis and headed for his home in late March 1865: "I was taken violently ill on the train with bronchitis, and on arrival at Harrisburg I was so weak I could not sit up and had to lie on the station platform until the train arrived for Pittsburg. I finally reached my home in Uniontown and after being confined to my bed for about three weeks I recovered sufficiently to rejoin my command at Arlington Heights after they had returned from Richmond. After completing our muster out rolls here we were moved to Harrisburg and I was there discharged after four years, two months and eleven days of constant and active service.[13] The slaveholders' rebellion was crushed; the Union was saved."[14]

In the years following the war, George Darby moved to Allegheny City (today the North Side neighborhood of Pittsburgh) where, on May 4, 1871, he married Sallie Ellen Hutchinson. He found employment with the P. F. W. & C. Railroad as an engineer, pursuing that occupation until 1903.[15] In that year, according to a physician's affidavit filed in support of his application for a pension increase, his "physical condition [had deteriorated] such as to incapacitate him from manual labor...and [diabetes] is now beginning to weaken him so much as to make it impossible for him to follow his usual occupation, that of locomotive engineer."[16]

George Darby passed away August 11, 1912, at 70 years of age. He was survived by Sallie Ellen Darby, his wife of 41 years.

James W. Eberhart hobbled out of the Salisbury Military Prison on February 22, 1865. He was one of 2,822 prisoners who had been released under parole by the Confederate authorities on that date. A column of prisoners two to three miles in length was marched under guard some fifty miles to Greensboro, North Carolina, arriving at that place February 26. From Greensboro, the prisoners were taken by train to Raleigh and then to Goldsboro. There they were transferred to another train that conveyed them to the Union lines at North East Bridge, about ten miles north of Wilmington. It was there that the prisoners were formally exchanged and turned over to the Federal authorities. James Eberhart recalled the scene vividly in his diary: "What a glorious Sight it was to see Old Glory a waving when we got off the Rebel cars."[17] Ironically, those "Rebel cars" that Eberhart spoke of traveled the line of the Wilmington and Weldon Railroad from Goldsboro to North East Bridge. It was near the northern terminus of the Wilmington and Weldon Railroad, at Globe Tavern, Virginia, that Eberhart and his fellow Fayette Guards had been captured on August 19, 1864. Barely half of them lived to see that "glorious Sight."

The newly liberated soldiers spent one night in Wilmington (the city having fallen to Union troops February 22, 1865, following the capture of Forts Fisher and Anderson) and left by steamship for Annapolis, Maryland, the next morning. Eberhart reached Camp Parole at Annapolis on March 14, 1865. He was granted a 30-day prisoner-of-war furlough and reached his home in Fayette City, Pennsylvania, four days later. A neighbor, Naoma Roley, recalled Eberhart's appearance upon his return: "I was present when he returned from prison about March 18, 1865. He...was then a living skeleton being supported by two canes. He was attended by Dr. Roberts...."[18]

Lieutenant Sturgis "saw [Eberhart] after he came from prison and before his discharge. He was then nothing but a skeleton. He had scurvy affecting his mouth....[19] He had rheumatism at that time and it seemed to affect him most in his legs and hips. He was not then in hospital, but he may have been in hospital before he rejoined his regiment [at Arlington Heights, Virginia]. He went on to Washington for to attend the General Review soon after he returned."[20]

The event Sturgis referred to was officially known as the Grand Review. It took place in the nation's capital over the course of two days in the latter part of May. President Andrew Johnson, in office barely a month since the assassination of Abraham Lincoln, reviewed Major General George G. Meade's Army of the Potomac on May 23. The next day, troops of General William T. Sherman's Army of the Tennessee and the Army of Georgia passed in review. One author described the events of May 23, 1865, with these poignant words: "Today the Army of the Potomac, after four long years of suffering defeat and then final victory over its old adversary, Gen. Robert E. Lee, marched in its last parade down Pennsylvania Avenue in Washington, D. C. The Grand Review, on its first day, contained seemingly endless lines of blue infantry and artillery and a constant clatter of cavalry as that proud army had its last hurrah. For most it was a day of unbounding joy. For others, it seemed that the ghosts of the thousands of fallen sat sadly in the reviewing stands unable to let the moment go without remembrance."[21]

One observer, surrounded by the ghosts of his own comrades—fallen on the slopes of Little Round Top at Gettysburg—was Brevet Major General Joshua Lawrence Chamberlain. He remarked upon the remnants of the old Pennsylvania Reserves as they marched past: "[H]ere comes the Third Division, with Crawford, of Fort Sumter fame; high gentleman, punctilious soldier, familiar to us all.... Their [insignia] is the blue cross,... And the men who in former days gave fame to that division—the Pennsylvania Reserves of the Peninsula, Antietam, and Gettysburg, with their strong *'esprit de corps'* and splendor of service—only the shadow of them now. But it is of sunset gold."[22]

It is not known whether either James Eberhart or George Darby marched in the Grand Review. Both returned to their regiment, then encamped at Arlington Heights, Virginia, upon the expiration of their prisoner-of-war furloughs in late April. Lieutenant Sturgis noted that Eberhart did go to Washington to attend the General Review. One would hope that, having survived the dark days in Libby, Belle Isle, and Salisbury, both men were sufficiently recovered to have taken part in the great parade. In any event, whether they marched with their regiment or merely cheered them on from the curb, the day surely must have been one of mixed emotions for them: on the one hand, joy at the celebration of final victory and the preservation of the Union, while on the other, sorrow at the remembrance of so many fallen comrades.

After his discharge, James Eberhart returned to Fayette City. He lived there for one and one-half years, before moving to Allegheny (today the North Side of Pittsburgh). Eberhart described his postwar employment history in an application for an increase in his military pension:

> I entered the employ of S. S. Marvin, the bakerman, as [a] travelling salesman, and was in their employ about 12 years.... I was on the road five of those 12 years and the remaining seven was on a wagon here in this city [Pittsburgh]. I went to Florida in 1877 or 1878 and was in that state about 7 months. I went down there to buy a farm [and] spent most of the 7 months at Bronson, Florida. I came back to this city and remained here until the latter part of 1879 or the first part of 1880 when I moved to a farm about 1 ½ miles from Grand Rapids, Mich. I remained there until...I went to California. I first went to Englewood.... Then I moved to Sierra Madre...where I lived three or four years. Then I moved to Los

Troops marching along Pennsylvania Avenue in Washington, D.C., during the Grand Review. Note the dome of the Capitol in the background.

Angeles City and remained there until 1897 when I came [back] to Allegheny, Pa. where I have resided ever since.

During all the time I lived in Michigan I ran a market garden.

At Englewood...I worked on ranches as a farm hand....[23]

In November 1868, James Wood Eberhart married Emma Helena Roberts in the Episcopal Church in Monongahela City, Pennsylvania. Between 1869 and 1879, they had five children—two boys and three girls. All but one lived to adulthood. Emma and the children traveled with Eberhart as he moved from Pennsylvania to Michigan to California. In 1897, James Eberhart left his wife and returned to Pennsylvania. He moved into the home of his sister in Allegheny. The circumstances surrounding Eberhart's return to Pennsylvania are unknown, but both he and Emma, who continued to live in Los Angeles, confirmed in documents filed in connection with pension applications that they were never divorced or legally separated, and that neither ever remarried.

In the late 1800s, James Eberhart applied for and received a pension of $10 per month, based upon disabilities he suffered as a result of his military service. The monthly stipend was increased to $25 in April of 1914, but Eberhart never saw any of the increase. He died less than one month later, passing away on May 5, 1914.[24]

Sergeant Isaac Moore limped out of Salisbury Prison alongside his friend, James Eberhart, on February 22, 1865. He, too, rode the cars down to North East Bridge on the same Weldon Railroad that his regiment had tried to destroy six months earlier. He, too, was sent to Camp Parole at Annapolis, where he was given a 30-day prisoner-of-war furlough. Moore reached Uniontown in late March and made his way to the farm of his maternal uncle, Andrew Hart Dutton. The uncle recalled his nephew's return: "In March, 1865 he was brought home on sick furlough after being paroled from rebel prison in Salisbury, North Carolina at which time he was almost a...moving skeleton and a total wreck of his former self, so much so that his own mother did not recognize him on making his appearance. Since that time continuous until May following he lay at [my] house sick with typhoid fever and a complication of diseases associated therewith."[25]

Dr. F. C. Robinson, who treated Isaac Moore following his return to Uniontown, stated: "[I] was the family physician of his mother's family for many years prior to the war and...knew [Isaac Moore] intimately and [knew] that prior to his enlistment his habits were unexceptionable and that his health was perfect.... His commanding size and soldierly bearing always attracted attention.... I saw him in the spring of 1865 after his release from Rebel prisons and he was then a mere skeleton I think weighing scarcely a hundred pounds...."[26]

While he stayed at his uncle's farm, Isaac Moore's first cousin, Lucinda Keffer Moore, cared for him and nursed him back to health. The two young cousins (she was 23 years old, he was 24) fell in love. They were married in the Methodist Episcopal Church in Ironton, Ohio, July 17, 1866. Ironton lay just across the Ohio River from Greenup County, Kentucky, where Isaac had gone to find work as a coal miner. Isaac and Lucinda had four children during the years they lived in Kentucky—two girls and two boys. One of the girls died in childhood, as did one of the boys, but the two surviving children lived to adulthood. After the death of their firstborn child in 1874, Isaac and Lucinda returned to Uniontown. They would live in Fayette County, Pennsylvania, for the remainder of their lives.

In the years that followed, Moore worked variously as a tanner, a woolen mill worker, a foundry worker, and a policeman. For a brief period of time he served as the chief of police in Uniontown. On January 1, 1917, an interesting article appeared in a Uniontown newspaper:

WRITES POEM ON HIS BIRTHDAY

I. A. Moore, former chief of police of Uniontown and veteran of the Civil War as a member of the 85th [*sic*] Pennsylvania regiment, celebrated his 76th birthday on January 1 at the National Soldiers Home in Tennessee. Mr. Moore, who is well known to all of the older residents of Uniontown, was born a short distance from Hopwood. He has been in the National Soldiers Home for several months and has written friends in Uniontown that his health is good and that he is enjoying life in Tennessee among the 1,400 old soldiers. He said that he keeps informed as to what is going on in Fayette County through the Herald.

On his birthday Mr. Moore briefly sketched his life in the following words:

> In good old Pennsylvania
> In Eighteen Forty One,
> In a happy little family
> By the stork was dropped a son.

> At the foot of Laurel Hill mountain,
> On that blustery New Year's morn;
> In a cottage by my father built,
> Where I, a babe was born.

> The dames and doctors all agreed,
> And father laughed with joy
> When was dropped upon the carpet
> A sixteen pounder boy.

> I am still upon the carpet
> In perhaps a better fix;
> In Nineteen Hundred and Seventeen
> I'm a youth of seventy six.

Please accept this little token,
And share with me my joy,
That in all these years unbroken,
At heart I'm still a boy.[27]

Lucinda Keffer Moore died in December 1909 at 67 years of age. She and Isaac had lived together as husband and wife for 43 years. Isaac Moore died on Christmas eve in 1921. His obituary appeared in the *Genius of Liberty* three days later: "Isaac A. Moore, aged 80 years, died at the home of his niece, Mrs. William Lytle, of Nicholson township Saturday [December] 24. Mr. Moore was one of the last surviving members of Company G, 8th Pennsylvania Reserves, one of the first companies to leave Fayette county at the outbreak of the Civil War. He was later transferred to the 191st Pennsylvania volunteers with which outfit he served until the close of the war. He was a member of the Will F. Stewart Post No. 180 G. A. R. of this city. The body will be brought to Uniontown and funeral services

In the years following the war, Isaac A. Moore served for a time as the chief of police in Uniontown, Pennsylvania.
Author's Collection

held this afternoon at 2 o'clock at the Episcopal church. Interment at Oak Grove Cemetery."[28]

Isaac Moore was laid to rest in the Circle of Honor surrounding the Civil War Soldiers' Monument in Oak Grove Cemetery in Uniontown.

Sergeant Ashbel Fairchild Hill, of course, returned to Fayette County, Pennsylvania, long before Isaac Moore or George Darby, a rebel bullet at Antietam sparing him the horror of Salisbury. As noted in Chapter Eight, he was honorably discharged December 20, 1862, at the Smoketown field hospital near Sharpsburg, Maryland, after recovering from the amputation of his left leg. He returned to Masontown, Pennsylvania, where he took up residence and began working on his memoir, *Our Boys*.[29]

Shortly thereafter, Hill left the Fayette County area, moving to Philadelphia where he completed *Our Boys* in 1864. In the final chapter, he offered a poignant remembrance of his former comrades in the 8th Regiment:

The Eighth is no more. The Pennsylvania Reserves are disbanded, and those left of them have returned to their homes....

Major Bailey [*sic*] became colonel of the Eighth; Captain Lemon, lieutenant-colonel; and Captain Gallop [*sic*], major.

Captain Conner resigned his commission in consequence of ill health, but has since won his way to distinction in the Western Army.

Lieutenant Cue became captain of Company 'D' [the Brownsville Grays].

Lieutenant Moth was killed in the Battle of Fredericksburg.

Sergeant Graham returned to the regiment, and was commissioned adjutant.

My brave messmates are still alive.

Dick and Haman became non-commissioned officers—the former being first-sergeant at the time the regiment was mustered out. Jim refused to accept any position—he resolutely adhered to his fife.

Gaskill is still alive. No bullet was ever made to kill *him*.

Dave Winder recovered from his fracture, re-enlisted, and entered the army in West Virginia.

Hare, Mayhorn, and Smith are still alive....

Dennis—brave fellow-passed unhurt through many battles, and at last fell a victim to disease. He sleeps in a quiet churchyard on the banks of the Monongahela; and the snow-white stones that mark his resting-place can be seen by travelers as the boats glide up and down the smooth stream.

Others whom I have not mentioned—though no less worthy of notice—have died of disease; but many more lie buried where they fell. The soil of Virginia and Maryland covers them, and green as ever is the sod above them. Yes, they are scattered over the fields of Cold Harbor, Glendale, Beaver Dam, South Mountain, Antietam, Gettysburg, Fredericksburg, and the Wilderness of Spotsylvania, where friend and foe...lie wrapped in the sleep that knows no earthly waking—the sleep that will only be broken when the last trump[et] shall wake the slumberers to new life in a land whose bright and happy skies are never veiled in the storm-clouds of war, and a land where the shriek of the shell and the whistle of the bullet are never heard.[30]

In later years, Hill traveled as far as San Francisco where he edited a publication entitled *Golden City*. By 1873, he had moved to Concord, New Hampshire, where, it is believed, he worked for a time as an editor for the *Daily Patriot*, a Concord newspaper of the period. During these postwar years, Hill also wrote several other books, including *White Rocks* and *Abel Gray, or A Romance of the National Road*, which was published in serial form in the *Genius of Liberty* in the summer of 1876. Sadly, while Hill's writing gained him a measure of notoriety, it did not suffice to enable him to prosper. He died in Uniontown in November 1876 without sufficient assets to enable the expenses of his last sickness and burial to be paid in full.[31] He was just 34 years of age and had never married. Hill's friends at the *Genius of Liberty* remembered him fondly in the following obituary:

ASHBEL FAIRCHILD HILL

With sorrow and regret we have to announce the death of Ashbel F. Hill, Esq., which took place at the McClelland House in this place, on Tuesday, November 7th, 1876, at 3 o'clock. P.M. He had taken an active part in the political campaign, and on Saturday afternoon, October 28th, delivered an address at Geneva during a drizzling rain, and his clothing became wetted through and through. In this condition he drove to Uniontown [by wagon], a distance of fifteen miles, and was completely be-numbed and exhausted upon his arrival here. A severe cold resulted, followed by intense fever, and although he had the best medical attention, his system never recovered from the severe attack, and he passed quietly away on Tuesday afternoon last. His remains were taken to Masontown on Wednesday morning, and will be buried there today at one o'clock.

Mr. Hill responded to the call of his country for volunteers, early in 1861, and was a member of Company D [the Brownsville Grays] raised in this county by Captain C. L. Conner, and attached to the Eighth Regiment of Pennsylvania Reserves, commanded by Col. Hays, afterwards by Cols. Oliphant and Baily. He was mustered in as a private, June 21, 1861, and promoted to Sergt. May 1, 1862. He participated in the engagements of Manassas, Bull Run, Hunter's Mills, Mechanicsville, Gaines' Mill, the battles of the Chickahominy, South Mountain and Antietam. At this last-named battle he lost a leg, and was discharged from the army by Surgeon's certificate in December 1862. Mr. Hill was a fine scholar and a writer of fine abilities; was at one time editor of the *Golden City* in San Francisco, assistant editor of the Philadelphia *Mercury*, and was a contributor to *Saturday Night* and other literary papers. He was the author of several widely read publications, most popular of which were "White Rocks," "Our Boys," "Secrets of the Sanctum," "John Smith's Funny Adventures on a Crutch," and of the serial published in the GENIUS OF LIBERTY entitled "Abel Gray, or a Romance of the National Road," which is still fresh in the minds of thousands of our readers. Mr. Hill was a candidate for the nomination for General Assembly in this county and lacked but a few votes of being successful. As a man, he was eminently social, generous, and full of noble impulses. He had a host of friends in this county who feel deeply grieved at his untimely departure.[32]

Sergeant Thomas Wathen Springer, of course, never did come home. He died at Salisbury just two months after his 20th birthday, mourned by his messmates, Isaac Moore and James Eberhart. Both had done their best to save him, but to no avail. He was buried anonymously in a mass grave outside the prison stockade, together with some four thousand other Union prisoners who died during the terrible winter of 1864–65. The loss of their oldest son was not the only cross that his bereaved parents would have to bear. Thomas Springer's younger brother, John, who had enlisted in the 101st Pennsylvania at 16 years of age, was captured at

Plymouth, North Carolina, in April 1864. He was imprisoned at Andersonville, Georgia, and died there June 28 of typhoid fever. He was but 18 years old.[33]

George Darby, James Eberhart, Isaac Moore, Ashbel Hill, Thomas Springer— five young men who marched out of Fayette County in the spring of 1861 to answer their country's call. Only four returned in the spring of 1865. Three of the four were so wasted by their months of confinement in Confederate prisons that it would take them years to fully recover. The fourth had been wounded so severely that he would live only a decade beyond the end of the war. But in that first spring of peace in four long years, Darby, Moore, and Hill undoubtedly would have echoed James Eberhart's sentiment, expressed so profoundly in his final diary entry: "Thanks be Mercifull God that brought me Home again."

"You Come to Honor the Soldiers of '61"

Pilgrimage to Salisbury

On November 16, 1910, James Eberhart and Isaac Moore returned to North Carolina. It was surely a bittersweet journey for the two old veterans. They were among 111 former prisoners of war from Pennsylvania who traveled to Salisbury to witness the dedication of a memorial commemorating the sacrifice of their comrades who had perished while imprisoned there.

The memorial was erected on the grounds of the Salisbury National Cemetery. Established by Congress shortly after the war, the cemetery, located just west of the old prison site, encompassed within its boundaries 18 trenches in which nearly four thousand Union prisoners of war were buried without coffins or markers. The trenches, approximately four feet deep, six feet wide, and 240 feet long, were dug largely by the prisoners themselves. Each day, those who had died were collected and counted at the dead house and then hauled "to the old field west of the Prison [in an] old rickety wagon...without anything to cover them."[1] One prisoner, George Swift, described the process in graphic detail. When the wagon pulled up to the dead house each afternoon, the guards "lift[ed] the bod[ies] between them and carried [them] feet foremost to the rear of the wagon [and], with one or two swings and a heave, would throw the almost naked corpse[s] into the wagon." The sight, according to Swift, "was most hideous to gaze upon. Some were stiff, while others again were pliant and limber and, as the wagon rolled over the ground, the heads of some, hanging out of the wagon, would roll or swing from side to side, their glassy eyes staring wide open which was as revolting as any demons could conceive."[2]

It was to honor the sacrifice of the thousands of Pennsylvania soldiers who died and were buried in such appalling circumstances that the Pennsylvania legislature passed an act "authorizing the erection of a memorial to the memory of the Pennsylvania dead interred in the National Cemetery at Salisbury, North Carolina, who died in the Confederate prison at that place while confined as Prisoners of War...."[3] Governor Edwin S. Stuart approved the act and appointed a commission to implement its provisions. The Pennsylvania Salisbury Memorial Commission consisted of five members, all of whom were Union veterans who had been confined in Confederate military prisons during the Civil War. Colonel James D. Walker of Pittsburgh was elected president of the commission.[4]

Over the course of the next two years, the commission reviewed various proposed designs for the memorial, finally selecting one that consisted of an arcade 24 feet square with circular arched entrances from the front and both sides. It was capped with a dome surmounted by a life-size bronze figure of a Union prisoner of war.[5] Within the arcade were mounted three bronze tablets, one of which featured a bas-relief depiction of the old prison stockade. The other two were inscribed as follows:

Tablet No. 1

THIS MONUMENT IS ERECTED BY AUTHORITY OF AN ACT OF THE PENNSYLVANIA LEGISLATURE APPROVED JUNE 13TH 1907,

To commemorate the patriotic devotion, heroism and self-sacrifice of the officers and soldiers of the Pennsylvania volunteers who died while confined as prisoners of war in the Confederate Military Prison at Salisbury, North Carolina, during the War of the Rebellion and were interred among the unknown Union soldiers and sailors in the eighteen trenches at the southeast of this monument. A grateful Commonwealth renders this tribute to their honor and memory.[6]

Tablet No. 2

MANY PENNSYLVANIA SOLDIERS ARE BURIED HERE.

They were citizens of a State whose founders came across the sea and established a Commonwealth where all men would be equal, and under just laws, free to enjoy their inalienable rights in the pursuit of happiness, unmolested by king or noble or prejudiced class. They used the sword only to preserve the peace and unity of their country. Twice on the soil of their State were crucial struggles for the Republic. First at Valley Forge that tested the courage and fortitude of the patriot army then at Gettysburg that proved the nation could not be broken. Respecting the example of the Romans, who never raised emblems of triumph over a foe, the Commonwealth of Pennsylvania erects this monument to perpetuate the memory of the dead and not as a commemoration of victory.

Their memory cannot be forgot.
Forever shall men's hearts revere
Their loyalty and hold this spot
Sacred because they perished here.[7]

In May of 1910, as the construction of the memorial neared completion, the commission published a notice advising the survivors of Salisbury that the memorial would be dedicated in November of that year and that the Commonwealth would

The Pennsylvania Memorial at the Salisbury National Cemetery, dedicated November 16, 1910.

provide free transportation to any survivor who wished to attend the ceremonies. One hundred fifty-two applications for transportation were approved. Of these, 111 veterans, including Isaac Moore and James Eberhart, actually journeyed to Salisbury and witnessed the dedication ceremonies.[8]

Moore and Eberhart traveled by rail from their homes in Uniontown and Pittsburgh to Harrisburg, where they transferred to a specially chartered Pennsylvania Railroad train. They pulled out of the state capital on Tuesday, November 15, and headed for Richmond, Virginia, the old Confederate capital. Arriving in Richmond just after midnight, the train was switched to the Southern Railway system and departed for Salisbury via Danville, Virginia, and Greensboro, North Carolina. The travelers were delayed between Richmond and the Virginia-North Carolina border when their locomotive broke down, and several hours were lost while a replacement engine was brought to the scene. One can imagine the governor of Pennsylvania and the various other dignitaries aboard the train pacing about in the middle of the night, wondering whether they would get to Salisbury in time for the scheduled ceremonies.

Eventually, the train resumed its journey, pulling into the Salisbury Depot shortly after noon on Wednesday, November 16, just three hours late: "The [Pennsylvania] party was met by the reception committee and conveyed to the Empire Hotel in automobiles and carriages, where dinner was served.... The meeting of the two Governors—Pennsylvania and of North Carolina—at the Empire was exceedingly cordial and gracious.... The procession formed at the hotel...about 2:30 P.M., and marched to the cemetery, led by the [Salisbury Brass] Band and the Pennsylvania survivors with the North Carolina veterans on foot, followed by the Governors of North Carolina and Pennsylvania, their staff and distinguished guests in automobiles and carriages."[9]

The Confederate veterans present for the occasion, largely from the Salisbury area, figured in an unscheduled display of comradeship that left an indelible impression with the Pennsylvania survivors: "While the parade was forming, the local Confederate veterans ordered the Union veterans to form in double file and, when the line was completed, the Johnny Rebs marched through the Yankee lines, shaking hands heartily right and left. It was an impromptu feature of the program and one that drew tears to the eyes of the gathered multitude...." "After marching through the Streets of Salisbury, the parade ended at the Pennsylvania Memorial in the National Cemetery where an immense concourse of the citizens of Salisbury [including local school children released from class for the occasion], Durham, Raleigh, and the surrounding country had assembled, and with a close and respectful attention remained during the entire proceedings."[10]

Beneath a crisp, clear southern sky, Isaac Moore and James Eberhart listened as Colonel Walker called for the invocation: "Comrades, gentlemen, ladies and friends, the exercises upon this occasion will be opened with an invocation to our God by the Reverend J. W. Sayers, Chaplain of the Department of Pennsylvania, Grand Army of the Republic."[11] Reverend Sayers rose from his seat and asked all those present to join him in prayer:

> Our heavenly Father, we thank Thee that Thou hast permitted us to see this hour.... We thank Thee for Thy sovereign care and protection in that, in the days that were shadowed with trouble, Thou didst lead us, and gavest Thy strength when the burden was heavy upon us, and gavest us courage and guidance, so that, after the conflict, we have come to these days of peace.
>
> We thank Thee that the wrath of war has been stilled, that brother no longer strives against brother, that once again we have one country and one flag.... We pray Thee to make our memories steadfast that we may never forget the generous sacrifices made for our country. May our dead be enshrined in our hearts! May their graves be the altars of our grateful and reverential patriotism.
>
> And now, O God, bless Thou this memorial; Bless it...in honor of mothers who bade their sons to brave deeds; in honor of wives who wept for husbands who should never come back again; in honor of children whose heritage is their fallen fathers' heroic names;... But, chiefly, O God, in honor of men who counted not their lives dear when their country needed them: of those alike who sleep beside the dust of their kindred...or in nameless graves, where only thine angels stand sentinel 'til the reveille of the resurrection morning.... Amen.[12]

Colonel Walker then introduced the governor of North Carolina, saying: "To us who have traveled so many miles from our grand old state, it surely is a pleasure to be met and welcomed by the Governor of the Old North State. Comrades, permit me to present to you the Honorable W. W. Kitchin, Governor of the State of North Carolina."[13] Governor Kitchin greeted the Pennsylvanians with remarks notable for their tone of harmony and remembrance:

> Your Excellency, Governor Stuart:... In the name of the people of North Carolina I welcome you to this state.... You come to honor the soldiers of '61.... They and their brave comrades, by sacrifice and courage, made your pilgrimage hither easy and pleasant, while their pilgrimage to the South was difficult and bitter. In the 60's their army required four years and four thousand miles of travel beset by danger and death to go from Washington to Richmond, but...they made the trip, where none but our fellow Americans could have succeeded. Then, we extended our arms to resist your hostile march, and now we extend our hearts to encourage your peaceful invasion....
>
> The State that furnished more slain in battle...than any other state of the Confederacy, this day rejoices to have in her borders the distinguished representatives

of the Union State on whose soil was fought the greatest conflict of that ever memorable struggle—the conflict that decided the destiny of the continent.

[F]rom Maine to Texas marble and granite and bronze point skyward in memory and in honor of American valor, patriotism, and sacrifice. What matters it whether they commemorate Northern or Southern heroism, whether Lee or Grant, whether blue or gray? They all typify noble, sincere, brave American impulse, spirit, endurance, devotion to duty, love of country, and fidelity to faith....

Pennsylvanians, your monument stands in no enemy's country. It stands...among your friends, who rejoice that you are displaying the highest sentiment and performing a sacred duty in perpetuating the memory of your heroes.... We know that you approve the monument standing in yonder street erected by the love of our great people in honor of our noble dead in a cause we lost,[14] as we approve this monument erected by the love of a great people to noble dead in a cause you won, both emblematic of civilized man's unconquerable affection and immeasurable regard for those who risk their all for principle and for it yield up their lives....

[A]s we were worthy of each other's steel in war, we are worthy of each other's friendship in peace, and this friendship we give unstintedly and without reserve. Again I extend the glad hand to Pennsylvania's Governor and his companions; again I wish for you and yours pleasure and success on this patriotic occasion, for Tarheels, generous and true, rejoice with you in this day's exercises....[15]

The lieutenant governor of Pennsylvania, Robert S. Murphy, offered a response to Governor Kitchin's remarks, calling to mind the comradeship of North and South in the perilous days of the Revolution:

Language fails upon this occasion to express properly the deep appreciation we all feel for the brilliant and eloquent welcome extended to us by your distinguished Governor. His words of splendid tribute to those who died here and to the bravery of the men in blue, who with their blood maintained the integrity of the Union, is only matched by our high esteem for the unflinching devotion of those soldiers who gave to the Army of Northern Virginia the laurel of imperishable renown. To say that there was anything but sincere belief upon the part of those contending on both sides in the great Civil War in the righteousness of their cause is an insult to the honesty of the intelligent and the brave, who risked and lost their all in support of their conviction of right....

In the great heart of the North there is no malice, no hatred, nothing but generous fraternal regard and regret for what seemed to be imperative necessity. Her eyes turn with appreciation to the Carolinas; to this land noted for its hospitality;... this land...where cotton blooms and fragrant tobacco grows, in answer to the persuasive power of sunshine warm and tender.... [W]e come here not as

An artist's impression of the dedicatory address at the Pennsylvania Memorial in Salisbury, North Carolina. One can imagine Isaac A. Moore and James Eberhart in the audience.

Courtesy of the artist, Grey Gamewell Carle

strangers, for in the veins of Pennsylvania and the Carolinas courses the same rich red blood....

We are standing today in a region...whose historic past is the common heritage of all. Here was first heard the notes of the Marseillaise of the Revolution of 1776 through the medium of the Mecklenburg resolutions. Here upon the Alamance was heard the opening gun that shouted defiance to kingly power. In yonder Carolina the conqueror of Burgoyne at Saratoga went down to overwhelming defeat at Camden. Hope and courage were again restored by the brilliant victory of Daniel Morgan at the famous Cowpens.

The very existence of American authority and control in the Carolinas was determined by that remarkable soldier, Nathaniel Greene, at Guilford Courthouse.... His wisdom and military genius foiled the efforts of Cornwallis to subjugate the Carolinas in the interest of King George.... In place of the King's authority he substituted that of the Continental Congress in the interest of liberty and independence, and to that great work we are largely indebted today for the liberty which we now enjoy.... The names of Marion, of Sumter, and of Pickens are as dear to us of the North as any that decorate the pages of history—splendid patriots, brilliant soldiers...their deeds and triumphs contributed much to our final success, and their fame and patriotism will ever be revered by a grateful country....

[F]rom that time when our arms were crowned with success, we enjoyed an era of uninterrupted [domestic] peace until we became embroiled in civil strife—North against South, South against North.

One of the incidents growing out of that frightful conflict summons us here today. We come here, in a spirit of tenderness and love, to pay the just tribute of a great Commonwealth to her sons who perished on this soil and who perished under circumstances that will ever excite the tenderest emotions of the human heart. For them it was not given to die upon the battlefield in the presence of a brave and courageous enemy and beneath the waving folds of the flag they loved;... to them it was not given in their dying moments to be surrounded by companions and friends, or encouraged by the stirring music of the bugle and the shouts of triumph; to them it was not given to be stimulated by the belief that their sacrifices would be appreciated by their countrymen, and that long afterward their bravery and noble conduct would be the subject of admiration. But it was their misfortune to become...prisoners of war, and to my mind no greater misfortune can come to any soldier...than that which came to these men. It was their misfortune to be confined within the...military prison which formerly stood upon this ground. A place...where men, even under favorable circumstances, found it extremely difficult to retain the qualities of manhood and maintain the courage of one's soul—a captivity which practically meant death and where exchange or liberty seemed almost out of the question. Yet, these men bore up unflinchingly against insidious disease, against privation of the most painful character, and unfalteringly bore the burden imposed upon them as soldiers of the great republic.... [T]hey gave up their lives and sank into unknown graves in order that we might live.

Today we commemorate in appropriate stone those who cheerfully surrendered life upon the altar of their country. Around about us lie men of Pennsylvania and of other states—soldiers, loyal and true. The memory of their sufferings and sorrows will never be forgotten by those who love manhood and revere courage. To those who died here was given the supreme privilege of contributing in the highest degree to the preservation of the Republic....

From the sacrifices of those who lie here...this great Union of indivisible states has been made possible.... Among the memories of the past there is nothing more grateful to the mind of the true patriot than the recollection of the contest that gave to us that great body of soldiers from the North and the South who stood by the side of the great LaFayette and the mighty Washington. Let it ever be remembered that in the hour of severest trial the Colonies stood together as one man; the soldiers of Virginia, of Georgia, and of the Carolinas were united with those of Massachusetts, of New York and of Pennsylvania at Valley Forge and at Yorktown—names dear to every American; occasions that excite the noblest impulses and bid us walk forward arm in arm together to the destiny which will be unfolded in the future. An unavoidable conflict turned us one from the other. All that need be remembered of that chaotic event are the bravery and courage of the men on both sides who, confident in their cause and executing the right as they believed God had given them to see the right, furnished to the world an example of heroism and devotion which has placed the fame of the American soldier on the topmost round of fame....

Let us [therefore] renew our devotion to our common country. Let us gather increased inspiration from the memory of those whose privations and sacrifices we today recall. Let us consecrate ourselves anew to the spirit of liberty, to the spirit of justice, to the spirit of nationalism upon which the glory and greatness of this splendid country must ever and always depend.[16]

Colonel Walker next introduced Mrs. J. Sharp McDonald, who led the audience in "Lorena," a song that was a favorite of both armies during the war.[17] After the singing of "Lorena," which undoubtedly brought back poignant memories to the old veterans present, the mayor of Salisbury delivered a welcoming address on behalf of the city:

Mr. Chairman, [Your] Excellency the Governor of Pennsylvania, Members of the Commission, Old Survivors, Ladies and Gentlemen: You have come today from the home of your birth to dedicate a memorial of marble and bronze to the memory of those who years ago left [that] same beloved land, to wander into what was then an enemy's country, and lay them down to die. They left at duty's call and, marching 'neath the Stars and Stripes, for weary miles they trod their rough and rugged way, where'er superiors bade them go.

Their only cheer in those dread days, the martial strains of bugle call; their only aim, to serve their country well; their fondest hopes, to soon return, and tell to loved ones left behind of glorious conquest, and of fame well earned through toil and strife and much sacrifice. Their warrior's dream was rudely shattered within yon prison walls when, after sufferings untold, hunger undescribed, sickness beyond endurance, their wasted forms were laid to rest beneath this green sward. 'Tis well you come...to pay respect to those who merit more than the living can give to them, who yielded up their lives that a nation riven through fratricidal strife might be united once again, to stay united until time shall be no more.

But Esteemed Sirs, and old survivors, the glory of this historic event shall not be yours alone. There comes to join with you in this good hour a remnant of another army—the Army of Northern Virginia—a remnant of an army that has made history equal to that of Waterloo or Ancient Thermopylae—a remnant of an army that left more comrades sleeping upon the heights of Gettysburg in your own Commonwealth, in unmarked graves, than sleep today in this silent city of the dead—a remnant, thank Heaven, that has long since buried the bitterness of that strife and comes today to extend to you a welcome that knows no bounds....

And others still in this vast throng...have come to bid you royal welcome, and join with you in dedicating this memorial, and at the same time to erect another, which shall surpass in grandeur and be more lasting than your bronze and stone. For we believe 'tis true, if erected of marble, it will perish; if we build it of brass, time will efface it; but if we construct it upon the fundamental principles of justice and virtue, friendship and hospitality, in the fear of God and with love towards men, we shall erect a memorial...that will live forever and brighten all eternity. And of these we would build it today, as we clasp glad hands across a chasm of half a century and give you a cordial welcome.

The noble sentiments you utter in the words inscribed on bronze—"The Commonwealth of Pennsylvania erects this monument to perpetuate the memory of the dead, and not as a commemoration of victory"—strikes a responsive chord within our hearts, and we throw open wide our doors with hospitality unbounded, with friendship unexcelled, with cordiality unrestrained and liberality limited only by circumstances and the time you have allotted to remain in our midst.

'Tis with genuine pleasure [that] I extend to you the keys of the city of Salisbury.... These keys will admit you to the best of all that is within our power to give. Our fondest aim shall be to make you feel that the old Salisbury prison has become indeed a myth, that this cemetery is now but a trysting place where lovers plight their troth, and this memorial prepared as a tribute to valor, having now served its purpose as such, hence forward shall remind us of a happy union of those who were once estranged, but are now forever reconciled. Thrice welcome to our city.[18]

Colonel Walker thanked Mayor Smoot for his remarks and introduced General Thomas J. Stewart, adjutant general of Pennsylvania, and a past National Commander of the Grand Army of the Republic for a response:

People of North Carolina, Ladies and Gentlemen: It is a great honor...to be designated to represent my comrades of the war, and the people of Pennsylvania assembled here, in voicing their appreciation of your gracious welcome so eloquently expressed by your distinguished Governor, and also by the Mayor of your beautiful city. Your welcome is indeed most gracious and cordial. We come joyously and gladly within the gates of the historic State of North Carolina; come to pay tribute, and to commemorate the valor and devotion to duty of the sons of Pennsylvania in days now long gone; days when war, cruel and relentless, kept us far apart; days in which men in blue and men in gray wrote with swords and bayonets dipped in blood the heroic chapters of the nation's martial history.

Pennsylvania was not always welcome in North Carolina, nor was North Carolina always welcome in Pennsylvania. We were on opposite sides in that mighty contest.... We and you had hopes that were shattered...hearts that were broken; enemies from 1861 to 1865, now friends. Since the days our visit commemorates, we and you have been marching away from war, away from its fields of blood, its hospitals of pain, its prisons of cruelty.

The seasons in their unceasing round have covered soldiers' graves, North and South, with sweet flowers, and moistened them with dewy tears, and as we look out over this silent camping ground of our heroic dead, in this far away Southland, we recall the words of the poet so beautiful in tribute,

> Oh little mounds that mean so much,
> We compass what you teach,
> And our worst grossness feels the touch
> Of your uplifting speech.
> You thrill us with the thoughts that flow
> Like eucharistic wine,
> And by our holy dead we know
> That life is still divine.

This is a pilgrimage of peace.... Today there is little of the bitterness, of the strife.... The gray are here with the blue, conqueror and conquered, all full of gratitude for the safety in our homes, the glory in our flag, the hope in the future so full of promise....

[W]e appreciate the warmth and cordiality of your welcome, but amid the exceeding pleasure of this occasion there is a feeling of sadness in the fact that all who wished to attend on this occasion are not here. Many of the veteran soldiers are detained at home by the infirmities of age...but I am sure that today in Pennsylvania those who in the days of war were round about this place, and felt its pain and privation and trials, will in imagination follow this goodly assemblage throughout the ceremonies of the day, and I bring you their kindly greeting for the cordial welcome and generous hospitality you this day extend....

This day, this ceremony, this pilgrimage, will fall far short of its purpose unless it shall strengthen the bond of unity between the people of North Carolina and Pennsylvania, unless the tribute we pay to the valor and devotion of the American soldier, whether he wore the blue, or whether he wore the gray, shall make and keep the children of the future as brave as their fathers were in the past...and make them in their day and time defenders of the flag and of the unity of the Republic, thus keeping us one people with one destiny, one hope, one country and all under one flag, and that our own Star Spangled Banner.

Honored Governor, Mr. Mayor, for all here, soldier and civilian, men and women of Pennsylvania, and for the great Commonwealth whose sons and daughters we are proud to be, I thank you for your generous, hearty welcome and for them all I express the wish and voice the prayer that this State and its people may be prosperous, her homes happy, her people loving, her fields be gardens of plenty, within her gates peace, and in this spirit and this wish we salute the people of North Carolina.[19]

Following General Stewart's comments, Mrs. McDonald sang "Columbia, the Gem of the Ocean," after which United States Senator Lee S. Overman, a Salisbury native, offered some impromptu remarks. Although not formally scheduled to speak, the senator pointed to the Stars and Stripes waving overhead and exclaimed:

Countrymen—The men of North Carolina love that flag, and when our glorious country needs defense, they will follow it to glory or to the grave. But you must not be unsympathetic with us for hallowing that other flag that once waved over this Southland. Gentlemen, our brave men followed it for four long years, and saw it go down in an ocean of tears—Forever.... But we are all at home now—one great, grand, undivided, indissoluble country....[20]

We once welcomed you with bouquets from the cannon's mouth and you welcomed us with bursts of lurid flames from the musket's muzzle; now we welcome you with open hearts and homes. Your comrades no longer rest on an enemy's soil, but on American soil.... The cotton fields, which are white to the harvest, wave you a welcome today. The thousands of spindles in our cotton mills whirl you a welcome. The children laugh you a welcome. The ladies smile you a welcome, and the men catch you by the hand and say "God bless you; we are glad you are here."[21]

Colonel Walker then closed the Welcomes and Responses portion of the program with the following comments: "On behalf of the Salisbury Memorial Commission...to you Governor Kitchin, Mayor Smoot and Senator Overman, for your many kind, loving and cheering words of greeting and welcome, to the 'Old Johnnies' present, for their open-handed, cordial and warm reception to the 'Yanks,' and to the ladies and citizens of Salisbury for their constant attention, and unbounded hospitality extended to our ladies, our guests, and ourselves, you have our thanks, and deep down in the hearts of every Pennsylvanian here, there will be a remembrance for years of the many courtesies received by them on this momentous and historical occasion...."[22] Walker directed his next remarks to the Pennsylvania veterans:

Soldiers of Pennsylvania and friends of our Grand Old Commonwealth: It is a pleasure indeed to be with you here, on a place made sacred by your sufferings, and on the scene of your trials, tribulations, and temptations, and of your Comrades who sacrificed their lives that these United States, as a Nation, should forever exist.

Of the long months of agonizing anxiety, suffering and torture, endured here by you men and your dead Comrades, much can be said, but little need be....

Comrades, were I gifted with the language of that Master of French Literature, Victor Hugo, my words would fail to adequately portray the agony and suffering of the helpless prisoners of war confined within the wooden walls of Salisbury prison. And yet you and the heroic martyrs to principle who are interred here, in the face of temptations stronger than the temptations of St. Anthony, remained steadfast and unswerving by the duty demanded of you by your country. Daily facing death in a more fearful and horrible form than that of any field of battle, firmly you stood on your oath of Allegiance to the United States and Old Glory. With a devotion sublime, an unselfish patriotism, an unflinching courage and a loyalty to duty unsurpassed, you made a most brilliant page in the history of your country that will forever redound to the credit and glory of Pennsylvania.

Pennsylvania has always been true to her soldiers, were they hungry she fed them, were they naked she clothed them. In sickness and distress or in prison she succored them, and when they returned to her bosom from battle triumphantly, she generously provided for them and nobly protected their off-spring. To her soldier dead, she paid magnificent tribute. From Gettysburg in our own fair state, to Vicksburg on the banks of the Mississippi, from Chickamauga to

Atlanta, from Shiloh to Andersonville, within and without her borders wherever her soldier dead lie, Pennsylvania has honored their memory by stones, tablets, monuments and memorials of everlasting marble, granite and bronze, and to honor the memory of her dead who lie here she has brought you, the remnant of her thousands who were imprisoned here, to participate in the dedicatory services of this, her most chaste and beautiful tribute to the memory of any of her Sons, and affords you a last opportunity to wreathe with laurel the resting places of your departed comrades. Pennsylvania will ever honor their memory, and you, survivors of Salisbury and soldiers of Pennsylvania, she will ever protect and care....

As the presiding officer of these ceremonies, it becomes my pleasant privilege to present to you one of your comrades, Captain Louis R. Fortescue, a brave and gallant officer of the Union Army who was confined for a great many months as a prisoner of war in various Confederate Prisons and a member of the Pennsylvania Salisbury Commission, [who] will tender the memorial to the Governor of Pennsylvania.[23]

Captain Fortescue's remarks were brief, but touching:

Your Excellency,...Comrades, Ladies and Gentlemen: In pursuance of the Act of the Legislature...which provided for the erection of a suitable monument in the National Cemetery at Salisbury, North Carolina, to commemorate the heroism, sacrifices and patriotism of the Pennsylvania Soldiers of the...War of the Rebellion, who died in the Salisbury Military Prison while confined there as prisoners of war, I have the honor of presenting to you, Governor...this beautiful memorial....

It represents a large following. So large indeed as to seem almost incredible. Eleven thousand, seven hundred [*sic*] soldiers of the Union Armies who died in this prison, lie buried in eighteen trenches near this monument.[24] There was no burial record ever found of this prison, and there was nothing to mark the individual resting place of any soldier. A hospital record was kept of those who died in the hospital and the names of 3,504 are recorded therein. If the same ratio prevailed throughout the prison as in the hospital, then 2,457 Pennsylvanians gave up their lives in this prison. No other prison or battlefield of the Civil War records so great a number from our State.

It had pleased the God of bidden heroes to lay them in unmarked ground that a whole nation might claim their burial place.... Little may it signify to them, but much to us that their memory should be sanctified by some enduring record. Therefore, in their honor, and in memory of their devotion to their Country, a grateful Commonwealth renders this tribute.

> Here in the camp of death,
> No sound their slumber breaks.

There is no fevered breath,
Nor wound that bleeds and aches.
All is repose and peace.
Untrampled lies the sod.
The shouts of battle have ceased.
It is the truce of God.[25]

During Captain Fortescue's address, the memorial, which until then had been covered, was unveiled by Colonel Walker's daughter, Miss Helen H. Walker. In an impromptu address following Fortescue's remarks, Governor Stuart accepted the memorial and in turn conveyed it to the safekeeping of the United States government.[26] Following the singing of "Tramp, Tramp, Tramp, the Boys are Marching," the memorial was accepted for the United States by General A. L. Mills:

> Governor Stuart, Governor Kitchin,...Veterans of the Blue and the Gray, Ladies and Gentlemen: The Honorable Secretary of War, who is...charged under the law with the supervision and control of our national cemeteries, having designated me to represent him at these ceremonies, I have the honor and great pleasure of accepting...this enduring memorial of granite and bronze to the memory of these brave soldiers of Pennsylvania whose lives were given here for their country. Governor Stuart, with this acceptance goes the assurance of the Secretary of War that the War Department will suitably and tenderly care for this monument,...preserving it not only as a memorial, but as an enduring lesson to foster in coming generations sentiments of patriotism and the obligations of our citizens to our country.[27]

Mrs. McDonald then led the audience in singing "The Star Spangled Banner," after which Colonel Walker introduced the orator of the day, General Harry White, who offered the following remarks:

> Comrades, Ladies, Fellow Citizens: Though late in the afternoon...your reception has been so hearty and cordial that I must recall a little occurrence, which the soldiers will appreciate, of one night on the picket line in front of Petersburg,...the lines then not far apart.... I heard a voice across the lines, "Hello Yank," then a quick response, "Hello Johnny, what do you want?" Then the inquiring reply, "Have you any oil?" To which the Yank replied, "None here, but plenty in camp." Then the Johnny...cried out, "Anoint yourself and slide over." Well, we...Yanks, have come over at last and your smooth, oily words have anointed us with the oil of gladness....
>
> Pennsylvania with her Governor...is here to honor the memory of Pennsylvania soldiers buried in yonder graves.... [T]here are here, also, many comrades who, imprisoned with the dead here, survived the severities and harshness of prison life.... Pennsylvania...always comes to North Carolina with no hesitating

step. These two states have much patriotic history in common. While the Mecklenburg Declaration of Independence of May 20, 1775 is not recognized officially and historically as the original adopted by the American Congress, yet the resolution...adopted there is so in harmony with the Declaration [adopted in] Independence Hall, that...[t]he man from North Carolina visits Philadelphia and with uncovered head stands in Independence Hall as at the Altar of American Liberty. [Likewise] [t]he man from Pennsylvania stands before the Battle Monument at King's Mountain and feels he is on hallowed ground.

The...sojourn here of the...citizens of Pennsylvania is not to a foreign land or in an enemy's country, but Americans visiting Americans in their own land and country. For a while, some years ago, such a visit would not have received welcome hospitality here.... [I]n 1861 the then Governor of North Carolina favored the state's seceding and joining the Confederacy, yet the mass of people were opposed to it.... The advocates of secession predicted no war would follow and ridiculed any thought of it. And it is narrated that one of its advocates, if not in this very city of Salisbury, yet in this part of the State, deprecated the fear or apprehension of war and at one point in his address sneeringly said of war, "Listen to me; spell the word, W A R, war, a very small word of only three letters." A voice in the audience instantly replied, "Hell has only four."

The great mass of this people hearkened to the pleadings of a distinguished statesman of the South in his efforts to turn the people from the maelstrom of secession and rebellion, as in public address he said in answer to the sneer that the Northern people would not fight, "I plant myself on the inflexible laws of human nature and the unvarying teaching of human experience and warn you this day that no government half as great as this Union can be dismembered... except through blood. You had as well expect the fierce lightning to rend the air and make no thunder...as to expect peace to follow the throes of dissolving government. I pass by the puerile taunts at my devotion to the best interests of the people among whom I was born and reared...and again tell you, dissolve the Union and war will come. I cannot tell when, but it will come and be to you a most unequal, fierce, vindictive and desolating war...."

Standing here...it is hard to realize the magnitude of the conflict. Time has mellowed, indeed, dispelled the asperities of that fighting time. That fight had to come.... On some things there was, indeed, an irrepressible conflict.... [I]t is instructive...to stand about the graves of those who have died in the great battle to settle the disputed questions that disturbed and ever would have disturbed the peace of the Republic....

Pennsylvania is here today with no hostile thought.... She has erected this monument to perpetuate the good deeds of her sons, many of whom lie in yonder graves.... Pennsylvania has never been unmindful of her citizen soldiers.... [I]t is her crowning glory that, during and after the war, she gathered the helpless and destitute orphans of her dead soldiers, adopted, maintained and educated them as her children, starting them panoplied and equipped for the battle of life. When the Pennsylvanians buried yonder died, this was called the enemy's country.... Pennsylvania and North Carolina never should have been, and are not today, enemies about the elementary principles of our republic. We leave here our dead, buried yonder, with no thought that they lie in an enemy's country or in a foreign land....[28]

As the afternoon's ceremonies drew to a close, the audience joined in singing "God be with You Till We Meet Again." The dignitaries and the survivors and veterans then made their way back to town where the governor of Pennsylvania and his delegation were feted at a reception in the home of Senator Overman. As the *Salisbury Post* put it: "Music, flowers, dainty refreshments and charming women all added to the pleasure of the guests, and the Pennsylvanians will long remember the hospitality extended to them."[29]

The survivors and the veterans repaired to the lobbies of the Empire and Ford Hotels, where they "gathered in groups and discussed the incidents of the terrible days in which they were confined in the prison. The Confederate veterans of the city and county mingled freely with their former enemies, many incidents of the old days [being] recalled and discussed with all of the halo that time has thrown around them."[30] A banquet for the Pennsylvania survivors was held at the Ford Hotel in the evening, and at its conclusion the North Carolinian delegation gave each of the Pennsylvanians a souvenir of the day's events. It was an open cotton boll, with a badge attached bearing the coats of arms of North Carolina and Pennsylvania on either side.[31] The Salisbury Memorial Association also gave each Pennsylvania veteran a medal especially struck to commemorate the occasion.

The Pennsylvanians' train left Salisbury late Wednesday evening, bound for Harrisburg and home. The old veterans undoubtedly slept soundly that night, their pilgrimage completed, their final respects paid to the memory of their long-departed brothers in arms. Perhaps Isaac Moore expressed the feelings of all of the old survivors best when, in a Christmas letter to his family in 1911, he wrote: "There is one portion [of my life] that shines brightly on memory's tablet, that is, four years engaged in the service of God and my country. I say in the service of God, because I hold that a man who serves his country loyally and faithfully, renders acceptable service to God.... Most people think that the old boys of my age are fit for nothing but the scrap heap, to be laid on the shelf to die. But that is a mistaken idea, a false conclusion, for the fire of life still burns, and that spark of Divinity implanted in every man's bosum by the Diety Himself, can never die."[32]

Written by an old soldier in the winter of his life, these words form a fitting eulogy for all of the young soldiers who marched off to war in the springtime of their own.

An artist's impression of the old veterans mingling outside the Empire Hotel in Salisbury following the ceremonies at the National Cemetery.

Courtesy of the artist, Grey Gamewell Carle

The commemorative medal issued to the Pennsylvania veterans during the ceremonies at Salisbury by the Pennsylvania Salisbury Memorial Commission.

Courtesy Kevin Carle

Two close-up views of the obverse and reverse of the commemorative medal presented to the Pennsylvania veterans November 16, 1910.

Courtesy Kevin Carle

Appendix A[1]

Petition from the Mayor and
Commissioners of Salisbury, North Carolina

HOUSE OF REPRESENTATIVES,
Richmond, Va., November 15, 1864.
Hon. J. A. SEDDON:

SIR: The inclosed petition from the mayor and commissioners of the town of Salisbury, N. C. has been sent to me, accompanied with a letter signed by one of the latter, urging me "to use my utmost influence to get the petition granted."

Representing the district in which this town is situated, and residing, as I do, in that neighborhood, I have a knowledge of the facts set forth in the petition, and beg leave to represent that they are not only true, but that the subject, in my opinion, commends itself to your immediate and favorable consideration. I have reason to believe that those prisoners are suffering, dying, and also escaping; but the fact that the people of the town and surrounding country are bearing far more than their fair proportion of the burdens of this establishment is with me a most weighty reason why the prayer of the petitioners should be granted.

Hoping that you will be aide [*sic*] in a short time to give a favorable response,
I am, most respectfully and very truly, yours,
JAMES G. RAMSAY.

Hon. JAMES A. SEDDON,
Secretary of War Confederate States of America:

The undersigned, mayor and commissioners of the town of Salisbury, State of North Carolina, would respectfully represent that there are now in the C. S. prison in this place nearly 10,000 Yankee prisoners; that the site of the prison is a most ineligible one, wanting in every facility for the secure confinement and proper subsistence of a large number of prisoners.

In the first place, the prison grounds are too small and the prisoners have to be crowded to an extent prejudicial to their comfort and health, causing dissatisfaction

303

and insubordination, and increasing the probabilities of concerted movements for their enlargement.

In the second place, the supply of water is wholly insufficient.

In the third place, a sufficient amount of wood cannot be obtained for the consumption of the prison during the winter months. Since the arrival of the prisoners the wagons and teams of the country have been impressed for the purpose of hauling wood to the prison. This has already been productive of much inconvenience and loss to the farmers in gathering their corn crops and in sowing their wheat, and if it has to be continued much longer will be ruinous to their interests. Besides, this means of transportation for wood cannot be relied on in the advanced part of the winter when wagoning becomes impracticable in consequence of bad roads, and there is no other means of procuring wood except from the Western North Carolina Railroad, which is an uncertain and precarious mode.

In the fourth place, there cannot be, under the existing system of impressment, a sufficient amount of flour, meal, and meat drawn from this region of country to subsist the prisoners. The commissary at this point has been making the most active and strenuous efforts to meet the demands upon him in the matter of subsistence for the prisoners, but as yet has not been able to more than meet the current exigencies, and cannot accumulate supplies. The wheat crop of the present year in this and surrounding counties did not reach more than one-third of an average crop, out of which, after seeding, there will be but a small surplus. The corn crop now being gathered will not amount to more than one-half of an average yield. This being the case the prisoners cannot be sustained here unless provisions are imported from other portions of the Confederacy where the season during the present year has been more propitious.

In view of the facts here stated we most respectfully ask that at least one-half of the prisoners confined in Salisbury be removed to some other prison.

> JON. I. SHAVER,
> *Mayor.*
> JAMES E. KERR,
> C. A. HENDERSON,
> THOS. E. BROWN,
> THOS. C. McNEELY,
> JOHN A. SNOW,
> S. FRANKFORD,
> JNO. A. HOLT,
> W. J. PLUMMER,
> *Commissioners.*

Appendix B[2]

Report of Inspection of Salisbury Prison by
Brigadier General Winder

HEADQUARTERS PRISONS EAST OF THE MISSISSIPPI,
Salisbury, N. C., December 13, 1864.
General S. COOPER,
Adjutant and Inspector General, Richmond, Va.:

GENERAL: I have the honor to report that having inspected at Florence, from whence my last communication was dated, I proceeded where I now am.

I am sorry to say I fear I shall be detained some days, as I find an unpleasant state of things among the officers. Indeed I fear I shall be obliged to assume command of the post for a short time, but this I shall not do unless forced to it.

In my communication from Florence I spoke of the unfitness of both that place and this as sites for prisons.

I will now state at some length the reasons why I hold that opinion.

The site at this place is very objectionable for six reasons, either of which I think conclusive:

1. There is a scarcity of water, as the wells fail and cannot afford a sufficient supply for the number of prisoners even now here.

2. There is not nor can there be a place for sinks, as there is no stream, and the sinks have to be dug inside, or if outside could only be removed a few feet. The stench is insupportable both to the prisoners and the people in the vicinity.

3. The soil is entirely unfit for a prison, being a stiff, sticky clay, and after a slight rain is over shoe-tops in mud, without a dry spot within the inclosure.

4. The prison is immediately within the town, and defenses could not be erected without destroying much property, and could not be defended when erected on account of the proximity to the buildings, which if fired would drive out the garrison. In the last outbreak one of three shots fired struck the principal hotel in the town.

5. Experience has proved that proximity to a town is extremely objectionable and injurious.

6. Wood is so distant that it is next to impossible to keep up a sufficient supply, and the expense is enormous. Thirty-nine wagons and teams are required, and then only a scant supply furnished to prison and guard. One hundred cords per day are required for troops and prison, which at $20 per cord is $60,000 per month or $720,000 per year.

In a month the saving would probably cover the expense of purchase. On the land proposed to be purchased the tops of the trees used for a stockade and the wood already on the ground would serve the post for more than a year.

A raid has reached within eighty miles of this place, and would, I am informed, have reached here but for the accidental escape of one of the prisoners captured.

I stated in my communication from Florence some reasons why I thought Florence unfit as a site for a prison. I will here repeat them. The site itself is entirely unfit for the purpose, as about one-fourth or more, probably one-third, is an impracticable morass, and cannot, without more labor and expense than building a new stockade, be in any manner reclaimed, as it would require the whole of the soil on the dry parts for three or four feet to cover the morass of marsh, and when covered would not be fit for use.

The prison at Florence is only sixty miles from Georgetown, S. C., with a good ridge road, and only one river intervening, which is ford-able in five or six places.

I see that spies have been captured, one having visited the prison at this place and the other the prison at Danville. From this we may fairly infer that Florence has not been neglected.

This would indicate a disposition on the part of the enemy to operate against the prisons.

Having said this much by way of objection to the present sites (most of which objections hold good in regard to Danville), I will take the liberty to suggest the remedy:

I proposed in my communication from Florence that I be permitted to purchase a tract of 900 acres at the fourteen-mile post from Columbia, S.C., on the railroad to Charlotte, N. C., for the purpose of erecting prisons. The purchase of that or some other tract instead of renting would save a large sum, as experience has shown at Andersonville. The place is, I think, as far removed from raids as any place I know, and such defensive work could be erected as would make it secure against any raid. This locality is situated in poor land, country thinly settled, and very few persons to be annoyed by the proximity of a prison. The prison at Andersonville, with a sufficient guard, could resist any raid that would be likely to be sent against it.

I would make this further suggestion: I think the property here (Salisbury) on which the prison is erected could be sold for at least $150,000. It cost originally $15,000 in bonds. This would pay the purchase money for another tract, complete the prison, and put up all necessary workshops to employ usefully to the Confederate States the labor of the prisoners. The purchase would have another advantage. All the labor bestowed and improvements made would be for the benefit of the Confederate States, and when prisons would be no longer required could be profitably employed or sold as thought best.

With this arrangement the prison at Andersonville, the prison at Camp Lawton, and the new prison, with the small prisons at Richmond and Cahaba, Ala., as receiving depots, would answer all purposes.

The ratio of mortality at Florence and Salisbury exceeds, I think that at Andersonville.

I feel satisfied that if authorized to carry out the above suggestions I could arrange the prisons to the entire satisfaction of the authorities, and by that means relieve the Confederate States of all expense connected with the prison, except, perhaps, feeding, and to a great extent pay for that.

I respectfully ask that as early an answer as possible be given, as it is very important to know exactly what course will be adopted.

Very respectfully, your obedient servant,
JNO. H. WINDER,
Brigadier-General.

Appendix C [3]

Correspondence from North Carolina
Governor Vance Regarding Conditions at Salisbury

State of North Carolina, Executive Department.
Raleigh, February 1, 1865.

Hon. I. A. Seddon. Secretary of War.

Dear Sir: I beg leave to call attention to the condition of the Federal prisoners of war at Salisbury, N. C. Accounts reach me of the most distressing character in regard to their suffering and destitution. I earnestly request you to have the matter inquired into and if in our power to relieve them that it be done. If they are willfully left to suffer when we can avoid it, it would not only be a blot upon our humanity, but would lay us open to a severe retaliation. I know how straitened our means are, however, and will cast no blame upon any one without further information.

Very respectfully, your obedient servant,
Z. B. VANCE.

* * *

State of North Carolina, Executive Department.
Raleigh, February 1, 1865.

General Bradley T. Johnson, Salisbury, N. C.

Most distressing accounts reach me of the suffering and destitution of the Yankee prisoners under your charge. If the half be true, it is disgraceful to our humanity and will provoke severe retaliation. I hope, however, it is not so bad as represented; but lest it be so, I hereby tender you any aid in my power to afford to make their condition more tolerable. I know the great scarcity of food which prevails, but shelter and warmth can certainly be provided, and I can spare you some clothing if the Yankees will deliver as much to North Carolina troops in Northern prisons. Please let me hear from you.

Respectfully yours,
Z. B. VANCE.

Appendix D[4]

Report of Inspection of Salisbury Prison
by T. W. Hall, with Indorsements

SALISBURY, *N. C., February* 17, 1865.

General S. COOPER,
Adjutant and Inspector General C. S. Army:

GENERAL: I have the honor to acknowledge the receipt at Charlotte on the 14th instant of letter of instructions of February 10, from Col. R. H. Chilton, inclosing a communication from His Excellency the Governor of North Carolina to the Honorable Secretary of War, in regard to the suffering condition of the Federal prisoners at this post, and directing me to make an immediate inspection of the prison and full report of the subject. I have the honor to state that acting under my previous general instructions of December 5, 1864, and January 19, 1865, I included the condition of the military prison and treatment of the prisoners of war there confined in the general inspection of the post, in which I was engaged from the 1st to the 10th of February, and the results of my observations would have been immediately forwarded to the Department but for the fact that the post commander, Brig. Gen. Bradley T. Johnson, happened to be absent from the post during the whole time of my inspection, and I deemed it not less in accordance with the spirit of my instructions than the dictates of military propriety to withhold my report until I should have an opportunity of conferring with him upon the subject and of ascertaining how far it might be in his power to remedy the evils found to exist. Pending his return I was engaged in an inspection of the post of Charlotte, but immediately upon the receipt of Colonel Chilton's letter returned to this place, and on the 16th instant made a second inspection of the prison in company with General Johnson. The results of my two visits of inspection are respectfully submitted as follows: I made three visits of inspection to the prison—January 31, in company with Maj. Mason Morfit, prison quartermaster; February 1, in company with Maj. J. H. Gee, prison commandant, and the medical officer of the prison, and again, as already stated, on the 16th of February, with General B. T. Johnson. On the two occasions first named the weather was particularly pleasant and I saw the prison under the most favorable circumstances. On the 16th of February, immediately after a fall of snow and sleet, I saw it again, probably in its worst aspect. In my report I have endeavored carefully to distinguish between those causes of suffering which are unavoidable, and for the existence of which, therefore, the Government and its officers cannot be held responsible, and such abuses as, in my opinion, are justly chargeable to the neglect or inefficiency of the prison management.

I. *Location and plan of the prison.*—The location of the prison I regard as an unfortunate one, though I presume this with the Government at the time was a matter not of choice but of necessity. That it was already used as a prison for civilians and military convicts should have been an argument against its selection, not in its favor, unless it had been at the same time determined to remove the former classes of prisoners. The general plan of the prison may be seen from the diagram accompanying this report. The area inclosed and constituting the main prison yard is about eleven acres. I do not think, especially with the present number of prisoners (5,476 of all classes), that there can be any reasonable ground of complaint on the score of want of room. Water is obtained from nine wells within the inclosure and from the creek, one mile and a half distant, to which the prisoners are allowed to go, a certain number at a time, under guard, with buckets and barrels. The supply obtained from all these sources, however, is not more than sufficient for cooking and drinking purposes. The want of a running stream within the prison inclosure, for the purposes of washing and general sewerage, is therefore a serious objection. The proximity of the prison to the railroad affords every necessary facility for obtaining an adequate supply of fuel, which can be deposited in any quantity needed within less than 100 yards of the prison, and unloaded and transported by the labor of the prisoners themselves. A memorandum statement of Major Morfit, prison quartermaster, accompanying this report, shows the amount of fuel received, issued, and due the prisoners from January 1 to February 15, 1865. That they have not received the full amount due them during a season of more than ordinary inclemency I think is chargeable more probably to want of energy on the part of the post quartermaster, Capt. J. M. Goodman, than to any other cause. Both Major Gee and Major Morfit profess to consider the actual supply sufficient, but in this I think they are mistaken. The fact cited by Major Gee that the prison sutler buys all his fuel from the prisoners proves nothing, no more than their willingness to part with their newly-received supplies of clothing, a practice to check which General Johnson has been obliged to publish a stringent order forbidding citizens or soldiers from purchasing, proves that they are not in want of clothes. The most serious objection to this choice of a site for a prison is, however, the character of the soil, which is a stiff, tenacious red clay, difficult of drainage and which remains wet for a long time, and after a rain or snow becomes a perfect bog. The system of drainage contemplates the double object of carrying off the surface water and cleansing the sinks, but cannot be said to be particularly successful in either point of view. In warm weather or in a season of drought the sinks would not fail to prove a source of great annoyance, and possibly of pestilence, not only in the prison, but in the town of Salisbury.

II. *The prison commissariat.*—Among the papers accompanying this report will be found a statement of the number of rations issued from February 1 to February 15, 1865, showing the component parts of the ration and the quantity of each. Compared in quantity and kind with the rations issued to our own troops in the field, it will be seen that on this score the prisoners have no cause to complain. The rations are cooked before they are issued, and pains have been taken by General Johnson to see that no frauds are committed in this department to the injury of the prisoners. Bread and meat (or sorghum in lieu of meat) are issued every morning, rice or pea soup in the afternoon. The bread which I inspected in the bakery was of average quality and of the average weight of five pounds to the double loaf. A half loaf, therefore, the daily allowance of each prisoner, will average twenty ounces of bread, the equivalent of sixteen ounces of flour.

III. *Clothing.*—More than from any other cause the prisoners have suffered this winter from the want of sufficient and suitable clothing, being generally destitute of blankets and having only such clothes as they wore when captured, which, in the case of many of them, was during warm weather. Recently 3,000 blankets and 1,000 pair of pants have been received from the United States and are now being distributed under the supervision of three Federal officers sent here from Danville for the purpose. Additional supplies are expected, and it is probable that one principal cause of suffering will therefore soon be removed, one for which, however, the Confederate Government is under no circumstances chargeable, but which is ascribable solely to the neglect of their own Government. As already stated, General Johnson has taken every necessary step to prevent speculation upon the necessities of the prisoners by prohibiting all purchases from them of articles of clothing by soldiers or citizens.

IV. *Prison quarters.*—Three hundred tents and flies of mixed sizes and patterns were issued for the use of the prisoners of war in October by Major Morfit, prison quartermaster, and constitute the only shelter provided during the winter for a number of prisoners, amounting on the 7th of November to 8,740, and the 15th of February to 5,070. Major Morfit showed me the frame of a large barrack, of which he told me he had contemplated erecting five for the accommodation of the prisoners, but was stopped by an order two months ago from the Commissary-General of Prisoners, intimating the possibility of a speedy removal of the prisoners, and ordering all work of the kind to be suspended. The prisoners were not removed, and in my judgment if General Winder's order had never been issued Major Morfit's plan would have been found, in its conception, to involve great and unnecessary expense to the Government, probably not less than $75,000 or $100,000, and in its execution would probably have consumed the entire winter, and therefore have resulted in little practical benefit to the prisoners. A better plan would have been, failing to obtain a sufficient supply of tents, to have constructed cabins of pine logs and shingles, for which the material was at hand in abundance, and labor could have been furnished by the troops, or, if necessary, by details of the prisoners themselves, working under guard. In this way the garrison who guard the prisoners have been made comfortable; so might have been the prisoners. I cannot consider it, therefore, a matter of choice on their own part, that at the time of my inspection I found one-third of the latter burrowing like animals in holes under ground or under the buildings in the inclosure.

V. *Prison hospitals.*—One of the most painful features connected with the prison is the absence of adequate provision or accommodation for the sick. There is no separate hospital inclosure, but with a few exceptions, as will be seen from the diagram, all the buildings in the prison yard are used as hospitals. The number sick in hospital February 15 was 546. There was an entire absence of hospital comforts—bedding, necessary utensils, &c. The reason assigned on the occasion of my first visit (February 1) was, that it was useless to supply these articles as no guard was kept inside of the prison yard and they would be inevitably stolen. Surg. John Wilson, Jr., the medical officer at present in charge, is endeavoring to supply these deficiencies, and in the short interval of two weeks between my first and second visits had succeeded in effecting several improvements. Still much remains to be done. There are bunks for not more than one-half of the sick, the rest lie upon the floor or ground, with nothing under them but a little straw, which on February 16 had not been changed for four weeks. For a period of nearly one month in December and January the hospitals, I was told, were without straw. For this there is no excuse. I am satisfied that straw could have been obtained in abundance at any time, the county (Rowan) being one of the largest wheat-growing counties in the State, and I am assured by Captain Crockford, inspector of field transportation in this department, that the field transportation at this post has been in excess heretofore of the requirements of the post; that in January, when no straw was furnished, he found thirty animals standing idle in Captain Goodman's stable, and consequently ordered them to be turned over. The excessive rate of mortality among the prisoners, as shown by the prison returns herewith forwarded, merits attention. Out of 10,321 prisoners of war received since October 5, 1864, according to the surgeon's report, 2,918 have died. According to the burial report, since the 21st of October, 1864, a less period by sixteen days, 3,479 have been buried. The discrepancy is explained by the fact that in addition to the deaths in hospital, six or eight die daily in their quarters without the knowledge of the surgeons, and of course without receiving attention from them. This discrepancy, which in December amounted to 223, and in January to 192, in the first two weeks of February had diminished to 21. The actual number of deaths, however, outside of hospital during that period would show probably little falling off, if any, from the number in previous months. Pneumonia and diseases of the bowels are the prevalent diseases. The prisoners appear to die, however, more from exposure and exhaustion than from actual disease.

VI. *Prison discipline.*—Inside of the prison there appears to be no proper system of discipline or police. The prisoners are divided into ten divisions, each division into as many squads, the divisions in charge of a sergeant-major of their own number, the squads under a sergeant. Two roll-calls are nominally observed, the one in the morning being usually neglected. In the afternoon the prisoners are mustered by squads and counted by the prison clerk and his assistants. No details are made for the purpose of policing the grounds, except one of a sergeant and twelve men, who report to the surgeon. All sorts of filth are allowed to be deposited and to remain anywhere and everywhere around the quarters, unsightly to the eye and generating offensive odors and in time, doubtless, disease. Since the outbreak of November 25 no guard is kept inside the inclosure, except at the gates. Robberies and murders even are said to be of not unfrequent occurrence among the prisoners, usually charged to an association of the worst characters among them, known as "Muggers." But a few days before my first visit a negro prisoner in one of the hospital wards was murdered by one of these ruffians, and such is the state of terrorism inspired that none of the patients or attendants in the ward who saw the deed would lodge information against the murderer, who was at last only discovered and arrested through the agency of a detective. The use of detectives and a counter association among the prisoners are the only dependence of the commandant for enforcing any kind of order, discipline, or police in the prison. The excuse given by Major Gee for not having the prison grounds properly policed was the want of tools and the danger of trusting picks, &c., in the hands of the prisoners. The excuse cannot be considered sufficient; wooden scrapers and hickory brooms, with wheelbarrows or boxes with rope handles, all of which can readily be furnished by the prison quartermaster, would answer every purpose. I subsequently brought the matter to the attention of General Johnson, who promised to issue the necessary orders upon the subject and see that they are enforced. Major Gee, the prison commandant, as an officer, is deficient in administrative ability, but in point of vigilance, fidelity, and in everything that concerns the security of the prison and the safe keeping of the prisoners, leaves nothing to be desired. As respects the general question of the condition of the prisoners I am of the opinion that so far as their sufferings have resulted from causes within the control of the Government or its officers they are chargeable (1) to the unfortunate location of the prison, which is wholly unsuitable for the purpose; (2) to the want of administrative capacity, proper energy and effort on the part of the officers of the Quartermaster's Department, charged with the duty of supplying the prison. To attempt an exact apportionment of the blame in this respect between Maj. Mason Morfit, the prison quartermaster, and Capt. James M. Goodman, the post quartermaster, would probably be irrelevant to the purpose of the present report. Having had occasion in a general inspection of the post of Salisbury to examine the affairs of both of these officers, I cannot say that I consider either of them as efficient in his present position. I have the honor to be, general, very respectfully, your obedient servant

T. W. HALL,
Assistant Adjutant and Inspector General.

[First indorsement.]

ADJUTANT AND INSPECTOR GENERAL'S OFFICE,
February 23, 1865.

Respectfully submitted to Honorable Secretary of War.

This is a "report of inspection of prison at Salisbury, N. C.," made in compliance with instructions from this office and based on complaints made by Governor Vance, of North Carolina. His Excellency the Governor only mentions in general terms that complaints of a distressing character had reached him of the destitute and suffering condition of the prisoners. The inspector reports that he made three visits to the prison; that on the first two visits the weather was pleasant, and that he saw the prison then in its most favorable aspect, but on the last the weather was bad, and that he saw it then in its worst aspect. He endeavors to distinguish between unavoidable causes of suffering and those justly chargeable to the neglect or inefficiency of the prison management, and furnishes a diagram of the plan and location of the prison, and reports that there can be no reasonable grounds of complaint for want of room, as the area is eleven acres, but that the water, supplied by wells and brought in buckets, &c., from a stream only half a mile from the prison, is only sufficient for drinking and cooking purposes, and that the want of a running stream within the prison is a serious objection; that the proximity of the prison to the railroad affords every facility for obtaining an adequate supply of fuel, and incloses a statement of Major Morfit, quartermaster, of issue of fuel and amount due from January 1 to February 15, 1865, and charges the want of a full supply during the inclement weather to want of energy on the part of Captain Goodman, post quartermaster; that the fact cited by Major Gee that the prison sutler buys all of his fuel from the prisoners proves nothing, no more than their willingness to part with their newly received supply of clothing, a practice to check which General Johnson has issued an order forbidding citizens or soldiers to purchase, proves that they are not in want of clothes. He reports that the most serious objection to the prison is the character of the soil, a stiff, tenacious red clay, difficult of drainage, remaining wet for a long time after a rain or snow, and becoming a perfect bog; that the system of drainage neither carries off the surface water nor cleanses the sinks, and in a season of drought the sinks would prove a source of annoyance and probably a pestilence. He reports in reference to the commissariat that, compared with the rations that are issued to our troops in the field, it will be seen from the inclosed statement of rations issued from February 1 to 15, instant, 1865, that the prisoners have no cause to complain, and in reference to clothing, that the prisoners have suffered from the want of suitable clothing and blankets, but that recently 3,000 blankets and 1,000 pants from United States were issued, and, respecting the prison quarters, that 300 tents and flies of mixed sizes and patterns were issued in October, 1864, and constitute the only shelter that was provided during the winter for a number of prisoners, amounting in November to 8,740, and in February, 1865, to 5,070; that Major Morfit, quartermaster, exhibited the frame of a large barrack, which he had contemplated building, but which was fortunately stopped by the Commissary-General of Prisoners; that a better plan would have been to have constructed cabins of logs and shingles, for which the material was at hand in abundance, and they could have been erected by the prisoners, and that in this way the prisoners would, like the guard, have been made comfortable, and would not have been forced to burrow in the ground like animals. That respecting the prison hospitals, one of the most painful features connected with the prison is the absence of adequate provisions and accommodations for the sick; that there is no separate hospital inclosure, but with a few exceptions (see diagram) all the buildings in the prison yard are used as hospitals; that there were no hospital comforts—bedding, necessary utensils, &c.; that the reason assigned to him on his first visit was that it was useless to supply these articles, as no guard was kept inside of the prison yard, and that they would be stolen.

Surgeon John Wilson, Jr., the medical officer at present in charge, is endeavoring to supply these deficiencies, and has succeeded in effecting several improvements; yet much remains to be done.

He reports that there are only enough bunks for one-half of the sick, and that the rest have to lie on the floor or ground, with nothing under them but a little straw, which, on February 16, instant, had not been changed for four weeks. He reports that for a period of nearly one month (December and January) the hospital was without straw, and that there is no excuse, for straw could have been procured in abundance at any time, and that he was assured by Captain Crockford, inspector of field transportation, that the transportation of the post had been in excess of the requirements of the post; that in January, 1865, when no straw was furnished, he found thirty animals standing idle in Captain Goodman's stable, and consequently ordered them to be turned over. He reports that the excessive rate of mortality (see reports herewith) merits attention; that out of 10,321 prisoners that were received since October 5, 1864, according to surgeon's report, 2,918 have died, but according to the burial report, that since October 21, 1864, a less period by sixteen days, 3,479 have died and been buried; that this discrepancy is explained by the fact that six or eight die daily in their quarters without the knowledge of the surgeons; that pneumonia and diseases of the bowels are prevalent, but that the prisoners appear to die more from exposure and exhaustion than from actual disease.

The inspector reports that there is no proper system of discipline and police of the prison; that all sorts of filth are allowed to be deposited and to remain anywhere and everywhere around the quarters, unsightly to the eye and generating offensive odors; that robberies and murders are said to be of frequent occurrence, and that the excuse for not having the grounds properly policed is the want of tools and the danger of trusting picks, &c., in the hands of the prisoners, but it is not good, for wooden scrapers and hickory brushes could have been furnished by the prison quartermaster, but that General Johnson has promised to have them provided.

In reference to the prison commandant, Major Gee, the inspector reports that he is deficient in administrative ability, though vigilant and faithful, and expresses the opinion that so far as the causes of their sufferings have been the result of want of attention on the part of the officers, they are chargeable (1) to the unfortunate location of the prison, which is wholly unsuited for the purpose; (2) to the want of administration, capacity, energy and proper efforts on the part of the officers of the Quartermaster's Department, who were charged with the duty of supplying the prison; and states that he does not consider either Major Morfit, the prison quartermaster, or Captain Goodman, post quartermaster, as efficient in their present positions.

R. H. CHILTON,
Assistant Adjutant and Inspector General

[Second indorsement.]

WAR DEPARTMENT, *March* 6, 1865.

Respectfully referred to the Quartermaster-General.

This report reflects upon the prison and post quartermasters at Salisbury, N. C., in such manner as to call for further action. If the report be correct they should at least be removed to positions of less responsibility.

By command Secretary of War
SAML. W. MELTON,
Assistant Adjutant-General.

[Third indorsement.]

QUARTERMASTER-GENERAL'S OFFICE, *March* 13, 1865.

Respectfully returned to the Adjutant and Inspector General. The prisoners formerly at Salisbury having been exchanged and Captain Goodman having been relieved from duty as post quartermaster at that point, no further action by this office seems to be necessary.

A. R. LAWTON,
Quartermaster. General.

Appendix E[5]

Enclosure 1 to Appendix D,
being a general plan of Salisbury Prison

Enclosure No. 1 to Report of T. W. Hall dated February 17, 1865 (See Appendix D)

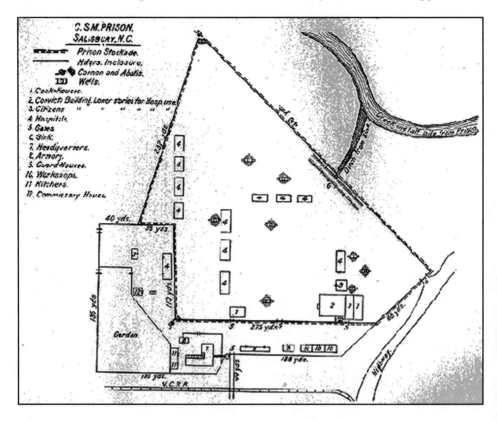

Dear Friends and Relatives,

I am happy to be with you here today to enjoy your society and participate in the festivities of the occasion. But first of all, let us call to mind and realize why this should be commemorated and celebrated above all other days in the year. There have been many noted personages born into the world at various times whose birth was celebrated with more or less pomp and ceremony, but only one whose Advent was heralded and proclaimed in the glorious words of the Holy Angel who said, "Behold, I bring you good tidings of great joy, which shall be to all people, for unto you is born this day in the city of David, a Savior, which is Christ the Lord!" And suddenly there was with the angels, a multitude of the Heavenly Host praising God in the highest, and on earth, peace, good will to men.

That song has been reverberated down through the ages, until now in the beginning of the twentieth century, in the blaze of Gospel light, we can the more realize and appreciate its significance. That is why we celebrate this as the holiest and happiest day of all the year. And while we ascribe glory to God in the highest and enjoy the peace proclaimed on earth, let us not hesitate to shed abroad the good will to all mankind and share it with all we meet. And my friends, while we are enjoying ourselves together, let me call your attention to a phenomenon of nature that I have discovered in our midst.... It is...the December lilly that blooms on Christmas!...

And friends, in after years, in happy remembrance of the present occasion, we will also remember that we witnessed the blooming, and enjoyed the hospitality of this same lilly of the Yuletide. And the entrance into this beautiful old world of your humble servant, which anniversary you have so kindly remembered this day was begun at the foot of Laurel Mountain one blustery New Year's morn in a cottage my father built, where I a babe was born....

I am told they had quite a hilarious time over my advent, though I cannot recall the scene, but I was there all the same. Since that time, seventy-one years have elapsed, and the blasts of as many winters have swept over this devoted head, as the sparse locks on this partially bald cranium can testify. In part of this more or less eventful life, some good was accomplished. In most of the remainder I fear, it was otherwise.

There is one portion that shines bright on memory's tablet, that is, four years engaged in the service of God and my country. I say in the service of God, because I hold that a man who serves his country loyally and faithfully, renders acceptable service to God.

As someone has wisely said: "Man serves God best who serves humanity." And I am here today not as was old Moses of sacred history, whose eye was not dimmed, nor his natural forces abated, but still capable of enjoying life and with thankful heart, the many blessings vouchsafed to us by the kind Father.

Most people think that the old boys of my age, are fit for nothing but the scrap heap, to be laid on the shelf to die. But it is a mistaken idea, a false conclusion, for the fire of life still burns, and that spark of Divinity implanted in every man's bosom by the Deity himself, can never die.

Isaac Andrew Moore

Acknowledgments

During the years we lived and worked in Washington, D.C., my wife, Katherine, volunteered as a docent at the National Archives. Among her many assignments, she worked as a charter member of the Civil War Conservation Corps. These dedicated men and women, volunteers all, labored long and diligently to prepare the original military records of soldiers in various Union regiments for microfilming. When not leading tours or poring over old muster rolls, Kathy found time to indulge her passion for family history. Her success at unearthing long-lost ancestors led me in time to ponder whether I had any relatives who fought in the Civil War. Not surprisingly, my pondering quickly turned to researching. To my great amazement, following several weekends filled with reams of musty documents and countless reels of microfilm, I discovered that no fewer than five of my great-great-grandfathers had served in Mr. Lincoln's Army of the Potomac. In this book I recount the story of one of them—and of his messmates and comrades who served alongside him during the defining period of our nation's history. And so, on behalf of the Moore and Springer Clans, I extend heartfelt thanks to my dear Katherine. Without her love of genealogy and her patient tutoring, the stories of Isaac Andrew Moore and Thomas Wathen Springer might never have been told.

My thanks are due as well to two other members of my family: to my daughter, Larissa, for reading the first draft of each chapter as I completed it and offering comments that, invariably, proved on the mark—the finished work is better (and shorter!) because of her efforts; and to my son, Robert III, for giving freely of his time and computer skills to help me combine the various individual chapters into an integrated whole, text reformatting being a concept as foreign to me as quantum mechanics. Without Robert's timely assistance, I would still be attempting to decipher Chapter Three of "Word Processing for Dummies."

A number of people helped me during the many sojourns I made while doing research for the book. In particular, I wish to thank Amy Port Reiter for kindly offering me a place to hang my hat whenever I traveled to Washington. I have many pleasant memories of the "Casa de Port." Thanks as well to Amy's brother, Louis Port, with whom I stayed during my final trek to D.C. Lou joined me for a memorable evening of "research" into the origins of the famed Irish brigade (conducted in several Irish pubs along Connecticut Avenue) that proved most enjoyable—if not particularly enlightening. Sankey and Margaret MacDonald and Wayne and Nancy Port graciously opened their homes to me whenever I had occasion to visit Fayette County, Pennsylvania.

Among the many individuals who provided assistance to me during the course of my research, my particular thanks go to Victoria Leonelli, Curator of the Pennsylvania Room at the Uniontown Public Library; to Sharon Watson-Mauro, Director of Library Services at the Historical Society of Western Pennsylvania; and to Dr. Richard J. Sommers, Assistant Director for Patron Services at the United States Army Military History Institute in Carlisle, Pennsylvania. Dr. Sommers, whose title does not do justice to his encyclopedic knowledge of the holdings of the Military History Institute, first called my attention to the pioneering work done by William Weidner on the 190th and 191st Pennsylvania Infantry Regiments. Bill's research, which I am happy to acknowledge, confirmed a hypothesis I had come to believe: that the great majority of the Pennsylvania Reserves veterans did not muster out at the end of their original terms of enlistment but, in fact, reenlisted and served to the war's end. Those fortunate few who were not captured during the fight for the Weldon Railroad in August of 1864 fought on and were witnesses to history at Appomattox Court House the following April. I also wish to acknowledge and thank Arthur Bergeron, a member of the Military History Institute staff, for his assistance in locating the James Longstreet quote on General McCall's capture at Glendale that appears in Chapter Five.

At the National Archives, my thanks are due Michael Musick, Trevor Plante, and David Wallace. Michael, of course, is a living legend among Civil War researchers. Trevor and David helped me pin down those last few missing source citations. Jane Douma Pearson, a genealogical researcher in Oak Hill, Virginia, provided valuable assistance in locating and copying Civil War pension records for me; I greatly appreciate her many kindnesses. Timothy Reese, author of *Sealed With Their Lives: The Battle for Crampton's Gap*, supplied much useful information about the Civil War era road network in the vicinity of Turner's Gap and took me on a memorable driving tour of the South Mountain battlefields. Kevin Carle of New London, North Carolina, shared information and photographs pertaining to James Carle, the commander of the 191st Pennsylvania. Kevin's wife, Grey, is an artist whose work I have admired for a long time. She graciously gave me permission to publish two of her illustrations that bring to life the old veterans' pilgrimage to Salisbury in 1910.

In addition to my daughter, mentioned above, a number of people reviewed various iterations of the manuscript and offered valuable criticism and advice. First and foremost, my thanks go to Edwin C. Bearss, Chief Historian Emeritus of the National Park Service. Ed took time from his incredibly busy schedule to not only read the manuscript in its entirety, but also to write the foreword to the book. Thank you, Ed, for everything. My thanks are also due to the following individuals, respectively, for reviewing the chapters on the Seven Days Battles, the Battle of Second Bull Run, the Maryland Campaign, the Battle of Fredericksburg, and Grant's Overland Campaign: Robert E. L. Krick, Historian at the Richmond National Battlefield Park and author of *Staff Officers in Gray*; John J. Hennessy, Chief Historian at the Fredericksburg and Spotsylvania National Military Park and author of *Return to Bull Run: The Campaign and Battle of Second Manassas*; Ted Alexander, Staff Historian at Antietam National Battlefield; Francis A. O'Reilly, Historian at the Fredericksburg and Spotsylvania National Military Park and author of *The Fredericksburg Campaign: Winter War on the Rappahannock*; and Gordon C. Rhea, author of *The Battle of the Wilderness: May 5-6, 1864* (and three other books that, taken together, constitute the definitive history of Grant's 1864 Overland Campaign). To Alana Morgan, a dear friend and editor extraordinaire, I extend my gratitude for her work on early drafts of the manuscript and on the page proofs. The final product is infinitely the better for her efforts. A thousand E-Hugs are winging your way, Miss Morgan. Dr. Diane R. Gordon of Columbia, Maryland, compiled the index to the book, and I thank her very much for her excellent work. Any errors that remain following the efforts of these dedicated individuals are, of course, solely my own responsibility.

Karl Feldmeyer of Boonsboro, Maryland, made all of the maps that appear in the book, and my thanks are due to him for that prodigious effort. Cartography is not Karl's only claim to fame, however. Known to his pards as "Sergeant Grumpy," Karl is also the founder and fearless leader of the 101st Pennsylvania Veteran Volunteers (Reconstituted), the unit with which I have reenacted for the past seven years. All of us who have been privileged to take the field with our beloved sergeant recall with pride the many exploits of the 101st PVV.

To Harold Collier, Marianne Zinn, Nicole Riley, and the wonderful staff at White Mane Publishing Company I extend heartfelt thanks. I made a promise to my ancestor, Thomas Wathen Springer, when I found his gravesite in Salisbury, North Carolina, some ten years ago—I vowed that someday I would tell his story. White Mane's decision to publish this book has enabled me to keep that promise and, in the process, to honor the service and sacrifice of all the boys of the 8th Pennsylvania Reserves.

To the late Lieutenant Colonel William Lemon, then captain commanding Company G of the 8th Reserves, go my sincere thanks for selecting my great-great-grandfather, Isaac Andrew Moore, to return to Fayette County on recruiting service in the summer of 1862. Corporal Moore left for home August 9 and did not return to his regiment until the end of October. During his absence, the Pennsylvania Reserves were in the thick of the fighting at Second Bull Run, South Mountain, and Antietam. But for Captain Lemon's perspicacity, I might not be here to tell this tale.

Finally, my thanks are due my late father for much more than I could ever put into words. I wish he were here to hold a copy of this book in his hands, but I take comfort in the knowledge that he read and enjoyed the final draft of the manuscript. I have vivid memories of going to Gettysburg with Dad when I was just a lad. I have taken my own son to that hallowed place and, as my father and I did so many years ago, we stood together on Cemetery Ridge and looked out across the Emmitsburg Road. The ghosts are still there, Dad.

Notes

PREFACE

1. Rogan H. Moore, *A History and Genealogy of the Moore Family of Fayette County, Pennsylvania* (Bowie, Md.: Heritage Books, Inc., 1999), 69–70 (hereafter cited as *A History of the Moore Family*).

2. Diary of James W. Eberhart, 122. The diary is held in the Library and Archives Division of the Historical Society of Western Pennsylvania, Pittsburgh, Pennsylvania. Excerpts from the diary are published by permission of the Historical Society of Western Pennsylvania.

3. *Pennsylvania at Salisbury, Ceremonies at the Dedication of the Memorial* (n.p.: C. E. Aughinbaugh, Printer to the State of Pennsylvania, 1912), 28 (hereafter cited as *Pennsylvania at Salisbury*).

4. Ibid., 29–30.

INTRODUCTION

1. Both states erected rival counties, and for a number of years competing court and county office systems held sway.

2. The Act provided that all colored persons born in Pennsylvania after March 1, 1780, would be considered to be free, provided that those who otherwise would have been held as slaves were required to act as servants to their masters until reaching the age of 28 years.

3. James Veech, *The Monongahela of Old* (Pittsburgh: Mrs. E. V. Blaine, 1892), 99–100.

4. In the first national census (1790), there were 12,995 free whites and 282 slaves listed in Fayette County. An 1803 registry of slaveholders listed 60 of Fayette County's best-known and wealthiest citizens. It was not until 1839 that these registries were discontinued, slavery finally having become virtually nonexistent in Pennsylvania by then.

5. Walter Storey, *Stories of Uniontown and Fayette County* (Dunbar, Pa.: Stefano's Printing, 1993), 55.

6. The Democratic candidate received a majority of the Fayette County vote in each of the seven presidential elections held between 1828 and 1852.

7. James Buchanan, Pennsylvania's only president, campaigned against the "Black Republicans" in 1856, asserting that the critical question before the electorate was union or disunion. He was elected with 174 electoral votes to 114 for the Republican candidate, John C. Fremont. Ironically, while Buchanan carried Pennsylvania, he lost 11 of the other so-called free states. It was only due to the votes of 14 Southern states, where he was regarded as a defender of the slave interests, that Buchanan assumed the presidency.

8. It must be borne in mind that relatively few Fayette Countians actually were qualified to vote. Under the Pennsylvania Constitution of 1838, only "white free[men] of the age of twenty-one years, having resided in the State one year...and within two years paid a State or county tax...[could] enjoy the rights of an elector." Pa Const (1838), Art III, Sec 1. Thus, out of a total county population of 39,909, only 6,933 votes were cast in the 1860 election.

9. Lincoln received 3,454 votes to Breckinridge's 3,308 (Breckinridge running with Douglas on a "Fusion" ticket). Bell received 147 votes (2.1 percent) and Douglas (running on a "Straight" ticket) received a mere 24 votes (0.3 percent).

10. Lincoln won 180 votes in the Electoral College to Breckinridge's 72. Bell received 39 electoral votes, while Douglas received 12.

CHAPTER 1: "HEADED FOR THE SEAT OF WAR"

1. "Fire-eaters" was the popular name given to those radical Southern planters and politicians who defended the institution of slavery and espoused secession in order to maintain their rights and property free from interference by Northern abolitionists and the national government. The noted diarist Mary Chesnut wrote of South Carolina in 1861 that "[n]obody could live in this state unless he were a fire-eater.... Bluffton, Rhetts, &c had exasperated and heated themselves into a fever that only bloodletting could ever cure...." Mary Chesnut, *Mary Chesnut's Civil War*, ed. C. Vann Woodward (New Haven, Conn.: Yale University Press, 1981), 4.

2. William A. DeGregorio, *The Complete Book of U. S. Presidents* (New York: Wing Books, 1984), 236.

3. Ibid.

4. Letter to the Editor, *Uniontown (Pa) Genius of Liberty*, April 4, 1861 (hereafter cited as *Genius of Liberty*). It is not known whether this is a nom de plume or simply refers to the home township of the writer.

5. Editorial, *Genius of Liberty*, April 4, 1861.

6. *Genius of Liberty*, April 11, 1861.

7. Clarence Clough Buel and Robert Underwood Johnson, eds., *Battles and Leaders of the Civil War*, 4 vols. (New York: n.p., 1884–1887; reprint, Secaucus, N.J.: Castle, n.d.) 2:76 (page citations are to the reprint edition) (hereafter cited as *Battles and Leaders*).

8. *Genius of Liberty*, April 18, 1861.

9. Ibid.

10. George Darby, *Incidents and Adventures in Rebeldom: Libby, Belle-Isle, Salisbury* (Pittsburgh: Press of Rawsthorne Engraving & Printing Company, 1899), 12–13 (hereafter cited as *Incidents and Adventures*). The term of service for the volunteers responding to Lincoln's April 15 call was three months, hence the appellation "three months' men." This would have serious implications in July of 1861, as the terms of many of the regiments thus raised were expiring on the eve of the Battle of First Bull Run. The "quota" that George Darby referred to was a state-by-state requirement for the provision of volunteers imposed by the War Department pursuant to Lincoln's call. Pennsylvania was assigned an initial quota of 16 regiments to serve for three months (later raised to 25). The response by the citizens of the Commonwealth was so overwhelming that all 25 regiments were quickly raised and accepted by the national government. Some thirty additional regiments were raised, but were refused initially by the War Department as being unnecessary. On the organization of the Pennsylvania Reserves generally, see Edward G. Everett, "Pennsylvania Raises an Army," *The Western Pennsylvania Historical Magazine* 39 (Summer 1956).

11. *Genius of Liberty*, April 25, 1861.

12. In June, Oliphant was presented a sword in a ceremony described in a Pittsburgh newspaper: "Last evening one of the large parlors of the Monongahela House was filled by a party of ladies and gentlemen to witness a pleasing and touching ceremony.... A beautiful sword was presented to Lieutenant-Colonel S. D. Oliphant by his friends as a token of their love for the man and their esteem for the virtues peculiar to the soldier which he so eminently possesses. In a speech conceived in most excellent taste, and delivered with true manly feeling, the sword was presented to Col. Oliphant by Algernon S. Bell, Esq., of this city. It was received by Col. Oliphant with deep feeling, and his reply was a model of calm eloquence, such as only comes when the heart speaks out. The gentlemen were college-mates together [and] are both members of the legal profession.... The occasion was one which called forth feeling allusions to bygone days.... We never recollect to have witnessed a similar ceremony more happily consummated. The audience sympathized heartily with the sentiments expressed by the speaker, and at the close of the ceremony gave their hearty congratulations to the officer whom they had assembled to honor." *Pittsburgh (Pa.) Daily Post*, June 17, 1861.

13. *Genius of Liberty*, May 2, 1861.

14. Darby, *Incidents and Adventures*, 13–14.

15. Camp Wilkins was named in honor of Judge William Wilkins, one of Pittsburgh's most distinguished civic and political leaders. He chaired the "Committee of One Hundred" that coordinated the provisioning and quartering of the large number of volunteers descending upon Pittsburgh in the spring of 1861. He was described by a reporter of the time as follows: "With his silvery locks, his animated eyes, his clarion voice, his patriotic fire which eighty winters failed to chill, he exhorted his fellow citizens to lay aside all former differences and rally around the President." *Pittsburgh Gazette*, April 16, 1861.

16. Andrew G. Curtin was elected governor of Pennsylvania in October 1860. He was the guiding force behind the formation of the Pennsylvania Reserve Volunteer Corps and was a staunch supporter of the Lincoln government and its policies throughout the war.

17. John and Mary McQuaide to Joseph McQuaide, 23 May 1862, Joseph L. McQuaide Papers, Library and Archives Division, Historical Society of Western Pennsylvania, Pittsburgh, Pa. (hereafter cited as "McQuaide Papers"). McQuaide's company, known as the Iron City Guards, was recruited in Allegheny County, Pennsylvania, at the outset of the war.

18. *Genius of Liberty*, May 2, 1861. It is telling to contrast this list of daily rations supplied for one company of 77 men with the rations supplied to one squad of 100 prisoners by the commissaries of the Confederate military prison at Salisbury, North Carolina, in the fall and winter of 1864. See, in this regard, Thomas W. Springer's diary entry for Tuesday, August 30th (and accompanying commentary) in Chapter Fourteen.

19. Amos M. Judson, *History of the Eighty-Third Regiment Pennsylvania Volunteers* (Erie, Pa.: B. F. H. Lynn, n.d.; reprint, Dayton, Ohio: Morningside, 1986), 22 (page citation is to the reprint edition).

20. Darby, *Incidents and Adventures*, 14.

21. *Genius of Liberty*, May 9, 1861.

22. Ibid., May 23, 1861.

23. Ibid., May 30, 1861.

24. Joseph A. Borkowski, "Camp Wilkins, Military Post, 1861," *The Western Pennsylvania Historical Magazine* 45 (September 1962): 235.

25. J. R. Sypher, *History of the Pennsylvania Reserve Corps* (Lancaster, Pa.: Elias Barr & Co., 1865), 52–53 (hereafter cited as *History of the Pa. Reserves*).

26. Governor Curtin's first choice for the position, George B. McClellan, had already accepted an offer to command Ohio's volunteer forces.

27. *Pittsburgh Gazette*, May 22, 1861.

28. *Genius of Liberty*, June 20, 1861.

29. A. F. Hill, *Our Boys: Personal Experiences of a Soldier in the Army of the Potomac* (Philadelphia: John E. Potter and Company, 1866; reprint, Mt. Vernon, Ind.: Windmill Publications, Inc., 1994), 13 (page citations are to the reprint edition) (hereafter cited as *Our Boys*).

30. Ibid., 14.

31. Ibid., 15.

32. Ibid., 18–19.

33. Ibid., 22–23.

34. Ibid., 25–26. Almost one year to the day from this humorous episode, the Brownsville Grays would repeat this exercise, only then it would be in deadly earnest at the Battle of Glendale on the Virginia Peninsula. See the discussion of this pivotal battle in Chapter Five.

35. Ibid., 30. One can only imagine what General McCall must have thought.

36. "A new regiment was formed on Saturday [June 15] for the purpose of improving the men in drill and better securing their acceptance into service. The following companies compose the regiment: Anderson Cadets, Capt. Hayes [Allegheny Co.]; Jefferson Light Guards, Capt. Kirk [Allegheny County]; Jefferson Riflemen, Capt. Johnston [Allegheny County]; Clarion Union Guards, Capt. Lemon [Clarion County]; Fayette Guards, Capt. Oliphant; Duncan Guards, Capt. Duncan [Allegheny County]; McKeesport Guards, Capt. Snodgrass [Allegheny County]; Hopkins Infantry, Capt. Wishart [Washington County]; Brownsville Greys, Capt. Conner; Greene County Rangers, Capt. Bailey...." *Genius of Liberty*, June 20, 1861 (reprinted from the *Pittsburgh Post*).

37. *Genius of Liberty*, July 4, 1861.

38. "Major J. C. Thornton was in town this week and informed us that the 8th Regiment, Col. Hayes' marched on Monday last [July 1, 1861] from Camp Wright back to Camp Wilkins, where they will await orders. He also informed us that after the election of S. D. Oliphant as Lieut. Col., Jesse B. Gardner was elected Captain, J. B. Ramsey, 1st Lieut., and H. W. Patterson 2d Lieut. by a unanimous vote." *Genius of Liberty*, July 4, 1861.

39. Hill, *Our Boys*, 32–33.

40. Ibid., 38–39.

41. Ibid., 44.

42. Ibid.

43. Ibid., 44–45.

44. Darby, *Incidents and Adventures*, 14. The *Genius of Liberty* relayed the news of the 8th Regiment's departure on July 25, 1861: "The Pittsburgh papers give glowing accounts of the departure of [the 8th] Regiment from Camp Wilkins on Sunday morning last. They marched from the Camp to the depot in the city where an immense crowd had assembled to see them off. In this Regiment our citizens feel a deep interest and pride; hundreds will watch with anxiety the movements of the Penna. Eighth.... Their destination is not yet known. The stirring events taking place in Eastern Virginia will doubtless change the orders very suddenly and perhaps frequently. We all who feel interested in their welfare invoke upon them without ceasing the blessings and protection of Heaven." *Genius of Liberty*, July 25, 1861.

CHAPTER 2: "WE MAY HAVE SOME TROUBLE IN BALTIMORE"

1. Hill, *Our Boys*, 45.

2. Ibid., 47. Not all of the thousands of recruits passing through Harrisburg were so well provided for. A Cambria County newspaper, the *Democrat & Sentinel*, commenting upon the plight of volunteers from that county who arrived in Washington without arms or uniforms, stated: "We learn that wherever our gallant volunteers appear, they are laughed at and pointed out as 'the ragged Pennsylvanians.'" Joseph Gibbs, *Three Years in the Bloody Eleventh: The Campaigns of a Pennsylvania Reserves Regiment* (University Park, Pa.: The Pennsylvania State University Press, 2002), 10.

3. Hill, *Our Boys*, 47.

4. Rumors of trouble in Baltimore were nothing new to the men of the 8th Regiment. Some three weeks earlier, the *Genius of Liberty* had reported that "[s]ince two o'clock this morning startling proceedings have been going on [in Baltimore]. Detachments of artillery and infantry were sent to various parts of the city, and are now posted in Monument Square, Exchange Place, the Eighth Ward, and other points. Before daylight all the members of the Board of Police Commissioners except the Mayor were arrested and sent to Fort McHenry. A multitude of rumors are afloat as to the cause of this sudden movement, but nothing definite is yet known. It is said that a plot has been discovered of an intended outbreak." *Genius of Liberty*, July 4, 1861.

5. In mid-July, Governor Curtin arranged for the delivery of a trainload of arms to the recruits at Camp Wright. Many of the troops stationed at Camp Wilkins received arms at about the same time. Most likely, these arms were old-style smoothbore muskets that had been converted from flintlock to percussion. See footnote 25 infra.

6. Hill, *Our Boys*, 47–49.

7. Ibid., 52.

8. Ibid., 53.

9. Ibid., 56.

10. Ibid., 56–57.

11. Buck and ball was a musket load intended for use at close quarters; it consisted of three .30 caliber balls added to the regular .69 caliber ball. The load created a shotgun effect when fired.

12. Darby, *Incidents and Adventures*, 17.

13. Mitchell was destined to be killed June 30,1862, at the Battle of Glendale.

14. Hill, *Our Boys*, 59.

15. Ibid., 66.

16. Ibid., 68.

17. Robert Taggert (later captain of Company C, 9th Regiment, P.R.V.C.) to "Friend Jarrett," 10 August, 1861, Jarrett Family Papers, Library and Archives Division, Historical Society of Western Pennsylvania, Pittsburgh, Pa. (hereafter cited as "Jarrett Family Papers").

18. The riflemen of this regiment were recruited from Elk, McKean, and Cameron Counties, where deer abounded. These experienced hunters carried their own weapons and ammunition early in the war and, later, were among the first to be issued the new Sharps breechloading rifles. They took their name from the bucks' tails that they pinned to their caps.

19. Hill, *Our Boys*, 68. In all, 15,856 officers and men of the Pennsylvania Reserves were mustered into Federal service at Meridian Hill and Tennallytown.

20. Albert Rake to his wife, 11 August 1861, Civil War Miscellaneous Collection, United States Army Military History Institute, Carlisle Barracks, Pennsylvania (hereafter cited as "Rake Papers"). The United States Army Military History Institute is hereafter cited as "USAMHI."

21. Michael Barton, ed., "The Civil War Letters of Captain Andrew Lewis and his Daughter," *The Western Pennsylvania Historical Magazine* 60, no. 4 (October 1977): 374–75 (hereafter cited as "Lewis Letters").

22. Ibid., 374.

23. Darby, *Incidents and Adventures*, 19.

24. Adam Bright, a private in the 9th Regiment, wrote to his brother from Camp Tennally: "You want to know how much duty we have to perform. Well, we have to drill 5 times every day and each drill is one hour and a half long. We have to stand guard about once every 5 days. We have our old muskets yet and I guess we will have to keep them." Aida Craig Truxall, *"Respects to All": Letters of Two Pennsylvania Boys in the War of the Rebellion* (Pittsburgh: University of Pittsburgh Press, 1962), 5 (hereafter cited as *Respects to All*).

25. In all probability, these guns were .69 caliber Model 1816 smoothbore muskets converted from flintlock to percussion by the Remington Arms Company and distributed to the new recruits from the various Pennsylvania arsenals. George Darby recalled them with little affection: "These muskets will be remembered by the old soldiers as the gun that the boys of '61 used to say, 'The fellow who stood at the butt end was in more danger than the one who was shot at.'" Darby, *Incidents and Adventures,* 14–15. McCall's plea met with mixed success. In a September 2, 1861, report to General McClellan on the condition of his command, General McCall stated that the 1st, 4th, 9th, 10th, and 11th Regiments were still armed with "the old altered flintlock musket, against which the feelings of prejudice and distrust are almost universal." Sypher, *History of the Pa. Reserves*, 111. The 8th Regiment (and several others) fared better, being "armed [by September] with rifles and muskets of improved patterns." Ibid, 112. Most likely these were the .69 caliber Model 1842 smoothbore muskets (with rifles for the flank companies) manufactured at the Harpers Ferry Armory. As to the evolution of rifles and muskets generally, see Earl J. Coates and Dean S. Thomas, *An Introduction to Civil War Small Arms* (Gettysburg, Pa.: Thomas, 1990).

26. National Archives and Records Administration, Washington, D.C. (hereafter cited as NARA), Record Group 94, Records of the Adjutant General's Office (hereafter cited as RG 94, AGO), Muster Rolls of Volunteer Organizations, 8th Pennsylvania Infantry, Regimental Papers.

27. John Strathern, *The Civil War Letters of Cpl. John H. Strathern, Eighth Pennsylvania Volunteer Corps*, comp. Marlene C. Bumbera (Apollo, Pa.: Closson Press, 1994), 5–6 (hereafter cited as *Civil War Letters*).

28. Florence C. McLaughlin, ed., "'Dear Sister Jennie-Dear Brother Jacob': The Correspondence Between a Northern Soldier and his Sister in Mechanicsburg, Pennsylvania, 1861–1864," *The Western Pennsylvania Historical Magazine*, 60, no. 2 (April 1977): 118–20.

29. Truxall, *Respects to All*, 3.

30. Sypher, *History of the Pa. Reserves*, 110.

31. Strathern, *Civil War Letters*, 9.

32. Sypher, *History of the Pa. Reserves*, 115–16. "The flags were made of blue silk, fringed with yellow; in the centre was embroidered the coat of arms of the State of Pennsylvania, surrounded by thirteen golden stars; the number of each regiment also appeared on the flag it received." Ibid., 116.

33. Ibid., 116–17.
34. Ibid., 117–18.
35. Hill, *Our Boys,* 76.
36. Ibid., 83.
37. Ibid., 83–84.
38. *Genius of Liberty,* September 26, 1861. This article, which originally appeared in the *Pittsburgh Chronicle,* was reprinted in the *Genius of Liberty* together with the following addendum: "The above is from the *Pittsburgh Chronicle.* Now the Pittsburgh papers have a queer way about them in crediting things connected with the war to Pittsburgh. It appears, however, from the record that the Greene County Rangers had a hand in this, and we believe the 'State of Greene' is not located in Pittsburgh. We have all along been of the opinion that Capt. Conner's company was from Brownsville, and Capt. Gardner's from Uniontown, and we know they are part of the 8th Regiment, but as quick as they do something nice they belong to Pittsburgh. Some time ago, these same papers published Col. S. D. Oliphant and Adjt. H. W. Patterson as Pittsburgh Lawyers. Now we are willing that Pittsburghers shall have all the credit they are entitled to, but we insist on them allowing other people their rights at least." Ibid.
39. *Genius of Liberty,* October 10, 1861.
40. This phrase was common among the soldiers on both sides during the war and referred to their first experience of battle.
41. Fort Pennsylvania was later renamed Fort Reno in honor of Major General Jesse Reno, a Virginia native who was killed September 14, 1862, at the Battle of South Mountain.
42. Strathern, *Civil War Letters,* 12–13. Another soldier described the construction of the fort in more prosaic terms: "We ar buzy building a battery it is mate werry strong & goot to protect our soldiers it holts about too thousand mens it is mounted with three canons. We expect more canons yet we cut down orchards with fine apple and peach trees and also some large corn fields we have destroyed too houses that wer in our way to build the battery." Letter from A. S. Bray dated August 30, 1861, quoted in Benjamin F. Cooling, III and Walter H. Owen, II, *Mr. Lincoln's Forts* (Shippensburg, Pa.: White Mane Publishing Company, 1988), 143.
43. Hill, *Our Boys,* 114–15.
44. Ibid., 131. John Strathern also mentioned this unusual encounter in a letter to his parents dated September 24, 1861: "During our stay we had an opportunity of seeing and talking to some [of] the Rebels. Those we saw belong to the 30th Virginia Regiment, and are men of refined manners and good education, and talked as if there was nothing between us. One of them with whom we conversed remarked that it seemed like foolishness for us to be fighting against each other.... [H]e expressed a wish that he might never meet us in arms, and wished that the war was over. They told us that they were at the fight at Bull Run and that we had them whipped three times, and that they were in full retreat when General Johnston came up and turned the fortunes of the day. They were all draped in citizens clothes except their officers. They say that they get enough to eat and drink, but that their garments are like Paddy's shirt.... One little incident I must notice: One of our men asked the Rebel Captain if he knew anything of this book, at the same time holding up a pack of cards. Said the Rebel, 'What book?' Said Blackley, 'The history of the four Kings.' 'No, Sir,' said the Rebel Captain, 'this is my book,' at the same time holding up a New Testament. This ought to make men that call themselves Union men blush, but I am sorry to say that he was so ignorant as not to be able to see the farce of the rebuke." Strathern, *Civil War Letters,* 14.

CHAPTER 3: "A BRUSH WITH THE REBELS"

1. Strathern, *Civil War Letters,* 20–21.
2. This movement by the Pennsylvania Reserves occurred October 9, 1861, with the regimental bands playing "Dixie's Land" as the troops marched across the Chain Bridge. Sypher, *History of the Pa. Reserves,* 123.
3. Hill, *Our Boys,* 139–40.
4. A. F. Hill was promoted to the rank of corporal October 1, 1861.
5. Hill, *Our Boys,* 141.
6. Ibid., 142.

7. Darby, *Incidents and Adventures*, 23.

8. Ibid., 17.

9. Hill, *Our Boys*, 150.

10. Ibid., 151–52.

11. *Genius of Liberty*, December 12, 1861.

12. Hill, *Our Boys*, 155.

13. Mark Reinsberg, ed., "A Bucktail Voice: Civil War Correspondence of Pvt. Cordello Collins," *The Western Pennsylvania Historical Magazine*, 48 (July 1965): 236–38 (hereafter cited as "A Bucktail Voice").

14. *Genius of Liberty*, January 9, 1862.

15. Sypher, *History of the Pa. Reserves*, 129.

16. Hill, *Our Boys*, 170.

17. Ibid., 171.

18. Ibid., 172.

19. Ibid., 173. Hill added the following commentary on his poetic effort: "The reader will think this scarcely sublime, and I perfectly agree; but it serves to express my feelings on the disappointment we were treated to, in not arriving in time to participate in that glorious little affair known as THE BATTLE OF DRAINESVILLE." Ibid., 174.

20. Albert Rake to his wife, 27 December 1861, Rake Papers. Private Rake could not have joined in the "fun," as A. F. Hill characterized the Battle of Dranesville, even if the first brigade had reached the field in time to have become engaged. He had been hospitalized with a leg injury since mid-November. His fighting spirit was undiminished, however, as illustrated by these lines from a letter to his wife dated November 27, 1861: "I was examined yesterday by two Doctors and the one thought he could cure my leg and I hope he can for it is very painful.... I could...get my discharge if I wanted to but I would like to have a pop or tow [*sic*] at the suns of bitches before I come home." Albert Rake to his wife, 27 November 1861, Rake Papers.

21. In late October, a Union brigade commanded by Edward D. Baker, a prominent senator from California, crossed the Potomac above Leesburg. It was surprised by a Confederate force and driven back into the river. Baker was killed, as were 48 other Union soldiers, and the wounded, captured and missing totaled nearly one half of the brigade. Southern losses were very light. This disaster resulted in the creation of the Congressional Joint Committee on the Conduct of the War.

22. James Randolf Simpson, a native of Huntington, Pennsylvania, enlisted in August of 1862 and was severely wounded at Antietam the following month. His brother, George, was killed in the same battle. Willoughby and Simpson (known as "Dol") corresponded with each other throughout the war.

23. Governor Curtin issued the following order, which General McCall caused to be read to the troops: "The gallantry of our troops in the late affair at Dranesville, demands a public acknowledgment. Their courage, conduct and high discipline are honorable to the corps and to the Commonwealth by whose forecast it was raised and formed, in anticipation of the exigencies of the country, and whose sons fill its ranks. General McCall and Brigadier-General Ord, and the officers and men who were engaged under their commands, may be assured that Pennsylvania is not insensible to their martial virtue, and from them and their fellows, confidently looks for as many further illustrations of it as there shall be opportunities afforded them." Sypher, *History of the Pa. Reserves*, 140–41.

24. James Mason and John Slidell, Confederate Commissioners to Great Britain and France, respectively, were bound for London on the British mail ship *Trent* when it was intercepted near the Bahamas by the Union warship *San Jacinto*. Mason and Slidell were forcibly removed from the *Trent* and taken to Massachusetts where they were imprisoned. The "*Trent* Affair," as the incident came to be known nearly precipitated a state of war between Great Britain and the Union. The crisis was ended when the Union acceded to British demands to release the two diplomats. Although Mason and Slidell sailed to Great Britain aboard a British warship, their efforts to enlist England and France in the Confederate cause ended in failure.

25. John A. Willoughby to James R. Simpson, 29 December 1861, Civil War Miscellaneous Collection, Cpl. James Randolf Simpson "Dear Dol" Civil War Letters, USAMHI (hereafter cited as Simpson Papers). Willoughby added an interesting postscript to this letter two nights later: "Evening 7 o'clock [New Year's Eve] Joe Stewart, Simon Weston, Keith, Geis, Dixey McCabe, and I are...talking about the review and the

subject of the day—War. Since beginning [this letter] I hear that a forage party goes out on Tuesday next. Should any secesh make their appearance, we will have a set-to. Tonight a year ago I spent the evening with Miss Sharar [of] Hollidaysburg. I would like to spend a few...nights in Philadelphia after being away from the female sex...."

26. Hill, *Our Boys*, 185.

27. Ibid., 187–88.

28. Ibid., 188. Throughout the Civil War, disease consistently exacted a deadlier toll among the troops on both sides than did battle. In the Union armies, two soldiers died of sickness and disease for every one killed in battle. Chronic diarrhea and typhoid fever were the great killers, with some 44,564 White Union soldiers dying from these two afflictions. See Alfred J. Bollet, M.D., *Civil War Medicine: Challenges and Triumphs* (Tucson, Ariz.: Galen Press, 2002), 365. Mortality rates among white Union troops from chronic diarrhea varied from a low of 3.5% in 1861 to a high of 23.6% in 1864 (the latter figure most probably reflecting the large number of Union soldiers being held in Confederate prisons at that time. Mortality rates among white Union troops for typhoid fever varied from a low of 25.7% in 1861 to a high of 59.5% in 1864 (the latter figure also resulting from the large number of Union soldiers held in Confederate prisons at that time). See Bollet, *Civil War Medicine*, 330. Mortality rates among black Union troops and Confederate troops were roughly comparable.

29. Strathern, *Civil War Letters*, 42–43.

30. A. F. Hill described this game of chance as follows: "This interesting species of gambling is much practiced in the army. For the edification of the non-military reader, I would just impart a slight idea as to how the game is played. It is as follows: Six cards—those from the ace to the six of any suit—are fastened to a table; the proprietor shakes his dice-box and upturns it upon the table; outsiders then bet that a certain number will come uppermost on the dice, laying their money upon a card containing the number on which they wish to try their luck—generally losing." Hill, *Our Boys*, 189.

31. Ibid., 190–91.

32. *Genius of Liberty*, February 20, 1862. The writer, whose identity is unknown, also related, in a rather blunt manner, his view of the common soldiers' opinion on the question of emancipation: "And I will just observe for the benefit of such as think with these gentry [abolitionists] in your midst, *that three-fourths of this army now assembled to fight for the Constitution and Government under the 'Old Flag,' can never be made by any power on earth, to fire a gun in the cause of 'Nigger Emancipation.'*" Ibid.

33. NARA, RG 94, AGO, Book Records of Volunteer Union Organizations, 8th Pennsylvania Reserve Infantry Regimental Order Book, Part 2, Vol. 3 of 4.

34. The capture of Fort Donelson on the Cumberland River and its sister, Fort Henry on the Tennessee River, by a combined infantry and naval force under the command of Ulysses S. Grant was significant in several respects: The border state of Kentucky was secured to the Union by the victory; Unionists in East Tennessee were encouraged to rally to the Union cause; Federal forces were freed to move, via the Tennessee River, deep into the heart of the Confederacy; and, perhaps most significantly, General U. S. Grant emerged as a capable combat commander in President Lincoln's eyes. It was at Fort Donelson that Grant first imposed upon a foe the terms of "unconditional and immediate surrender" that would give rise later to his nickname, "Unconditional Surrender Grant."

35. The Battle of Glendale, fought June 30, 1862, is discussed in Chapter Five.

36. Hill, *Our Boys*, 198–99.

37. Ibid., 199.

38. Strathern, *Civil War Letters*, 51.

CHAPTER 4: "AWAY DOWN SOUTH IN DIXIE"

1. Hill, *Our Boys*, 200.

2. Fearing that the Union army would commence offensive operations with the coming of spring, Confederate President Jefferson Davis directed that the Southern forces then stationed at Manassas fall back to a defensive perimeter closer to Richmond so as to better protect the Southern capital. During the weekend of March 8–9, the Confederates under General Joseph Johnston slipped quietly out of their lines at Manassas and withdrew to a new position behind the Rappahannock River.

3. The phrase "Burnside stick-in-the-mud" is a reference to the infamous "Mud March" of January 1863. This debacle is described in Chapter Ten.

4. Darby, *Incidents and Adventures*, 23–24. This series of movements and countermovements actually consumed an entire month. Leaving Camp Pierpont on March 10, the 8th Regiment headed for Manassas, marching 16 miles to Hunter's Mills where it camped for three days. It then reversed direction and marched toward Alexandria, arriving there March 16. The regiment remained in Alexandria until April 9, when it moved by rail to Manassas. It stayed there until April 17, when General Reynolds's brigade led the advance of McCall's division to Catlett Station. Throughout all of this time, the weather was generally dreadful and the marching very severe. Darby's account of these movements, while compressing them in time, is unfortunately all too accurate in its description of the prevailing conditions.

5. Hill, *Our Boys*, 226.

6. Albert Rake to his wife, 20 April 1862, Rake Papers.

7. George Darby remembered this incident, and recounted what he believed to be the cause of the widespread sickness: "During our stay [at Manassas] some of our soldier boys entered a car, which lay at the station freighted with hospital stores, and proceeded to confiscate some of said goods, but unfortunately for them among the things which they stole was some wine, and of course they proceeded to fill up on this product of the vine, but alas! It proved to be wine of antimony, and the result was that they paid the penalty of their escapade with their lives." Darby, *Incidents and Adventures*, 25. Antimony is a silver-white metallic element related to arsenic and tin, and, in small doses, was often prescribed for medicinal purposes during the 19th century.

8. Hill, *Our Boys*, 229–30.

9. Ibid., 230–31. It was an experience that almost certainly convinced Hill never to take another horn. Upon recovering sufficiently to return to active duty, Hill noted: "How thankful I felt as I found myself shouldering my musket once more; for I fully understood what fearful peril I had passed through in being placed under the doctor's hand." Ibid., 231.

10. McClellan's Peninsula campaign and the part played in it by the Pennsylvania Reserves is the subject of Chapter Five.

11. Strathern, *Civil War Letters*, 61–62.

12. Hill, *Our Boys*, 236–38.

13. Ibid., 240.

14. The Confederate forces defending Fredericksburg withdrew from the town when they learned of the approach of McDowell's corps but, as noted by Albert Rake in a letter to his wife dated June 1, 1862, they remained within threatening distance: "[W]e crossed the river on last Monday and fell back on this side again yesterday. I don't know but we will be attacked here yet for there is plenty of them in this country. But let them come on. We will try them a hack." Albert Rake to his wife, 1 June 1862, Rake Papers.

15. Joseph L. McQuaide to his parents, 12 May 1862, McQuaide Papers.

16. Darby, *Incidents and Adventures*, 25–26.

17. On contrabands generally, see Ervin L. Jordan, Jr., *Black Confederates and Afro-Yankees in Civil War Virginia* (Charlottesville, Va.: University Press of Virginia, 1995), 82–90. Jordan notes that "[t]he first contrabands were three Virginia slave field hands who appeared at [Fort Monroe] on 23 May 1861.... They informed Union officials that they were about to be shipped to North Carolina to labor on Confederate fortifications. Their owner, Confederate colonel Charles F. Mallory, 115th Virginia Militia, demanded their return under the...Fugitive Slave Act of 1850 and appealed to Major General Benjamin F. Butler.... [Mallory's emissary] and Butler met under a flag of truce...near Hampton to discuss the situation; Butler initially denied the request in order to confer with his superiors. By the end of May, Butler formally refused to return the three slaves, pointing out that since Virginia had seceded, it could no longer claim the protection and privileges of Federal law: 'I am under no constitutional obligations to a foreign country, which Virginia now claims to be.' [Butler] proclaimed as 'contrabands of war' any slave who reached Union lines or had previously been employed as military labor for the Confederacy." Ibid., 83.

18. Hill, *Our Boys*, 243.

19. In late May, with the bridges over the Rappahannock rebuilt, General Reynolds's first brigade crossed the river and occupied Fredericksburg. Reynolds was appointed military governor of the town on May 26 and served as such until he joined McClellan on the Peninsula.

20. Hill, *Our Boys*, 242–44.

21. Ibid., 244–45. George Darby also visited the memorial site and was shocked by what he saw: "In a neglected cemetery near our camp lie the mortal remains of the mother of the first president of the United States of America, and as I stood by the neglected grave of the mother of America's great chieftain, and saw the marble shaft which had evidently been designed to perpetuate her illustrious name, lying prone upon the ground, pitted by bullet marks from rebel guns, I could but think what a sad commentary upon human greatness as exemplified in this rebel respect for the mother of the Father of the Country." Darby, *Incidents and Adventures*, 26.

22. Since landing at Fort Monroe in late March, McClellan's army had been advancing methodically up the peninsula toward Richmond. Yorktown fell May 4, and Williamsburg, two days later. By May 31, McClellan had reached Fair Oaks, where Johnston finally stood and fought.

23. Hill, *Our Boys*, 263.

24. Darby, *Incidents and Adventures*, 29.

25. Hill, *Our Boys*, 269.

CHAPTER 5: "NOW, BOYS, LET THEM HAVE IT!"

1. Hill was promoted to the rank of sergeant May 1, 1862.

2. Hill, *Our Boys*, 269.

3. John W. Urban, *Battle Field and Prison Pen, or Through the War, and Thrice a Prisoner in Rebel Dungeons* (Philadelphia: Hubbard Brothers, Publishers, 1882), 98–99 (hereafter cited as *Battle Field and Prison Pen*).

4. Hill, *Our Boys*, 271.

5. On January 27, 1862, Lincoln, finally out of patience with McClellan's inaction, issued General War Order No. 1 that declared that all land and naval forces would attack the enemy on February 1. The president supplemented this order with Special War Order No. 1, directed specifically at McClellan. It ordered McClellan to commence offensive action against Manassas prior to February 22.

6. The movement to Fort Monroe was the largest amphibious operation in American military history until the Normandy invasion in 1944. In addition to the troops, some 270 artillery pieces, 15,000 horses and mules, 3,500 wagons and thousands of head of cattle made the voyage from Alexandria to Fortress Monroe.

7. The Confederates had abandoned their positions at Manassas Junction and Centreville and had established a new defensive line behind the Rappahannock River.

8. Early in the war, Northern newspapers lauded McClellan's performance in western Virginia. The *New York Times* wrote, "'We feel very proud of our wise and brave young Major-General. There is a future before him....'" And the *New York Herald* led a column with a headline that read, "'Gen. McClellan, the Napoleon of the Present War.'" Stephen W. Sears, *George B. McClellan: The Young Napoleon* (New York: Ticknor & Fields, 1988), 93. Following the *Herald*'s lead, other newspapers "began praising [McClellan] as the 'Napoleon of America' or the 'Young Napoleon' and comparing his rapid climb to high command with Bonaparte's." Ibid., 101.

9. Urban, *Battle Field and Prison Pen*, 97–98.

10. John Urban of the 1st Regiment commented on the fraternization between the opposing pickets: "[A]n amazing amount of good feeling, and even jollity, cropped out between these opposed pickets at times. A brisk trade in newspapers was kept up almost continually. The exchange of coffee for tobacco was a very usual thing. Among the facetious things of these perilous posts was the conference between the 'Reb,' who called out 'Hello, Yank! What regiment do you belong to?' 'To the Ninety-Ninth Rhode Island,' was the ready reply. 'The Ninety-Ninth *Rhode Island!* Good Heavens!' cried the astonished questioner. 'How many regiments must New York have, if Rhode Island has ninety-nine?'" Urban, *Battle Field and Prison Pen*, 103.

11. Joseph L. McQuaide to his parents, 24 June 1862, McQuaide Papers. Fayette Countians were as anxious for news from "the seat of war" as were Corporal McQuaide's parents. The following article appeared in the *Genius of Liberty* June 26, 1862: "Several of our citizens have returned from the Army of the Potomac during the past week: Drum Major J. Duncan Ramsey, Joseph O. Thornton and John Nesmith of the 8th

Regiment...have all returned on account of ill health. From them we gather the following items. The 8th and 11th Regiments are at Dispatch Station 13 miles from Richmond. It will be recalled by our readers that the 'Oliphant Company,' the first to leave this place, is in the 8th Regiment, and is now commanded by Capt. Henry C. Dawson. Capt. E. Bierer's company is in the 11th Regiment. The health of these regiments, and especially the two companies from here, is very good. The 8th Regiment is now under the command of Lieut. Col. S. D. Oliphant, who it is thought, will be promoted if an opportunity offers. S. Milton Baily has been elected major of the 8th Regiment.... H. H. McQuilken has been elected 2nd Lieutenant of Company G, 8th Reg.... Several wagons, teams and prisoners were captured by the rebel raid that was made along our lines several days ago. Among the prisoners were James Crawford and Zadoc Springer, from North Union Township...." *Genius of Liberty*, June 26, 1862. Zadoc Springer was a relative of Thomas W. Springer of Uniontown.

12. Barton, ed., "Lewis Letters," 383–84.

13. McCall, in turn, posted Reynolds's first brigade on the right of his line. Thus, the Fayette Guards and the Brownsville Grays, together with the other eight companies of the 8th Regiment, would bear the brunt of any Confederate attempt to turn the Union army's right flank.

14. In addition to the time-honored precaution of pickets on the ground, the Federals also employed the very latest in military technology to help them ascertain the enemy's intentions: "While at dinner we saw a balloon slowly ascend to the height of a hundred and fifty feet, where it remained. It was held to the ground by means of three guy-ropes. We could see a man in the car; he raised a telescope and proceeded to take a survey of Mechanicsville and rebeldom in general. Suddenly he lowered his glass, and in the most feeling and eloquent manner signaled to those below to draw him down quickly. The balloon had just begun to descend, when bang! Bang! Went two cannon in quick succession, seemingly in the vicinity of the rebel earthworks beyond the river, and a shell and a solid shot came shrieking through the air over our heads flying past the balloon—the shell exploding just beyond." Hill, *Our Boys*, 282.

15. Barton, ed., "Lewis Letters," 386–89.

16. Hill, *Our Boys*, 284.

17. Franklin Ellis, *History of Fayette County, Pennsylvania* (Philadelphia: L. H. Everts & Co., 1882), 196, quoting from the *Uniontown (Pa.) American Standard*.

18. Hill, *Our Boys*, 286–87.

19. Darby, *Incidents and Adventures*, 32–33. Commenting on the loss of the haversacks, Darby noted: "While the loss of our grub was a serious one, for we were mighty hungry after a hard battle and a night of fasting, the comical way in which Coon puckered his mouth, and by sucking in and expelling the air, gave a perfect imitation of the sounds produced by the different sized shot and shells, in their passage through the air, was so laughable that we forgave him for losing the grub." Ibid., 33.

20. Hill, *Our Boys*, 289.

21. Urban, *Battle Field and Prison Pen*, 111.

22. One of the Union soldiers killed at Mechanicsville predicted his own demise. Henry Flick, a private in the 1st Regiment, related the story in a privately printed memoir: "The first battle was Mechanicsville, in front of Richmond.... I was in that battle and my bunk-mate was Jacob Getz from Dillersville, Lancaster County. He always said that he would be killed in the first battle and the last shot that night from the Confederate side was a shell that bursted and killed him." Henry Flick, *Enlisted Man's Published Memoirs, 1861–1865*, Harrisburg Civil War Round Table Collection & Leigh Collection, Book 24:96, USAMHI.

23. George B. McClellan, *The Civil War Papers of George B. McClellan, Selected Correspondence 1860–1865*, ed. Stephen W. Sears (New York: Da Capo Press, 1989), 316 (hereafter cited as *The Civil War Papers of George B. McClellan*).

24. Hill, *Our Boys*, 291.

25. Following the duel between the USS *Monitor* and the CSS *Virginia* in March, Union forces threatened Norfolk. The retreating Confederates blew up the *Virginia* as her draft was too deep to allow her to steam up the James River toward Richmond. Thus, the James was open to the Union navy all the way up to the Confederate defenses at Drewry's Bluff.

26. In their haste to withdraw, many soldiers of the 8th Regiment left their knapsacks behind. Ashbel Hill was among the unfortunates: "Yes, I left my knapsack...hoping to return to it; but I never saw it again. Some

grim rebel I suppose, soon after took possession of it, and gloried over its contents, which were as follows: A woolen blanket, a tent-blanket, a change of under garments, a 'Lloyd Map of Virginia,' a copy of the New Testament, a port-folio containing ample writing materials and stamps, a photograph, an ambrotype, and a half a dozen letters from my darling." Hill, *Our Boys*, 293.

27. Ibid., 299–300. Hill described the terror that sustained artillery fire instilled among the infantry: "The infantry fighting abated, while that of the artillery was resumed with redoubled fury. There was not a second that the air above our heads was free from either shot or shell. They were sent one after another so rapidly, that a constant, prolonged, and connected whizzing, shrieking and screaming was maintained. Shells were exploding every second—now in front of us, now in our rear, and frequently over our heads. Grape and canister came whistling shrilly about us; while solid shot came rushing madly along, now flying a few feet above our heads, now striking the hillside with a dull crash, and ricocheting a hundred feet into the air, and falling far in our rear. When a shell explodes in the air above one's head, many fragments fly upward, and are heard singing and whistling in the air for half a minute before they drop. During this half minute the suspense of those beneath it is horrible to endure. How is a poor mortal to know that it is not going to drop plumb upon his head? Every one is sure to think that, judging by the sound, it is descending in a straight line for his head." Ibid., 300–301.

28. Ibid., 303–5.

29. Darby, *Incidents and Adventures*, 35.

30. Hill, *Our Boys*, 306.

31. Darby, *Incidents and Adventures*, 50.

32. Urban, *Battle Field and Prison Pen*, 122

33. Ibid., 124.

34. Sypher, *History of the Pa. Reserves*, 232.

35. General Porter, in his official report to General McClellan on the battle of Gaines's Mill, stated: "I desire especially to call the commanding general's attention to the conduct of...General McCall and his brigade commanders Reynolds, Meade and Seymour, who successfully led their regiments into the thickest of the fight to support and relieve [Brigadier General George W. Morrell's division]. Sypher, *History of the Pa. Reserves*, 243. Of Reynolds, the first brigade commander, Porter said: "Reynolds, having repulsed the enemy in his front, and hearing the tremendous contest on his left...moved to the sound of cannon, and led his men regiment after regiment where our hard pressed forces required most assistance. As each regiment entered the woods to the relief of their exhausted companions, the effect was immediately shown by the enemy being driven before them...." Ibid., 241.

36. Hill, *Our Boys*, 307.

37. Urban, *Battlefield and Prison Pen*, 129–30. Conducted to a position of safety by the Pennsylvania Reserves, these guns would be used to devastating effect two days later at the Battle of Malvern Hill.

38. The New Market Road connected Richmond with the village of New Market 15 miles southeast of the Confederate capital. Just east of New Market, the road forked, one spur continuing southward toward Turkey Bridge, the other leading toward Glendale some seven miles to the east. This latter road was variously referred to as the New Market Road and the Long Bridge Road. See George B. Davis, Leslie J. Perry, Joseph W. Kirkley, *The Official Military Atlas of the Civil War*, comp. Calvin D. Cowles (New York: Gramercy Books, 1983), Plate XX, Map No. 1.

39. Urban, *Battle Field and Prison Pen*, 146–48. Private Urban would be wounded during the fighting on June 30 and captured the following morning.

40. Hill, *Our Boys*, 315.

41. Four other divisions, three under Stonewall Jackson and one under Theophilus Holmes, were to threaten the Federal rear at White Oak Swamp (Jackson) and intercept the Union trains near Malvern Hill (Holmes). For various reasons, none of these four divisions was able to participate in the day's action to any meaningful extent.

42. It was here that McCall threw the first brigade forward to establish the picket line that Private Urban spoke of.

43. Darby, *Incidents and Adventures*, 38.

44. "General Porter [later] explained his conduct by saying that, 'he no longer considered McCall's troops as attached to his command.' Yet no order had been issued detaching them from the Fifth Corps." Sypher, *History of the Pa. Reserves*, 255.

45. George A. McCall, *The Seven Days' Contests: Pennsylvania Reserves: General McCall's Report and Accompanying Documents* (New York: Office of the Rebellion Record, 1864), 669.

46. This disposition of the artillery would contribute to the near disaster that befell McCall's left flank during the battle that followed. See Stephen W. Sears, "Glendale: Opportunity Squandered," *North and South: The Official Magazine of the Civil War Society* 5 no. 1 (Dec. 2001): 12–24 (hereafter cited as *Glendale*).

47. Evan M. Woodward, *Our Campaigns; the Second Regiment Pennsylvania Volunteers* (Philadelphia: J. E. Porter, 1865; reprint, ed. Stanley W. Zamonski, Shippensburg, Pa.: Burd Street Press, 1995), 102–3 (page citations are to the reprint edition) (hereafter cited as *Our Campaigns*). This disposition of the four Union divisions left both flanks of McCall's division "in the air."

48. Sears, *Glendale*, 16.

49. Hill, *Our Boys*, 316.

50. It is unlikely that the 6th Georgia opposed the 8th Regiment on McCall's left flank. Kemper's brigade of Longstreet's division (all Virginians) made the initial assault. Branch's brigade of A. P. Hill's division (all North Carolinians) and Pickett's brigade of Longstreet's division (all Virginians, commanded by Eppa Hunton) followed up Kemper's initial advance. Archer's brigade and Pender's brigade (both of A. P. Hill's division) also became engaged on McCall's left, but the only Georgia troops in either of these brigades were Archer's 19th Georgia Infantry.

51. Hill, *Our Boys*, 317.

52. Ibid., 319–20.

53. Ibid., 321. Colonel Simmons was not killed outright but, rather, was mortally wounded and taken prisoner. He later died of his wounds, having first given his sword to an officer of Jenkins's brigade in gratitude for the solicitous attention and care he had received while in Confederate hands. See James J. Baldwin, III, *The Struck Eagle: A Biography of Brigadier General Micah Jenkins* (Shippensburg, Pa.: Burd Street Press, 1996), 140.

54. Brian K. Burton, *Extraordinary Circumstances: The Seven Days Battles* (Bloomington, Ind.: Indiana University Press, 2001), 285 (hereafter cited as *Extraordinary Circumstances*).

55. Darby, *Incidents and Adventures*, 39.

56. George A. McCall, *The Seven Days Contests: Pennsylvania Reserves: General McCall's Report and Accompanying Documents* (New York: Office of the Rebellion Record, 1864), 668.

57. *Confederate Veteran*, Vol. 1, No. 11, November 1893 (Reprint: Broadfoot's Bookmark, Wendell, N.C.), 334.

58. In his Official Report on the action at Glendale, General Kearny accused McCall's division of having abandoned their position. In a July 10, 1862, letter to his wife, Kearny wrote: "General McCall's Pennsylvanians ran to a man." Philip Kearny, *Letters from the Peninsula: The Civil War Letters of General Philip Kearny*, William B. Styple, ed. (Kearny, N.J.: Belle Grove Publishing Co., 1988), 125. McCall responded forcefully to this criticism in the publication cited in footnote 56.

59. See Burton, *Extraordinary Circumstances*, 298.

60. The action on June 30, 1862, has been referred to variously as the Battle of Glendale, New Market Crossroads, Frayser's Farm, Nelson's Farm, Charles City Crossroads, and Willis Church.

61. Douglas Southall Freeman, *R. E. Lee* (New York: Charles Scribner's Sons, 1934; abridged, Richard Harwell, New York: Charles Scribner's Sons, 1961), 214 (page citations are to the abridged edition). General Lee himself, in his Official Report on the action, wrote: "Could the other commands [of the Confederate army] have co-operated in the action the result would have proved most disastrous to the enemy." *The War of the Rebellion: Official Records of the Union and Confederate Armies*, XI, Pt. 2, 495 (hereafter cited as *O.R.*) (unless otherwise noted, all further references to the *O. R.* are to Series One).

62. Edward Porter Alexander, *Fighting for the Confederacy: The Personal Recollections of General Edward Porter Alexander*, ed. Gary W. Gallagher (Chapel Hill, N.C.: The University of North Carolina Press, 1989), 109–10.

63. McCall was captured as he rode along the original battle line late in the day. General Longstreet noted that "It was the Forty-seventh Virginia Regiment that caught and invited General McCall to quarter with the Confederates. Although his gallant division had been forced from the fight, the brave head and heart of the general were not fallen till he found himself on his lonely ride. He was more tenacious of his battle than anyone who came within my experience during the war, if I except D. H. Hill at Sharpsburg. In years gone by I had known [General McCall] in pleasant army service, part of the time as a brevet lieutenant of his company. When the name was announced, and as he dismounted, I approached to offer my hand and such amenities as were admissible under the circumstances, but he drew up with haughty mien, which forbade nearer approach, so that the courtesies were concluded by the offer of staff officers to escort him to...Richmond." James Longstreet, *From Manassas to Appomattox: Memoirs of the Civil War in America* (Philadelphia: J. B. Lippincott Co., 1896), 138–39.

64. *O. R.*, XI, Pt. 2, 397. The Union surgeon, N. F. Marsh, wrote to General McCall in November of 1862 relaying Longstreet's remarks. He added that "[o]n Thursday, July 3d, General Roger A Pryor [a brigade commander in Longstreet's division] came into the church (hospital) and we had a long conversation. He repeated in substance what Longstreet had said, and spoke in the highest terms of the 'pluck' displayed by McCall's Pennsylvania troops." William H. Powell, *The Fifth Army Corps: Army of the Potomac, A Record of Operations During the Civil War in the United States of America, 1861–1865* (n.p., n.d.; reprint, Dayton, Ohio: Press of Morningside Bookshop, 1984), 147 (page citations are to the reprint edition) (hereafter cited as *The Fifth Army Corps*).

65. Hill, *Our Boys*, 323.

66. Ibid., 325.

CHAPTER 6: "THE SACREDNESS OF THE FAMILY CIRCLE IS BROKEN"

1. Prominent among these were the 13 batteries of Hunt's Artillery Reserve that McCall's division had escorted safely through White Oak Swamp three days earlier.

2. Hill, *Our Boys*, 326–27.

3. Ibid., 327–28. Confederate General Daniel H. Hill noted the impact of the Federal gunboats on the fighting at Malvern Hill in a postwar article published in *Battles and Leaders of the Civil War*: "As General Holmes marched down the river, his troops became visible to the gun-boats, which opened fire upon them, throwing those awe-inspiring shells familiarly called by our men 'lamp-posts,' on account of their size and appearance. Their explosion was very much like that of a small volcano, and had a very demoralizing effect upon new troops, one of whom expressed the general sentiment by saying: 'The Yankees throwed them lamp-posts about too careless like.' The roaring, howling gun-boat shells were usually harmless to flesh, blood and bones, but they had a wonderful effect upon the nervous system." Daniel Harvey Hill, "McClellan's Change of Base and Malvern Hill," *Battles and Leaders*, 2:390.

4. Woodward, *Our Campaigns*, 114.

5. Daniel Harvey Hill, "McClellan's Change of Base and Malvern Hill," *Battles and Leaders*, 2:394.

6. Woodward, *Our Campaigns*, 115–16.

7. Hill, *Our Boys*, 331.

8. Urban, *Battle Field and Prison Pen*, 173–75.

9. Claimant's Testimony, November 9, 1885; Jacob D. Moore, Sergeant, Soldier's Certificate No. 340,231, Company E, 85th Pennsylvania Infantry; Case Files of Approved Pension Applications of Veterans who Served in the Army and Navy Mainly in the Civil War and the War with Spain ("Civil War and Later Survivor's Certificates"), 1861–1934; Civil War and Later Pension Files; Records of the Veterans Administration, Record Group 15; NARA (the Series Title, Subgroup Title, Record Group Title and Number, Repository, and Location are hereafter collectively cited as RG 15).

10. Affidavit of Isaac A. Moore, November 9, 1885; Jacob D. Moore, Sergeant, Soldier's Certificate No. 340,231, Company E, 85th Pennsylvania Infantry; NARA, RG 15. Eventually, Jacob Moore was evacuated from the Peninsula by ocean transport and taken to St. David's Island Hospital near New York City where he recovered from his wound. He was honorably discharged on disability in August 1862. He reenlisted in the 5th Regiment, United States Light Artillery, in March 1864.

11. Hill, *Our Boys*, 333–34.

12. *Genius of Liberty*, July 17, 1862.

13. *Genius of Liberty*, July 10, 1862. It was noted in this article that Patrick Tuhey of Uniontown and James McNamee, a printer from Connellsville, were among those killed.

14. Powell, *The Fifth Army Corps*, 185–86. See also Burton, *Extraordinary Circumstances*, 387.

15. Powell, *The Fifth Army Corps*, 185.

16. Barton, ed., "Lewis Letters," 389–90.

17. Joseph L. McQuaide to his parents, 26 July 1862, McQuaide Papers. Tragically, McQuaide's wish to meet his departed comrade once again, expressed in the lines with which he concluded this letter, would be fulfilled barely one month later. He was killed August 30, 1862, at the Battle of Second Bull Run.

18. Hill, *Our Boys*, 335.

19. Ibid., 337–38.

20. Ibid., 350–51.

21. General McClellan referred to the midnight shelling in a letter to his wife, Mary Ellen, written later that same night: "As I was just about comfortably asleep about ¾ of an hour ago I was awakened by a tremendous shelling—the rascals...opened on us with field guns from the other side of the river & kept up a tremendous fire. It is now pretty much over.... Still some firing—now heavy again—gun boats at work.... A queer thing this, writing a letter to my wife at this time of night to the music of shells...." George B. McClellan, *The Civil War Papers of George B. McClellan*, ed. Stephen W. Sears (New York: Da Capo Press, 1992), 379–80.

22. In burning one of these homes, McClellan's men settled an old score: "Edmund Ruffin, that conspicuous traitor who had journeyed to Charleston to earn a cheap notoriety by firing the first shot at Sumpter, lived here and all his property was totally destroyed. And thus, partially at least, was this blatant rebel repaid for firing the shot that plunged a happy country into a fratricidal war." Darby, *Incidents and Adventures*, 40.

23. Hill, *Our Boys*, 352.

24. Many of the Pennsylvania Reserves had been forced to go into battle on the Peninsula with antiquated muskets; indeed, they had been complaining of the inadequacy of their weapons since their arrival at Camp Tennally the preceding summer (see Chapter Two). The Springfield rifled muskets that Hill mentioned were most likely .58 caliber Model 1861s. Of their rearmament, A. F. Hill wrote: "[W]e were now a rifle regiment. We were highly pleased at this; for it cannot be doubted that the rifle is a more effective weapon than the musket." Ibid.

25. Woodward, *Our Campaigns*, 125.

26. Belle Isle, as it was commonly known, was situated in the James River within sight of Richmond and was used by the Confederates to hold the overflow from the various prisons in downtown Richmond (such as the Libby prison). Sadly, many of these men would find themselves sent there once again after being captured at the Battle of the Weldon Railroad in August 1864. See generally Chapter Thirteen.

27. Hill, *Our Boys*, 346–49.

28. Truxall, *Respects to All*, 28–29.

29. Sypher, *History of the Pa. Reserves*, 323.

30. The *Genius of Liberty* noted Oliphant's return to Uniontown in its July 31, 1862, edition: "Lieut. Col. Oliphant, of the 8th Pa. Regiment, returned to this place on Wednesday evening last, considerably prostrated by the arduous duties and privations through which he has passed. He passed safely and honorably through the battles before Richmond in which the Pennsylvania Reserves occupied a prominent position. A few days after the battles he was taken with partial paralysis, losing his hearing entirely, and the use of his limbs partially. Under the quiet and comforts of home, and the treatment of skilfull physicians, he seems to be improving. He moves about with but little pain and converses freely; but can only receive communications from his friends in writing. He hopes soon to be sufficiently recovered to resume his command, of which he is justifiably very proud, speaking in the highest terms of the gallantry and good conduct of the men of his command. Fayette County may well feel proud of the noble bearing of her noble representatives in the battles of the Chicahominy." *Genius of Liberty*, July 31, 1862.

31. NARA, RG 94, AGO, Muster Rolls of Volunteer Organizations, 8th Pennsylvania Infantry Regimental papers.

32. *Genius of Liberty*, August 21, 1862. Moore was promoted to sergeant September 1, 1862. He returned to his regiment in November, his bravery on the Peninsula having spared him the horrors of Second Bull Run, South Mountain, and Antietam.

CHAPTER 7: "WE HAVE HAD A PRETTY HARD TIME OF IT"

1. Hill, *Our Boys*, 355. On March 8, 1862, the CSS *Virginia* (better known as the *Merrimack*) steamed out of Norfolk and engaged Union warships lying in the James River off Newport News. The wooden frigates USS *Cumberland* and USS *Congress* were destroyed and a third, the USS *Minnesota*, was damaged and run aground. One day later, in Hampton Roads, the *Virginia* and the USS *Monitor* fought to a draw in the first clash of ironclads in naval history.

2. Ibid., 359.

3. Ibid., 363.

4. Ibid., 363–64.

5. General Meade had recovered quickly from his Glendale wounds and rejoined the Army of the Potomac on August 17, 1862. He assumed command of the Pennsylvania Reserves' first brigade, comprised of the 3rd, 4th, 7th, 8th, and 13th Reserves.

6. Darby, *Incidents and Adventures*, 46–47.

7. John J. Hennessy, *Return to Bull Run: The Campaign and Battle of Second Manassas* (New York: Simon & Schuster, 1993), 139 (hereafter cited as *Return to Bull Run*).

8. Darby, *Incidents and Adventures*, 47. Darby recovered from his wound and rejoined his regiment in September 1862.

9. E. M. Woodward, *History of the Third Pennsylvania Reserve: Being a Complete Record of the Regiment, with Incidents of the Camp, Marches, Bivouacs, Skirmishes and Battles* (Trenton, N.J.: MacCrellish & Quigley, 1883), 148 (hereafter cited as *History of the Third Pennsylvania Reserve*).

10. *O. R.*, XII, Pt. 2, 394.

11. Hennessy, *Return to Bull Run*, 259.

12. Hill, *Our Boys,* 377.

13. Woodward, *History of the Third Reserve*, 154–55.

14. Hill, *Our Boys*, 380.

15. *O. R.*, XII, Pt. 2, 394.

16. When McCall's division marched out of Camp Tennally and crossed into Virginia some ten months earlier, the command consisted of 11,255 men. See Sypher, *History of the Pa. Reserves*, 121. By the time of Second Bull Run, the Pennsylvania Reserves had been reduced to some 2,500 men. They lost 653 more killed, wounded, captured, and missing between August 16 and September 2, 1862.

17. Case shot, or shrapnel, was manufactured in both spherical and rifled configurations. The hollow projectile was filled with small lead or iron balls mixed with asphalt or sulphur. A small fused bursting charge blew open the thin walled casing and scattered the balls at high velocity in a wide pattern.

18. Hill, *Our Boys*, 383.

19. O. R. Howard Thompson and William H. Rauch, *History of the "Bucktails": Kane Rifle Regiment of the Pennsylvania Reserve Corps (13th Pennsylvania Reserves, 42nd of the Line)*, (1906; reprint, with an introduction by Michael A. Cavanaugh, Dayton, Ohio: Morningside House, Inc., 1988), 192 (page citation is to the reprint edition).

20. Hill, *Our Boys*, 384.

21. In his official report on the battle, General Pope stated: "Brig. Gen. John F. Reynolds, commanding the Pennsylvania Reserves, merits the highest commendation at my hands. Prompt, active, and energetic, he commanded his division with distinguished ability...and performed his duties in all situations with zeal and fidelity. Generals Seymour and Meade, of that division, in like manner performed their duties with ability and gallantry and in all fidelity to the Government and to the army." *O. R.*, XII, Pt. 2, 48.

22. *O. R.*, XII, Pt. 2, 398.

23. Hill, *Our Boys*, 386–87.

24. Reinsberg, ed., "A Bucktail Voice," 241–42.

25. In the same issue of the *Genius of Liberty* the following obituary appeared: "It becomes our painful duty to announce the death of Wm. H. Leithead, of Co. G, 8th Penna. Reserves. He was killed on the 28th of August while on a march from Warrenton to Manassas. Having seated himself to rest for a few minutes, a shell exploded in his lap literally tearing him to pieces. Thus fell an estimable young man in whom we felt a deep interest. He had learned in this office 'the art preservative of arts,' and learned it well, and remained several years as an esteemed and useful employee, and here we desired and expected, as he also did, that he should remain. At the breaking out of the rebellion he was among the first to enlist, and left in April, '61, with the first company from this county [the Fayette Guards]. He has participated in all the severe battles, and endured all the hardships to which the gallant Pa. Reserves have been exposed, acquitting himself honorably on every occasion, and enjoying, in a high degree, the respect and confidence of his officers and companions in arms. His remains were interred by his brother soldiers near Gaines' Mills [*sic*: Gainesville] close to the spot where his noble spirit was yielded up, and the resting place of a true friend and gallant soldier was marked by every evidence of respect and affection within the reach of those who survived and loved him...." *Genius of Liberty*, September 11, 1862.

26. Ibid.

27. Springer was promoted to the rank of corporal in March 1862.

CHAPTER 8: "DIE LIKE MEN; DON'T RUN LIKE DOGS!"

1. Robert E. Lee, *The Wartime Papers of Robert E. Lee*, ed. Clifford Dowdy and Louis H. Manarin (Boston: Little, Brown, 1961; reprint, New York: Da Capo Press, n.d.), 292–93 (hereafter cited as *Wartime Papers*) (page citations are to the reprint edition).

2. Stephen Sears, *Bloodiest Day: The Battle of Antietam* (Yorktown, Va.: Eastern Acorn Press, 1990; Reprint. Original edition Harrisburg, Pa.: Historical Times, Inc., 1987), 4 (hereafter cited as *Bloodiest Day*) (page citations are to the reprint edition).

3. Stephen W. Sears, *Landscape Turned Red: The Battle of Antietam* (Boston: Houghton Mifflin Company, 1983), 72 (hereafter cited as *Landscape Turned Red*).

4. Leo W. Faller and John I. Faller, *Dear Folks at Home: The Civil War Letters of Leo W. and John I. Faller*, ed. Milton E. Flower (Harrisburg, Pa.: The Telegraph Press, 1963), 87–89 (hereafter cited as *Dear Folks at Home*). Leo was a private and his brother John a sergeant in the 7th Regiment of the Pennsylvania Reserves.

5. Hill, *Our Boys*, 394.

6. Woodward, *History of the Third Pennsylvania Reserve*, 173.

7. Capt. Samuel Waters's (6th Reserves) brief sketch including excerpts from his diary, Civil War Miscellaneous Collection, 3d Series; USAMHI.

8. Woodward, *Our Campaigns*, 150.

9. Sears, *Landscape Turned Red*, 115.

10. Ibid., 126.

11. Hill, *Our Boys*, 395–96.

12. Darby, *Incidents and Adventures*, 49. Joseph Sturgis and the Confederate major met again following the end of the war and renewed their prior acquaintance on decidedly friendlier terms.

13. *O. R.*, XIX, Pt. 1, 945.

14. Frank Holsinger, "South Mountain, and the Part the Pennsylvania Reserves Took in the Battle," *The National Tribune*, September 27, 1883, p. 7.

15. Hill, *Our Boys*, 397.

16. Darby, *Incidents and Adventures*, 50.

17. *The Confederate Veteran*, Vol. 23, No. 2, February, 1915 (Reprint: Broadfoot's Bookmark, Wendell, N.C.), 72.

18. Sears, *Landscape Turned Red*, 143.

19. Hill, *Our Boys*, 398.

20. Ibid., 399–400.

21. Bates Alexander, "Sergeant's Memoir," 1861–1864, Pennsylvania Save the Flags Collection, USAMHI (hereafter cited as "Sergeant's Memoir"). This "memoir" was published in the form of a series of articles in the *Hummelstown Sun* in the 1890s. The article from which the quotation is taken is dated September 20, 1895.

22. Sears, *Bloodiest Day*, 12.

23. Hill, *Our Boys*, 402.

24. Ibid., 403.

25. The regiment that surprised the second brigade was the 6th North Carolina, not the 6th Georgia. See John Michael Priest, *Antietam, The Soldiers' Battle* (New York: Oxford University Press, 1989), 348 n. 47.

26. Henry Steele Commager, *The Blue and the Gray* (New York: The Fairfax Press, 1950), 306.

27. Silas Milton Baily was born in Brownsville and raised in Uniontown. At the outbreak of the war, he raised an infantry company known as the Greene County Rangers (subsequently Company I of the 8th Regiment of Pennsylvania Reserves) and was elected its captain. Promoted to the rank of major in May 1862, he was seriously wounded at the Battle of Gaines's Mill. After recuperating, he assumed overall command of the 8th Regiment, leading it at the Battles of South Mountain and Antietam, where he had his horse shot out from under him. He was subsequently promoted to the rank of colonel and was wounded again at Fredericksburg. Baily returned to active duty in time to participate in Grant's Overland campaign in the spring of 1864, and in May 1865, he was promoted to the rank of brevet brigadier general of volunteers. After the war, Baily worked as a jeweler and silversmith in Uniontown. He died there in 1900.

28. *O. R.*, XIX, Pt. 1, 274. Major Baily, in his own report, stated that as the 8th Regiment "[p]ass[ed] from their first position, through an open field, they were thrown beneath the galling fire of the unnatural foe. Still, without faltering, they pressed forward to the woods beyond, which they held against superior numbers until relieved. Our loss was less than could have been expected; 11 fell to rise no more; 40 received wounds.... Coolness and great firmness characterized both officers and men." *O. R.*, XIX, Pt. 1, 1093.

29. Hill, *Our Boys*, 404.

30. Ibid., 403–4.

31. Ibid., 405.

32. Darby, *Incidents and Adventures*, 51.

33. This regiment actually was the 1st Texas, part of Hood's brigade commanded by Col. William T. Wofford.

34. Darby, *Incidents and Adventures*, 51. In his Official Report on the Battle of Antietam, General Hooker, the I Corps commander, wrote of the terrible effect of Federal artillery fire on the Confederate troops in the cornfield: "In the time I am writing every stalk of corn in the northern and greater part of the field was cut as closely as could have been done with a knife, and the slain lay in rows precisely as they had stood in their ranks a few moments before. It was never my fortune to witness a more bloody, dismal battle-field." *O. R.*, XIX, Pt. 1, 218.

35. Hill, *Our Boys*, 406–7.

36. Sears, *Landscape Turned Red*, 202.

37. Reinsberg, ed., "A Bucktail Voice," 244. Cordello Collins survived the carnage of Antietam, only to be severely wounded at Gettysburg. On July 2, 1863, the Bucktails fought in the Wheat Field and at Devil's Den. The next day they were posted near Little Round Top and, after the repulse of Pickett's Charge, they were ordered to take out a rebel battery posted beyond the Wheat Field. It was during this action that Collins was wounded. He died August 8, 1863, in the Two Taverns Hospital.

38. Darby, *Incidents and Adventures*, 51–52.

39. Hill, *Our Boys*, 408–9.

40. When Lee withdrew across the Potomac River, a number of Confederate surgeons stayed behind to care for the Southern soldiers who had been too badly wounded to be moved. Of course, both doctors and patients were considered to be prisoners of war, but all could expect to be paroled. One such surgeon, James Mercer Greene of the 17th Mississippi, reflected on how the war had changed him: "My head had whitened and my very soul turned into stone.... A long vista of human blood shuts out the dearest past and a boundless expanse of the same crimson fluid stretches before us in the future. I see no end to it...." James M. Green, letter of September 21, 1862, to Miss Annie R. Shoemaker, Manuscript Department, Duke

University Library, Durham, N.C., quoted in John Michael Priest, *Antietam: The Soldiers' Battle* (New York: Oxford University Press, 1989), 316.

41. Darby, *Incidents and Adventures*, 57. While the field hospitals of both sides more nearly resembled abattoirs in the days following the battle, the surgeons' grim work was interrupted occasionally by a ray of humor. Sergeant Alexander of the 7th Reserves recounted one such occasion: "Confederate surgeons and nurses cared for their wounded, of whom there were about 200. There were some warmly contested arguments on war questions, while a broad streak of good humor was discernable on both sides. A slightly wounded [Confederate] Lt. told Lt. Lantz [of the 7th Reserves], 'Your Gen. Porter was our friend at Bull Run.' 'How so?' 'In not coming up when Pope ordered him.' Says Lantz, 'Well we will conquer you all the same.' The Confederate replied, 'After you Yankees may have killed...all of our men, our women would turn out and fight you with broom sticks.'" Alexander, "Sergeant's Memoir," article dated October 11, 1895.

42. Darby, *Incidents and Adventures*, 58.

43. *Confederate Veteran*, Vol. 4, No. 8, August, 1896 (Reprint: Broadfoot's Bookmark, Wendell, N.C.), 276.

44. Robert Taggart to "Friend George," 3 October 1862, Jarrett Family Papers.

45. Strathern, *Civil War Letters*, 84–85.

46. Ibid., 86–87.

47. Sears, *Landscape Turned Red*, 334.

48. Ibid.

CHAPTER 9: "WE PASSED THROUGH A TERRIBLE FIGHT"

1. Jacob Heffelfinger, 36th Pennsylvania Infantry Regiment, Diaries (Typescript), 30 October 1862 entry, 88, Civil War Times Illustrated Collection, USAMHI (hereafter cited as Heffelfinger Diary).

2. "Handy Jack" was the soldiers' nickname for a small pouch, usually made of leather, which contained thread, buttons, and scissors.

3. Florence C. McLaughlin, ed., "'Dear Sister Jennie-Dear Brother Jacob': The Correspondence Between a Northern Soldier and his Sister in Mechanicsburg, Pennsylvania, 1861–1864," *The Western Pennsylvania Historical Magazine*, 60, no. 3 (July 1977): 215–16 (hereafter cited as "Dear Sister Jennie"). Heffelfinger was promoted to the rank of sergeant December 1, 1861.

4. McClellan, *The Civil War Papers of George B. McClellan*, 482.

5. Alexander, "Sergeant's Memoir," article dated October 25, 1895.

6. Ibid. The regimental officers attempted to put a stop to such plundering, but to no avail, as Alexander recalled: "At halting in evening there were sometimes fences nearby, but by morning, well, what a change was there, no fences in sight. Guards were at times posted to prevent the soldiery moving the rails, but the wondrous change occurred all the same, while no one was censured. Each guard reported 'No rails taken that I saw,' while the last man on post reported 'I found no rails there.'" Ibid.

7. Heffelfinger Diary, 7 November 1862 entry, 90.

8. Woodward, *Our Campaigns*, 178–79.

9. Darby, *Incidents and Adventures*, 65–66.

10. Woodward, *History of the Third Pennsylvania Reserve*, 204.

11. William Marvel, *The Battle of Fredericksburg* (n.p.: Eastern National Park and Monument Association, 1993), 15. As the shelling increased in intensity, Miss Beale and many other residents fled their homes and took refuge in the nearby countryside: "[C]rowds of women and children had sought refuge in this sheltered spot and as night drew on they were in great distress, they could not return to the town which was already in possession of the enemy, and they had fled too hastily to bring with them the...necessities of life. Some few had stretched blue yarn counterpanes or pieces of old carpet over sticks, stuck in the ground—and the little ones were huddled together under these tents, the women were weeping the children crying loudly, I saw one walking along with a baby in her arms and another little one not three years old clinging to her dress and crying 'I want to go home.' My heart ached for them...." Ibid.

12. *O. R.*, XXI, 71.

13. Alexander, "Sergeant's Memoir," article dated November 3, 1895.

14. Henry Flick Military Record, Civil War Miscellaneous Collection, USAMHI. Other than this account, there is no evidence that the Confederate artillerists actually drove stakes in the ground as range markers.

15. Alexander, "Sergeant's Memoir," article dated November 10, 1895.

16. Francis Augustin O'Reilly, *The Fredericksburg Campaign: Winter War on the Rappahannock* (Baton Rouge, La.: Louisiana State University Press, 2003), 172 (hereafter cited as *The Fredericksburg Campaign*).

17. Alexander, "Sergeant's Memoir," articles dated December 6, 1895, and December 10, 1895. In 1895, Alexander wrote that the "dying Georgian at Fredericksburg can never pass from my memory. 'Tis as vivid in mind to-day as then." Ibid., article dated December 6, 1895.

18. Heffelfinger Diary, 13 December 1862 entry, 97–98.

19. Woodward, *History of the Third Pennsylvania Reserve*, 212.

20. Sypher, *History of the Pa Reserves*, 415.

21. *O. R.*, XXI, 140.

22. Ibid., 139.

23. O'Reilly, *The Fredericksburg Campaign*, 173.

24. NARA, RG 94, AGO, Muster Rolls of Volunteer Organizations, 8th Pennsylvania Infantry, Regimental Papers.

25. Lee, *Wartime Papers*, 373.

26. Woodward, *History of the Third Reserve*, 218–19.

27. *Genius of Liberty*, January 3, 1863.

CHAPTER 10: "BURNSIDE'S STUCK IN THE MUD"

1. Alexander, "Sergeant's Memoir," article dated July 10, 1896. "Some of the men dug pits, about two feet deep, which they logged up above ground, and stretched their shelter tents over. Comfortable fire-places and chimneys were built, and, with abundance of dry leaves to sleep upon, they got along quite comfortably. Two or four generally bunked together; and by splicing blankets, and lying spoon-fashion, slept quite warm." Woodward, *History of the Third Reserve*, 221.

2. Woodward, *History of the Third Reserve*, 221–22.

3. Freeman Cleaves, *Meade of Gettysburg* (Norman, Okla.: University of Oklahoma Press, 1960), 97.

4. Following General Meade's promotion to command of the V Corps, Colonel Horatio G. Sickel of the 3rd Regiment was given temporary command of the Pennsylvania Reserves.

5. Truxall, *Respects to All*, 34–36.

6. Strathern, *Civil War Letters*, 91.

7. Heffelfinger Diary, 31 December 1862 entry, 102.

8. Strathern, *Civil War Letters*, 93.

9. Darby, *Incidents and Adventures*, 69.

10. Alexander, "Sergeant's Memoir," article dated July 17, 1896.

11. Truxall, *Respects to All*, 37–38. For several years prior to the Civil War, Adam Bright and his brother, Michael, both of whom had been orphaned, made their home with their uncle and guardian, Emanuel Stotler, on his farm in Penn Township, some fifteen miles east of Pittsburgh. Adam survived the war, married twice, had several children and died in 1888. Michael was killed September 19, 1863, at the Battle of Chickamauga.

12. Hill, *Our Boys*, 204.

13. Affidavit of James W. Eberhart, May 13, 1890; Isaac A. Moore, Sergeant, Soldier's Certificate No. 783,682, Company G, 37th Pennsylvania Infantry and Company G, 191st Pennsylvania Infantry; NARA, RG 15 (hereafter cited as "I. A. Moore Pension Papers"). Captain H. G. Dawson, Moore's commanding officer, noted that "this [was] the first time I had ever known Sergt. Moore to complain. He was one of the largest and ablest young men in the Co. Upon other occasions afterwards, specifically after exposure to cold wet weather, Sergt. Moore was partially disabled by reason of rheumatism.... My recollection now is that Sergt. Moore was unable for duty from this cause...in the Spring 1863, probably in March or April.... I think he suffered severely at times during this period. I always missed him greatly when he was off duty." Affidavit of H. G. Dawson, June 2, 1890; I. A. Moore Pension Papers.

14. McLaughlin, ed., "Dear Sister Jennie," 216–18.

CHAPTER 11: "WHO STOLE BAER'S DUCK?"

1. Colonel H. G. Sickel of the 3rd Regiment had assumed temporary command of the Pennsylvania Reserves when General Meade was assigned to the command of the V Corps. General Abner Doubleday succeeded Sickel and briefly commanded the division until replaced by Brigadier General Samuel W. Crawford on June 3, 1863. General Crawford commanded the Pennsylvania Reserves through the end of their three-year term of service on June 1, 1864.

2. Woodward, *History of the Third Reserve*, 224–25.

3. Darby, *Incidents and Adventures*, 21.

4. Faller and Faller, *Dear Folks at Home*, 101–2.

5. Burke Station was located 12 miles west of Alexandria, approximately midway between Alexandria and Manassas Junction.

6. Darby, *Incidents and Adventures*, 33–34.

7. Ibid., 34.

8. McLaughlin, ed., "Dear Sister Jennie," 219.

9. Sypher, *History of the Pa. Reserves*, 448.

10. On June 15, 1863, Pennsylvania Governor Andrew G. Curtin issued a proclamation that stated: "The State of Pennsylvania is again threatened with invasion, and an army of rebels is approaching our border.... I now appeal to all the citizens of Pennsylvania who love liberty and are mindful of the history and traditions of their revolutionary fathers, and who feel that it is a sacred duty to guard and maintain the free institutions of our country, who hate treason and its abettors, and who are willing to defend their homes and their firesides, and do invoke them, to rise in their might, and rush to the rescue in this hour of imminent peril.... It is now to be determined by deeds, and not by words alone, who are for us and who are against us. That it is the purpose of the enemy to invade our borders with all the strength he can command is now apparent. Our only dependence rests upon the determined action of the citizens of our free Commonwealth. I now, therefore, call upon the people of Pennsylvania capable of bearing arms to enroll themselves in military organizations, and to encourage all others to give aid and assistance to the efforts which will be put forth for the protection of the State and the salvation of our common country." *O. R.*, XXVII, Pt. 3, 145.

11. Faller and Faller, *Dear Folks at Home*, 105–6. Despite being taken prisoner at the Battle of the Wilderness and being sent to Andersonville, John Faller survived the war. He returned to his hometown of Carlisle where he spent nearly fifty years working for the Carlisle Deposit Bank.

12. Heffelfinger Diary, 27 June 1863 entry, 118.

13. Sypher, *History of the Pa. Reserves*, 489.

14. Woodward, *Our Campaigns*, 208.

15. Jeffrey F. Sherry, "'The Terrible Impetuosity': The Pennsylvania Reserves at Gettysburg," *The Gettysburg Magazine* 16 (1997): 73.

16. Sypher, *History of the Pa. Reserves*, 460.

17. Jeffrey F. Sherry, "'The Terrible Impetuosity': The Pennsylvania Reserves at Gettysburg," *The Gettysburg Magazine*, 16 (1997): 74.

18. George Meade, *The Life and Letters of George Gordon Meade*, ed. George Gordon Meade (New York: Charles Scribner's Sons, 1913; reprint, Baltimore: Butternut and Blue, 1994), 122–23 (page citations are to the reprint edition).

19. McLaughlin, ed., "Dear Sister Jennie," 221.

20. The first and third brigades of the Pennsylvania Reserves remained with the Army of the Potomac as the third division of the V Corps through the pursuit of Lee's army into Virginia and the Mine Run campaign of late November 1863. On December 2 the third division crossed the Rapidan River and headed for the line of the Orange & Alexandria Railroad and winter quarters. Rejoining their comrades in the second brigade, the weary Pennsylvanians were posted as follows: the first brigade, under Colonel McCandless, at Bristoe Station; the third brigade, under Colonel Fisher, at Manassas; and the second brigade, under Colonel Sickel, at Alexandria.

21. McLaughlin, ed., "Dear Sister Jennie," 221.

22. Darby, *Incidents and Adventures*, 70.

23. Heffelfinger Diary, 2 November 1863 entry, 135.

24. Colonel Elmer E. Ellsworth was the first Union officer killed after the commencement of hostilities in April 1861. Ellsworth was shot to death by James Jackson, the manager of the Marshall House, an Alexandria Hotel, after he had entered the hotel and removed a Confederate flag from its roof. Ellsworth's body lay in state in the East Room of the White House, and the President and Mrs. Lincoln attended his funeral. Ellsworth quickly became a martyr and was widely celebrated in story and song. Jackson, who was killed as well in the exchange of gunfire, was promptly elevated to similar status in the South.

25. Darby, *Incidents and Adventures*, 71–72.

26. Heffelfinger Diary, 18 October 1863 entry, 133–34. After the war, Jacob Heffelfinger moved to Hampton, Virginia, where he entered the lumber business. He married there, had three children (two of whom died in childhood), and served for a time as president of the local bank. In 1867 he received a commission as a brevet captain for gallant conduct at the Battle of the Wilderness.

27. *Uniontown (Pa.) The American Standard*, April 23, 1863. The meetings to which the writer refers were held in many parts of Fayette County during the early months of 1863 in response to the unbroken string of battlefield disasters suffered by the Army of the Potomac. Many of the speakers blamed the Lincoln administration for such egregious mismanagement of the military that it was "drenching our once happy land with the blood of her sons." *Genius of Liberty*, March 12, 1863. The majority of the resolutions passed at these meetings called for the Federal government to abandon its goal of preserving the Union through force of arms and to commence discussions with the Confederacy to bring the war to a close through a negotiated settlement. A number of the resolutions also dealt with the consequences of President Lincoln's Emancipation Proclamation. There was a widespread fear that freed slaves would stream into the Northern states. The feeling among many Fayette County citizens was that "those who want the niggar ought to have him, pay for him and keep him." *Genius of Liberty*, March 26, 1863.

28. Darby, *Incidents and Adventures*, 76.

29. Ibid., 73–74.

30. Ibid., 76–77.

31. Ibid., 77.

32. Ibid., 79.

33. Ibid., 79–80.

CHAPTER 12: "WE SORROWFULLY LAID HIM TO REST"

1. Cleaves, *Meade of Gettysburg*, 232.

2. U. S. Grant, *Personal Memoirs of U. S. Grant* (New York: Charles Webster & Company, 1886), 2:141 (hereafter cited as *Personal Memoirs*).

3. Andrew J. Elliott, "Corporal and Sergeant's Diary," January 1, 1860—December 31, 1865), entry of May 4, 1864, Pennsylvania Save the Flags Collection, USAMHI (hereafter cited as "Corporal and Sergeant's Diary").

4. Joseph P. Cullen, *Wilderness and Spotsylvania* (Harrisburg, Pa.: Historical Times, Inc., n.d.; reprint, n.p.: Eastern Acorn Press, 1985), 6 (page citations are to the reprint edition).

5. Elliott, "Corporal and Sergeant's Diary," entry of May 5, 1864.

6. John Michael Priest, *Nowhere to Run: The Wilderness, May 4th & 5th, 1864* (Shippensburg, Pa.: White Mane Publishing Company, Inc., 1995), 113. During the withdrawal, the 7th Regiment was deceived into surrendering en masse by two companies of the 61st Georgia.

7. Robert J. McBride, *In the Ranks from the Wilderness to Appomattox Court-House: The War as Seen and Experienced by a Private Soldier in the Army of the Potomac* (Cincinnati: Walden & Stowe, 1881), 31 (hereafter cited as *In the Ranks*).

8. Elliott, "Corporal and Sergeant's Diary," entry of May 6, 1864.

9. *O. R.*, XXXVI, Pt. 1, 540. Other accounts of this action suggest that Sedgwick had managed to restore his lines before the Pennsylvanians arrived on the scene. See Sypher, *History of the Pa. Reserves*, 517.

10. Elliott, "Corporal and Sergeant's Diary," entry of May 7, 1864.

11. Noah Andre Trudeau, *Bloody Roads South: The Wilderness to Cold Harbor, May–June 1864* (Boston: Little, Brown and Company, 1989), 117 (hereafter cited as *Bloody Roads South*).

12. Grant, *Personal Memoirs*, 2:211.

13. Elliott, "Corporal and Sergeant's Diary," entry of May 8, 1864.

14. Trudeau, *Bloody Roads South*, 141.

15. Ibid., 143.

16. Darby, *Incidents and Adventures*, 81–83. After the war, John Sisler's body was removed to the National Cemetery at Fredericksburg, Va.

17. Elliott, "Corporal and Sergeant's Diary," entry of May 10, 1864.

18. Trudeau, *Bloody Roads South*, 152, 154.

19. Ibid., 155.

20. Ibid., 163–64.

21. Elliott, "Corporal and Sergeant's Diary," entry of May 12, 1864.

22. Trudeau, *Bloody Roads South*, 182.

23. Ibid., 181.

24. John A. Willoughby to James R. Simpson, 13 May 1864, Simpson Papers. "Jack" Willoughby was one of three Willoughby brothers who fought in the Civil War. After the war, he returned to Huntington, Pa. where he married and had at least one son. He later moved to Colorado where he died.

25. Emory M. Thomas, *Bold Dragoon, the Life of J. E. B. Stuart* (New York: Vintage Books, 1986), 297.

26. Elliott, "Corporal and Sergeant's Diary," entry of May 14, 1864.

27. Ibid., entry of May 15, 1864.

28. Sypher, *History of the Pa. Reserves*, 534. *O. R.*, XXXVI, Pt. 2, 819.

29. *Genius of Liberty,* June 2, 1864. Those who returned included Capt. H. C. Dawson, 1st Lieut. Jesse B. Ramsey, 2nd Lieut. H. H. McQuilkin, Cpl. Geo. B. Rutter, George H. Ashcraft, James P. Ashcraft, Wm. Peters and Isaac Sampsell, all of Uniontown, and Daniel F. Darr and Joseph L. Warrick of West Newton.

30. See Bill Weidner, "After the Reserves (An Unofficial Regimental History of 190th & 191st Regiments, Pennsylvania Volunteer Infantry)," Manuscript Archive, USAMHI (hereafter cited as Weidner Papers).

31. M. D. Hardin, *History of the Twelfth Regiment Pennsylvania Reserve Volunteer Corps (41st Regiment of the Line), from its Muster into the United States Service, August 10th, 1861, to its Muster Out June 11th, 1864* (New York: M. D. Hardin, 1890), 186 (hereafter cited as *History of the Twelfth Regiment*).

32. McBride, *In the Ranks*, 67.

33. Darby, *Incidents and Adventures*, 85–86.

34. *Southern Historical Society Papers*, Vol. 33 (Richmond, Va.: The Southern Historical Society, 1905; Reprint: Broadfoot Publishing Company, 1991), 59–60.

35. Ibid.

36. McBride, *In the Ranks*, 68–69.

37. Sypher, *History of the Pa. Reserves*, 546–47. Other historians have taken a more skeptical view of the part played by the Reserves at Bethesda Church. For example, Noah Andre Trudeau wrote of them: "These veteran soldiers had an honorable history with the Army of the Potomac, though their fighting quality at this moment [May 30, 1864] was very much open to question. The Pennsylvanians had only one day remaining in their term of enlistment.... Federals in other regiments who had, unlike the Pennsylvanians, re-upped for the duration harbored the suspicion that these once vaunted troops were no longer to be trusted in combat." Trudeau, *Bloody Roads South*, 254. Trudeau fails to note, however, that more than 2,200 soldiers from the various Pennsylvania Reserve regiments had reenlisted for the duration of the war prior to the fight at Bethesda Church on May 30, 1864, or had time remaining on their original enlistments as of that date. These veterans fought their way through to Petersburg, only to be captured almost to a man at Globe Tavern in August 1864. Many of them would die in Confederate prisons before the year was out. See the Weidner Papers for a detailed accounting of the composition of the 190th and 191st

Pennsylvania Volunteer Infantry Regiments, to which these veterans of the Pennsylvania Reserves were transferred. Thirty-four soldiers from Company G of the old 8th Reserves (who initially were transferred to the 12th Reserves on May 15, 1864) were assigned to the new 191st PVI, the great majority of them to its Company G. Only about 75 8th Regiment veterans whose terms of enlistment had expired as of May 16, 1864, left the front and headed for home. See *O. R.*, XXXVI, Pt. 2, 818–19.

38. McBride, *In the Ranks*, 70–71.

39. Thomas Chamberlin, *History of the One Hundred and Fiftieth Regiment Pennsylvania Volunteers: Second Regiment, Bucktail Brigade* (Philadelphia: F. McManus Jr. & Co., 1905), 254. George Darby said: "After the battle the division marched away to the tune of 'Home again, home again, from a foreign shore,' and the organization known as the Pennsylvania Reserves passed out of existence in the full tide of battle." Darby, *Incidents and Adventures*, 86.

CHAPTER 13: "I GUESS I'LL RIDE THAT HORSE AGAIN NOW!"

1. Sypher, *History of the Pa. Reserves*, 548.

2. Weidner Papers, USAMHI, 1–1. The figure of 2,231 includes a number of soldiers whose original terms of enlistment had not then expired.

3. These two regiments were also known as the First and Second Veteran Reserves. The 190th Regiment was comprised of veterans from the old 1st, 7th, and 9th Reserve Regiments, with several companies of the 10th, 11th, 12th, and 13th Regiments. The 191st Regiment was comprised of men from the old 2nd, 5th, 6th , and 8th Reserves, and the remaining companies of the 10th Regiment. See Weidner Papers, USAMHI, 1–3, n. 2.

4. Grant, *Personal Memoirs*, 2:276.

5. Commenting upon the fraternization between the two sides, General Meade noted: "I believe these two armies would...make peace in an hour, if the matter rested with them; not on terms to suit politicians on either side, but such as the world at large would acknowledge as honorable...." George Meade, *The Life and Letters of George Gordon Meade*, ed. George Gordon Meade (New York: Charles Scribner's Sons, 1913), 2:207.

6. Darby, *Incidents and Adventures*, 93–94.

7. *O. R.*, XL, Pt. 1, 472.

8. Grant, *Personal Memoirs*, 2:324.

9. Darby, *Incidents and Adventures*, 100.

10. *Washington (D.C.) National Tribune*, August 9, 1900 (hereafter cited as *National Tribune*).

11. Darby, *Incidents and Adventures*, 100.

12. *National Tribune*, August 9, 1900.

13. Darby, *Incidents and Adventures*, 100–101. It is questionable whether it was, in fact, General Mahone who was taken prisoner, albeit temporarily. There is no indication in the *Official Records* that such was the case. It is more likely that it was one of Mahone's staff officers who was the unfortunate detainee. John Horn, in his account of the destruction of the Weldon Railroad, describes such an occurrence involving two staff officers whom General Mahone had sent to contact A. P. Hill: "One after the other, the two staff officers took a short road...[that] took them over the ground that Mahone's Brigade had just crossed. Though by this time most of Clingman's and Colquitt's men bringing off the Federal prisoners had reentered Confederate lines, many stragglers and fugitives of both sides still roamed the woods. A squad of Union fugitives captured the lead staff officer. The other staffer saw his colleague captured, rallied a few Confederate stragglers, and in turn captured the Federals, thus releasing his colleague. Moments later another group of Federals captured this whole party and took it with them through the rear of Mahone's Brigade toward Union lines. Observing this, Mahone put himself at the head of a group of his men and rushed on the Federals. Capturing them, the Major General freed the captive rebel staffers and stragglers." John Horn, *The Destruction of the Weldon Railroad, Deep Bottom, Globe Tavern, and Reams Station, August 14–25, 1864* (Lynchburg, Va.: H. E. Howard, Inc., 1991), 84.

14. Powell, *The Fifth Army Corps*, 713.

15. McBride, *In the Ranks*, 118–19.

16. *Confederate Veteran*, Vol. 29, No. 6, June, 1921 (Reprint: Broadfoot's Mark, Wendell, N.C.), 216.

17. *Genius of Liberty*, August 25, 1864. The seriousness with which Confederate General Robert E. Lee viewed the loss of the Weldon Railroad is revealed in a communication that he sent to Jefferson Davis August 21, 1864. In it, Lee stated, "I think it is [the enemy's] purpose to endeavor to compel the evacuation of our present position by cutting off our supplies, and that he will not renew the attempt to drive us away by force." Robert E. Lee, *The Wartime Papers of Robert E. Lee,* eds. Clifford Dowdey and Louis Manarin (Boston: Little, Brown, 196; reprint, New York: Da Capo Press, n.d.), 842.

18. Grant, *Personal Memoirs*, 2:325.

19. Samuel P. Bates, *History of Pennsylvania Volunteers* (Harrisburg, Pa.: B. Singerly, State Printer, 1871), 5:281.

CHAPTER 14: "TODAY I AM TWENTY YEARS OLD"

1. The diary of Thomas W. Springer (Call No. 7093-V) is held by the University of Virginia, Charlottesville, Va., in the Albert and Shirley Small Special Collections Library. Publication of the diary is with the permission of the University of Virginia, the grant of which is gratefully acknowledged. In this chapter supplemental material and/or citations that normally would appear in endnotes is referenced by one or more asterisks within the text of the daily diary entries. Such material is then presented immediately following the relevant diary entry.

CHAPTER 15: "TIS A HARD CHRISTMAS FOR US"

1. The diary of James W. Eberhart is held by the Historical Society of Western Pennsylvania, Pittsburgh, Pa., in their Library and Archives Division. Publication of excerpts from the diary is with the permission of the Historical Society of Western Pennsylvania, the grant of which is gratefully acknowledged. In this chapter, supplemental material and/or citations that normally would appear in endnotes are referenced by one or more asterisks within the text of the daily diary entries. Such material is then presented immediately following the relevant diary entry.

CHAPTER 16: "THE PEACE THEIR VALOR HAD ESTABLISHED"

1. *The American Standard*, March 30, 1865. It is believed that "S," the author of this letter, was Joseph W. Sturgis, one of the original Fayette Guards. Sturgis reenlisted as a veteran volunteer, avoided capture at Weldon Railroad and was still on active duty in March 1865. Also, he authored the earlier letter that is referenced in the second paragraph of the instant letter.

2. Ibid.

3. Ibid. It should be noted that Isaac A. Moore was a sergeant, not a private as stated, having been promoted to that rank September 1, 1862.

4. Darby, *Incidents and Adventures*, 120.

5. See the entry for October 7, 1864, in Thomas W. Springer's diary, Chapter Fourteen. Sergeant Isaac A. Moore was among the escapees.

6. Darby, *Incidents and Adventures*, 144–45.

7. Ibid., 155, 155–56.

8. Ibid., 167–68.

9. Ibid., 176–77.

10. Darby's actual date of parole was March 13, 1865, according to his Company Muster-out Roll.

11. Darby, *Incidents and Adventures*, 183.

12. Ibid., 184, 185. George Darby reminisced at length about his friend, James Eberhart, in his book: "Among the rank and file composing a company of American volunteers may be found men of such sterling qualities of both head and heart as to command the admiration and respect of the entire company. Such a man was Sergeant James W. Eberhart, of Company G. Generous, kind-hearted and uncomplaining, he cheerfully performed any duty assigned to him, however arduous or dangerous it may have been. Brave and courageous at all times, yet so gentle and kind to all that he never aroused the ire of anyone. His grandfather was a patriotic soldier during the 'Times that tried men's souls' at Valley Forge, and the

grandson was not a whit behind the grandsire in soldierly qualities during the war of the Great Rebellion.... In that hell-hole of misery, starvation and death, Salisbury, [Eberhart] was the Good Samaritan, visiting the hospital, cheering the despondent and despairing and relieving the misery of the sick and dying comrades. Although starving, with a devotion sublime, a self-abnegation unequalled, he deprived himself of his rations of bread that he might make poultices for those desperate sufferings were greater even than his own. He was attacked by the scurvy and his teeth one by one dropped from his jaws...but under all trying conditions whatsoever he remained the same kind, congenial and uncomplaining [comrade]." Ibid., 185–87.

13. George W. Darby was promoted to the rank of corporal May 5, 1865, to sergeant June 1, 1865, and was honorably discharged June 28, 1865.

14. Darby, *Incidents and Adventures*, 188.

15. It was in the mid-1890s that Darby wrote *Incidents and Adventures in Rebeldom*. The book was published in Pittsburgh in 1899.

16. Physician's Affidavit, Dr. James R. McCarrell, M.D.; George W. Darby, Sergeant, Soldier's Certificate No. 972,179, Company G, 191st Pennsylvania Infantry; NARA, RG 15. Darby was first pensioned at the rate of $8.00 per month based upon partial disability related to his Civil War service. This was increased in 1904 to $12.00 per month based upon total disability. In 1906, Darby was awarded a pension of $24.00 per month by virtue of a private bill enacted by the United States Congress.

17. In an out-of-sequence entry not included in Chapter Fifteen, Eberhart noted that the prisoners "left prison about 2 pm [February 22, 1865]. Reached our lines about 8 or 10 of March at Wilmington N.C. What a glorious Sight it was to see Old Glory a waving when we got off the Rebel cars. The first troops we seen was the Colored troops and they would give you anything you wanted that they had."

18. Affidavit of Naoma Roley, August 5, 1890; James W. Eberhart, Sergeant, Soldier's Certificate No. 857, 807, Company G, 191st Pennsylvania Infantry; NARA, RG 15 (hereafter cited as Eberhart Pension Papers). Roley added that Eberhart "never recovered to his former health, for I saw him in Pittsburgh [in 1881]. He was then trying to sell carpet sweepers for a living."

19. Eberhart stated in a deposition taken in connection with his application for pension increase that "I had scurvy while in Salisbury Prison. I first suffered from it in Dec. 1864 and suffered from it the rest of the time I was in prison. My teeth got loose and my gums swelled and bled.... I lost some teeth while I was in Salisbury Prison, not more than two or three. I now have but eight teeth on my lower jaw, they are front teeth, and none on my upper jaw. I lost almost all of the missing teeth during the five years right after discharge." Deposition of James W. Eberhart, April 14, 1901; Eberhart Pension Papers.

20. Deposition of Joseph W. Sturgis, August 22, 1901; Eberhart Pension Papers.

21. Robert E. Denny, *The Civil War Years: A Day-by-Day Chronicle of the Life of a Nation* (New York: Sterling Publishing Company, 1992), 570. One participant, Sergeant Locus Barber of the 15th Illinois Volunteer Infantry, recalled the day's festivities: "'cleared off pleasant during the night. Moved camp to day to the south side of the Potomac in full view of the City of Washington. The Capitol towers up majestically above all the other buildings. We can see the White House, War Department, Washington Monument, and Smithsonian.... To day the army of the Potomac was reviewed by [General U. S.] Grant, [General George G.] Meade, President [Johnson], Secretary of War [Stanton] and other high government officials. The army was dressed in its gayest suit. The soldiers appeared splendid, showing the effects of good discipline.... Their step was elastic and guided by a strict military gait, quite different from the free step of Sherman's army. To-morrow Sherman's army appears upon the stage. Thousands of visitors from all parts of the United States are flocking to the Capital to witness these grand reviews, the largest and most brilliant ever known....'" Ibid., 571.

22. Joshua Lawrence Chamberlain, *The Passing of the Armies: An Account of the Final Campaign of the Army of the Potomac, Based upon Personal Reminiscences of the Fifth Army Corps* (New York: G. P. Putnam's Sons, 1915), 347.

23. Deposition of James W. Eberhart, April 14, 1901; Eberhart Pension Papers.

24. In 1920, Emma Eberhart, then 81 years of age and still living in Los Angeles, filed an application for a widow's pension. In a supporting letter, she advised the pension commissioner that "[a]t the time my husband left me...I had some money left to me by an Aunt which I am using it is nearly gone, even necessities are so costly. I think I can now honorably request a pension. I do not wish to be a burden on

anyone. I have only two sons, both married, [who] were not called out in the last war. I hope to enclose the papers that you require. I remain yours respectfully. Mrs. Emma H. Eberhart." Emma H. Eberhart to G. M. Saltzgaber, May 11, 1920; Eberhart Pension Papers. On May 1, 1920, Emma Eberhart began to receive a monthly widow's pension of $30.

25. Affidavit of Andrew H. Dutton, April 22, 1890; I. A. Moore Pension Papers. In a similar affidavit, James Eberhart described the conditions that led to his friend's physical reduction: "[I] was with him [Moore] a prisoner of war at Richmond, Belle Island and Sailsbury N.C. and saw him, one of the stoutest & healthiest men we had, virtually and a mere wreck when released. I often thought that he would of never lived 30 days longer when he was a going so fast from exposure, starvation and diarrhea. Why I know he had it is because me and him boiled oak bark to check it on both of us as it was a very hard matter to get anything from the Rebel doctors." Affidavit of James W. Eberhart, May 13, 1890; I. A. Moore Pension Papers.

26. Affidavit of Dr. F. C. Robinson, n.d.; I. A. Moore Pension Papers.. Dr. Robinson noted in his affidavit that Moore suffered from chronic diarrhea and rheumatism in his back and lower extremities. Robinson also stated: "I was medical examiner for pensions here for thirteen years and during that time I was so thoroughly convinced that his disabilities were pensionable that I several times suggested to him to make an application, but he was reluctant to do so and procrastinated and deferred until the present time when he finds that with the advance of age his attacks become more frequent and severe." Ibid.

27. "Scrap Book," 3:98. Call No. PR974.884, held in the Pennsylvania Room, Uniontown Public Library, Uniontown, Pa.

28. *Genius of Liberty*, December 27, 1921.

29. In the years following his discharge, Hill was unable to engage in any form of manual labor due to the severity of his injury. He described his disability as follows in a Declaration for Increase of an Invalid Pension filed in May 1873: "By amputation of the left thigh-upper third-or about three inches from the hip joint, in consequence of a gunshot wound received in the Battle of Antietam, that he [Hill] has never been able to wear an artificial leg, and that he is obliged to walk with the aid of a pair of crutches, or with one crutch and a cane." Declaration of Ashbel F. Hill, May 14, 1873; Ashbel F. Hill, Sergeant, Soldier's Certificate No. 19921, Company D, 37th Pennsylvania Infantry (the Pennsylvania Reserves); NARA, RG 15 (hereafter cited as Hill Pension Papers). An examining surgeon verified the nature of Hill's condition in a certificate filed in support of the declaration: "The leg was amputated very high up and subsequently the bone was sawed again as it protruded through [the] flaps. The stump is less than three inches in length and he cannot wear an artificial substitute." Examining Surgeon's Certificate No. 17721; Hill Pension Papers.

30. Hill, *Our Boys*, 410–12.

31. In February 1879, Hill's personal representative, William A. Coffman, filed with the Federal Bureau of Pensions a "Petition for Allowance from Arrears due a Deceased Pensioner to Defray Expenses of Last Sickness and Burial," stating that "the expenses of the last sickness and burial of said Ashbel Hill were borne by me...and that the entire assets of the decedent are insufficient to pay the above expenses [because] he has no estate." Petition of William A. Coffman, February 7, 1879; Hill Pension Papers.

32. *Genius of Liberty*, November 9, 1876.

33. In an article on Uniontown's role in the Civil War published in 1896, C. H. Livingston remembered the Springer boys: "In the years gone by I was a young man in Uniontown and among my young friends I remember three bright, intelligent, happy-hearted young fellows who are today sleeping their long sleep, two at Andersonville and one at Salisbury prison cemeteries. John Springer and his brother Thomas, sons of D. Merch. Springer, and John (Tude) Rutter, son of John Rutter, born in Uniontown, died victims of southern prisons." *Uniontown (Pa.) Daily News Standard*, July 4, 1896, Third Part, 17.

CHAPTER 17: "YOU COME TO HONOR THE SOLDIERS OF '61"

1. Louis A. Brown, *The Salisbury Prison: A Case Study of Confederate Military Prisons 1861–1865* (Wilmington, N.C.: Broadfoot Publishing Company, 1992), 141 (hereafter cited as *The Salisbury Prison*), quoting from the diary of Augustus H. Ferris, entry for October 27, 1864.

2. Brown, *The Salisbury Prison*, 141, quoting George W. Swift, *Experiences of a Falmouth Boy in Rebel Prisons* (Falmouth, Mass.: The Independent Press, 1899), 17–20. Any usable clothing worn by deceased prisoners was removed and distributed among the ill-clothed prisoners who remained alive.

3. *Pennsylvania at Salisbury*, 7.

4. Colonel Walker served during the Civil War with Knap's Independent Battery E, Pennsylvania Light Artillery.

5. The *Salisbury Post* described the figure thusly: "Surmounting the arch is a bronze figure, representing a forlorn prisoner, with head bent, arms hanging limply and having a general appearance of dejection and despair that makes the cold bronze to seem almost alive." *Salisbury (N.C.) The Salisbury Post*, November 18, 1910 (hereafter cited as *The Salisbury Post*).

6. *Pennsylvania at Salisbury*,17 (facing illustration).

7. Ibid.

8. The *Uniontown Morning Herald* reported that: "I. A. Moore, one of the Civil War veterans who languished in the military prison at Salisbury, N. C., has been invited by the United States government to assist in the dedication of a monument erected at Salisbury. The ceremonies will be held November 16 at noon and Mr. Moore will start this morning. The entire expense of the trip will be borne by the government. All the survivors who were incarcerated in the prison have been given free transportation. Mr. Moore is one of the few survivors of the 25 Fayette Countians who were imprisoned in the Salisbury pen during the war. He spent four months there. Many of the state officials will be present." *Uniontown (Pa) Uniontown Morning Herald*, November 15, 1910.

9. *The Salisbury Post*, November 18, 1910.

10. *Pennsylvania at Salisbury*, 18, 11.

11. Ibid., 26. Mass communication via radio and television were unknown in 1910. Indeed, public speakers could not even avail themselves of the public address systems so familiar to us today. It was an age of oratory. In the remainder of this chapter, I have tried to place the reader in the audience with the old veterans as they listened to the various speakers and took part in a ceremony that surely evoked their deepest emotions.

12. Ibid., 27.

13. Ibid.

14. In May 1909, a magnificent monument had been erected to the memory of the Confederate dead of Rowan County, N.C. It stands today at the intersection of West Innes and Church Streets in Historic Downtown Salisbury.

15. *Pennsylvania at Salisbury*, 28–29.

16. Ibid., 29–33.

17. Mrs. McDonald, of Pittsburgh, was widely known among the members of the Pennsylvania Chapters of the Grand Army of the Republic as "Comrade Bob." The song, "Lorena," one of the best-loved ballads of the Civil War era, was generally considered to be a Southern song, but it was widely sung in the camps of the Union army as well.

18. *Pennsylvania at Salisbury*, 33–34. One may wonder whether Isaac Moore and James Eberhart were inclined to consider "the old Salisbury prison" a myth. Their memories of the harsh months they spent there in the winter of 1864–65 were unlikely to have dimmed with the passage of time.

19. Ibid., 35–36.

20. Ibid., 36–37.

21. *The Salisbury Post*, November 18, 1910.

22. *Pennsylvania at Salisbury*, 37.

23. Ibid., 37–41.

24. Recent scholarly research has placed the number of Union dead at Salisbury at approximately four thousand. See generally Brown, *The Salisbury Prison*, 142–45, and, in particular, Appendices R and U thereto.

25. *Pennsylvania at Salisbury*, 43–44.

26. In language representative of the era, the editor of *Pennsylvania at Salisbury* noted that "[t]he absence of a stenographer at the dedication ceremonies was very much regretted, it preventing us from inserting the masterly, patriotic and scholarly address of Governor Edwin S. Stuart.... It was a field day of oratory and of all the speakers that addressed the assembly, no one was more happily and enthusiastically received

than the handsome, stalwart Governor of Pennsylvania. The reputation of Pennsylvania's sons suffered none at his hands, and in no wise was it dimmed or lessened by him; only additional lustre added laurels to the fame of Pennsylvania resulting." Ibid., 45.

27. Ibid.

28. Ibid., 46–53.

29. *The Salisbury Post*, November 18, 1910.

30. Ibid.

31. "The old soldiers prized these souvenirs very highly. The beautiful white cotton was an emblem of peace, and with the red, white and blue of North Carolina mingled with the yellow of Pennsylvania made very beautiful souvenirs." Ibid.

32. Isaac Andrew Moore's letter appears in its entirety at Appendix F.

APPENDICES

1. *O. R., Series II*, VII, 1128–30.

2. Ibid., 1219–21.

3. *O. R., Series II*, VIII, 167, 168.

4. Ibid., 245–51.

5. Ibid., 252.

6. Moore, *A History of the Moore Family*, 68–70.

Bibliography

Published Sources

Books

Alexander, Edward Porter. *Fighting for the Confederacy: The Personal Recollections of General Edward Porter Alexander*. Ed. Gary W. Gallagher. Chapel Hill: University of North Carolina Press, 1989.

Baldwin, James J., III. *The Struck Eagle: A Biography of Brigadier General Micah Jenkins*. Shippensburg, Pa.: Burd Street Press, 1996.

Barnes, William. *The Diary of a Civil War Soldier: Private William Barnes....* Comp. Charlotte Palmer. Washington, Pa.: Washington County Historical Society, 2002.

Bates, Samuel P. *History of the Pennsylvania Volunteers 1861–65*. 5 vols. Harrisburg, Pa.: B. Singerly, State Printer, 1871.

Bollet, Alfred Jay, M.D. *Civil War Medicine: Challenges and Triumphs*. Tucson: Galen Press, 2002.

Brown, Louis A. *The Salisbury Prison: A Case Study of Confederate Military Prisons 1861–1865*. Wilmington, N.C.: Broadfoot Publishing Co., 1992.

Buel, Clarence C., and Robert U. Johnson, eds. *Battles and Leaders of the Civil War*. 4 vols. 1884–1887; Reprint, Secaucus, N.J.: Castle, n.d.

Burton, Brian K. *Extraordinary Circumstances: The Seven Days Battles*. Bloomington, Ind.: Indiana University Press, 2001.

Catton, Bruce. *Mr. Lincoln's Army*. New York: Anchor Books, Doubleday, 1951.

———. *The American Heritage Picture History of the Civil War*. New York: American Heritage Publishing Co., 1960.

Chamberlain, Joshua Lawrence. *The Passing of the Armies....* New York: G. P. Putnam's Sons, 1915.

Chamberlin, Thomas. *History of the One Hundred and Fiftieth Regiment Pennsylvania Volunteers: Second Regiment, Bucktail Brigade*. Philadelphia: F. McManus Jr. & Co., 1905.

Christian, C. B. "The Battle at Bethesda Church." In *Southern Historical Society Papers*. Ed. R. A. Brock. 1905. Reprint, n.p.: Broadfoot Publishing Co., 1991.

Cleaves, Freeman. *Meade of Gettysburg*. Norman, Okla.: University of Oklahoma Press, 1960.

Coates, Earl J., and Dean S. Thomas. *An Introduction to Civil War Small Arms*. Gettysburg, Pa.: Thomas Publications, 1990.

Commager, Henry Steele, ed. *The Blue and the Gray*. 1950. Reprint, New York: The Fairfax Press, 1982.

Cooling, Benjamin Franklin, III, and Walter H. Owen, II. *Mr. Lincoln's Forts: A Guide to the Civil War Defenses of Washington*. Shippensburg, Pa.: White Mane Publishing Co., 1988.

Cooling, Benjamin Franklin, III. *Symbol, Sword, and Shield: Defending Washington during the Civil War*. Shippensburg, Pa.: White Mane Publishing Co., 1991.

Cullen, Joseph P. "Battle of the Wilderness." In *Wilderness and Spotsylvania*. Conshohocken, Pa.: Eastern Acorn Press, 1985. Reissued with permission of Historical Times, Inc. Originally published in *Civil War Times Illustrated*.

Darby, George. *Incidents and Adventures in Rebeldom: Libby, Belle-Isle, Salisbury*. Pittsburgh: Press of Rawsthorne Engraving & Printing Co., 1899.

Davis, George B., Leslie J. Perry, and Joseph W. Kirkley. *The Official Military Atlas of the Civil War*. Comp. Calvin D. Coles. 1891. Reprint, New York: Gramercy Books, 1983.

DeGregorio, William A. *The Complete Book of U.S. Presidents*. Rev. and exp. ed. New York: Wings Books, 1993.

Denny, Robert E. *The Civil War Years: A Day-by-Day Chronicle of the Life of a Nation*. New York: Sterling Publishing Co., 1992.

———. *Civil War Prisons and Escapes: A Day-by-Day Chronicle*. New York: Sterling Publishing Co., 1993.

———. *Civil War Medicine: Care and Comfort of the Wounded*. New York: Sterling Publishing Co., 1994.

Edwards, William B. *Civil War Guns: The Complete Story of Federal and Confederate Small Arms....* Rev. ed. Gettysburg, Pa.: Thomas Publications, 1997.

Ellis, Franklin. *History of Fayette County, Pennsylvania....* 1882. Reprint, Evansville, Ind.: whipporwill publications, 1988.

Faller, Leo W., and John I. Faller. *Dear Folks at Home: The Civil War Letters of Leo W. and John I. Faller.* Ed. Milton E. Flower. Harrisburg, Pa.: Telegraph Press, 1963.

Fox, Arthur B. *Pittsburgh During the American Civil War.* Chicora, Pa.: Mechling Bookbinding, 2002.

Freeman, Douglas Southall. *Lee.* Abridgment in one volume by Richard Harwell of the 4-vol. *R. E. Lee.* New York: Charles Scribner's Sons, 1961.

Garrison, Webb, with Cheryl Garrison. *The Encyclopedia of Civil War Usage: An Illustrated Compendium of the Everyday Language of Soldiers and Civilians.* Nashville, Tenn.: Cumberland House Publishing, 2001.

Gibbs, Joseph. *Three Years in the Bloody Eleventh: The Campaigns of a Pennsylvania Reserves Regiment.* University Park, Pa.: Pennsylvania State University Press, 2002.

Gienapp, William E. *The Origins of the Republican Party: 1852–1856.* New York: Oxford University Press, 1987.

Glass, Paul. *Singing Soldiers: A History of the Civil War in Song.* New York: Da Capo Press, 1986.

Grant, U. S. *Personal Memoirs of U. S. Grant.* 2 vols. New York: Charles L. Webster & Co., 1886.

Hadden, James. *A History of Uniontown, the County Seat of Fayette County, Pennsylvania.* 1913. Reprint, Evansville, Ind.: whipporwill publications, 1987.

Hennessy, John J. *Return to Bull Run: The Campaign and Battle of Second Manassas.* New York: Simon & Schuster, 1993.

Hill, A. F. *Our Boys: Personal Experiences of a Soldier in the Army of the Potomac.* 1886. Reprint, Mt. Vernon, Ind.: Windmill Publications, 1994.

Horn, John. *The Petersburg Campaign: The Destruction of the Weldon Railroad, Deep Bottom, Globe Tavern, and Reams Station, August 14–25, 1864.* Lynchburg, Va.: H. E. Howard, 1991.

Jordan, Ervin L., Jr. *Black Confederates and Afro-Yankees in Civil War Virginia.* Charlottesville: University Press of Virginia, 1995.

Judson, Amos M. *History of the Eighty-Third Regiment Pennsylvania Volunteers.* N.d. Reprint, Dayton, Ohio: Morningside House, 1986.

Kearny, Philip. *Letters from the Peninsula: The Civil War Letters of General Philip Kearny.* Ed. William B. Styple. Kearny, N.J.: Belle Grove Publishing Co., 1988.

Lee, Robert E. *The Wartime Papers of Robert E. Lee.* Ed. Clifford Dowdy and Louis Manarin. 1961. Reprint, New York: Da Capo Press, n.d.

Longstreet, James. *From Manassas to Appomattox: Memoirs of the Civil War in America*. Philadelphia: J. B. Lippincott Co., 1896.

Mangum, A. W. "Salisbury Prison." *Histories of the Several Regiments and Battalions from North Carolina in the Great War 1861–'65*. Ed. Walter Clark. Vol. 4. Goldsboro, N.C.: Nash Brothers, 1901.

Marvel, William. *The Battle of Fredericksburg*. N.p.: Eastern National Park and Monument Association, 1993.

McBride, Robert J. *In the Ranks from the Wilderness to Appomattox Court House: The War as Seen and Experienced by a Private Soldier in the Army of the Potomac*. Cincinnati: Waldon & Stowe, 1881.

McCall, George A. *The Seven Days Contests: Pennsylvania Reserves, General McCall's Report and Accompanying Documents*. New York: Office of the Rebellion Record, 1864.

Meade, George. *The Life and Letters of George Gordon Meade*. Ed. George Gordon Meade. 1913. 2 vols. Army of the Potomac Series. Reprint, Baltimore: Butternut & Blue, 1994.

Miller, William J. *Civil War City: Harrisburg, Pennsylvania, 1861–1865*. Shippensburg, Pa.: White Mane Publishing Co., 1990.

Minnigh, H. N. *History of Company K: 1st Penn'a Reserves*. 1891. Reprint, with new introductory material, Gettysburg, Pa.: Thomas Publications, 1998.

Moore, Rogan H. *A History and Genealogy of the Moore Family of Fayette County, Pennsylvania*. Bowie, Md.: Heritage Books, 1999.

Murfin, James V. *The Gleam of Bayonets: The Battle of Antietam and the Maryland Campaign of 1862*. New York: Yoseloff, 1965.

Nichols, Edward J. *Toward Gettysburg: A Biography of General John F. Reynolds*. University Park, Pa.: Pennsylvania State University Press, 1958. Reprint, Gaithersburg, Md.: Olde Soldier Books, 1987.

O'Reilly, Frank A. *The Fredericksburg Campaign: "Stonewall" Jackson at Fredericksburg, The Battle of Prospect Hill, December 13, 1862*. Lynchburg, Va.: H. E. Howard, 1993.

O'Reilly, Francis Augustin. *The Fredericksburg Campaign: Winter War on the Rappahannock*. Baton Rouge: Louisiana State University Press, 2003.

Pennsylvania at Salisbury, North Carolina: Ceremonies at the Dedication of the Memorial. N.p.: C. E. Aughinbaugh, Printer to the State of Pennsylvania, 1912.

Pennypacker, Isaac R. *General Meade*. 1901. Reprint, Gaithersburg, Md.: Olde Soldier Books, 1987.

Phillips, David. *Maps of the Civil War: The Roads They Took*. New York: Barnes & Noble Books, 1999.

Powell, William H. *The Fifth Army Corps....* 1895. Reprint, Dayton, Ohio: Press of Morningside Bookshop, 1984.

Priest, John Michael. *Antietam: The Soldiers' Battle*. Shippensburg, Pa.: White Mane Publishing Co., 1989. Reprint, New York: Oxford University Press, 1993.

———. *Before Antietam: The Battle for South Mountain*. Shippensburg, Pa.: White Mane Publishing Co., 1992.

———. *Nowhere to Run: The Wilderness, May 4th & 5th, 1864*. Shippensburg, Pa.: White Mane Publishing Co., 1995.

Rhea, Gordon C. *The Battle of the Wilderness: May 5–6, 1864*. Baton Rouge: Louisiana State University Press, 1994.

———. *The Battles for Spotsylvania Court House and the Road to Yellow Tavern: May 7–12, 1864*. Baton Rouge: Louisiana State University Press, 1997.

———. *To the North Anna River: Grant and Lee, May 13–25, 1864*. Baton Rouge: Louisiana State University Press, 2000.

———. *Cold Harbor: Grant and Lee, May 26–June 3, 1864*. Baton Rouge: Louisiana State University Press, 2002.

Sauers, Richard A. "The Pennsylvania Reserves: George A. McCall's Division on the Peninsula." In *The Peninsula Campaign of 1862: Yorktown to the Seven Days*. Ed. William Miller. Campbell, Calif.: Savas Woodbury Publishers, 1993.

Sears, Stephen W. *Landscape Turned Red*. Boston: Houghton Mifflin Co., 1983.

———. *George B. McClellan: The Young Napoleon*. New York: Ticknor & Fields, 1988.

———. *The Civil War Papers of George B. McClellan: Selected Correspondence, 1860–1865*. New York: Ticknor & Fields, 1989. Reprint, New York: Da Capo Press, 1992.

———. *To the Gates of Richmond: The Peninsula Campaign*. New York: Ticknor & Fields, 1992.

———. *Bloodiest Day: The Battle of Antietam*. Yorktown, Va.: Eastern Acorn Press, 1990. Issued with permission of Historical Times, Inc., the original publisher.

Sneden, Robert Knox. *Eye of the Storm*. Ed. Charles F. Bryan, Jr. and Nelson D. Lankford. New York: Simon & Schuster, Touchstone, 2002.

Speer, Lonnie. *Portals to Hell: Military Prisons of the Civil War*. Mechanicsburg, Pa.: Stackpole Books, 1997.

Stevens, Sylvester. *Pennsylvania: Birthplace of a Nation*. New York: Random House, 1964.

Storey, Walter. *Stories of Uniontown and Fayette County*. Dunbar, Pa.: Stefano's Printing, 1993.

Strathern, John H. *The Civil War Letters of Cpl. John H. Strathern*. Comp. Marlene C. Bumbera. Apollo, Pa.: Closson Press, 1994.

Sypher, J. R. *History of the Pennsylvania Reserve Corps....* Lancaster, Pa.: Elias Barr & Co., 1865.

Thomas, Emory M. *Bold Dragoon: The Life of J. E. B. Stuart*. New York: Random House, 1988.

Thomson, O. R. Howard, and William H. Rauch. *History of the "Bucktails:" Kane Rifle Regiment of the Pennsylvania Reserve Corps....* 1906. Reprint, Dayton, Ohio: Morningside House, 1988.

Trudeau, Noah Andre. *Bloody Roads South: The Wilderness to Cold Harbor, May–June 1864*. Boston: Little, Brown & Co., 1989.

Truxall, Aida Craig. *Respects to All: Letters of Two Pennsylvania Boys in the War of the Rebellion*. Pittsburgh: University of Pittsburgh Press, 1962.

Turner, George Edgar. *Victory Rode the Rails: The Strategic Place of Railroads in the Civil War*. Indianapolis: Bobbs-Merrill, 1953. Reprint, Lincoln, Nebr.: University of Nebraska Press, 1992.

Ulrich, Robert Schell. *To See the Elephant*. N.p., 2000.

Urban, John W. *Battle Field and Prison Pen, or Through the War, and Thrice a Prisoner in Rebel Dungeons*. Philadelphia: Hubbard Brothers, Publishers, 1882.

Veech, James. *The Monongahela of Old; or Historical Sketches of South-Western Pennsylvania to the Year 1800*. Pittsburgh: n.p., 1892.

War of the Rebellion: A Compilation of the Official Records of the Union and Confederate Armies. 130 vols. Washington, D.C.: Government Printing Office, 1880–1901.

Wert, Jeffry D. *General James Longstreet: The Confederacy's Most Controversial Soldier—A Biography*. New York: Simon & Schuster, Touchstone, 1994.

Wheeler, Richard. *Sword Over Richmond: An Eyewitness History of McClellan's Peninsula Campaign*. N.p.: Harper & Row, 1986. Reprint, New York: HarperCollins, HarperPerennial, 1991.

Wiley, Bell Irvin. *The Life of Johnny Reb: The Common Soldier of the Confederacy*. Baton Rouge: 1943. Reissued by Louisiana State University Press in 1978 by special arrangement with the author.

Woodward, C. Vann. *Mary Chesnut's Civil War.* New Haven, Conn.: Yale University Press, 1981.

Woodward, E. M. *History of the Third Pennsylvania Reserve: Being a Complete Record of the Regiment, with Incidents of the Camp, Marches, Bivouacs, Skirmishes and Battles....* Trenton, N.J.: MacCrellish & Quigley, 1883.

———. *Our Campaigns: The Second Regiment Pennsylvania Reserve Volunteers, or the Marches, Bivouacs, Battles, Incidents of Camp Life and History of our Regiment During its Three Years Term of Service....* 1865. Reprint, ed. Stanley W. Zamonski, Shippensburg, Pa.: Burd Street Press, 1995.

Periodicals

Barton, Michael. Ed. "The Civil War Letters of Captain Andrew Lewis and his Daughter." *The Western Pennsylvania Historical Magazine* 60 (October 1977).

Borkowski, Joseph A. "Camp Wilkins, Military Post, 1861." *The Western Pennsylvania Historical Magazine* 45 (September 1962).

Everett, Edward G. "Pennsylvania Raises an Army." *The Western Pennsylvania Historical Magazine* 39 (summer 1956).

McLaughlin, Florence C. Ed. "'Dear Sister Jennie-Dear Brother Jacob:' The Correspondence between a Northern soldier and his Sister in Mechanicsburg, Pennsylvania, 1861–1864." *The Western Pennsylvania Historical Magazine* 60 (April & July 1977).

Reinsburg, Mark. Ed. "A Bucktail Voice: Civil War Correspondence of Pvt. Cordello Collins." *The Western Pennsylvania Historical Magazine* 48 (July 1965).

Sears, Stephen W. "Glendale: Opportunity Squandered." *North and South: The Official Magazine of the Civil War Society* 5 no. 1 (December 2001).

Sherry, Jeffrey F. "The Terrible Impetuosity." *The Gettysburg Magazine* 16 (1997).

National Tribune, September 27, 1883.

National Tribune, August 9, 1900.

National Tribune, August 16, 1900.

National Tribune, August 23, 1900.

National Tribune, August 30, 1900.

National Tribune, September 6, 1900.

National Tribune, September 20, 1900.

Confederate Veteran, Vol. 1, No. 11, November 1893.

Confederate Veteran, Vol. 4, No. 8. August 1896.

Confederate Veteran, Vol. 23, No. 2, February 1915.

Confederate Veteran, Vol. 29, No. 6, June 1921.

Newspapers

Uniontown (Pa.) Genius of Liberty, April 4, 1861.

Uniontown (Pa.) Genius of Liberty, April 11, 1861.

Uniontown (Pa.) Genius of Liberty, April 18, 1861.

Uniontown (Pa.) Genius of Liberty, April 25, 1861.

Uniontown (Pa.) Genius of Liberty, May 2, 1861.

Uniontown (Pa.) Genius of Liberty, May 9, 1861.

Uniontown (Pa.) Genius of Liberty, May 23, 1861.

Uniontown (Pa.) Genius of Liberty, May 30, 1861.

Uniontown (Pa.) Genius of Liberty, June 20, 1861.

Uniontown (Pa.) Genius of Liberty, July 4, 1861.

Uniontown (Pa.) Genius of Liberty, July 25, 1861.

Uniontown (Pa.) Genius of Liberty, September 26, 1861.

Uniontown (Pa.) Genius of Liberty, October 10, 1861.

Uniontown (Pa.) Genius of Liberty, December 12, 1861.

Uniontown (Pa.) Genius of Liberty, January 9, 1862.

Uniontown (Pa.) Genius of Liberty, February 20, 1862.

Uniontown (Pa.) Genius of Liberty, June 26, 1862.

Uniontown (Pa.) Genius of Liberty, July 10, 1862.

Uniontown (Pa.) Genius of Liberty, July 17, 1862.

Uniontown (Pa.) Genius of Liberty, July 31, 1862.

Uniontown (Pa.) Genius of Liberty, August 21, 1862.

Uniontown (Pa.) Genius of Liberty, September 11, 1862.

Uniontown (Pa.) Genius of Liberty, March 26, 1863.

Uniontown (Pa.) Genius of Liberty, April 25, 1864.

Uniontown (Pa.) Genius of Liberty, June 2, 1864.

Uniontown (Pa.) Genius of Liberty, September 15, 1864.

Uniontown (Pa.) Genius of Liberty, March 9, 1865.

Uniontown (Pa.) Genius of Liberty, September 9, 1876.

Uniontown (Pa.) Genius of Liberty, December 27, 1921.

Pittsburgh Gazette, April 16, 1861.

Pittsburgh Gazette, May 22, 1861.

Pittsburgh Daily Post, June 17, 1861.

Uniontown (Pa.) The American Standard, April 23, 1863.

Uniontown (Pa.) The American Standard, March 30, 1865.

Uniontown (Pa.) Daily News Standard, July 4, 1896.

Uniontown (Pa.) Morning Herald, November 15, 1910.

Salisbury (N.C.) The Salisbury Post, November 18, 1910.

Unpublished Sources

Manuscripts

National Archives, Washington, D.C.

    George W. Darby Combined Service Record, Record Group 94.

    George W. Darby Pension Record, Record Group 15.

    James W. Eberhart Combined Service Record, Record Group 94.

    James W. Eberhart Pension Record, Record Group 15.

    Ashbel F. Hill Combined Service Record, Record Group 94.

    Ashbel F. Hill Pension Record, Record Group 15.

    Isaac A. Moore Combined Service Record, Record Group 94.

    Isaac A. Moore Pension Record, Record Group 15.

    Thomas W. Springer Combined Service Record, Record Group 94.

    Thomas W. Springer Pension Record, Record Group 15.

United States Army Military History Institute, Carlisle, Pennsylvania

    Albert Rake Papers, Civil War Miscellaneous Collection.

    James Randolf Simpson "Dear Dol" Letters, Civil War Miscellaneous Collection.

    Henry Flick Memoirs, Civil War Round Table Collection & Leigh Collection.

    Samuel Waters Diary, Civil War Miscellaneous Collection.

    Bates Alexander "Sergeant's Memoir," Pennsylvania Save the Flags Collection.

    Jacob Heffelfinger Diary (Typescript), Civil War Times Illustrated Collection.

    Andrew J. Elliott Diary, Pennsylvania Save the Flags Collection.

    William Weidner "After the Reserves (Unofficial Regimental History of the 190th & 191st Regts. Pa. Vol. Inf.)," Manuscript Archive.

Historical Society of Western Pennsylvania, Pittsburgh, Pennsylvania

    Joseph L. McQuaide Papers, Library & Archives Division.

    Jarrett Family Papers, Library & Archives Division.

    James W. Eberhart "Diary of Sailsbury [sic] Prison," Library & Archives Division.

University of Virginia, The Albert & Shirley Small Special Collections Library

    Thomas W. Springer Diary.

Uniontown Public Library, Uniontown Pennsylvania

    "Scrap Book" 3: 98. Call No. PR974.884. Held in the Pennsylvania Room.

Index